HEIDEGGER'S ANALYTIC

This book offers a new interpretation of Heidegger's major work, *Being and Time*. Taylor Carman places Heidegger's early philosophy in a broadly Kantian context, describes its departure from Husserl's phenomenology, and contrasts it with recent theories of intentionality, notably those of Dennett and Searle. Unlike others who view Heidegger as a Kantian idealist, however, Carman defends a realist interpretation. The book also examines the status of linguistic and nonlinguistic discourse in *Being and Time* and concludes with a discussion of Heidegger's concepts of guilt, death, and authenticity.

Rigorous, jargon-free, and deftly argued, this book will be necessary reading for all serious students of Heidegger.

Taylor Carman is Assistant Professor of Philosophy at Barnard College, Columbia University.

MODERN EUROPEAN PHILOSOPHY

General Editor
Robert B. Pippin, *University of Chicago*

Advisory Board
Gary Gutting, *University of Notre Dame*
Rolf-Peter Horstmann, *Humboldt University, Berlin*
Mark Sacks, *University of Essex*

Some Recent Titles

HEIDEGGER'S ANALYTIC

Interpretation, Discourse, and Authenticity in *Being and Time*

TAYLOR CARMAN

Barnard College, Columbia University

CAMBRIDGE
UNIVERSITY PRESS

CAMBRIDGE UNIVERSITY PRESS
Cambridge, New York, Melbourne, Madrid, Cape Town, Singapore, São Paulo

Cambridge University Press
The Edinburgh Building, Cambridge CB2 8RU, UK

Published in the United States of America by Cambridge University Press, New York

www.cambridge.org
Information on this title: www.cambridge.org/9780521820455

First published 2003
This digitally printed version 2007

A catalogue record for this publication is available from the British Library

Library of Congress Cataloguing in Publication data
Carman, Taylor, 1965–
Heidegger's analytic : interpretation, discourse, and authenticity in Being and time /
Taylor Carman.
p. cm. – (Modern European philosophy)
Includes bibliographical references and index.
ISBN 0-521-82045-6
1. Heidegger, Martin, 1889–1976. Sein und Zeit. 2. Ontology. I. Title. II. Series.
B3279.H48 S459 2003
111–dc21   2002067417

ISBN 978-0-521-82045-5 hardback
ISBN 978-0-521-03893-5 paperback

For Claudia and Caleb

And for my mother
gone but with us

Denn es scheint, daß uns alles
verheimlicht. Siehe, die Bäume sind; *die Häuser,*
die wir bewohnen, bestehn noch. Wir nur
ziehen allem vorbei wie ein luftiger Austausch.
Und alles ist einig, uns zu verschweigen.

For it seems that everything
hides us. Look, the trees *are*; the houses
we dwell in are still standing. But we
drift past them all like some foreign wind.
And everything conspires to cover us in silence.

Rilke, *Duino Elegies*

CONTENTS

ACKNOWLEDGMENTS

While writing this book I received financial support from Barnard College in the form of a leave from teaching duties for the duration of 1997, and from the National Endowment for the Humanities in the form of a stipend for participation in the Summer Institute on "Background Practices" in Santa Cruz in 1997.

This book has benefited immeasurably from all the friends and colleagues with whom I have spoken over the past decade or so, directly or indirectly, about Heidegger and *Being and Time*. Among them I especially want to thank Dave Cerbone, Dagfinn Føllesdal, Eckart Förster, Charlie Guignon, Richard Howey, Pierre Keller, Sean Kelly, Cristina Lafont, Mark Okrent, John Richardson, Joe Rouse, David Woodruff Smith, Gianfranco Soldati, Iain Thompson, and Mark Wrathall. I am grateful to two anonymous referees whose comments and criticisms improved the manuscript considerably. Bill Blattner has my special heartfelt thanks for his intellectual patience and generosity, and for going over an earlier draft of the first five chapters with a fine-tooth comb, saving me from countless blunders. He has been enormously supportive, even and especially in the midst of philosophical disagreement. My greatest intellectual debt, however, is undoubtedly to Bert Dreyfus, whose constant encouragement and disarming candor over the years have been nearly overwhelming. Writing this book would have been impossible without his inspiration. Finally, I want to thank my entire family for their unconditional affection and support, above all my wife, Claudia, whose love is impossible to measure or repay.

ABBREVIATIONS

Kant

KRV   *Kritik der reinen Vernunft*

Husserl

Hu IX   *Phänomenologische Psychologie. Husserliana* IX
Id I   *Ideen zu einer reinen Phänomenologie und phänomenologischen*
         Philosophie, Erstes Buch
Krisis   *Die Krisis der europäischen Wissenschaften und die*
         transzendentale Phänomenologie
LU   *Logische Untersuchungen*
PTP   *Psychological and Transcendental Phenomenology and the*
         Confrontation with Heidegger (1927–1931)

Heidegger

GM   *Die Grundbegriffe der Metaphysik. Welt-Endlichkeit-Einsamkeit*
GP   *Grundprobleme der Phänomenologie*
KPM   *Kant und das Problem der Metaphysik*
MAL   *Metaphysische Anfangsgründe der Logik im Ausgang von*
         Leibniz
PGZ   *Prolegomena zur Geschichte des Zeitbegriffs*
SZ   *Sein und Zeit*
ZSD   *Zur Sache des Denkens*

INTRODUCTION

Philosophy is at once historical and programmatic, its roots always planted in tradition even as it moves into new, uncharted terrain. There are undeniably great works all along the spectrum, some immersed in intellectual history at the expense of contemporary problems, some fixated on current problems, forgetful of their histories. But philosophy misunderstands itself at either extreme.

In writing this book, I have tried to steer a middle course between Scylla and Charybdis. The result is a reading of *Being and Time* that is, I hope, neither antiquarian nor anachronistic. I have focused on some problems at the expense of others, many of them fed by discussions in contemporary Anglo-American philosophy, though I have tried to deal with them within what strike me as the conceptual horizons proper to Heidegger's thinking. The book is therefore neither a commentary on *Being and Time* nor simply a Heideggerian approach to some independently defined philosophical domain.

It is instead an account of the substantive and methodological role of the concept of interpretation (*Auslegung*) in Heidegger's project of "fundamental ontology" in *Being and Time*. Interpretation runs like a thread through the entire fabric of the text, and I have tried to point up its philosophical importance for the existential analytic of Dasein. Substantively, Heidegger maintains that interpretation – by which he means *explicit understanding* – is definitive of human existence: Human beings have an understanding of what it means to be, and that understanding is or can be made explicit, at least in part. *Homo sapiens* may or may not be alone in this capacity. In any case, what is distinctive about *us*, however widely or narrowly we construe the community of inquirers, culturally or biologically, is our ability to understand explicitly *that* and *what* entities *are*.

1

Methodologically, moreover, I shall argue, it is precisely the phenomenon of explicit understanding that forms the explanatory target of Heidegger's argument in *Being and Time*. It is the very *possibility* of interpretation that Heidegger wants to account for in his phenomenological interpretation of human existence. What *Being and Time* describes, then, is not some random heap of phenomena, just any old thing that happened to strike its author as interesting or important about us. Rather, the book aims to provide an account of the existential conditions constitutive of interpretation, or what I shall call *hermeneutic conditions*. On my account, then, *Being and Time* is an interpretive description of the conditions of interpretation, that is, the conditions of our ability to understand explicitly *that* and *what* entities, including ourselves, *are*. Chapter 1 introduces this approach to the text and concludes with some remarks concerning the scope of the term 'Dasein' and what I take to be Heidegger's conception of animal intentionality in the absence of an understanding of being like ours.

The prehistory of this book lies in the dissertation I wrote nearly a decade ago on Husserl and Heidegger. My central concern at the time was whether and how one could decide between their respective conceptions of intentionality, which struck me as obviously incompatible. Had either Husserl or Heidegger simply gotten the phenomena wrong? Perhaps. My thesis, however, was that their accounts of intentionality rest on fundamentally different conceptions of meaning and linguistic practice. I found support and inspiration for this idea in Dagfinn Føllesdal's semantic interpretation of Husserl's notion of the *noema*, though I could never accept his subsequent conclusion that Heidegger's phenomenology remains largely parasitic on Husserl's, a mere variation on a dominant Husserlian theme. The two seemed to me worlds apart, perhaps ultimately incommensurable.

Only several years after having written the dissertation was I able to put my finger on what had always struck me as peculiarly insular and dogmatic about Husserl's view. It is not simply that his phenomenology is at times cramped and uninspired or that he advances implausible accounts of meaning and experience. The problem with Husserl's phenomenology is rather that the method he enlists presupposes substantial commitments about mind and meaning, which he then defends on the grounds that phenomenological inquiry reveals them to be as he says they are. The method seems to vouchsafe the results, yet the results must be taken for granted before the method itself can seem plausible. This, in a nutshell, is the argument of Chapter 2. The internal incoherence threatening Husserl's phenomenology, it now seems to me, flows directly from his critical disregard of the problem of hermeneutic conditions, in particular the external social conditions that necessarily inform all phenomenological interpretations of intentional phenomena.

But Husserl is in good company, for most contemporary theories of intentionality are no less neglectful of their own hermeneutic conditions. In Chapter 3, I contrast Heidegger's explicitly hermeneutical approach to intentionality, which regards it as just one aspect of our being-in-the-world, with two contemporary theories in analytic philosophy: Daniel Dennett's, which relativizes intentional phenomena to the theoretical attitude or attitudes involved in an explanatory strategy he calls the "intentional stance"; and John Searle's, which seems to acknowledge the external, extramental conditions of intentionality, conditions he calls the "Background." Dennett and Searle both say things that sound superficially friendly to Heidegger's position. Dennett's "stances" (the physical stance, the design stance, and the intentional stance) for example, appear at first glance to run parallel to the three modes of being in *Being and Time*: objective "occurrentness" (*Vorhandenheit*), instrumental "availability" (*Zuhandenheit*), and human "being-in-the-world" (*In-der-Welt-sein*). Similarly, Searle's notion of the Background seems to echo Heidegger's insistence on the embeddedness or situatedness of intentional attitudes in a wider physical and social environment.

But in fact, neither Dennett nor Searle asks the *transcendental* question inspiring and animating Heidegger's analytic, namely, What are the conditions informing our very idea of intentional phenomena *as* intentional? What, for example, makes it possible for us even to conceive of anything like the theoretical attitudes involved in the explanatory strategies of science and common sense? And what are the conditions already internal to our understanding of the contents of our own minds, over and beyond the merely physiological conditions of conscious awareness, of which we may be utterly ignorant? Chapter 3 concludes with a discussion of Heidegger's account of the social conditions of meaning and understanding. As I read it, Heidegger's conception of the normativity of "the one" (*das Man*) in *Being and Time* commits him to a form of social externalism broadly similar in effect, though neither in aim nor in method, to the anti-individualism of Tyler Burge.

As I have just indicated, and as my title suggests, I read Heidegger's early project as belonging to a broadly Kantian tradition of transcendental philosophy. Unlike other recent commentators, however, I do not infer from that affiliation that Heidegger was himself any kind of transcendental idealist. On the contrary, in Chapter 4 I try to explain and defend his avowed realism about entities, what I call his *ontic realism*. Heidegger was a realist, I believe, in part simply because he took our ordinary prereflective attitudes seriously and sought to resist philosophical arguments purporting to subvert or discredit them. Constructing arguments for or against realism or idealism, however, was clearly not Heidegger's chief concern. Rather, his transcendentalism lay in a different effort, namely, to spell out the conditions that make it possible for us to understand entities explicitly as we do. No conclusion about the hermeneutic conditions of human understanding directly implies any metaphysical thesis concerning the ontological status of the entities we interpret – for example, whether or in what ways they depend on us and our practices or attitudes. Some do, some do not.

It is plausible, for example, to insist that things defined by their usefulness are what they are only within some domain of human practices, whereas mere objects and natural kinds exist independently of us. Reading *Being and Time* as an account of hermeneutic conditions rather than as straightforward metaphysics, then, takes some of the pressure off the problem of realism and idealism, since Heidegger's point is not to advance or defend any particular metaphysical thesis, but simply to say what falls within the conditions of interpretation peculiar to human existence and what does not. Brute nature, as Heidegger describes it, falls outside those conditions. Our ordinary, untutored realism about the natural world, then, is both plausible in itself and consistent with the account of hermeneutic conditions in *Being and Time*. Such hermeneutic conditions, by contrast, comprise the world of human artifacts, practices, and institutions. It therefore makes little sense to be a realist about such things, for *what* (and even *that*) they *are* is bound up essentially with the practices and attitudes in which they are implicated. Being (*Sein*) depends on Dasein, Heidegger insists, but what is (*das Seiende*) – more precisely, what is "occurrent" (*vorhanden*) – does not. Chapter 4 ends with a plea that we not confuse matters by wondering whether being, in addition to entities, might itself *be*. Being is not an entity, so it cannot *be* in addition to them. Rather, on Heidegger's view, being is simply what we understand when we understand *what* and *that* things *are*.

Chapter 5 is an account of what I take to be the hermeneutic condition, the condition of interpretation, par excellence in *Being and Time*, namely, discourse (*Rede*). Surprisingly little has been said about this concept, though it plays a vital role in both divisions of the treatise. But what *is* discourse? Scholars disagree dramatically about what the term even means. Many assume that discourse, as Heidegger understands it, is simply language taken in a properly broad context to include the full range of semantic and pragmatic phenomena associated with speech, in addition to words and sentences themselves. Others take it to be the underlying pragmatic structure of all meaningful activity, linguistic and otherwise, thus rendering any direct connection between discourse and language virtually accidental.

I think both approaches miss Heidegger's point, and they do so precisely by missing the phenomenon itself. Discourse is not essentially linguistic, but neither is it simply an aspect of the purposive structure of meaningful activity. It is rather a wider spectrum of irreducibly expressive and communicative comportments that constitute a distinct, nonpurposive dimension of meaning in addition to the instrumental goal-directedness of practical activity. It is that expressive-communicative dimension of meaning that makes language and semantic phenomena in general possible. Discourse is not language, then, but it is a privileged conditio sine qua non of language precisely because it is the conditio sine qua non of expression generally, and expression is the essence of interpretation. Interpretation is the express or explicit (*ausdrücklich*) understanding of something *as* something, and it is the communicative dimension of discourse that allows expressive phenomena to stand out from the background of practical significance and lay claim to an altogether different form of intelligibility. In the absence of some primitive form of communicative comportment, no gesture can distinguish itself as expressive rather than merely useful or appropriate. Understanding and discourse are thus "equiprimordial" (*gleichursprünglich*), Heidegger insists, inasmuch as they run orthogonally along different dimensions in the fabric of intelligibility, as it were, neither reducible to the other.

What this account of discourse reveals, then, is a level of meaning midway between the instrumentality of practice and the semantic contents of propositions expressed by assertions. This intermediate domain of significance amounts to a kind of *hermeneutic salience* that makes a particular cultural world intelligible in some expressible way by opening up some linguistic and semantic possibilities and closing down others. Only against a background of hermeneutic salience, for instance, can assertions be intelligible as either true or false. It is this preassertoric domain of expressive significance, I argue, that Heidegger describes in his account of truth as "unconcealment" in §44 of *Being and Time*. This approach to Heidegger's account of truth, I hope, steers a middle course between critics who are prone to dismiss it as either obviously false or nonsensical, on the one hand, and those who would transpose it into something innocuous, perhaps even trivial, on the other. Heidegger's point, as I understand it, is neither to analyze propositional truth in some revisionary way nor simply to insist that entities must be given to us in order for our assertions to be true of them. Rather, in my jargon, the hermeneutic salience in which entities are revealed to us in discourse is itself a condition of the interpretability of assertions as true or false. Discourse is a hermeneutic condition of the truth of assertions.

In Chapter 6, however, I argue that to construe interpretation as expressibility, and so the conditions of interpretation as the conditions of expressibility, is not to say that we should read Heidegger as an "expressivist," that is, as belonging to a tradition arising in the late eighteenth and early nineteenth centuries according to which expressive achievements of various kinds bridge real gaps between the self and the world and restore it to a form of social and psychological, indeed metaphysical, integrity. Heidegger's fundamental ontology marks a radical break with that tradition, I believe, since he interprets Dasein as the sort of entity for whom any such ideal of unity or completion amounts to an ontological category mistake. Dasein is in principle never a finished thing, and so neither does it remain tragically unfinished or incomplete in the absence of properly expressive practices and institutions. Expression and expressive practices as such have no *telos* in anything like the wholeness of selfhood or character, nor is the self the kind of entity that can in principle ever be a finished whole.

The incoherence of that normative ideal is what motivates Heidegger's account of death in Division II of *Being and Time*. Death, as Heidegger understands it, is neither the mere terminus of a biological process nor the dénouement of a life story, but rather the fact that as we project into some future possibilities, we at once constantly and unavoidably project into the closing down and extinction of others. All projection is in principle attended by the shutting down of possibilities, which is to say "dying" in the existential sense of the word. Authenticity, understood as "forerunning resoluteness" (*vorlaufende Entschlossenheit*), lies in owning up to one's concrete situation and pushing forward into one's death, that is, projecting wholeheartedly into the simultaneous flourishing and perishing of possibilities. The possibility of forerunning resoluteness is intelligible only in light of an irreducible first-person point of view on *oneself*, as opposed to any objective or impersonal view one might have of oneself as *a self*. Heidegger's account of authenticity, that is, recognizes a profound asymmetry between first-person and second- and third-person modes of interpretation.

The question *Being and Time* does not address, let alone answer, however, is how those asymmetrical aspects of selfhood are in fact bound up with one another in a more general concept of self or person. Is a self no more than what it understands itself to be in authentic forerunning resoluteness, or is that first-person understanding always tied in complex ways to an understanding others have of us, both as discursive partners and as unfamiliar third parties? Is it possible to reintegrate a second- or third-person interpretation of ourselves into our own self-understanding without losing sight of the very asymmetry that makes authenticity intelligible? What, in other words, are the hermeneutic conditions of our more general, perspectively complex concept of the self? As it stands, the account of authentic selfhood in *Being and Time* remains at best radically incomplete. For it remains to be seen whether and how the irreducibility of our first-person self-interpretations can be reconciled with an account of the hermeneutic conditions of a concept of person applicable both to ourselves and to others, but without in effect disowning and defacing our defining commitments by surrendering them to the averageness of public understanding, thus rendering them anonymous and impersonal – in short, inauthentic.

WHAT IS FUNDAMENTAL ONTOLOGY?

God does not philosophize.
Heidegger

The central theme of Heidegger's philosophy is the question concerning the meaning (*Sinn*) of being (*Sein*).[1] The "fundamental ontology" he advances in *Being and Time* departs dramatically from traditional ontology in that it asks not *what there is*, nor *why there is what there is*, nor even *why there is anything at all and not nothing*. The last of those questions, most famously associated with Leibniz and Schelling, is what Heidegger calls "the fundamental question of metaphysics."[2] It is a deep and important question, but it is not the question of fundamental ontology, for what it asks about is the totality of *entities*, not the meaning of *being*.

Heidegger's question, then, is not, Why is there anything? but rather, What does it *mean* for something to be? – or simply (redundantly), What *is* it to be? "What does 'being' mean?" Heidegger asks in his lectures of 1928. "This is quite simply the fundamental question of philosophy" (*MAL* 171).[3] So, whereas traditional ontology was merely "ontic," in that it occupied itself exclusively with entities, or what is (*das Seiende*), Heidegger's own project is "ontological" in a radically new sense in

---

[1] I translate *Sein* as 'being' and *Seiende* as 'entity' or 'entities,' thus avoiding the common but confusing and unnecessary distinction between uppercase 'Being' and lowercase 'being.'

[2] Heidegger, *Introduction to Metaphysics*, chapter 1.

[3] Ernst Tudenghat objects that Heidegger conflates the question of the meaning of being with the question of the meaning of (the word) 'being' (see *SZ* 1, 11). Heidegger does admittedly use the two formulations interchangeably, but the distinction strikes me as irrelevant to his treatment of the question, since his argument has nothing to do with linguistic usage as such. For Heidegger's purposes, asking about the meaning of (the word) 'being' is simply another rhetorical way of asking what it means *to be*.

asking not just about what there is, but about being as such. Fundamental ontology is fundamental relative to traditional ontology, then, in the sense that it has to do with what any understanding of entities necessarily presupposes, namely, our understanding of that in virtue of which entities *are* entities. Heidegger's originality consists in part in having raised the question at all, perhaps more explicitly and systematically than ever before. Philosophy begins in wonder, Plato and Aristotle say,[4] and in the course of his inquiry into the meaning of being, Heidegger can fairly be credited with reminding modern philosophy of what may be the most wondrous fact of all – that there *is* anything, and moreover that we understand something definite, however obscure, in understanding that there is.

Over and beyond having posed the question of being, though, Heidegger continues to command our attention because of the originality with which he approaches it, the philosophical strategy and the style of thought he thinks it demands, and finally the conclusions he draws in pursuing, if not exactly answering, the question. For the question of being, as Heidegger conceives it, is inseparable from questions concerning the understanding and the existence of those entities for which, or rather for whom, the question of being can be a question at all, namely, ourselves, human beings. The argument of *Being and Time* therefore begins by referring ontology back to what Heidegger calls an "existential analytic of Dasein," that is, an account of the basic structures of human existence: "*fundamental ontology*, from which all others can first arise, must . . . be sought in the *existential analytic of Dasein*" (*SZ* 13), which offers a means of "uncovering the horizon for an interpretation of the meaning of being in general" (*SZ* 15). For Heidegger, "An analytic of Dasein must therefore remain the principal matter of concern in the question of being" (*SZ* 16).[5]

But how are we to understand such a project? What does the meaning of being have to do specifically with the existence of human beings? What unique link between being and human being requires that fundamental ontology proceed by means of an analytic of Dasein? Heidegger

---

[4] Plato, *Theaetetus*, 155d. Aristotle, *Metaphysics*, A 2, 982b12.

[5] But compare Heidegger's remark earlier in the text that "even the possibility of carrying out the analytic of Dasein depends on the prior working out of the question concerning the meaning of being in general" (*SZ* 13). Although an adequate answer to the question of being calls for an analytic of Dasein, that is, the analytic of Dasein in turn presupposes some initial articulation of the question of being itself. Heidegger's project is therefore inherently, but not viciously, circular.

tries to answer this question in the opening pages of *Being and Time,*
but it is worth reminding ourselves of the strangeness of the very idea
of fundamental ontology if we are to gain philosophical insight into
Heidegger's enterprise. For while the question of being, with its echoes
of ancient and medieval ontology, lies at the very heart of his thinking,
early and late, Heidegger was no less preoccupied with philosophical
questions concerning the conditions of intentionality and the ontological status of agency and subjectivity, uniquely modern problems that
lend his work a degree of contemporary relevance unmatched by all
but a few philosophical texts of the same period. What, then, is the connection between these two central motivating concerns in Heidegger's
thought? Why should the renewal and explication of the question of
being demand a critique of the concepts of subjectivity and intentionality? How does Heidegger propose to ground ontology as a whole in
an account of the phenomenal structure of everyday experience, and
why does he insist that "Ontology is possible only as phenomenology"
(*SZ* 35)? Why, in short, does Heidegger pursue the question of being
in the context of an "analytic of Dasein" at all?

The best short answer to these questions, I believe, lies in an unmistakable analogy between Heidegger's fundamental ontology in *Being
and Time* and the "Copernican revolution" in philosophy Kant claimed
to have brought about in the *Critique of Pure Reason* (*KRV* Bxvi).
Heidegger offered lectures on Kant's philosophy throughout the 1920s
and 1930s. He even published a book, *Kant and the Problem of Metaphysics,*
in 1929, just two years after the publication of *Being and Time* itself,
which I shall discuss further later in this chapter. In a word, Heidegger's
existential "analytic" of Dasein is a self-conscious allusion to the Transcendental Analytic that makes up the central constructive core of the
first *Critique.* The reference is crucially important, for an "analytic" in
Kant's sense is not an analysis of the contents of our thoughts, but a
kind of "dissection" (*Zergliederung*) – a "critique" in the original sense
of the word – of the faculty of understanding (*KRV* A64–5/B89–90).[6]

---

[6] Herman Philipse is therefore wrong to assimilate Heidegger's phenomenological interpretations in *Being and Time* to the sort of conceptual analysis practiced by J. L. Austin,
Gilbert Ryle, and P. F. Strawson. See *Heidegger's Philosophy of Being,* 321, 341, 386.
Heidegger's substantive positions do at times coincide with theirs, but his methods are crucially different. What Heidegger sets out to interpet is neither ordinary language nor the
logic of our concepts, but the prelinguistic, preconceptual forms of understanding and
interpretation that linguistic practices and conceptual categories presuppose. For a more
detailed critique of Philipse, see my "On Making Sense (and Nonsense) of Heidegger."

Admittedly, the analogy is not perfect. For example, although fundamental ontology and the analytic of Dasein are distinct, they are apparently coextensive: Fundamental ontology must be sought in, and so must proceed *as,* an analytic of Dasein. The analytic of Dasein, then, unlike Kant's Transcendental Analytic, is not one discrete chapter in Heidegger's project but describes the enterprise as a whole. Certain aspects of Heidegger's analytic therefore have greater affinities with the Transcendental Aesthetic and the Transcendental Dialectic in the first *Critique* than with the Analytic proper. For example, Kant's critique of the *metaphysica specialis* of the Leibniz–Wolff tradition (which included rational psychology, cosmology, and theology) finds no close analogue in Heidegger's thought, apart from his constant insistence that Dasein cannot be understood in terms of the ontological categories of functional utility and objectivity. On the other hand, Kant's critique of the "logic of illusion" in the Dialectic can be seen as a distant ancestor of Heidegger's account of the perpetual "falling" (*Verfallen*),[7] and the occasional motivated "flight" (*Flucht*) into inauthenticity, which tell us something essential about Dasein (*SZ* 184–6). Just as, for Kant, human reason is burdened with questions that it can neither dismiss nor answer, so too, for Heidegger, Dasein is in under constant, if at times only subtle, threat of diversion and temptation away from a proper "authentic" (*eigentlich*) understanding of itself. Notwithstanding the differences in detail, however, Heidegger's "project of a dismantling (*Destruktion*) of the history of ontology" (*SZ* 6)[8] by means of an analytic of Dasein

---

[7] 'Falling' is not a perfect translation of *Verfallen,* which literally means wasting, rotting, deterioration, decline, decay, addiction. Nevertheless, the bland English word does seem to capture the phenomenon Heidegger has in mind precisely because he repudiates those negative connotations: "The term expresses no negative evaluation," he insists (*SZ* 176). Indeed, falling is nothing like "a bad and deplorable ontic property, which could possibly be eliminated in more advanced stages of human culture" (*SZ* 176). Rather, "Falling reveals an essential ontological structure of Dasein itself, which, far from characterizing its nocturnal side, constitutes all its days in their everydayness" (*SZ* 179). "The term 'falling' ... once again must not be taken as a value judgment, as if the term marked something like an occasionally occurring defect of Dasein's that is to be deplored and perhaps rectified in advanced stages of human culture" (*PGZ* 378).

[8] In his 1927 lectures Heidegger also uses the term *Abbau* (*GP* 31), which Derrida renders as '*déconstruction*.' Using Derrida's terminology to translate Heidegger's can be misleading, however, for whereas Derrida regards all intelligibility as self-undermining, and so essentially "undecidable," Heidegger is instead advocating a dismantling or building down of the distortions and obscurities of the metaphysical tradition in favor of a more coherent ontology rooted in Dasein's understanding of itself as being-in-the-world. Fundamental ontology thus in no way suggests, indeed it is profoundly averse to, the skeptical spirit of Derrida's deconstructive technique.

is an obvious tribute to Kant's effort to supplant Leibnizian-Wolffian "ontology" (*metaphysica generalis*) with the Aesthetic and the Analytic of the first *Critique*: "[T]he proud name of ontology," Kant writes, "must give way to the modest one of a mere analytic of the pure understanding" (*KRV* A247/B303).[9]

So, just as Kant is concerned not with the empirical contents of our beliefs, but with the subjective conditions of knowledge, Heidegger, I shall argue, is interested not in our particular practices and understandings, but in the conditions of the possibility of interpretation (*Auslegung*). Interpretation, for Heidegger, means explicit understanding, making sense of something *as* something – primitively *entities as entities,* that is, as *being.* According to Heidegger, then, the question of the meaning of being, the question concerning what we understand when we understand entities *as entities,* presupposes some general account of our ability to understand anything explicitly as anything. So, while Henry Allison has construed Kant's transcendental idealism as an account of "epistemic conditions," or conditions of knowledge,[10] I read Heidegger's fundamental ontology as an account of what I shall call *hermeneutic conditions,* that is, conditions of interpretation or explicit understanding. The notion of hermeneutic conditions implicit in *Being and Time* is important especially because traditional philosophy, and in particular modern theories of knowledge and intentionality, have so consistently taken for granted the possibility of interpretation by appeal to such things as subjects and subjectivity, consciousness, ideas, representations, semantic content, and the "aspectual shape" of intentional states.[11]

But how is anything like subjectivity, representation, consciousness, content, or even *aspect* intelligible to us *as such?* This is the question Heidegger intends his fundamental ontology to address. And just as Kant's critique of reason could claim to undercut the "way of ideas" of early modern epistemology, turning its attention instead to the conditions of anything, even an idea or representation, counting as an object of knowledge, so too Heidegger's phenomenology of everydayness challenges traditional assumptions about the mind, mental representation, and intentionality in favor of an inquiry into the conditions of anything

[9] For an account of Kant's own changing conception of transcendental philosophy and its relation to metaphysics, see Eckart Förster, "Kant's Notion of Philosophy."

[10] Allison, *Kant's Transcendental Idealism,* and "Transcendental Idealism: A Retrospective," in *Idealism and Freedom: Essays on Kant's Theoretical and Practical Philosophy.*

[11] The phrase is John Searle's. See *The Rediscovery of the Mind,* 155.

making sense to us *as* anything. What follows in this chapter, then, is a sketch of the interpretation of fundamental ontology that will inform the rest of the book, namely, as an account of the conditions of our having an explicit understanding of being, that is, an interpretation of entities *as* entities.

The Meaning of Being

Heidegger's invocation of the notion of being is often dismissed by critics who regard it as a conflation of three different senses of the verb 'to be': existence, predication, and identity.[12] Heidegger usually seems to have existence in mind, though several sections of *Being and Time* are concerned explicitly with the nature and conditions of predication (*SZ* §§31–3).[13]

Does Heidegger's entire enterprise rest on a grammatical confusion? One reason to think not is that there is no reason to deny that being comprises all three semantic contexts. After all, what it means for something to be *such-and-such,* or to be *identical with* or *distinct from* something else is no less intelligible to us in everyday life, yet enigmatic upon reflection, than what it means for something to *exist.* That there are three distinct logical senses of the verb 'to be,' and so perhaps three distinct dimensions of our understanding of being, is no reason not to ask *what* it is we understand in each case. The question of being is in this way perfectly general and so in principle neutral about whether there is one sense or several. In any case, Heidegger does not assume that there is just one meaning. Indeed, one of the central tenets of *Being and Time* is precisely that being, in whichever grammatical form, means something fundamentally different for different kinds of entities – *Existenz* or "being-in-the-world" (*In-der-Welt-sein*) for human beings, "availability" (*Zuhandenheit*) for things defined by their use, and "occurrentness" (*Vorhandenheit*) for objects, properties, and relations. The only unity Heidegger claims for the meaning of being has to do with its general intelligibility in terms of some temporal framework, or "horizon." Time, Heidegger proposes, constitutes "the transcendental horizon for

---

[12] Concerning the various senses of 'to be,' see Plato's *Sophist* and (more recently) Rudolf Carnap, "The Elimination of Metaphysics Through Logical Analysis of Language," 73–4. Carnap insisted that Heidegger's question is a mere grammatical conundrum. See my "On Making Sense (and Nonsense) of Heidegger."

[13] Heidegger devoted an essay to "The Principle of Identity" in 1957, in *Identity and Difference,* but the subject hardly arises at all in his early thought.

the question of being" (*SZ* Part One)[14]; indeed, it is "the horizon for any understanding of being at all" (*SZ* 1).

But this response to the standard objection may be too easy, for the point of the objection is that Heidegger's question is not one question at all, but three, each of which would best be served by its own separate line of inquiry. Ernst Tugendhat has responded to the standard criticism in another way by arguing that the universality of the question of being, for Heidegger and the ancients alike, stems not from any assumption about the unified sense of the verb 'to be,' but instead from the universal phenomenon of *affirmation*. Affirmation is implicit in utterances and so ordinarily goes unexpressed, yet both affirmation and negation apply universally to speech acts of all kinds, not just to assertions and not just to sentences containing the verb 'to be.' The word 'is' can serve a variety of different linguistic functions, but optatives, imperatives, and indicatives all contain affirmations and negations, if only tacitly. And as Tugendhat points out, "It has never been doubted that the word 'not,' for its part, has a unified meaning."[15]

Tugendhat's proposal has several compelling points to recommend it, but I think it is misleading as an approach to the question of being. Tugendhat is right to suggest that Heidegger's question has to do with the primitive structures of understanding, and his analysis of the question of being in terms of the affirmability and negatability of linguistic expressions contextualizes the global scope of ontology in "a dimension of *praxis*," which is of course crucial to Heidegger's conception of being-in-the-world.[16]

The problem with Tugendhat's account is that it confines intelligibility and practice to an exclusively linguistic context. For example, Tugendhat simply folds the pragmatic notions of acceptance and refusal, or assent and dissent, into the specifically semantic concepts of affirmation and negation, assertion and denial. But, of course, we can reject what someone says by uttering affirmative statements, just as we can embrace what they say using negations. Tugendhat's "linguistic-analytical" reconstruction of the question of being therefore tends to

---

[14] The first two-thirds of Part One of *Being and Time* constitute the two divisions of the published book. See §8, "The Design of the Treatise."

[15] Tugendhat, "Die sprachanalytische Kritik der Ontologie," 492. See also lectures 8–10 in *Self-Consciousness and Self-Determination*, where Tugendhat candidly admits that his analysis "certainly does not correspond exactly to Heidegger's self-understanding, but it is the best I could make of Heidegger's question of being" (150).

[16] Ibid., 492.

suppress the distinction between pragmatic and linguistic intelligibility on which, as we shall see, Heidegger insists. For Heidegger, by contrast, being is not restricted to the intelligibility we can explicitly affirm or deny in linguistic utterances; it is more fundamentally the intelligibility in virtue of which we treat things as the things they are – as human beings, as environments or practical artifacts, or as mere objects, properties, or relations. Not all practice is linguistic practice, nor does treating things appropriately necessarily involve affirming or denying anything about them.[17]

But although his interpretation fails to capture something essential in Heidegger's question of being, Tugendhat's account does nonetheless express something true and important about the question and its relation to the analytic of Dasein and the critique of intentionality. Tugendhat is wrong to confine Heidegger's notions of intelligibility and practice to linguistic meaning and linguistic practice, but he is right to construe being as intelligibility and to identify human practice as its proper domain.

What, then, is Heidegger asking about when he asks about the meaning of being? The closest thing to a definition of being in *Being and Time* is Heidegger's gloss of it as "that which defines entities as entities, that on the basis of which entities . . . are in each case already understood" (*SZ* 6). Being is the intelligibility, or more precisely the condition of the intelligibility, of entities as entities. Furthermore, that intelligibility has two aspects: "[E]very entity can, as an entity, be examined in a twofold question: what it is and whether it is" (*GP* 123). Heidegger's notions of "whatness" (*Washeit*) or "being such-and-so" (*Sosein*) and "thatness" (*Daß-sein*) echo the scholastic distinction between *essentia* and *existentia*, but Heidegger rejects those terms as inadequate for an inquiry into the being of human beings, whose whatness or essence cannot be understood apart from the thatness or fact of their existence (*SZ* 42).[18] Heidegger therefore abandons the traditional vocabulary and instead

---

[17] I will argue in Chapter 6 that "discourse" (*Rede*) is not language or linguistic practice, but the expressive-communicative dimension of practical understanding at large, which conditions interpretation. All language is discourse, then, but not all discourse is language.

[18] This is also why in the "Letter on 'Humanism'" Heidegger rejects Sartre's formula that, for human beings, "existence precedes essence." Sartre, *L'Existentialisme est un humanisme*, 17 passim. According to Heidegger, Sartre "takes *existentia* and *essentia* in the sense of metaphysics, which since Plato has said that *essentia* precedes *existentia*. Sartre reverses this proposition. But the reversal of a metaphysical proposition remains a metaphysical proposition." *Wegmarken* 159.

rests the analytic of Dasein on a distinction between the general "existential" (ontological) structures of human existence, on the one hand, and the particular "who" (*SZ* 113–30) of Dasein in its various "existentiel" (ontic) modes, on the other (*SZ* 12).[19]

One further point is worth noting. Heidegger might seem to be drawing a distinction between being and the meaning (*Sinn*) of being when he analyzes all inquiry, and so too his own question, into three constitutive elements, namely, what the inquiry asks about (*das Gefragte*), what it directly questions or investigates (*das Befragte*), and finally, what it tries to find out or ascertain (*das Erfragte*) (*SZ* 5). The question of being, Heidegger says, asks about being by directly questioning entities, particularly Dasein, in order to ascertain the meaning of being. Does this schematic sketch of the inquiry and its formal distinction between being and the meaning of being entail any substantive or systematic distinction between them?[20]

I think not, and to see why not, consider by way of analogy asking about a foreign or ancient word by addressing or "interrogating" a text in order to ascertain the word's meaning. One can distinguish the word from its meaning in this merely formal and provisional way without denying that the meaning is, after all, constitutive of the word, that the meaning is what makes the word the word it is, and that to understand the word is in effect to understand its meaning. So too, for Heidegger, being is constituted by the meaning of being, so that an understanding of being is in effect the same as an understanding of its meaning. As he says later in *Being and Time,* meaning is not an entity at all over and beyond that of which it is the meaning; therefore, grasping the meaning of anything simply consists in understanding the thing itself: "[S]trictly speaking, what is understood is not the meaning, but the entity" (*SZ* 151). The meaning of being is likewise nothing distinct from or additional to being itself; to understand being is simply to grasp its meaning. Hence, "when we ask about the meaning of being, the inquiry neither becomes deep nor broods on anything that stands behind being, but rather asks about being itself insofar as it enters into the

---

[19] Heidegger's account of Dasein's "whoness" (*Werheit*) (*GP* 108–71) is a deliberate departure from the traditional metaphysical assumption that all entities are defined in terms of their *essentia*, nature, or whatness.

[20] Mark Okrent and William Blattner argue for versions of such a distinction. See Okrent's *Heidegger's Pragmatism: Understanding, Being, and the Critique of Metaphysics,* 225, and his essay "The Truth of Being and the History of Philosophy." See Blattner's *Heidegger's Temporal Idealism,* 5–6. I think the distinction Heidegger draws is merely formal.

intelligibility of Dasein" (*SZ* 152). Moreover, when Heidegger later defines meaning (*Sinn*), what he says is virtually identical with what he says about being. Being is "that which defines entities as entities, that on the basis of which entities . . . are in each case already understood" (*SZ* 6). And what is meaning? "Meaning is the whereupon of projection . . . in terms of which something becomes intelligible as something" (*SZ* 151). The two notions thus play essentially the same functional role in Heidegger's thought, notwithstanding the formal distinction one can in principle draw between what one is asking about and what more specifically one wants to know.

The question of being is thus equivalent to the question concerning the meaning of being, and the question What does it mean to be? is in turn equivalent to the question What do we understand when we understand what and that (or whether) something is? The question concerning the meaning of being therefore reduces to the question concerning our understanding of being. Indeed, for Heidegger, "there is" no being apart from or independent of our understanding of it:

> being "is" only in the understanding of the entity to whose being something like an understanding of being belongs. Being can therefore remain unconceptualized, but it is never not understood at all. . . . [There is a] necessary connection between being and understanding. (*SZ* 183)[21]

In short, "only as long as Dasein *is* . . . 'is there' (*gibt es*) being" (*SZ* 212).[22] As Heidegger repeatedly insists, this is not to say that entities in general exist only if and when human beings exist; indeed, Heidegger is what in Chapter 4 I shall call an *ontic realist,* that is, a realist with regard to physical nature. The point is rather that being – that is, the intelligibility of entities, their making sense *as* entities – depends on human beings, whose own being, Heidegger maintains, consists essentially in having an understanding of being. Being, then, is always and only being of which Dasein has an understanding: " 'There is' (*gibt es*) being only in the specific disclosedness that characterizes the understanding of being. . . . There is being only . . . if Dasein exists" (*GP* 24–5). For

---

[21] Heidegger uses inverted commas or reverts to the locution "*es gibt*" (there is), whenever he says that being "is," since being is not an entity and so cannot strictly speaking "be."

[22] Interestingly, Heidegger says exactly the same things about truth: "Dasein, as constituted by disclosedness, is essentially in the truth. *'There is' truth only insofar and as long as Dasein is.* Entities are only uncovered *when,* and only disclosed *as long as,* Dasein itself *is.* Newton's laws, the principle of noncontradiction, all truths in general are only true as long as Dasein *is*" (*SZ* 226). See Chapter 4.

Heidegger, the relation between being and our understanding of being is internal, not external, so the two are strictly correlative. One cannot "be" without the other.[23]

Fundamental ontology therefore deals explicitly with human understanding, existence, and intentionality in a way that traditional ontology could not, just as traditional theories of understanding and intentionality have failed to come to terms with the ontological presuppositions lurking at their own foundations. To sustain an interpretation of the analytic of Dasein as an account of hermeneutic conditions, however, requires spelling out more precisely what Heidegger takes those conditions to be and exactly what it is they are supposed to condition. In short, what is the analytic of Dasein an analytic *of,* and what phenomenon is it in the service of rendering intelligible?

Understanding and the *As*-Structure of Interpretation

In his Marburg lectures of 1927, immediately following the publication of *Being and Time,* Heidegger says, "Our aim is to clarify fundamentally the possibility of the understanding of being in general" (*GP* 397), to "inquire into the condition of the possibility of the understanding of being as such" (*GP* 399). Heidegger's conclusion is that "temporality must be the condition of the possibility of the understanding of being" (*GP* 397). Indeed, the conclusion of *Being and Time,* if there is one, and again the justification of its title, is that we understand being in terms of time.

What then is understanding? As Heidegger uses the term (usually *Verstehen,* sometimes *Verständnis*), understanding is nothing necessarily

---

[23] Frederick Olafson is therefore not altogether wrong in *Heidegger and the Philosophy of Mind* when he says that Heidegger's notion of being "would not rule out the possibility that there could be entities without being" (136). In one sense, of course, it is plainly contradictory to suppose that there could *be* entities without *being,* just as it is contradictory to suppose that a person could walk without walking. But being is not an entity, neither a property nor an event like walking, so the analogy fails. To say that there could be entities without being is simply to say that there could be entities in the absence of any understanding of being, hence any understanding of entities *as* entities, in which case there would be no answer to the question What does it *mean* to be? or How is the being of anything to be *understood?* This last formulation especially reveals the essential normativity of the question of being. Olafson unfortunately lapses into talking about being as if it were a kind of entity, thus blurring the ontological difference, when he refers to what he imagines must be its "unity and singularity" (137; cf. 70–4). Only entities can be unitary and singular or binary and plural. I discuss this further in Chapter 4.

cognitive, but rather the entire scope of our ability to make sense of things by availing ourselves of them competently, even if unreflectively, in practice. Understanding means competence, skill, know-how: "In speaking ontically we sometimes use the expression 'to understand something' in the sense of 'managing (*vorstehen*) an affair,' 'being up to it,' 'being able to'" (*SZ* 143). Whereas traditional epistemology assumes that human understanding essentially amounts to cognition, the theoretical grasp of propositions, Heidegger construes it instead as practical ability. Heidegger therefore rejects traditional conceptions of understanding in favor of the more familiar common notion drawn from ordinary language:

> *understanding oneself in the being of one's ownmost ability to be (Seinkönnen) is the primordial existential concept of understanding.* Its terminological meaning goes back to common linguistic usage, when we say: someone can manage a thing (*einer Sache vorstehen*), i.e. he has an understanding of it (*versteht sich darauf*). (*GP* 391–2)

Simply put, understanding consists in knowing *how*, not knowing *that*.[24] More specifically, understanding means *getting it*, where the "it" in question can be anything from a bodily technique to an esoteric joke.

---

[24] Gilbert Ryle wrote a rather uneven review of *Being and Time* for the journal *Mind* in 1929, and then some twenty years later, in chapter 2 of *The Concept of Mind*, wound up drawing much this same distinction between intelligent practical skill and theoretical cognition. In his review, ironically, he complains that in Heidegger's account "*knowledge* of some reality . . . is surreptitiously imported . . . into such terms as 'understanding,'" for the language of *Being and Time* "surely implies that *underlying* our other reactions and attitudes there is *knowledge.*" Consequently, he argues, "the attempt to derive our knowledge of 'things' from our practical attitude towards tools breaks down; for to use a tool involves knowledge of what it is, what can be done with it, and what wants doing" (369). It is unclear if Ryle is here contradicting his own later account, which insists on the irreducibility of knowing-how to knowing-that, or if he means 'knowledge' in a distinct practical sense. If the latter, then he is not disagreeing with Heidegger. For what they both deplore is precisely what Ryle calls the "intellectualist legend," according to which intelligent, skillful practices are supposed to be explained by our theoretical grasp of propositions. On the contrary, knowing how to do something lies in the ability to do it. Some critics have objected that agents might still be said to know how to do something even after they have lost the ability to do it, for example musicians who meet with debilitating injuries. But in that case, the knowledge in question is still arguably bound up analytically with the ability that the agents had and then lost. Finally, of course, some uses of the expression 'know how' do not refer to practical skill at all, for example when I say that I know how a machine works or how someone does something. In cases of this sort, what I know is *that,* say, the spring pushes the lever or *that* she disengages the clutch with her left foot. I can therefore consistently know *how to do* things practically without knowing theoretically *how I do them.*

The concept forms the very linchpin of the project of fundamental ontology, naming as it does the most basic connection between the meaning of being and the human beings whose being consists in their understanding of it.

'Understanding,' then, is a success verb inasmuch as it presupposes the meaningfulness of the thing understood: You can't understand something that doesn't make any sense. Still, notwithstanding the implication of success, it is important to recognize that understanding is itself nonetheless an intentional notion. I shall discuss the structure of understanding in more detail later, but suffice it here to say that it involves the purposive use of available (*zuhanden*) things in practical situations. The notion of use does not by itself satisfy one traditional criterion of intentionality, since the things we use cannot fail to figure somehow into our use of them: If the thing is not there, you're not using it. The possible nonexistence of things is inadequate as a criterion of intentionality, however, since by that standard, seeing would also fail to count as intentional: If it's not there, after all, you're not *seeing* it. In any case, even if the mere use of things is not by itself intentional, the practical understanding with which we use them is, for we often find ourselves in situations and take up projects that turn out to be radically different from what we had understood them to be. By referring cognitive attitudes back to the practical context of everyday understanding, then, Heidegger is emphatically not proposing a behavioristic reduction of intentionality to anything nonintentional.

Yet in spite of the ontological primacy and systematic prominence of understanding in *Being and Time,* I want to suggest that methodologically the concept plays a secondary role to Heidegger's notion of interpretation (*Auslegung*). Understanding is the more primordial phenomenon, yet it is interpretation that figures as the guiding thread in the analytic of Dasein taken as a whole. What Heidegger is trying to account for is not just our capacity to understand entities in their being, but more precisely our capacity to understand things explicitly, as such, *as being.* Interpretation is understanding made explicit. What we understand explicitly in interpretation, Heidegger says, "has the structure of *something as something.* . . . The 'as' makes up the structure of the explicitness of something understood; it constitutes interpretation" (*SZ* 149). Interpretation is thus a 'development' or 'cultivation' (*Ausbildung*) of understanding (*SZ* 148), "the working-out (*Ausarbeiten*) and appropriation (*Zueignen*) of an understanding" (*SZ* 231).

Interpretation therefore presupposes understanding, not vice versa: "[I]nterpretation is grounded existentially in understanding, nor does the latter arise from the former" (*SZ* 148). Understanding is the more primordial phenomenon, yet it is interpretation – that is, the fact that we (at least sometimes) understand things explicitly or as such – that figures as a premise in the analytic of Dasein. For recall that being consists in the condition of the intelligibility of entities as entities: It is "that which defines entities as entities" (*SZ* 6). Interpretation is constituted by the *as*-structure, which is, I want to suggest, the deep central concern of Heidegger's argument in *Being and Time*. What we understand explicitly in interpretation, he says, "has the structure of something as something.... The 'as' makes up the structure of the explicitness of something understood; it constitutes interpretation" (*SZ* 149).

But interpretation is not an element in all our comportment and all our dealings with things and with each other.[25] Dasein is ordinarily far from understanding itself or its being in explicit, perspicuous, or even fully coherent terms. Nonetheless, since a positive understanding of being is constitutive of the very being of Dasein, Heidegger insists that our understanding is always, at least in part, thematic:

> it belongs to the constitution of the being (*Seinsverfassung*) of Dasein that in its being it has a relation of being (*Seinsverhältnis*) to that being. And this in turn means that Dasein understands itself in its being in some particular way and to some extent explicitly (*in irgendeiner Weise und Ausdrücklichkeit*). (*SZ* 12)

Moreover, "it belongs to its ownmost being to have an understanding of that being and to comport itself in each case as already interpreted in some particular way in its being" (*SZ* 15).[26] So, although *most of*

---

[25] It has to be, according to those who construe the understanding–interpretation distinction as a distinction between the ontological structure of significance, on the one hand, which is something like an abiding capacity, and its ontic actualization, on the other, that is, some particular exercise of that capacity. Since our understanding of being always has some particular ontic manifestation in our actual encounter with and treatment of entities, reading the text in this way implies that interpretation is a more or less constantly ongoing phenomenon. See Richardson, *Existential Epistemology*, 30; Okrent, *Heidegger's Pragmatism*, 55.

[26] "As in each case already interpreted in some particular way in its being" translates *je schon in einer gewissen Ausgelegtheit seines Seins*. The Macquarrie and Robinson translation misleadingly inserts the subjunctive "already...in each case *as if* its Being has been interpreted in some manner" (emphasis added), which casts unwarranted doubt on whether Dasein has in fact been interpreted or just seems to have been. The abiding

our understanding is tacit and unthematic, we are never entirely without *some* explicit interpretation of ourselves and the world. Indeed, Heidegger refers to "the specific disclosive function of interpretation" (*SZ* 150), which suggests that interpretation plays more than just a contingent or epiphenomenal role in Dasein's disclosedness at large. For example, interpretations frequently sink back down into the prethematic context of intelligibility, essentially transforming it by leaving traces or deposits of an understanding that was once explicit. The totality of involvements situating available equipment (*Zeug*), for instance, "need not be grasped explicitly by any thematic interpretation. Even if it has undergone such an interpretation, it recedes again into an unobtrusive understanding" (*SZ* 150). Heidegger does not rule out the possibility that the totality of involvements might remain entirely unaltered by its being made explicit in interpretation, but the idea that our background understanding might remain entirely untouched hermeneutically in this way seems unlikely. Just as most of an iceberg remains submerged, but only because a portion of it rises above the surface, so too, although our understanding of being remains largely hidden from view and beyond our immediate interpretive grasp, its very inconspicuousness may well be owing in part to the fact that we do sometimes interpret things concretely and explicitly in some particular way.

Finally, the phenomenon of interpretation is crucial for Heidegger's purposes since in its absence there would be no criteria identifying an understanding of being as an understanding of being at all. Understanding is itself defined by criteria provided by its own explicitness in interpretation. This is what I take Heidegger to mean when he says that in interpretation "understanding does not become something different, it becomes itself" (*SZ* 148). Interpretation is no mere contingent or inessential modification of understanding; it is rather the explicit realization or manifestation of the content and substance of understanding itself. Interpretation therefore serves Heidegger's argument in *Being and Time* precisely because it makes explicit the intelligibility essential to our ordinary understanding of being at large. We understand entities as entities, as such, as *being*. Interpretation therefore marks the point of departure for fundamental ontology as a whole, and the dawning of the question of the meaning of being is its exemplary instance.

presence and effects of prior interpretations in our everyday understanding of being are of central importance to Heidegger's conceptions of discourse and authenticity.

The Analytic of Dasein as an Account of Hermeneutic Conditions

I read Division I of *Being and Time*, then, as an account of *hermeneutic conditions*, which is to say conditions of interpretation, conditions of our understanding something *as* something. Foremost among hermeneutic conditions, of course, is the phenomenon of understanding itself, in particular our understanding of being. Heidegger's conception of understanding as practical competence, that is, informs his account of the availability of the things we use in our everyday practices, the anonymous social norms that govern those practices – what he calls "the one" (*das Man*) – and finally the temporal structure of existence itself: our "thrownness" (*Geworfenheit*) into a world with an already defined past and our "projection" (*Entwurf*) into the possibilities or options that give shape to our future. The constitutive structures of human being figure in the argument of *Being and Time*, then, as conditions of the sort of explicit understanding manifest in its primitive form in the question of the meaning of being. What I am calling hermeneutic conditions are, in short, what Heidegger calls "existentials" (*Existentiale*).

My notion of hermeneutic conditions is based, albeit loosely, on the concept of epistemic conditions, which Henry Allison invokes in his interpretation of Kant's transcendental idealism.[27] Epistemic conditions are, as the terms implies, conditions of our knowledge of objects and states of affairs such as space and time, and categories such as substance and causality. In their specific reference to our knowledge as finite beings, Allison suggests, epistemic conditions differ from the logical conditions of thought, from the causal conditions of thinking taken as a psychological or physiological process, and finally from ontological conditions, which is to say the way things are "in themselves," independent of the conditions of our knowing them. Heideggerian hermeneutic conditions are like Kantian epistemic conditions in the first two respects but not in the third, since the point of fundamental ontology is precisely to deny any sense of ontological commitment independent of an account of our own everyday, preontological understanding of being. So, although the analytic of Dasein is "transcendental" inasmuch as it inquires into the conditions of interpretation in general, it does not pretend to any sort of ontological neutrality. Indeed, for Heidegger,

---

[27] Allison, *Kant's Transcendental Idealism*, 10–13, 334 n20. The two cases differ widely, of course, but I think the analogy sheds some light on the sources and intentions of Heidegger's early project. I am not assuming that Allison would endorse the comparison, nor do I think the success of my own argument depends on the success of his.

"Every disclosure of being as the *transcendens*" – including fundamental ontology itself, of course – "is transcendental knowledge" (*SZ* 38).

First, then, consider what hermeneutic conditions have in common with epistemic conditions as Allison conceives them. To begin with, hermeneutic conditions must themselves *be* epistemic conditions, for knowledge is itself a form of interpretation, and conditions of interpretation are a fortiori conditions of knowledge. Knowledge and cognition, indeed propositional attitudes in general, presuppose interpretation, since it is only by understanding something *as* something that we are ever in a position to attribute properties to particulars and hold claims to be true or false of them in the first place. The converse, however, does not hold: Conditions specific to knowledge are not necessarily conditions of interpretation generally. What is necessary for propositional thought might not be necessary for having an understanding of things being, and being such and such. The conditions of *knowing that* are not identical with the conditions of *knowing how,* then, since the latter include the former but not vice versa.

This is not to say that Heidegger's position simply subsumes Kant's on all points, for Kant's account of epistemic conditions is itself rooted in an ontology whose basic assumptions Heidegger rejects. In his 1928 lectures, for example, he maintains that the objective and naturalistic orientation of epistemology has blinded modern philosophers to the salient features of the phenomena they themselves set out to describe and explain:

> it is characteristic of Kant, no less than his successors, and especially the present-day epigones, to inquire all too hastily into the ground of the possibility of the relation of consciousness to the object, without first of all adequately clarifying what is meant by this relation whose possibility is to be explained, between what this relation obtains, and what sort of being applies to it. (*MAL* 163)

Kant's successors and "present-day epigones," of course, include Brentano and Husserl:

> The theory of knowledge in the second half of the nineteenth century and in recent decades has repeatedly made the subject–object relation the basis of its inquiries, yet idealistic as well as realistic attempts at an explanation had to fail since what was to be explained was never adequately defined. (*MAL* 163–4)

Heidegger's account of hermeneutic conditions therefore not only claims priority over the Kantian account of epistemic conditions, it also challenges the presuppositions underlying Kant's conception of knowledge as a relation between a subject and an object. By inquiring into the conditions not of knowledge but of Dasein's explicit understanding of being, fundamental ontology moves beyond the orbit of both epistemology and traditional transcendental philosophy: "The transcendence of Dasein is the central problem – with a view to clarifying not just 'knowledge' (*Erkenntnis*), but Dasein and its existence as such" (*MAL* 170). But again, since knowledge itself is a form of interpretation, any genuine account of the conditions of the former presupposes an account of the conditions of the latter.

Second, like Kantian epistemic conditions, Heideggerian hermeneutic conditions are not the causal conditions of interpretation, understood as a psychological, physiological, or even social process. Of course, Heidegger does not deny that there are causal conditions of interpretation, but these are the concern of the empirical sciences, not of fundamental ontology. For Heidegger, as for Husserl, phenomenology concerns itself with conditions specific to understanding and – human – intentionality as such, not with what brings them about or causes them to persist. This is why, notwithstanding Heidegger's aversion to the doctrines and methods of orthodox phenomenology, he enthusiastically endorsed Husserl's critique of psychologism in *Logical Investigations*. Logic, indeed all intentional content per se, Husserl argued, is irreducibly normative. It is not just an empirical fact about the cognitive activity of human beings, for example, that when we add 2 and 2, we get 4. Rather, it is a rule of mathematical calculation that the addition of 2 and 2 *ought* to yield 4. Moreover, the laws of mathematics are exact and knowable with certainty a priori, whereas all knowledge in empirical psychology is inexact, inductive, and merely probable. Likewise, the contents of our thoughts generally are normative inasmuch as they are governed by logical norms of reasoning and epistemic norms of evidence. The intentional contents of our mental states are not just brute factual occurrences; rather, they impose complex normative constraints on one another, and it is precisely in virtue of those constraints that they manage to refer to objects and states of affairs beyond themselves at all. No purely nonnormative empirical description of thought understood as a causal process can capture what is essential to it qua intentional.

So, for example, in the same spirit, in his 1928 lectures Heidegger criticizes Leibniz for attempting "to justify a general norm for thought by appeal to facts of experience," attempting, that is, "to justify empirically an a priori proposition. Husserl's critique of psychologism,

Logical Investigations, Vol. 1, demonstrates the absurdity of such an attempted justification." Heidegger adds, however, that Husserl's "argument is of course only relatively compelling and merely negative. For
the question remains, what in general are a priori propositions, and
is a normative proposition then an a priori proposition, and in what
sense?" (*MAL* 151). Husserl's critique rules out any reduction of the
normative to the nonnormative, that is, but it does not tell us whether
the norms constituting intentional content must have a basis in a priori
knowledge, and if so, what the a priori itself amounts to.

The distinction between causal and hermeneutic conditions remains
essential to Heidegger's fundamental ontology – for example, the distinction between availability and occurrentness as categories definitive
of nonhuman entities. For that distinction is no mere logical distinction
between concepts we use in our fully conceptualized thoughts about
equipment and objects, nor is it merely a reminder of the relatively uninteresting empirical fact that we make unreflective use of things before
ever acquiring full-blown propositional knowledge about them. The
distinction is instead part of Heidegger's account of hermeneutic conditions, the point of which is neither logical nor psychological, strictly
speaking. The point of the distinction is rather that our unreflective use
of things constitutes a form of understanding whose normative structure always already conditions and informs the norms governing the way
we talk and think about objects and states of affairs. The hermeneutic
conditions inherent in practical understanding are not merely causal
conditions and so cannot be captured in any nonnormative description
of mere behavior or mentality.

Can this distinction between causal and hermeneutic conditions be
drawn more precisely? What is essential to hermeneutic conditions, I
want to suggest, is that they are constitutive of what they condition in
a way that causal conditions are not. That is, whereas causal conditions
bring it about that one as a matter of fact has some interpretive understanding of something as something, hermeneutic conditions constitute what it is for something to fall under an aspect, and thus to be interpretable, at all. For a condition to be constitutive of what it conditions,
it is not enough that it merely bring the thing about. It must also figure
into an adequate understanding of the conditioned phenomenon as
the thing it is. For hermeneutic conditions to be constitutive of the
interpretability of entities, then, any explicit understanding of those
entities as the entities they are must also involve some understanding,
however unthematic, of the hermeneutic conditions that render them

intelligible. So, although we can remain perfectly oblivious of the causal conditions bringing about or sustaining our understanding of things, we must have at least some prephilosophical inkling, however primitive and inarticulate, of the hermeneutic conditions that constitute their ordinary intelligibility for us.

So, for example, Heidegger identifies temporality as the most fundamental of all hermeneutic conditions, since understanding useful things and objects presupposes an understanding of such things as things we encounter in the present, while understanding human beings presupposes an understanding of them as interpreting themselves in light of their past and with an eye to their future. Without such tacit temporal frameworks of interpretation already in place, those entities would not be intelligible to us as they are. So too, the practical availability of useful things is a hermeneutic condition, since our understanding of anything as anything presupposes some mastery of the ways in which that understanding is put into practice in normal circumstances. Heidegger's distinction between availability and occurrentness, then, is not concerned with the psychological or social histories of our acquisition of skills and knowledge; rather, it specifies what is involved in or what it means to understand objects *as* objects, useful things *as* useful, useless things *as* useless, and human beings *as* human. Purposive activity, responsiveness to social norms, moods, and expressive and communicative competence are likewise hermeneutic conditions, since being able to interpret human beings in their average everydayness presupposes an understanding of them as practically situated, attuned social agents whose self-interpretations are manifest in their discursive interactions with one another.

Construing mundane practical phenomena of this sort as constitutive conditions of the interpretability of entities as such, then, is something essentially different from specifying the de facto causal conditions in the absence of which interpretation could or would not occur. Causal conditions are what bring it about that interpretation in fact happens. Hermeneutic conditions, by contrast, are what constitute a thing's being intelligible at all as potentially accessible to our interpretative practices, *as* the thing it is.

Finally, like epistemic conditions, hermeneutic conditions are not mere logical conditions of thought, independent of the way things are in fact given to us to understand. Consequently, the central claims of the analytic of Dasein are in no way meant to approach merely analytic or conceptual truths. Heidegger's analytic is no more "analytic" in that sense than is Kant's. Kant regarded Aristotelian logic as "a closed and completed body of doctrine" specifying legitimate but wholly formal, materially empty conditions of thought (*KRV* Bviii). It was the uncritical assumption of rationalist metaphysics, he argued, that such logical conditions could simply be read back into the world as ontological conditions inherent in the order of things, and so as the sole conditions of our, or for that matter God's, knowledge of them. But logic is too weak to specify anything like the conditions peculiar to our form of knowledge as finite beings. Over and beyond the purely formal requirements of "general logic," therefore, a "transcendental logic" would specify the conditions peculiar to our knowledge of objects (*KRV* A50ff/B74ff). Of course, Kantian epistemic conditions are themselves "formal" inasmuch as they abstract from all empirically contingent features of objects, but they go beyond the general requirements of logic in being fitted specifically to our knowledge, which is confined to appearances, that is, things represented as substances causally interacting with one another in space and time. Kant therefore suspended traditional metaphysical questions concerning the logical-cum-ontological conditions of objects as things in themselves, and set out instead to describe the conditions specific to our knowledge as finite subjects. Kant thus claimed to have answered skepticism by reversing the order of explanation, asking not how our knowledge manages to track objects, but rather how objects manage to conform to the conditions of our knowledge (*KRV* Bxvi–xvii). In so doing, he also took the first steps toward what we would nowadays call an account of intentionality, that is, an account of the directedness of consciousness or cognition toward objects in general.

Reading the analytic of Dasein as an account of hermeneutic conditions might seem to promise a series of knock-down transcendental arguments that would demonstrate their necessity in true Kantian fashion.[28] I do not believe that Heidegger provides such arguments, but neither do I think that his project avoids them as a matter of principle.

---

[28] For the most ambitious effort of this kind, see Okrent's *Heidegger's Pragmatism*. Okrent not only purports to find transcendental arguments in Heidegger's texts, he also endorses Barry Stroud's claim that such arguments presuppose verificationism. Okrent therefore concludes that "it is an essential premise of the transcendental argument that Heidegger constructs concerning the necessary conditions for intentionality that the meaning of any overt act, intention, or assertion is a function of the evidence that would count in favor of its truth or success" (ibid., 5). If Stroud is right that transcendental arguments presuppose verificationism, however, then it seems to me that the fact that there is no textual evidence supporting a verificationist reading of *Being and Time* casts doubt on Okrent's claim that Heidegger is advancing transcendental arguments.

And like the necessity of the forms of intuition and the categories in Kant, the necessity of the hermeneutic conditions Heidegger advances in the form of existential structures of Dasein, though stronger than mere causal necessity, will of course be considerably weaker than logical necessity. Unlike Kant, however, Heidegger insists that traditional or general logic dictates not too little but too much by way of the conditions of interpretation. Indeed, much of Heidegger's project in *Being and Time* is motivated by the insight that traditional logic itself harbors substantive metaphysical presuppositions about the being of all possible objects of discourse, so not even it can legitimately claim the kind of ontological neutrality that one might be tempted to ascribe to interpretation understood as a condition of knowledge in general.

As we have seen, Heidegger regards the *Critique of Pure Reason* as a kind of predecessor to *Being and Time*, rendering all dogmatic metaphysics obsolete, just as his own fundamental ontology aims at a dismantling of the metaphysical tradition. Yet Heidegger considers Kant no less guilty than his rationalist predecessors of taking logical categories for granted as the framework for the interpretation of the world and of ourselves. Heidegger credits Kant with unseating logic from its unquestioned preeminence in ancient and medieval philosophy (*KPM* 236), but he also maintains that in the second edition of the first *Critique* Kant effectively granted the intellect a position of overweening dominance once again, though in a new way. For whereas earlier metaphysicians had read the apparent demands of logic directly into their theories of the world, Kant fit them instead into his account of our faculties and only indirectly allowed them to dictate the order of things qua appearance. So, while Heidegger reads the *Critique of Pure Reason* as in part anticipating the conclusion of his own fundamental ontology – namely, that time constitutes the most general horizon or condition of our understanding of being – he also sees Kant as still entangled in a metaphysical tradition beholden to the ontological authority of logic.

Heideggerian hermeneutic conditions therefore make no pretense to the sort of ontological neutrality of epistemic conditions in Kant, since Heidegger thinks that both Kantian epistemology and traditional logic harbor ontological commitments to which they themselves remain blind. As we shall see in Chapter 2, Husserl modeled his transcendental and eidetic "reductions" on the supposed methodological autonomy and ontological neutrality of the Kantian paradigm, so it is not surprising that Heidegger attacks Husserl's enterprise by way of rejecting that tradition as a whole.

What Is Metaphysics?

Henry Allison's interpretation of transcendental idealism as an account of epistemic conditions sheds light on the scope and significance of Kant's "Copernican revolution" in philosophy, that is, his reorientation of inquiry away from the question of how knowledge manages to reach objects in favor of questions concerning the conditions under which objects can be objects of our knowledge.

Of course, Allison's reading of Kant is controversial. Karl Ameriks, for instance, associates it, albeit with some qualifications, with what he calls the "short argument" to idealism, which he traces back to Kant's immediate successors, Reinhold, Fichte, and Hegel, but which he thinks departs sharply from Kant's own considerably longer line of reasoning via the transcendental deduction and the antinomies in the first *Critique.* The short argument originally envisioned by Reinhold infers the ideality of objects of experience directly from the mere fact of their being represented.[29] Paul Guyer has argued in the same vein, but more emphatically, that substituting a purely methodological distinction between phenomena and noumena for the more robust dualism traditionally ascribed to Kant, as Allison does, in effect trivializes the thesis of the unknowability of things in themselves.[30]

Yet the incoherence of Kant's position according to what Allison calls the "standard picture" has been obvious to readers of the first *Critique* since its publication. Moreover, it is well known that Kant always strenuously denied that his own transcendental or "critical" idealism was equivalent to Berkeley's "empirical" idealism, or phenomenalism.[31] Allison's "double-aspect" construal of appearances and things in themselves allows him to take seriously, as proponents of the traditional "two-worlds" interpretation cannot, Kant's insistence that transcendental idealism is at once an empirical realism, that is, that the things we experience and have knowledge of are not just mental representations, but are perfectly "real," mind-independent objects.[32]

[29] See Ameriks, "Kantian Idealism Today" and *Kant and the Fate of Autonomy,* chapters 2 and 3.
[30] Guyer, *Kant and the Claims of Knowledge,* 336–42.
[31] See Kant's "Refutation of Idealism" in *KRV* and *Prolegomena,* 293, 374–5.
[32] Allison, *Kant's Transcendental Idealism,* 7.

Allison's interpretation of Kant is thus comparable to Dagfinn Føllesdal's account of Husserl's theory of intentionality, specifically Husserl's conception of the content or *noema* of an intentional state, in contrast to its object.[33] For Føllesdal, the *noema* of an intentional state is not a kind of intermediary psychological particular, or object of awareness, but the ideal semantic or "intensional" (with an *s*) content that directs consciousness to its putative objects, which are themselves none other than the standard inventory of naive realism and common sense. The objects of our intentional states are not the contents of our minds, or rather they are so only once we reflect on our own consciousness. Rather, it is the internal content of a mental state that makes possible an awareness of external objects. As Husserl himself said, "No ordinary 'realist' has ever been as realistic and as concrete as I, the phenomenological 'idealist' (a word which, by the way, I no longer use)."[34] Similarly, for Allison, Kantian appearances and things in themselves constitute not two classes of entities but rather two ways of regarding things: as represented by us, on the one hand, and in abstraction from our representations, on the other. Appearances are therefore not "mere representations," as Kant sometimes seems to suggest, but rather objects qua represented.[35] Allison thereby claims to save Kant, just as Føllesdal claims to save Husserl, from a dualism of appearance and reality and its looming skeptical implications.

It is plausible to insist, however, as Allison's critics have, that Kant's idealism remains incoherent even on the double-aspect interpretation. For how are we to understand the idea of things in themselves existing outside of space and time? What can such existence amount to, even in thought? And even if it offered a more intelligible notion of things in themselves, why should we begin our philosophical inquiry by doubting or denying the possibility of knowing them?[36] Kant's argument for idealism remains problematic, then, even on Allison's reading. Much of the contemporary appeal of Allison's approach lies in its apparent ontological neutrality, since on his interpretation Kant is not caught

---

33 Føllesdal, "Husserl's Notion of *Noema*."
34 Letter to Abbé Baudin, 1934. Quoted in Kern, *Husserl und Kant,* 276n.
35 Allison, *Idealism and Freedom,* 13.
36 Again, according to Ameriks, the unknowability thesis was not a premise for Kant at all, but rather the conclusion of a lengthy argument, whereas his contemporaries and successors sought to infer the unknowability, or even the incoherence of the very idea, of things in themselves solely from the concept of representation.

awkwardly asserting both the existence and the unknowability of entities numerically distinct from the physical objects we perceive in space
and time.[37] Instead, on this view, Kant merely points out the impossibility of our knowing things independently of the epistemic conditions
peculiar to our knowledge as finite beings.[38] But this seems either trivial
or false: Of course we cannot know things without relying on the conditions of our knowing them, but why should we not be able to know things
as they are, independent of our means of knowing them?[39] Allison may
well have purchased some increased plausibility for Kant's theory, but
perhaps only by reducing things in themselves to innocuous conceptual placeholders for the very objects of which we do have knowledge.
And as Guyer says, that does seem to take the wind out of the sails of
Kant's otherwise dramatic pronouncements concerning the real limits
of human knowledge.

Yet even if he fails to rescue transcendental idealism from its critics,
Allison's interpretation has the virtue of throwing an especially stark
light on Kant's wholesale rejection of the theocentric conception of
knowledge that had dominated the epistemological tradition for centuries. After Kant, that is, it could no longer be the task of epistemology to try to measure human knowledge against God's omniscience,
as philosophers had done at least since St. Augustine. Kant's transcendental idealism is thus radically anthropocentric inasmuch as it takes
for granted no concept of knowledge beyond our concept of our own
knowledge and the conditions peculiar to it.

Now what I want to suggest is that Heidegger's fundamental ontology is philosophically revolutionary in much the same way as Kant's
Copernican turn. For just as Kant redirected philosophical reflection on knowledge back to the sensible and conceptual conditions
specific to human knowledge, Heidegger envisions a "destruction,"
or more precisely a dismantling (*Destruktion*), of the history ontology

---

[37] In the first *Critique*, of course, "existence" (Dasein) is one of the categories of the
understanding.

[38] Allison has more recently acknowledged that the acceptance of epistemic conditions
is not by itself a sufficient argument for transcendental idealism. What is necessary in
addition is Kant's distinction between sensibility and understanding, so that considering
things as they are in themselves amounts to regarding them in abstraction from their
appearance in intuition, that is, apart from the sensible but not the conceptual conditions
of knowledge. Allison, *Idealism and Freedom*, 6–8.

[39] I defend what I take to be Heidegger's realism along these lines at greater length in
Chapter 4.

(*SZ* §6) by referring it back to the hermeneutic conditions specific to our understanding of being. And just as Kant moves beyond the skeptical question of how, or even whether, our knowledge conforms to objects, by insisting instead that objects must somehow conform to the conditions of our knowledge (*KRV* Bxvi–xvii), so too Heidegger closes the gap between ontology and phenomenology by taking for granted no understanding of being beyond that which is already at work and familiar to us in our mundane understanding. For Heidegger, "Ontology is possible only as phenomenology" (*SZ* 35). The immediate effect of this innovation is twofold, for not only does it cast suspicion on all naive or dogmatic ontologies that proceed without reference to hermeneutic conditions, it also undermines traditional subjectivist conceptions of understanding and interpretation that purport to leave all metaphysical or ontological questions untouched.

One perhaps ironic result of this is that Heidegger's own interpretation of Kant differs radically from Allison's own. For Heidegger rejects all pretense of ontological neutrality, not just in Kant but in the modern tradition at large in all its forms, from Descartes to Hegel and Nietzsche, including above all Husserl. This is why in *Being and Time* Heidegger writes, "the positive outcome of Kant's *Critique of Pure Reason* lies not in a 'theory' of knowledge but in its contribution to a working out of what belongs to nature in general. His transcendental logic is an a priori material logic of nature as a region of being" (*SZ* 11). In his lectures of 1927 he reiterates, "The interpretation of Kant's *Critique of Pure Reason* as epistemology completely misses the true meaning" (*GP* 181). Heidegger carries this point to an implausible extreme in *Kant and the Problem of Metaphysics* when he goes so far as to say that "The *Critique of Pure Reason* has nothing to do with a 'theory of knowledge'" (*KPM* 17). Yet the untenability of that claim should not deflect attention from Heidegger's main point, which is to deny that anything like a theory of knowledge is conceivable in an ontological vacuum, absent any conception of what it *means* for entities – for instance, minds and their objects – *to be*.

In his 1927 lectures Heidegger elaborates his notion of the ontological commitments latent in Kant's epistemology by identifying the phenomenological interpretation of being tacitly at work in Kant's thought as a whole (*GP* 35–107). For although Kant may have succeeded in overcoming the traditional theocentric conception of knowledge, Heidegger insists that he never abandoned the ancient metaphysical interpretation of being as presence (*Anwesen, Anwesenheit, Präsenz*).[40] Unlike Plato and Aristotle, of course, Kant refers the presence of entities specifically back to the "positing" mental attitudes of self-conscious subjects. He therefore maintains that "The concept of position or positing is totally simple and on the whole identical with the concept of being in general."[41] What Kant calls the "absolute position," namely existence, as opposed to the "relative position" of a predicate in relation to a logical subject, has its basis in the bare givenness of things in intuition: "For that the concept precedes the perception signifies its mere possibility; but perception, which yields the material for the concept, is the sole characteristic of actuality" (*KRV* B272–3). Heidegger therefore concludes that, for Kant, "being equals presentness, presence" (*GP* 448), so that "Kant's basic ontological orientation – in spite of all the differences of such a new inquiry – remains that of the Greeks" (*SZ* 26).

Heidegger's dismantling of traditional ontology is aimed principally at the metaphysical interpretation of being as presence, which underlies ancient as well as modern metaphysics and epistemology. The fundamental ontology of *Being and Time,* however, is aimed more specifically at the subjectivist versions of the interpretation of being that have dominated modern philosophy since Descartes, including Nietzsche's and Husserl's. Reading the analytic of Dasein as an account of hermeneutic conditions allows us to see the specific force of Heidegger's argument against all attempts to reduce our understanding of the world to representational states in the mind of the subject. For whereas the dogmatism of traditional metaphysics lay in its taking for granted as unproblematic the objectivity of objects, the corresponding dogmatism of subjectivist and cognitivist theories of intentionality consists in taking the being of the mind and the mental for granted and so forgoing any "preliminary ontological analytic of the subjectivity of the subject" (*SZ* 24). To take the *cogito,* the will, or even intentionality itself as primitive is to forgo any account of the hermeneutic conditions underlying the phenomena themselves.

[40] For a more detailed account of Heidegger's interpretation of traditional ontology and his own conception of the ontological presence of entities in the temporal present, see my article "Heidegger's Concept of Presence."

[41] Kant, "The Only Possible Argument in Support of a Demonstration of the Existence of God," in *Theoretical Philosophy, 1755–1770.*

What *Is* Dasein?

To understand Heidegger's fundamental ontology, we must finally ask what exactly the existential analytic of Dasein is an analytic *of.* I conclude this chapter, then, with an account of how we ought to understand the term 'Dasein' itself. What *is* Dasein? What kind of entity exists in such a way that its existence involves an understanding of being, and consequently rests on the conditions of the interpretability of entities as entities? My thesis is simply that the term 'Dasein' refers to any individual human being or person. My arguments thus aim merely to uphold what already amounts to widely received view concerning the extension, if not the intension, of the term.

'Dasein' is an ordinary German word meaning existence – literally, "being there" ('there' in a neutral sense, not the opposite of 'here'). In common parlance it often, but not always, denotes a human being's existence, or one's "living" or "daily bread."[42] Heidegger uses the word to refer to an individual human being or person. In appropriating the term for his own purposes, he is exploiting its conventional meanings but also drawing attention to what he regards as the essential relation between Dasein and *Sein,* that is, between human being and being itself. Indeed, the ordinary English expression 'human being' not only names what 'Dasein' names, it can also be read as intimating, as Heidegger's choice of the German word intimates, that human beings are defined in their being by their relation to being, specifically by their understanding of being. It is fitting, that is, that in German and in English the term referring to us is one that itself makes reference to being.[43]

Heidegger is at great pains to distinguish the analytic of Dasein both from "common sense" (so called) and from empirical sciences such as anthropology, psychology, and biology (*SZ* 10). He therefore eschews all conventional vocabularies that might insinuate presuppositions from those domains into the ontological inquiry as such, for

---

[42] Kant uses the term throughout the first *Critique* in the standard neutral sense, for example in the Table of Categories (*KRV* A80/B106) and in reference to the existence of God (*KRV* A583ff/B611ff).

[43] It has become standard practice to leave the term untranslated in English texts, and I shall do so too, if only because the word 'Dasein' functions as a generic representative term in a way that is impossible for the English expression, 'human being.' Grammatically, 'Dasein' is more like the distributive term 'man,' as in "Man is a rational animal."

example terms like 'ego,' 'subject,' 'soul,' 'consciousness,' 'spirit,' even 'person':

> These terms all denote determinate, "formable" spheres of phenomena, but their application always goes hand in hand with a curious modesty in asking about the being of the entities in question. It is not willfulness in terminology, then, if we avoid these terms as well as the expressions "life" and "man" to designate the entity that we ourselves are. (*SZ* 46)

Heidegger rejects the traditional terminology in favor of the philosophically unspoiled, ontologically resonant 'Dasein.' The new word has a radically different sense from those more conventional terms; still, it refers to the same entities that 'person,' 'human being,' and 'man' – though not 'ego,' 'soul,' 'consciousness,' 'spirit,' or even 'subject' – refer to, namely, embodied human agents understood as concrete particulars.[44] Of course, as we shall see, what it means to *be* a concrete particular differs fundamentally for human and nonhuman entities. So, for example, Dasein is *concrete* not by being usable or objective but by finding itself in its "facticity" (*Faktizität*), that is, in a given, externally determined practical situation. So too, Dasein is *particular* by being neither conventionally nor objectively individuated but by having "mineness" (*Jemeinigkeit*), that is, by always having a reflexive understanding of itself, however unthematic, in its understanding of the world.

But Heidegger's use of the term has had surprising consequences. On the one hand, Ernst Tugendhat has observed that 'Dasein' deviates grammatically from its extensional equivalents in ordinary language: 'human being,' 'person,' 'man.' Like the term '*Bewußtsein*' (consciousness), for example, 'Dasein' admits of no plural form. Consequently, although Heidegger talks about Dasein's relation to others, Tugendhat complains that "a peculiar and misguided egocentrism nonetheless survives as a result of this reliance on a *singularum tantum*." His verdict is severe: "I cannot see how the introduction of the term *Dasein* has had any positive sense. It is only a stylistic device that has

---

[44] Heidegger says explicitly that "subject and object do not coincide with Dasein and the world" (*SZ* 60) and that the Cartesian *res cogitans* "coincides neither ontically nor ontologically with Dasein" (*SZ* 66), which means not only that Descartes misinterpreted the being of Dasein (ontologically), but that a Dasein is not the same thing as a thinking subject (ontically).

unfortunate consequences, and we can better appropriate Heidegger's contribution ... if we refrain as far as possible from the use of this term."[45]

Tugendhat is right that we should beware the vagaries of philosophical jargon, but I think that in this case his worries are misplaced. Heidegger's ontological interpretation of one's relation to others may be problematic, but his approach departs so radically from traditional treatments of the problem of other minds, including Husserl's own analogical account in *Cartesian Meditations,* that it is hard to regard its shortcomings as owing simply to its surface grammar. If it begins to sound "egocentric," it ought to be enough to remind ourselves that the analytic of Dasein is emphatically not a description of anything like an isolated consciousness or ego, but rather an account of the conditions of the explicit intelligibility of entities of all kinds, including human beings in all their plurality.

It is even harder to charge the term 'Dasein' with solipsistic implications, considering the radically different inferences other philosophers have drawn from the same grammatical peculiarities. For example, John Haugeland has advanced what he candidly calls a "free-wheeling" interpretation of *Being and Time* by radically reconstruing Heidegger's reluctance to equate 'Dasein' with any ordinary or technical term referring to human individuals. Haugeland is right that Heidegger insists that the impersonal one (*das Man*) (*SZ* 126–30),[46] the world itself (*SZ* 64, 364, 380), and even the sciences (*SZ* 11) all have Dasein's "kind of being" (*Seinsart*).[47] In Haugeland's view, this is because "each of them *is* Dasein." The term 'Dasein,' he argues, refers not just to human individuals but to "a vast intricate pattern ... of norms, normal dispositions, customs, sorts, roles, referral relations, public institutions, and so on." Not only are norms and the world itself Dasein, "chemistry is Dasein – and so

[45] Tudendhat, *Self-Consciousness and Self-Determination,* 152 (translation modified).

[46] See Chapters 3 and 6 for further discussion of the one and its role in Heidegger's account of understanding, interpretation, and discourse. Like Haugeland and Dreyfus, and contrary to the standard Kierkegaardian interpretation, I regard the one as constitutive of the practical intelligibility of the world, and so of Dasein's being. Unlike Haugeland, I think the one is not an entity in its own right, a fortiori not itself Dasein.

[47] Haugeland adds language to the list (*SZ* 166). Heidegger, however, does not assert that language has Dasein's kind of being. He merely poses the possibility in a rhetorical question and leaves the matter undecided.

are philately, Christmas, and Cincinnati."[48] The trouble, as Haugeland sees it, is that

> readers have surmised that 'Dasein' is just a newfangled term for 'person' (or 'ego' or 'mind') – in other words, that each of us is or has one Dasein, and there is a Dasein for each of us. This is wrong; and the first indication is a simple textual point. 'Person' is a count noun (we can "count" a person, several people, and so on); Dasein is (virtually) never used as a count noun.[49] On the other hand, it isn't a mass noun either (such as 'water' or 'gold'); Dasein can no more be measured out (e.g., in gallons or ounces) than it can be counted. Grammatically, 'tuberculosis' is a closer analogy. We neither count "tuberculoses" nor measure amounts of it; it comes, rather, in distinct occurrences or cases (which can, of course, be counted). A person is like an occurrence or "case" of *Dasein*.[50]

A "case" of Dasein, Haugeland goes on to say, is a "unit of accountability" or "an institution."[51] Haugeland has elaborated his interpretation by appealing to Heidegger's claim that "*Dasein is its disclosedness*" (*SZ* 133). "This formula," he admits, is "not exactly an equation"[52]; nevertheless, it leads him to reassert his thesis that "'Dasein' is not equivalent, not even extensionally, with 'person' or 'individual subject.'" Instead, "Dasein is a 'living' (currently being lived) *way of life*."[53]

I think this reading cannot be right for several reasons. To begin with – *pace* both Tugendhat and Haugeland – it is not at all obvious that 'Dasein' is not a count noun. Haugeland concedes that in several instances in *Being and Time* it occurs with the indefinite

---

[48] Haugeland, "Heidegger on Being a Person," 19. Though he still takes ongoing traditions like chemistry to be instances of Dasein, Haugeland has more recently conceded that philately, Christmas, and General Motors are not.

[49] According to Haugeland, Heidegger occasionally "slips up," for example at *SZ* 240 and 336 (cf. 239).

[50] Ibid., 19–20.

[51] Ibid., 21. Haugeland also distinguishes between ordinary and "primordial" institutions, namely, those exhibiting what Heidegger calls "mineness" (*Jemeinigkeit*), which is to say persons.

[52] Haugeland, "Dasein's Disclosedness," 27.

[53] Ibid., 35. Charles Guignon adopts essentially the same position: "In the description of everyday Being-in-the-world, what emerges is a picture of Dasein which is closer to Dilthey's conception of 'objective mind' than it is to the Cartesian subject or a monad. From this standpoint we see that the technical term 'Dasein' cannot be taken as shorthand for 'human being' as this term is generally used." *Heidegger and the Problem of Knowledge*, 104.

article (*SZ* 239, 240, 336). The indefinite article appears at several points in his 1927 lectures, too (*GP* 240, 241, 410), and Heidegger even says, "We are always, each of us (*jeweils*), a Dasein" (*GP* 36). Moreover, the expression 'every Dasein,' the universal quantifier being another syntactic indicator of count-noun status, occurs in both texts as well (*SZ* 317; *GP* 421, 422). Haugeland is right that in certain respects 'Dasein' functions as a generic term like 'tuberculosis.' But the two cases are disanalogous precisely because 'Dasein' admits of paraphrase with indefinite articles and quantifiers, whereas 'tuberculosis' does not.

Another mark against Haugeland's syntactic argument rests on the parallel that Tugendhat points out between 'Dasein' and '*Bewußtsein*' (consciousness). The latter is perhaps an even less typical count noun than the former, though here, too, indefinite articles and quantifiers are not unheard of. In some psychological contexts the term functions as a mass noun, so that it makes sense to talk about amounts or degrees or consciousness. But in philosophical contexts, where the word means something like *mind,* philosophers typically take it for granted that the term refers to conscious individuals. Anything other than an individual, distributive reference would demand special pleading. And nothing distinguishes 'Dasein' from '*Bewußtsein*' in this respect. In any case, the *syntax* of such terms, whatever it turns out to be, is not enough to answer the *semantic* question of their reference.

So, what does 'Dasein' refer to? As it happens, the decisive clue to both its syntax and its semantics occurs when Heidegger first introduces the term at the beginning of §4 of *Being and Time.* He writes: "As comportments of man (*des Menschen*), sciences have the kind of being of this entity (man) (*Mensch*). This entity we refer to terminologically as Dasein" (*SZ* 11). Dasein is "this entity (man)." Indeed, grammatically speaking, 'Dasein' mirrors the traditional (by now quaintly sexist) generic term 'man.' Of course, 'man' sometimes refers collectively like a mass noun, sometimes distributively like a count noun. Collectively or distributively, though, the term refers either to particular human individuals or to the species. When the reference is distributive, 'man' picks out an arbitrary particular exhibiting features typical or definitive of the group. To say that man has opposable thumbs is just to say that *a* (typical) man does or that *all* men do. Similarly, to say that Dasein comports itself toward its being is just to say that this is what a Dasein does or what all Daseins do. Both syntactically and semantically, then, what goes for 'man' goes for 'Dasein.'

Furthermore, as Haugeland's critics have pointed out,[54] to say that the world, the sciences, and perhaps even language, have "Dasein's kind of being" is not to say that they *are* Dasein. What Heidegger has in mind with such claims, I think, is that human practices and institutions must be made sense of in the way one makes sense of human beings, which is radically different from the way one makes sense of nonhuman entities, namely, things defined by their objective occurrentness or by their practical availability. Practices and institutions are not objective entities, nor do we strictly speaking make use of them. They are rather aspects of our collective social existence. To say that institutions have Dasein's kind of being, then, is simply to say that they are *human* institutions, not that they are Dasein.[55]

Finally, Haugeland's conception of Dasein as a "pattern" of normative behavior or a "way of life" cannot be reconciled with the personal particularity evidently implied by Heidegger's concept of mineness: "We ourselves are, each of us, the entity to be analyzed. The being of this entity is *in each case mine*" (*SZ* 41). Moreover, "Addressing Dasein must always, in virtue of this entity's character of mineness, invoke a *personal* pronoun: 'I am,' 'you are'" (*SZ* 42). If Dasein is always "mine" and requires the use of personal pronouns, surely this is because a Dasein is a concrete personal particular. Haugeland is right to object to Macquarrie and Robinson's translation of *das Seiende* by the plural 'entities,' but in fact in the margin alongside the sentence in question – "We ourselves are, each of us, the entity to be analyzed" (*Das Seiende, dessen Analyse zur Aufgabe steht, sind wir je selbst*) (*SZ* 41) – Heidegger himself later wrote "in each case 'I'" (*SZ* 440). Heidegger also refers to "the I, Dasein in our terminology" (*GP* 77), and says explicitly, "we reserve the term 'Dasein' for the human entity" (*das menschliche Seiende*) (*GP* 78). Finally, in his 1928 lectures Heidegger says, "Dasein, as factical, is in each case, among other things, dispersed into a body and, with that, among other things, in each case differentiated (*zwiespältig*) into a particular sexuality" (*MAL* 173). Haugeland does not deny that Dasein is an entity, or even that it depends ontically on persons and their bodies. But passages like these make it clear that Heidegger meant the term to refer not just to human phenomena dependent on persons, but to individual human beings as such.

---

[54] See Stewart, "Intentionality and the Semantics of 'Dasein,'" and Dreyfus, *Being-in-the-World*, 14.

[55] Stewart righly points out that Heidegger refers to practices and institutions not as Dasein, but as "Dasein-like" (*daseinsmäßig*). Ibid., 98–9.

The fatal error underlying Haugeland's interpretation, it seems to me, lies in a blurring of what Heidegger calls the "ontological difference" between being and entities (*GP* 22, 322ff), a distinction that stands at the very center of Heidegger's philosophy as a whole. Haugeland admits that the claim that "Dasein is its disclosedness" is "not exactly an equation," but he adds that "each can be understood only with, and indeed *as*, the other"; "being-in-the-world is a single entity with two interdependent structural aspects: self and world and like two sides of one coin"; "Dasein *is* being-in-the-world."[56] But being-in-the-world is *not* an entity, nor "is" Dasein its being-in-the-world, in the sense of identity. It is tempting to read sentences like "Dasein . . . *is* its past" (*SZ* 20), "Dasein is, in each case, its possibility" (*SZ* 42), "Dasein is its disclosedness" (*SZ* 133), "Dasein is its there (*Da*)" (*SZ* 135), and "Dasein *is* its world existingly" (*SZ* 364) as if they were identity statements. But they cannot be. For identity statements can only assert the identity of entities, and neither the past nor possibility nor disclosedness nor the world, understood as worldliness, is an entity. Each is rather an "existential" (*Existenzial*), that is, a constitutive structural dimension of Dasein's being. Existentials are conceptually inseparable from Dasein, since they are precisely what make a Dasein a Dasein, but they are not entities in their own right, so they cannot strictly speaking be identical with (or distinct from) Dasein. Dasein cannot be identical with its disclosedness, its "there," or being-in-the-world, for the simple reason that no entity can be identical with its mode of being, since modes of being are not themselves entities.

As I have said, the term 'Dasein,' like 'human being,' contains a reference to being (*Sein*). Indeed, much of its terminological appeal lies in the way it mirrors what Heidegger insists is essential to Dasein itself, for 'Dasein' is defined in its relation to '*Sein*,' just as Dasein itself is defined by its relation to being: "Dasein is an entity that, *in its being, comports itself* understandingly toward that being" (*SZ* 52–3, emphasis added). The point of such a construction is clearly that the being consists in the comporting. Dasein is therefore more eventlike than objectlike, its 'being' more like a gerund than a substantive.[57] Comportment is not something that Dasein just happens to be capable of, or subject to, as if its comporting itself toward its being were distinct from its being. Dasein just *is* its

---

[56] Haugeland, "Dasein's Disclosedness," 27, 35, 42–3 n27.

[57] Similarly, "clearing," the English translation of Heidegger's word *Lichtung*, can be instructively misread as a gerund rather than a substantive (see *SZ* 133, 170).

comporting itself toward its own being. Of course, appealing to gerund verb constructions is by itself insufficient to distinguish Dasein from anything else, since obviously not every event or happening is Dasein. Heidegger's point, though, is that our being is not that of a self-contained object (or subject) but rather lies in our understanding of being. Again, "Dasein . . . in its being, comports itself understandingly toward that being."[58] But this is not to say that Dasein is *identical with* its being.

The most plausible reading of sentences like "Dasein is its disclosedness," I want to suggest, is to construe them not as identity statements but as elliptical for the claim that Dasein's being consists in its comporting itself understandingly *toward* its being, indeed toward being generally. The 'is' in the sentence, then, is not the 'is' of identity but functions instead as a somewhat peculiar transitive verb, analogous to the verb 'to live' in the expression 'to live one's life.' To "be" your disclosedness is not to be identical with it, but to *live* it or *exist* it. It may be trivially true that we live our lives, but it is far from trivial to maintain, as Heidegger does, that our very being consists not in our being physical objects or organisms, or even functional or intentional systems, but lies solely in the living of our lives. Dasein is not a way of life, then, as Haugeland proposes; rather, particular Daseins are particular livings of particular lives. Of course, Heidegger also maintains that the being of every particular Dasein consists essentially in "being-with" others (*Mitsein*), so his account is not individualistic in any traditional sense. Still, the entity whose being is being-with is a human particular, not a pattern of norms, institutions, or behaviors.

The analytic of Dasein, then, is an account of the existential structures of concrete human particulars, that is, individual persons. More specifically, it is an analytic of persons with respect to their being, which consists in their understanding of being, their own and in general. As Heidegger says, however, "Being is always the being of an entity" (*SZ* 9),

---

[58] Fichte and Kierkegaard might appear to have anticipated Heidegger in this, except that they conceive of human beings in terms of the reflexive structure of subjectivity, while Heidegger understands them as embodied social agents. For Fichte and Kierkegaard, then, as in the twentieth century for Sartre, a human being is defined by its consciousness of itself, not by its practical comportment toward its own being. See Kierkegaard, *The Sickness unto Death*, 43. There is no doubt that in his early work Heidegger borrows heavily from Kierkegaard, often without acknowledging the debt, but he is right to insist that the existential problematic as such remained fundamentally "alien" to his Danish precursor (*SZ* 235n).

so any account of our understanding of being will necessarily be an account of our understanding of or comportment (*Verhaltung*) toward entities, which is to say our moods and our understanding and interpretation of them.

Intentionality and the "World-Poverty" of Animals

If the analytic of Dasein ought to be read as an account of hermeneutic conditions, it is worthwhile trying to say how and why it does not just amount to a description of consciousness or a theory of intentionality, albeit in an exotic idiom. Heidegger makes it clear that consciousness is not the subject of the existential analytic, if only by resolutely avoiding any systematic mention of the term itself. It would be no less mistaken, however, to infer that he doubts or denies the existence of consciousness, or that he regards the notion as somehow philosophically corrupt or illegitimate.[59] It is far more plausible to suppose that Heidegger takes it for granted, as most of us do, that consciousness is a perfectly real phenomenon, but that he thinks it has needlessly preoccupied philosophers and led them away from the wider context within which it figures as just one aspect among others of being-in-the-world. More specifically, as Heidegger himself does say, what is lacking in traditional philosophical appeals to consciousness is an account of its *being*, which I understand as the conditions under which it is intelligible and interpretable as such.

So, for example, "in his idealistic epistemology," Heidegger says, "Husserl does not further ask the question about the entity constituted as consciousness" (*MAL* 167). Similarly, a few years later, in his exchange with Husserl on the occasion of their ill-fated collaboration on the *Encyclopaedia Britannica* article on phenomenology, Heidegger asks, "what is the mode of being of the entity in which the 'world' is constituted? This is the central problem of *Being and Time* – i.e. a fundamental ontology of Dasein" (*Hu* IX 601; *PTP* 138). Unlike Brentano and Husserl, and more recently John Searle,[60] that is, Heidegger does

---

[59] Frederick Olafson is right, then, that "it would be a mistake to infer that because he subjects the concept of consciousness to such a rigorous critique and effectively abandons its use, all connections between Heidegger's thought and the concept were severed." *Heidegger and the Philosophy of Mind*, 14. I think Olafson concedes too much, however, when he identifies the *concept* of Dasein with the *concepts* of the subject and the I. See Chapter 6 and my "On Being Social: A Reply to Olafson."

[60] Searle, *The Rediscovery of the Mind*, chapter 7.

not take for granted that there is any essential or necessary connection between consciousness and intentionality, and it is natural to read his description of everyday understanding as leaving room for the possibility of genuinely unconscious attitudes. Like perception and embodiment, consciousness simply does not fall within the orbit of Heidegger's concerns, nor does he assume that the question of being and the analytic of Dasein demand some preliminary account of it. On the contrary, it is precisely by assuming the ontological primacy and epistemic transparency of consciousness, subjectivity, and selfhood that philosophers have so often passed over both the question of being and the conditions of Dasein's understanding of being. Of course, none of this is to say that Heidegger doubts the reality or centrality of consciousness in our experience, any more than he doubts the reality and importance of pleasure or appetite. The question is whether consciousness deserves pride of place in an account of the structure of being-in-the-world at large.

It is somewhat more promising to interpret the analytic of Dasein as part of a global theory of intentionality. But what *is* intentionality? Here too, Heidegger thinks philosophers have failed to ask about the *being* of the entity evidently exhibiting the phenomenon: "We must," he says, "make intentionality itself into a problem" (*MAL* 168). Doing so means, at a minimum, challenging the Cartesian–Husserlian assumption that intentionality resides exclusively or even primarily in mental representation: "When relating-to, which is what is meant by the term 'intentionality,' is correctly understood, then it cannot be taken to be a feature of representing, a representing that remains with the mental, as it would seem to be in Brentano." So, Heidegger concludes,

> the previous concept of intentionality proves to be a truncated conception.... [E]very act of directing oneself toward something receives the characteristic of knowing, for example, in Husserl, who describes the basic structure of all intentional relating as *noēsis,* thus all intentionality is first of all a cognitive intending, upon which other modes of active relation to entities are later built. (*MAL* 168–9)

If we restrict the term 'intentionality' to the cognitive domain in this way, following Brentano and Husserl, then Heidegger's analytic is not, at least not primarily, an account of the conditions of intentionality. Indeed, it is precisely because intentionality typically lends itself to such a mentalistic construal that Heidegger is at pains to exclude the term from his own vocabulary. Again, this is not to deny the importance of cognition and mentality, any more than the turn away from consciousness amounted to a philosophically principled rejection of that concept. Heidegger's point is rather that traditional theoretical fixations on consciousness and cognition have truncated and distorted our interpretation of human existence by insisting that our distinctive relation to the world must itself reside in such subjective mental states.

Heidegger's fundamental ontology, then, is no more a theory of cognitive intention than it is a description of conscious experience. Instead, it is an account of the structures and conditions peculiar to human understanding and interpretation, that is, competent, socialized know-how and discursive expression and communication. The analytic of Dasein is not a theory of intentionality with a view to the explanation and prediction of behavior, but has to do instead with the hermeneutic conditions distinctive of human understanding as such, informed as it is by our understanding of being, which is constitutive of our being-in-the-world, and which Heidegger refers to elsewhere as "original transcendence." In his 1928 lectures he therefore says explicitly, "The problem of transcendence as such is not at all identical with the problem of intentionality" (*MAL* 170). Indeed, "Transcendence, being-in-the-world, is never to be equated or identified with intentionality" (*MAL* 214–15). Heidegger goes on to say that intentionality "is itself only possible on the basis of original transcendence, on the basis of being-in-the-world. This primordial transcendence makes possible every intentional relation to entities" (*MAL* 170).

Heidegger then spells this out by saying that it is our understanding of being that makes possible every intentional relation as an apprehension of entities *as such,* that is, *as entities.* "The relation is based on a preliminary understanding of the being of entities. This understanding of being . . . first secures the possibility of entities manifesting themselves as entities" (*MAL* 170). I take this to mean that original transcendence, or our understanding of being, is the condition of the possibility of intentionality *understood as a mode of interpretation,* which is to say the explicit understanding of entities as such, that is, *as entities.*

That is a strong claim, but perhaps not as strong as it might sound to contemporary ears, for it assumes a concept of intentionality applicable specifically to human beings in their capacity to recognize and deal with entities as the entities they are. Another way of putting this is to say that it construes intentionality as a form of knowledge, namely, knowledge of *what* and *that* entities *are.* I believe it says nothing, indeed deliberately so, concerning the intentional states of animals. Unlike the naturalistic theories of mind so prevalent today, especially among cognitive scientists, Heidegger's approach follows Brentano and Husserl in conceiving of the structure of intentionality in terms of its distinctive manifestation in human beings, not as a general biological phenomenon. To say that original transcendence, or our understanding of being, is a condition of the possibility of fully intentional attitudes, then, is to regard it as a hermeneutic condition, a condition of explicit practical understanding, not necessarily a condition of the object-directedness of mental states in any species of organism whatever.

Mark Okrent is right, then, to qualify his "interpretation of the early Heidegger which sees him as giving a transcendental argument concerning the necessary conditions for the possibility of intentionality" with the reminder that, for Heidegger, "the primary form of intending is doing something for a purpose rather than being conscious of something."[61] On Okrent's reading, an epistemic state such as a perception turns out to be a special case of practical intentionality, since "all perception involves understanding"; indeed, "Perception has the structure of understanding and interpretation built into it."[62] As Heidegger himself says, "All prepredicative simple seeing of the available is in itself already understanding-interpreting." Even in the case of "a pure perception of something," he insists, "The seeing of this sight is already understanding-interpreting" (*SZ* 149). Okrent's approach is thus made plausible by Heidegger's insistence on the dependence of intentionality on practical understanding. It is misleading, however, inasmuch as it obscures the gap – nay, the abyss – separating the mental life of animals from the robust intentional phenomena peculiar to the interpretive practices of human beings. For to say that perception always bears within it the structure of practical understanding and interpretation is not to say that all biological instances of perceptual consciousness, even the consciousness of animals, presuppose an understanding of being, only that *ours* does.

This raises a profound and difficult question, namely, What kinds of experience or understanding (if any) do "mere animals" have? The form of the question in contemporary philosophy of mind concerns the attribution of intentional states, in particular intentional states with propositional contents, to nonhuman organisms, even artifacts. And it

---

[61] Okrent, *Heidegger's Pragmatism*, 4, 10.   [62] Ibid., 75, 76.

is a question Heidegger himself dwells on at length in his lectures of 1929–30, though he frames it not in terms of intentional states, but in the language of fundamental ontology.

What Heidegger proposes, in short, is that animals have a kind of "access" (*Zugang*) to entities and that they exhibit a kind of "behavior" (*Benehmen*), but that they have no understanding of being. Behavior is something that falls short of action but is more than the mere occurrence of events (*GM* §§58–61). Accordingly, organisms of all kinds evidently perceive things and even deal with them intelligently, if only instinctively, but they have no understanding of *what* – or *that* – things *are,* or again what it *means* for anything to be. They are consequently unable to interpret entities as entities, since their experience lacks the *as*-structure constitutive of our understanding of being. Heidegger says:

> The lizard . . . basks in the sun. This is what we say, though it is doubtful that it comports itself as we do when we lie in the sun, that the sun is accessible to it *as* sun, that it experiences the rock *as* rock. Yet . . . it has *its own relation* to the rock and the sun and other things. One is tempted to say: what we come across here as rock and sun are for the lizard just lizard-things. When we say that the lizard lies on the rock, we ought to cross out the word "rock" to indicate that what it lies on is indeed given to it *somehow,* but is nonetheless not known to it *as* rock. Crossing the word out does not just mean: something else, taken as something else, but rather: not accessible *as an entity* at all. (*GM* 291–2)

> Thus a number of things are accessible to the animal, and not just any old things with no particular limits. Its *way of being,* which we call "*life,*" is *not without access* to the things around it . . . the animal has its environment and moves within it. (*GM* 292)

So, too, a bee's "sucking at a blossom is *not a comporting itself* toward the blossom *as something occurrent or not occurrent*" (*GM* 353). And though it finds its way back to the hive, presumably by navigating with reference to the position of the sun, "The bee is *simply given over* to the sun and to the duration of its flight *without grasping either of these as such* and without turning to a consideration of them as grasped" (*GM* 359).

What the mere animal lacks, Heidegger concludes, is the possibility of "comporting and relating itself to another thing *as* such-and-such at all, *as* something occurrent, *as* an entity" (*GM* 360). So, although animals have a kind of access to entities, they have no understanding of entities as entities, hence no understanding of being, hence no being-in-the-world. Unlike mere stones, they are not altogether "worldless," but neither are they fully "world-constituting" or "world-forming" (*weltbildend*), like Dasein. Instead, Heidegger proposes, animals are "world-poor" (*GM* 250–396), that is, they do not encounter or understand entities *as entities*, though neither do they lack a kind of "access" to things in their environments altogether.

But does such "access" to entities amount to what we would call intentionality? If so, it is certainly not the sort of intentionality that Brentano and Husserl had in mind, namely, the conceptual apprehension of objects as objects, as either being or not being. But neither is it mere qualitative nervous sensitivity, for Heidegger insists that it constitutes a kind of purposive "behavior," as well as an animal's distinctive "captivation" (*Benommenheit*) by things in the environment, though again not under any thematizable aspect – not "as such." Short of any understanding of being, that is, Heidegger does seem to credit animals with something like intentionality in the primitive sense of a "directedness" toward objects, which Brentano himself famously deemed "the mark of the mental."[63]

What I want to suggest is that Heidegger's ontological conception of "world-poverty" amounts to a kind of *analogical* approach to questions concerning the intentionality of mere animals. Robert Brandom has drawn a distinction between analogical and relational conceptions of the connection between language and intentionality.[64] Unlike intentionalists like Husserl, Grice, and Searle, all of whom try in different ways to analyze linguistic meaning in terms of the mental states of speakers – mental states whose intentional contents they must therefore simply take as given – Heidegger, like Brandom and Davidson, is a contextualist and so insists that content is inseparable from the practical and discursive setting in which it occurs. Whereas intentionalists like Grice and Searle conceive of intentionality in terms of rational agency, and so construe linguistic action as just one kind of reason-driven action,

---

[63] It is important to keep in mind that whereas many contemporary philosophers and psychologists conceive of intentionality as necessarily involving *propositional* content, Brentano and Husserl emphatically do not. Heidegger's apparent denial that animals have anything like propositional attitudes or knowledge therefore by itself says nothing against his granting them a more primitive form of preconceptual, preepistemic directedness toward objects.

[64] Brandom, *Making It Explicit*, 150–3. Brandom takes his point of departure from Robert Stalnaker's distinction between pragmatic and linguistic approaches to the question concerning animal intentionality. The analogical and relational views are two versions of what Stalnaker calls the "linguistic approach." Stalnaker, *Inquiry*, 4ff.

contextualists like Davidson and Brandom construe rationality itself in terms of linguistic competence and mental representation in terms of linguistic expression. Brandom adds, however, that this linguistic approach itself is free to conceive of the primacy of language in either analogical or relational terms. On the analogical view, we make sense of the content of intentional states in general by analogy with, or by appeal to their resembling, the content of speech. On the relational view, the content of particular intentional states just consists in, and so in a more robust sense depends upon, the content of the speech acts in which they are in fact concretely expressed.

Although Heidegger himself does not analyze intentional attitudes in terms of either rational agency or linguistic expression per se, his view is nonetheless close to that of Davidson and Brandom inasmuch as he conceives of intentionality in terms of the way it manifests itself in situated practical understanding. Moreover, it is expressive and communicative practice, or "discourse" (*Rede*), not reason or action, that he identifies as the distinguishing mark of human understanding, over against mere animal experience and behavior. This is why he explicitly rejects the Latin rendering of the Greek *zōon logon echon* as *animal rationale* in favor of the somewhat more homely observation that "Man shows himself as the entity that talks (*redet*)" (*SZ* 165; cf. 48). Like Davidson and Brandom, then, Heidegger is willing to regard the practice of assertion as constitutive of our understanding of conceptual and propositional content, and so too of belief. Unlike them, however, he treats assertion itself as "a derivative mode of interpretation" (*SZ* 33). He is thus free to countenance the possibility of genuinely meaningful expressive and communicative practice in the absence of the fully propositional contents of linguistic assertions and intentional states. Discourse is not identical with language, so although Heidegger considers human understanding and interpretation to be bound up with communication and expression broadly construed, he grants no pride of place to language as such, except in the articulation of specifically propositional contents, which are parasitic on the interpretive practice of assertion (*SZ* 33).

Notwithstanding the limited role of language in Heidegger's early thought, then, his approach to the intentionality of animals is still, broadly speaking, "analogical" in spirit. Brandom points out that the alternative "relational" linguistic view, which he shares with Davidson,[65]

---

[65] See Davidson, "Thought and Talk," in *Inquiries into Truth and Interpretation.*

entails that the intentional states of nonlinguistic animals must be assigned a kind of second-class status relative to our own, since only ours are in fact tied to linguistic expression, which constitutes content.[66] The analogical view, by contrast, allows for a more generous realism concerning the intentional states of brutes, since it claims only that we understand those states on analogy with our own discursive expressions, not that they could have content only if the animals themselves could talk. Brandom dismisses the analogical version of the linguistic picture because it seems to entail a mere reversal in the traditional order of explanation, obliging one instead to account for linguistic practice absent any appeal to intentionality. Like Davidson, though, Brandom thinks of intentionality and linguistic meaning as two sides of a single coin: neither reducible to the other, both essentially involving propositional content. He admits no notion of intentionality involving nonconceptual or prepropositional content, so any account of intentionality seems to him to take for granted a robust conception of linguistic meaning. For Brandom, "sapience, discursive intentionality, is concept-mongering."[67] In supposing that propositional content exhausts intentionality and discursive meaning, Brandom in effect subscribes to a kind of pragmatic *rationalism* that Heidegger rejects.

Heidegger's position, I want to suggest, amounts to a modified version of the analogical approach to animal intentionality. World-poverty, understood as mere behavioral access to things in an environment, absent any understanding of being, clearly falls short of the "world-forming" understanding of being that is unique to and definitive of Dasein. Animals therefore no doubt lack the forms of intentionality that are dependent on or constituted by such an understanding. This is why Heidegger proposes that, in saying that the lizard lies on the rock, we ought to cross out the word 'rock,' since although the rock is "given" to the lizard somehow, it cannot be given to the lizard as it is given to those of us who know *what* a rock *is,* and *that* it is. For the very word, just by being a word in a human language, already smuggles in too much of our own understanding of being to capture the peculiar poverty of the lizard's apprehension of the entity. Yet the analogy between the lizard's experience and our own understanding, thanks in part to our competent use of words like

---

[66] Brandom, *Making It Explicit,* 151.   [67] Ibid., 8.

'sun' and 'rock,' does provide us with a way – the only possible way – of making sense of the lizard as more than just a blind biological mechanism.

Whereas Davidson and Brandom conceive of all intentionality in terms of propositional content, then, and so treat the ascription of such content to mere animals as a kind of fiction or metaphor, Heidegger appears to regard the world-poverty of animals on analogy with being-in-the-world, and so treats such ascriptions as legitimate comparisons. The analogical view, of course, makes no commitment concerning the quality or convincingness of the comparisons in question; indeed, Heidegger often suggests that even our preontological understanding of animals is profoundly problematic and perhaps doomed to obscurity. Nevertheless, all efforts to make sense of what it means to have an "impoverished" world, or indeed to lack a world altogether, presuppose some ontological account of what a world is and what it means to "have" a world in the proper sense. In order to specify what human beings and other organisms have in common, that is, it is necessary first to get clear about the conditions of the kind of intentionality we have in virtue of our understanding of being. Relative to our own discursive and interpretive understanding, Heidegger suggests, the phenomena of "life" and "living" make sense only as "privative" modifications, intelligible only by subtracting something from our more basic understanding of being-in-the-world (*SZ* 50, 194, 246, 346). So, for example, he insists that only human beings "die" (*sterben*); animals merely "perish" (*verenden*) (*SZ* 240–1, 247, 251).[68] As he would say in the 1947 "Letter on 'Humanism,'"

> Of all the entities that are, presumably the most difficult for us to think about are living creatures (*das Lebe-Wesen*), because on the one hand they are in a certain way most closely related to us, and on the other hand are at once separated from our ek-sistent essence by an abyss. By contrast, it must appear as though the essence of the divine is nearer to us than what is foreign to us in living creatures, nearer, that is, in its essential distance, which as distance is nonetheless more familiar to our eksistent essence than our scarcely conceivable, abysmal (*abgründige*) kinship with the animal. (*Wegmarken* 157)

[68] The term 'animals' is deliberately vague, since the point is to specify an ontological distinction between the world-forming and the world-poor, not to speculate about where the division occurs biologically among species. For more on Heidegger's distinctions among perishing, demise, and death, see Chapter 6.

So, although animals may be like us in having at least primitive intentional relations to things, they lack the understanding of being that allows us to make sense of entities *as* entities and of our attitudes *as* intentional. What is fundamentally mysterious about mere animal intentionality, one might say, is precisely that it lacks the kind of understanding in virtue of which alone we can try to imagine what it must be like.

2

THE CRITIQUE OF HUSSERL

But there is no sharp boundary between methodological propositions and propositions within a method.

Wittgenstein

Perhaps no single philosophical influence on Heidegger is at once so important and yet so complex and controversial as that of his elder friend, colleague, and mentor, Edmund Husserl. Any serious discussion of Heidegger's thought presupposes some familiarity with Husserl's phenomenological method, his critique of naturalism, and his theory of intentionality. Husserl's phenomenology was of paramount importance for the conception and composition of *Being and Time,* yet it is difficult to say exactly what the nature and scope of his influence on Heidegger amounted to in the end.

Scholars have consequently advanced radically different accounts of the sources and implications of Husserl's and Heidegger's ideas, their conceptions of phenomenology, their philosophical commitments, and their apparent agreements and disagreements on a wide range of issues. Rather than address the question of their relation directly, some have simply given up drawing them onto the same intellectual maps at all, concentrating their efforts on one to the exclusion of the other, or else concluding that they were speaking such different philosophical languages as to share virtually no common conceptual ground. The historical and stylistic jump from Husserlian to Heideggerian phenomenology is, as one commentator has rightly said, something like a "Gestalt switch."[1] There is certainly no neat account to give of a smooth

---

[1] Theodore Kisiel, "Heidegger (1907–1927): The Transformation of the Categorial," 185.

transition from Husserl's notions of a presuppositionless description of pure consciousness, and of phenomenology as a "rigorous science" (*strenge Wissenschaft*),[2] to Heidegger's existential analytic of human existence by means of a "hermeneutic of facticity."[3] Indeed, their respective aims and assumptions seem so profoundly different that Husserl and Heidegger at times seem to occupy altogether incommensurable philosophical worlds.

Yet reducing their philosophical disagreements to a mere contrast of aspects threatens to obscure the substantive issues at stake between them. It also tends to conceal the motivation underlying Heidegger's project and the force of the "immanent critique" of Husserl's phenomenology that he spells out in his lectures in the 1920s (see *PGZ*). In this chapter I will try to say where and how far Heidegger departs from Husserl and what his critique amounts to. Husserl and Heidegger are worlds apart in both style and substance, but the abyss between them is not so deep as to render them literally incomparable.

Moreover, it seems to me, Heidegger's critique is compelling. What it suggests, in short, is that Husserl's phenomenology is at once uncritical and incoherent: uncritical in its appropriation of the Cartesian conception of the subject and the Platonic–Aristotelian interpretation of being as presence (*Anwesen*); incoherent because it purports to ground those prejudices in a rigorous philosophical method that can itself be made intelligible only by taking them for granted. Husserl's project is thus caught in a vicious circle, for its results presuppose its methods and its methods presuppose its results. Neither genuinely radical nor free of substantive presuppositions, Husserl's phenomenology is simply not the "rigorous science" it claims to be.

---

[2] The German word '*Wissenschaft*' has wider scope than the English word 'science,' so it can be misleading to say that Husserl conceived of philosophy as a kind of "science." One might say instead that he conceived of it as a rigorous "discipline." That is, he did not suppose that philosophy can or should strive to emulate the natural, mathematical, or social sciences, but that it is, or ought to be, a methodical exercise undertaken by a rational community of inquirers, proceeding from the observation of intuitively given evidence and aspiring to objectively valid results subject to strict, intersubjective confirmation. "Science," in this wide sense, then, has nothing in particular to do with the so-called hypothetico-deductive method, the quantification and analysis of data, experimental procedures, or the discovery of laws. What it does demand is a firm basis in intuitively given evidence. What it therefore rules out, I shall argue, is any approach, like Heidegger's, unabashedly caught up in the circularity of interpretation.

[3] See Heidegger's lectures of 1923, *Ontology: The Hermeneutics of Facticity*.

What it offers is, on the contrary, an instance of precisely the sort of circular interpretation that Heidegger thinks phenomenology, indeed philosophy in general, cannot avoid. For any method one initially articulates must remain open to revision under pressure from the observations and insights to which it leads, just as any of those observations and insights themselves must be sensitive to methodological considerations at the outset. It is impossible simply to establish a method a priori and then insulate it from one's concrete findings. Heidegger makes this point already around 1920 in his "Comments on Karl Jaspers's *Psychology of Worldviews*," where he writes,

> prior conceptions (*Vorgriffe*)[4] "are" everywhere in factical life experience (thus also in the sciences and in philosophizing).... Every problem of prior conception (*Vorgriffsproblematik*) is a problem of "method."...One must therefore let the sense of method be given with the prior conception itself; the one arises with the other from the same source and with the same significance (*aus derselben Sinnquelle*). Any fixing of the sense of "method" must be left open in a formally indicative meaning (e.g. "way") for authentic concrete determinations. (*Weg/GA9*, 9)

Philosophical discourse is essentially interpretive, and its content impinges on its "way" of proceeding, just as its way of proceeding shapes and informs its content.

But Husserl never acknowledges the interpretive character of his own inquiry, and his pretense of scientific rigor has the effect of concealing the substantive and methodological assumptions underlying his phenomenological claims. Moreover, Husserl's claims to have grounded his observations in pure eidetic intuition merely obscure the issue. In what is clearly a reference to Husserl, Heidegger remarks,

> The path to the "things themselves" under consideration in philosophy is a long one, so that the excessive liberties that certain phenomenologists have taken recently with essential intuition appear in a highly dubious light, which hardly accords with the "openness" and "devotion" they preach. (*Weg/GA9*, 5)

On the one hand, then, in his Marburg lectures of 1923–4, Heidegger credits Brentano and Husserl with genuine philosophical breakthroughs without which fundamental ontology would never have been

---

[4] As we shall see in Chapter 5, the concept of *Vorgriff* (fore-conception) comes to play a systematic role in Heidegger's account of understanding and interpretation in *Being and Time*.

possible: "With this discovery of intentionality, a path has been given for a radical ontological inquiry for the first time explicitly in the entire history of philosophy."[5] On the other hand, "In the fundamental task of determining its proper field," he concludes, "phenomenology is *unphenomenological!*" (*PGZ* 178).

Apart from the question of method and its relation to the putative findings of phenomenological inquiry, Heidegger also challenges Husserl on a number of substantive points. To begin with, although Heidegger undeniably attached great importance to the sixth of the *Logical Investigations* and Husserl's doctrine of "categorial intuition," he rejects the doctrine precisely because he regards all forms of intuition as parasitic on engaged practical forms of understanding whose function is not to present objects to a subject, but to guide and orient an agent's practical activity. Heidegger thus denies the primacy of what Husserl calls objectifying or "positing" attitudes, such as perception and assertion, and criticizes Husserl's continual reliance on what Heidegger regards as an ontologically obscure distinction between "real" (existing in time) and "ideal" (abstract or timeless) entities (*SZ* 156, 217, 229). Heidegger also repudiates the reductions, the "eidetic" and the phenomenological or "transcendental" reductions, and at least implicitly the "reduction to ownness," which Husserl would elaborate in *Cartesian Meditations* (§§44–7). For Heidegger, all the reductions represent a failure to acknowledge the hermeneutic constraints on any adequate understanding of human being as being-in-the-world, as opposed to mere objecthood or detached subjectivity. In contrast to Husserl's Platonism, mentalism, and methodological solipsism, then, Heidegger is best understood as a kind of pragmatic externalist. For in his view, it is not mental states that constitute our primitive relation to the world, nor can intentionality be understood in terms of ideal semantic contents in abstraction from social practice and communicative discourse.

What distinguishes Heidegger from Husserl most profoundly, however, is his recognition of the hermeneutic conditions of phenomenological inquiry itself. Far from the purely descriptive discipline Husserl envisioned, phenomenology is irreducibly interpretive and so must acknowledge and embrace the circularity inherent in his own claims. The "hermeneutic circle" essential to all interpretation, including the phenomenological interpretation of intentionality, is what Husserl's

---

[5] Heidegger, *Einführung in die phänomenologische Forschung*, 260.

enterprise fails to recognize and accommodate. Indeed, acknowledging the inescapable circularity of human understanding entails a radical reassessment of the nature of the philosophical enterprise itself.

A Plea for Discontinuity

Being and Time was published in the spring of 1927 as the seventh volume of Husserl's *Jahrbuch für Phänomenologie und phänomenologische Forschung* and in a separate edition inscribed with a dedication to Husserl composed the previous April: "in admiration and friendship." In a footnote in the Introduction of the text, Heidegger writes,

> If the following inquiry has taken any steps forward in disclosing the "things themselves," the author must above all thank E. Husserl, who, by his incisive personal guidance and by freely turning over his unpublished investigations, familiarized the author with the most diverse areas of phenomenological research during his years as a student in Freiburg. (*SZ* 38n)[6]

But Heidegger's personal and intellectual attitude toward Husserl and his work was always profoundly ambivalent. In fact, notwithstanding his philosophical and professional debt to his elder colleague and mentor, and in spite of what he always described as the "decisive influence" of Husserl's *Logical Investigations* (1900–1) on his own philosophical development,[7] Heidegger apparently held Husserl in low esteem as a teacher and philosopher. As early as 1916, before the two had met, Heidegger wrote to a friend regretting Husserl's appointment to the chair in philosophy at Freiburg, describing him as "lacking the necessary breadth of vision."[8] By the early 1920s Heidegger could write to Karl Löwith, referring to his assault on Husserl in his lectures,

> In the final hours of the seminar, I publicly burned and destroyed the *Ideas* to such an extent that I dare say that the essential foundations for the whole [of my work] are now clearly laid out. Looking back from this vantage point to the *Logical Investigations,* I am now convinced that

---

[6] Heidegger complied with the publisher's request to omit the dedication in the seventh edition of 1941 on the grounds that Husserl was Jewish. The footnote quoted here, however, was retained.

[7] From Heidegger's curriculum vitae, composed for his habilitation in 1915. Ott, *Martin Heidegger: A Political Life,* 84. Heidegger acknowledged the debt again nearly a half century later, in 1963, in "My Way to Phenomenology," in *ZSD.*

[8] Letter to Ernst Laslowski, January 1916. Quoted in Ott, *Martin Heidegger,* 90.

Husserl was never a philosopher, not even for one second in his life. He becomes ever more ludicrous.[9]

Similarly, in his correspondence with Jaspers in the 1920s, Heidegger imagines Jaspers and himself as "comrades in arms" (*ein Kampfgemeinschaft*) seeking to overthrow the academic establishment and eradicate "all the medicine men of contemporary philosophy."[10] The epithet clearly refers to his own mentor, among others, for just a few months later Heidegger writes:

Husserl has gone completely off his rocker – if he was ever really "all there" at all, which has become increasingly doubtful to me recently. He runs around saying such trivial things, it's pitiful. He thrives on his mission of being the "founder of phenomenology," no one knows what that is. Anyone who's here for a semester knows the problem. He begins to suspect that people are no longer following. Naturally he thinks it's too difficult. Naturally no one understands a "mathematics of the ethical" (the latest thing!) – even someone more advanced than Heidegger, of whom he *now* says, Well, he had to give lectures of his own and couldn't attend mine, otherwise he'd be farther along.[11]

A few months earlier, Heidegger had written to Löwith that his lectures in the spring of 1923, *Ontology: The Hermeneutics of Facticity,* had sundered all ties to Husserl, who would surely no longer support him professionally, particularly not in his aspiring to the chair at Freiburg. The course, he writes,

strikes the main blows against phenomenology. I now stand completely on my own feet. . . . There is no chance of getting an appointment. And after I have published, my prospects will be finished. The old man will then realize that I am wringing his neck – and then the question of succeeding him is out. But I can't help myself.[12]

Ironically, a month later – with Husserl's enthusiastic support – Heidegger was offered an "associate professorship with the status and rights of a full professor" at Marburg.[13] Nevertheless, he continued to attack Husserl philosophically in his lectures throughout the 1920s. And

[9] Letter to Löwith, 20 February 1923. Quoted by Sheehan, *PTP* 17.
[10] Letter to Jaspers, 19 November 1922. This and other cited letters to Jaspers are in Martin Heidegger/Karl Jaspers, *Briefwechsel 1920–1963*.
[11] Letter to Jaspers, 14 July 1923.
[12] Letter to Löwith, 8 May 1923. Quoted by Sheehan, *PTP* 17.
[13] Ott, *Martin Heidegger,* 124.

in December 1926, still working furiously to prepare the manuscript of *Being and Time* for publication, Heidegger confided to Jaspers, "If the treatise is written 'against' anyone, it's against Husserl, and he saw it immediately but clung to the positive from the outset. What I write against, only indirectly of course, is pseudophilosophy (*Scheinphilosophie*)."[14] Years later, in his letter to William Richardson, Heidegger would make the same basic point, though more diplomatically: "'phenomenology' in Husserl's sense was elaborated into a particular philosophical position already anticipated by Descartes, Kant, and Fichte. The historicity of thinking remained utterly foreign to it." Heidegger refers at this point to Husserl's essay "Philosophy as Rigorous Science" and then continues: "The question of being developed in *Being and Time* set itself against this philosophical position and on the basis of what I still today believe to be a more faithful adherence to the principle of phenomenology."[15]

In 1928 Heidegger did in fact take over the chair at Freiburg upon Husserl's retirement and promptly cut off all personal contact with his former friend and mentor. Only at that point, apparently, did Husserl become aware of the full extent of Heidegger's hostility to his entire philosophical orientation. In 1931 he wrote to Alexander Pfänder:

> I had been warned often enough: Heidegger's phenomenology is something totally different from mine; rather than further the development of my scientific works, his university lectures as well as his book are, on the contrary, open or veiled attacks on my works, directed at discrediting them on the most essential points. When I used to relate such things to Heidegger in a friendly way, he would just laugh and say: "Nonsense!"[16]

Husserl initially regarded Heidegger's philosophy as an inspired continuation of his own. Later, he considered it an obscure, pretentious, "anthropological" transposition of his transcendental philosophy, "so that everything deep becomes unclear and loses its philosophical value." In the margins of his copy of *Being and Time*, for instance, he complains, "Everything said here is just my own theory, but without any

---

[14] Letter to Jaspers, 26 December 1926. This scenario exposes the appalling disingenuousness of Heidegger's remarks in the interview with *Der Spiegel* forty years later concerning his relations with Husserl: "In the beginning of the thirties, Husserl settled accounts with Max Scheler and me in public. I could never find out what persuaded Husserl to set himself against my thinking in such a public manner." Neske and Kettering, *Martin Heidegger and National Socialism*, 48.

[15] Heidegger, Preface to Richardson's *Heidegger: Through Phenomenology to Thought*, xiv.

[16] Letter to Alexander Pfänder, 6 January 1931. Translated by B. Hopkins, *PTP* 481.

deeper argument."[17] In the end, he came to view Heidegger's thought as a dangerous outburst of irrationalism that was utterly foreign to the spirit and letter of his own life's work.[18] None of these estimates was correct, yet each has been taken up and reaffirmed by scholars broadly sympathetic to Husserl's philosophical program.

Dagfinn Føllesdal, for example, though he credits Heidegger with "a major advance upon Husserl" in his emphasis on action as constitutive of intentionality, in the end concludes that "Heidegger's philosophy is basically isomorphic to that of Husserl," even "down to small details." Føllesdal concludes: "There seems to me to be every reason to hold, as Husserl did, that the main framework of Heidegger's philosophy in *Being and Time* is a translation of Husserl's."[19] Barry Smith and David Woodruff Smith go further by seeming to deny as a matter of principle that Heidegger's philosophy can have departed very far from Husserl's:

> Evolution is a piecemeal affair, in philosophy as in nature, and sharp breaks between philosophical epochs are artificial constructs. . . .
> [A]rguments purporting to establish a radical rejection of Husserlian thought by Heidegger and others often prove, on closer inspection, to rest on the exploitation of ideas worked out in advance by Husserl himself or by his early realist disciples. Such "breaks" serve mainly to give intellectual history an easy handle on continuities and complexities in the slow evolution of ideas.[20]

Apart from the fact that Smith and Smith do not say which ideas and disciples they have in mind, what are we to make of their suggestion

---

[17] Quoted in Diemer, *Edmund Husserl*, 19–20; cf. *PTP* 310.

[18] In the same 1931 letter to Pfänder, Husserl confesses: "My ever-increasing impression of his extraordinary natural talent, of his absolute devotion to philosophy, of the powerful energy of this young man's thought finally led me to an excessive assessment of his future importance for scientific phenomenology in my sense of the term" (*PTP* 480). Upon rereading *Being and Time* and *Kant and the Problem of Metaphysics*, however, he writes, "I arrived at the distressing conclusion that philosophically I have nothing to do with this Heideggerian profundity, with this brilliant unscientific genius; that Heidegger's criticism, both open and veiled, is based upon a gross misunderstanding; that he may be involved in the formation of a philosophical system of the kind which I have always considered it my life's work to make forever impossible. Everyone except me has realized this for a long time. I have not withheld my conclusion from Heidegger. . . . This reversal in professional esteem and personal relations was one of the most difficult ordeals of my life" (*PTP* 482). *PPT* also contains a complete catalogue of Husserl's marginal notes on Heidegger's *Being and Time* and *Kant and the Problem of Metaphysics*.

[19] Føllesdal, "Husserl and Heidegger on the Role of Actions in the Constitution of the World," 365, 369, 376.

[20] Smith and Smith, *The Cambridge Companion to Husserl*, Introduction, 2–3.

that apparent breaks in the history of philosophy are at best fictions, mere heuristic devices instrumental for grasping the real underlying continuity and "slow evolution of ideas"?

One could reply, of course, that the notion of slow, continuous evolution is as much an "artificial construct" as the idea of revolutionary change, and that any a priori assumption of gradualism serves no less to impose a comforting appearance of order and uniformity on the abrupt and unpredictable shifts that often occur in intellectual history. Moreover, dismissing the possibility of irreducible discontinuities in the history of philosophy is, if anything, less plausible than the corresponding assumption in evolutionary biology. For whereas the theory of natural selection describes environmental accidents and adaptations in large populations of organisms over vast stretches of time, philosophy concerns itself with the original creative insights of exceptional, often idiosyncratic, individuals. In both cases, anyway, gradualism remains no more than an assumption, and surely we ought to remain open to the possibility of genuine novelty and discontinuity in the history of ideas.

Robert Dostal offers a milder, but I think still misleading, version of the same argument. Challenging what he calls the "standard story," Dostal argues that "Husserlian phenomenology provides the framework for Heidegger's approach," indeed that "Heidegger's *Being and Time,* with its explicit task of relating being to time, follows in the footsteps of Husserl's project."[21] This is wrong, it seems to me, for two reasons. First, as we shall see, Husserlian phenomenology scarcely even addresses the question of being, in Heidegger's sense, so the account of being and time in *Being and Time* cannot plausibly be read as a continuation of Husserl's project. Second, Heidegger's account of temporality is based on a rejection of the standard assumption of the primacy of the present, which Husserl's theory of time consciousness takes entirely for granted. It is true that inauthentic Dasein tends to lose itself in the temporal present by falling into a lingering concern with things present in its environment, but the tendency itself is possible, Heidegger maintains, only because *"The primary phenomenon of primordial and authentic temporality is the future."* Consequently, "The primacy of the future will vary according to the modified temporalizing of inauthentic temporality itself, but will still come to the fore even in derivative 'time' " (*SZ* 329).[22]

---

[21] Dostal, "Time and Phenomenology in Husserl and Heidegger," 142.

[22] William Blattner is right, it seems to me, to insist on the modal indifference of primordial temporality, that is, that it is neither authentic nor inauthentic, so that the primacy of

What then does Heidegger's personal relationship with Husserl tell us indirectly about the philosophical content of his work? First, it is clear that Heidegger himself in no way thought of his own project as a repetition, an extension, or a restatement of Husserl's. On the contrary, he seems to have had a rather low opinion of Husserl philosophically, whose patronage he nonetheless cultivated and whose professional rank and international reputation conferred considerable prestige on his own early career.[23] Second, it appears that having gone back and reread *Being and Time* and *Kant and the Problem of Metaphysics,* Husserl himself was eventually disabused of any illusion that Heidegger had ever really been a loyal or sympathetic disciple. The principal parties to the dispute themselves, then, testify to the prima facie implausibility of suggestions that their projects were methodologically or substantively continuous with one another.

Indeed, as I hope to show, Heidegger's fundamental ontology cannot be understood as a mere supplement or continuation, let alone "translation," of Husserl's philosophy. Construed as an account of hermeneutic conditions, the analytic of Dasein denies any identification of intentionality with transcendental subjectivity or "pure" consciousness. As we shall see, not only are their respective projects deeply at odds, but in his lectures Heidegger even says explicitly what he regards as the fatal flaws in Husserl's enterprise. In a word, the hermeneutic phenomenology of *Being and Time* amounts to a wholesale rejection of the transcendental and eidetic reductions by means of which Husserl seeks to establish pure consciousness as the privileged locus of intentional phenomena. Before examining his critique of the reductions, however, it is important to point out that Heidegger also criticizes two crucially interrelated elements in Husserl's theory of intentionality: the doctrine

the future is a general fact about temporality, not just something peculiar to authentic existence. See *Heidegger's Temporal Idealism,* 98–102, 117 n31. Chapter 4 of Blattner's book moreover contains the best account I have read of the relation between Husserl's and Heidegger's phenomenologies of time. As Blattner shows, Heidegger regards the temporal phenomenon Husserl describes as an already disengaged, derivative, leveled-off form of time.

[23] The subsequent story of their personal and political relationship makes for sad reading. After assuming the chair at Freiburg, Heidegger shunned Husserl, and by 1930 they ceased to have any real contact with each other. Heidegger joined the Nazi Party in May 1933 and then became rector of the University. Contrary to his own subsequent account of events, he assumed the position with evident zeal, stepping in for Wilhelm von Möllendorf, who had resigned after only a few days in office, in part in response to the scandal surrounding the persecution of Jewish emeriti professors, notably Husserl, in April of that year.

of intellectual or categorial intuition and the primacy of what Husserl calls "positing" acts of consciousness.

Categorial Intuition

Heidegger himself always acknowledged the importance of Husserl's *Logical Investigations* for his own philosophical development, citing in particular the Sixth Investigation, "Elements of a Phenomenological Elucidation of Cognition (*Erkenntnis*)." That Heidegger's recollections of reading the *Investigations* in his youth were bound up with his fond feelings about the past is evident from the way he later blended philosophical remarks about phenomenology with memories of the material qualities, even the typeface, of the volumes themselves: "[B]oth volumes of Husserl's *Logical Investigations* sat on my desk ever since my first semester in the [Freiburg] Theological Seminary," he recalled a half century later. "The magic that emanated from the work extended to the outer appearance of the sentence structure and the title page" (*ZSD* 81–2). The books clearly had a special place in Heidegger's heart: "Even after the appearance of *Ideas Pertaining to a Pure Phenomenology*, the never-waning spell emanating from the *Logical Investigations* held me captive" (*ZSD* 85).

Part of that spell no doubt lay in the very idea of a philosophical discipline that fell between the a priori analysis of concepts and judgments, on the one hand, and the empirical study of cognition, on the other. But what lies between those two domains of traditional inquiry? "Wherein consists what is proper to phenomenology, if it is neither logic nor psychology?" (*ZSD* 83). Crucial to this new philosophical approach was Husserl's contention that we can intuit logical and conceptual structures inherent in the world and in our own attitudes: "Husserl's teaching took place in the form of a step-by-step practicing of phenomenological 'seeing.' " The idea struck Heidegger as an inspiration for his own interest in ancient philosophy: "Meanwhile, I could separate myself less and less from Aristotle and the other Greek thinkers, the more clearly my growing familiarity with phenomenological seeing proved fruitful for the interpretation of the Aristotelian writings."

This new style of thinking led Heidegger back to the doctrine that purports to justify it, namely, Husserl's theory of categorial intuition:

As I myself practiced phenomenological seeing, teaching and learning in Husserl's presence since 1919 . . . my interest inclined anew toward the

Logical Investigations, above all the Sixth in the first edition. The distinction worked out there between sensuous and categorial intuition revealed
itself to me in all its importance for the determination of the "manifold
meaning of being (*Seiende*)." (*ZSD* 86)[24]

Husserl's theory rests on the scheme underlying his early theory of
intentionality, according to which intentions are either empty signifying
acts, for example expecting or imagining something, or else fulfilling
acts in which something is given in intuition. Perception is therefore not
wholly passive, for sensuous intuitions, unless they strike us as utterly
unfamiliar, typically satisfy prior anticipations, or signifying acts, of some
kind. Seeing an ordinary white piece of paper, for example, fulfills a
prior intention with the contents *white* and *paper.*

Of course, what I anticipate is probably not just *white* and *paper,* but
that the paper *is* white. What, Husserl wonders, could satisfy the logical or propositional elements of that prior signifying act, in particular the copula 'is'? He insists that such structured intentions are satis-
fied in acts of intuitive givenness, and these acts he calls "categorial,"
as opposed to sensuous, intuitions. Categorial intuitions, then, fulfill
signifying acts whose contents include purely formal elements such
as *is* and *not,* the logical connectives *if, then, and,* and *or,* and quantifiers like *all, some, many, few, a,* and *none.* Sensuous intuition alone,
he argues, cannot fulfill acts whose contents have propositional structure. We cannot, *pace* the empiricists, simply abstract our logical understanding of the world from perceptions of sensuously given particulars. Rather, a higher form of intuition affords us insight into the fully
structured states of affairs that make our beliefs true or false (*LU* II/2,
§40).

Of particular importance for Heidegger, of course, is Husserl's subsequent account of "the origin of the concept of being" in §44 of the Sixth
Investigation. Husserl's main point is to deny that we derive a notion
of being from reflection on our own mental acts. We do not discover
upon introspection some distinct psychological process corresponding
to our understanding that the paper *is* white. Rather, the *is* is "meant,
i.e. signitively intended, in the little word 'is.' But it is *itself given,* or at
least putatively given, in the *fulfillment* that in some cases attaches to the

---

[24] Heidegger is referring here to the title of Brentano's dissertation of 1862, *Von der mannig-
    fachen Bedeutung des Seienden nach Aristoteles,* which Heidegger credits with first sparking
    his philosophical interest in the question of being.

judgment: the *becoming aware* of the intended state of affairs" (*LU* II/2, 140). Husserl concludes:

> *Not in reflection on judgments, nor on the fulfillments of judgments, but in the fulfillments of judgments themselves lies the true source of the concepts state of affairs and being* (in the sense of the copula); not in these *acts as objects,* but in the *objects of these acts,* do we find the basis of abstraction for the realization of those concepts. (*LU* II/2, 141)

Our understanding of being, according to Husserl, is grounded in categorially structured intuitions of states of affairs, not in sensuous intuitions of external objects or internal psychological states.

Some have supposed that Heidegger simply inherits this doctrine from Husserl and embraces it, for better or worse.[25] Heidegger does quote the preceding passage from the *Investigations,* approvingly it seems, in his 1925 lectures (*PGZ* 79). But his qualified approval of the idea of categorial intuition can be misleading. Indeed, far from representing a full-fledged endorsement of Husserl's position, I believe it represents instead a merely negative or oblique point against the competing intellectualist assumption of the neo-Kantians that all our experience of the world is structured by concepts and judgments. What Heidegger liked in Husserl's theory, then, had nothing to do with the supposed primacy of intuition, but lay rather in the idea that our understanding of being – not just existence, but also predication and identity – is something essentially nonconceptual, prior not just to reflection and introspection, but even to the formation of judgment and propositional thought.

That Heidegger's initial enthusiasm for Husserl's notion of categorial intuition was in no way a wholehearted commitment to the doctrine in

---

[25] See, for example, Okrent, *Heidegger's Pragmatism,* 121–2, 125, 208–13. Herman Philipse, in "Heidegger's Question of Being and the 'Augustinian Picture' of Language," and then in his book, *Heidegger's Philosophy of Being,* argues, somewhat differently, that Heidegger uncritically embraces the "principle of referentiality" that motives Husserl's theory of meaning, which Philipse also identifies with the "Augustinian picture" of language Wittgenstein sets up as a foil at the beginning of *Philosophical Investigations.* It seems to me, on the contrary, that Heidegger's denial of the primacy of the occurrent in our everyday understanding of being anticipates Wittgenstein's rejection of purely referential theories of meaning. However, I think Philipse is right that being qua phenomenon in Heidegger cannot be what is given in categorial intuition, as Husserl describes it, since the *is* in Husserl is purely formal and the same in all regions, whereas Heidegger is a pluralist about the meanings of being for different kinds of entities.

any very concrete sense becomes clear when we recall his additional remark that the ancient Greek philosophers seemed to him to have understood the self-manifesting presence of phenomena in an even clearer and deeper way than Husserl himself. Husserl's basic insight, he insists, "is even more primordially thought by Aristotle and in the whole of Greek thought," which brings into relief the specifically modern prejudices underlying Husserl's theory. Heidegger continues:

> The more decisively this insight became clear to me, the more pressing became the question, Whence and how is it determined what is to be experienced as "the thing itself" (*die Sache selbst*) in accordance with the principle of phenomenology? Is it consciousness and its objectivity or is it the being of entities in its unconcealedness and concealment? (*ZSD* 87)

This, of course, is just a way of reiterating his departure from Husserl. *Being and Time* reconceives intentionality by removing it from the theory of consciousness and cognition in Husserl's work, in particular the "Elucidation of Cognition" in the Sixth Investigation, and resituating it in an account of worldly practical activity. Methodologically, as we shall see, Heidegger regards phenomenology itself as an interpretive rather than a purely descriptive enterprise. But that is just a special case of a more general claim that practical understanding at large is more basic than the kind of intuitive or cognitive grasp of objects that the tradition, including Husserl, has taken as primitive:

> Under the unbroken hegemony of traditional ontology, the genuine mode of registering what truly is has been decided in advance. It lies in *noein*, "intuition" in the widest sense, from which *dianoein*, "thinking" (*Denken*), is simply derived as a founded form. And it is from this fundamental ontological orientation that Descartes gives his "critique" of the still possible intuitively apprehending mode of access to what is, *sensatio* (*aisthēsis*) as opposed to *intellectio*. (*SZ* 96)

The conventional restriction of the concept of intentionality to the phenomena of thought and intuition goes hand in hand with the emphasis of traditional ontology on the occurrentness of objects, and Heidegger clearly regards Husserlian phenomenology as the most recent egregious embodiment of that fixation on intuition, presence, and the present:

> The thesis that all cognition has its goal in "intuition" has the temporal meaning that all cognition is a making present (*Gegenwärtigen*). Whether every science, or even philosophical thought, aims at a making present shall remain undecided here. – Husserl uses the expression

'making present' (*Gegenwärtigen*) to characterize sense perception. . . . It was no doubt the *intentional* analysis of perception and intuition in general that suggested this "temporal" characterization of the phenomenon. The following division will show that and how the intentionality of "consciousness" is *grounded* in the ecstatic temporality of Dasein. (*SZ* 363n)

It is the burden of *Being and Time*, that is, to dislodge those metaphysical and epistemological prejudices and replace them with a phenomenological account of understanding as a future-directed projection into practical possibilities. Such an existential account of understanding effectively undermines the notion that interpretation and understanding rest on pure intuitions of objects and objective states of affairs:

> By showing how all sight is grounded primarily in understanding ... we have robbed pure intuition of its privilege, which corresponds noetically to the privileging of the occurrent in traditional ontology. "Intuition" (*Anschauung*) and "thought" are both derivatives of understanding, indeed rather remote ones. Even the phenomenological "intuition of essences" (*Wesensschau*) is grounded in existential understanding. (*SZ* 147)

Like his later notion of "essential intuition" (*Wesenserschauung*) (*Id I* 10ff), then, Husserl's theory of categorial intuition remains alien to the substance and method of Heidegger's phenomenology.

The Concept of Positing

More fundamentally, though, Heidegger denies that the most basic intentional attitudes are what Husserl calls "positing" acts of consciousness. Husserl inherits the concept of positing (*setzen*) from Kant and Fichte, who use the term to mean our cognitive apprehension of objects as actual or existent, for example in perception. Thus Kant distinguishes between "absolute position," or existence, and "relative position," the relation of a predicate to a subject.[26] This distinction provides the basis for his refutation of the ontological proof for the existence of God in the *Critique of Pure Reason*, namely, his observation that existence, though it may be a logical or linguistic predicate, is not a "real predicate" (*KRV* A598/B626).[27] Notwithstanding the grammatical similarity of sentences like *Water boils* and *Water exists*, that is, existence claims do

---

[26] Kant, "The Only Possible Argument in Support of a Demonstration of the Existence of God," in *Theoretical Philosophy, 1755–1770*.

[27] See Chapter 3, n47, and the final section of Chapter 4.

not in fact predicate a property of anything; rather, they say that some properties (in this case the properties of water) are in fact instantiated. In contrast to predicative judgment, then, thinking or asserting the existence of something just amounts to "positing" it. For Kant and Fichte, then, positing is a modal notion tied to the category of existence (*Dasein*),[28] and Husserl often uses the term in this classical sense, particularly in *Logical Investigations*.

But the concept of positing takes on a different, wider sense in the First Book of *Ideas* (1913), the magnum opus of Husserl's middle period. To understand the notion of positing in this its distinctively Husserlian sense, it is necessary to appreciate the semantic orientation of Husserl's theory of intentionality generally. His theory of intentionality is semantic in the sense that it attempts to account for the directedness or "aboutness" of consciousness by appeal to the ideal or abstract meanings that he believes constitute the content of our subjective mental states. In *Ideas I* Husserl calls a concrete mental act or state a "*noesis*" and its ideal intentional content a "*noema*." Although my *noesis* and your *noesis* will always be numerically distinct, they can in principle share one and the same *noema*. Of course, since the *noema* encompasses every intentional element of my conscious experience of myself and the world, the chances of such a complete coincidence are vanishingly small. Føllesdal has argued that for Husserl the *noema*, or strictly speaking the noematic "sense" (*Sinn*), is not the object of consciousness, but rather an intensional (with an *s*) or semantic entity, much like Frege's notion of the sense (*Sinn*) of a linguistic expression, as distinct from its meaning, or referent (*Bedeutung*). Indeed, in the Third Book of *Ideas* Husserl writes, "the noema in general is nothing other than the generalization of the idea of [linguistic] meaning (*Bedeutung*) to all act-domains."[29]

---

[28] In the Table of Categories (*KRV* A80/B106) Kant distinguishes between existence (*Dasein*) and reality (*Realität*). See Heidegger's lectures from the summer of 1927 (*Grundprobleme der Phänomenologie*) for an extensive discussion of the implications of Kant's conception of being as positedness in perception and my article, "Heidegger's Concept of Presence."

[29] Husserl, *Ideen III*, 89. Quoted in Føllesdal, "Husserl's Notion of *Noema*." It is important to keep in mind that Frege's use of the word '*Bedeutung*' is idiosyncratic and that Husserl is using it here in its ordinary sense, which is closer to what Frege means by '*Sinn*'. In *Logical Investigations* Husserl criticizes Frege's choice of words and points out that in ordinary language '*Sinn*' and '*Bedeutung*' are synonymous. Later, however, Husserl himself uses '*Sinn*' in a wide sense to refer to intentional content and reserves '*Bedeutung*' for linguistic meaning. Complicating matters somewhat, in his article Føllesdal has inserted the word '*Sinn*' where Husserl has written '*Bedeutung*'. But since Føllesdal's claim is precisely that

I want to suggest that, just as, according to Føllesdal, Husserl's notion of *noema* is a generalization of the concept of linguistic meaning to all intentional acts, so too his notion of the positing character of consciousness is a generalization of what J. L. Austin calls the "illocutionary force" of a speech act. The illocutionary force of an utterance is not part of its propositional content but of its pragmatic import in speech. The assertoric force of an assertion, for example, is not itself asserted; it is what makes the utterance an assertion. Nor is the interrogative force of a question expressed in the question itself, nor the imperative force of a command in the command itself – unless one transforms such locutions into assertions of the form *I am asking you* . . . or *I order you*. . . . So, just as speech acts have an illocutionary force in addition to their propositional content, intentional acts in general have a "thetic quality" or "positing character" (*Setzungscharakter*) that marks them as asserting, doubting, denying, wishing, or imagining some content (*Id I* §§103–7, §113).

In *Logical Investigations* Husserl refers to force and content as "act-quality" and "act-matter" (*LU* II/1, §20, 411–16). A variety of act-qualities can attend one and the same act-matter, just as different act-matters can be combined with a single act-quality. Among act-qualities, Husserl draws a further distinction between positing and nonpositing attitudes. Positing attitudes – for example, perception, judgment, memory, and anticipation – are directed toward objects *as existing*, whether in the past, present, or future. Wishing and imagining are therefore examples of nonpositing attitudes, as are the mental states that give sense to optative, interrogative, and imperative speech acts.[30]

By the time of *Ideas I*, however, Husserl had recast his entire terminological apparatus, introducing the notions of *noesis* and *noema*, together with a new "universal concept of positing" (*Id I* §117), according to which *all* intentional acts can be said to have some positing character or other: "Even in valuing, wishing, willing, something is 'posited' " (*Id I* 241). What Husserl had called "nonpositing" acts in *Logical Investigations* are now "positing" acts in the language of *Ideas I,* and what he called "positing" acts before he now calls "doxic" positings, or "proto-doxa" (*Id I* 216).

---

the *noema* is an intensional entity and that Husserl conceives of intentional content in semantic terms, the text does indeed support his reading.
[30] Husserl alters his view of this matter considerably between the first and second editions of *LU*.

In the Kantian–Fichtean sense, then, which is still largely preserved in the *Investigations,* what gets posited is an *object* of consciousness. In the later sense of the term, by contrast, what gets posited is not an object but a *content,* a noematic sense (*Sinn*). In judgment, for example, *what* I judge is not the intentional object of my awareness, but a proposition, namely, *that the object is such and such.* Similarly, *what* I ask is not an object or a person but *whether such and such,* just as *what* I wish or command is not a thing but *that such and such.* While judgments, questions, commands, wishes, and fantasies all direct my consciousness toward intentional objects of various kinds, whether things or states of affairs, what they posit are not objects but the contents of my consciousness of objects. Even when our intentional contents are nominal rather than propositional, for example in bare perception without judgment, the positing character of the act qualifies its contents in such a way that I am aware of the object as actually existing before me, rather than as remembered, anticipated, or fantasized.

In both senses of the term, however, and so in both *Logical Investigations* and *Ideas I,* Husserl takes it for granted that all intentional states are based on original doxic positings, that is, attitudes of "primal belief" in the existence of objects. Primal belief is not belief in the received sense, since it is not predicative or propositional, not believing *that S is p.* It is rather the spontaneous conviction in the existence of objects given in intuition, for instance the "bodily presence" of physical objects in perception. Doxic positings, or "protodoxa," thus constitute a primitive form of intentionality, and Husserl insists that our belief in the existence of things is in no way derivative of any more basic mental state. We do not infer that objects exist; we just perceive them as actual, as existing. The primitive function of the positing character of our most basic intentional states thus suggests a reply to, if not exactly a refutation of, skepticism:[31]

> As what confronts me, I continually find the one spatiotemporal actuality to which I belong like all other human beings who are to be found in it and who are related to it as I am. I find the "actuality" – the word already says it – as a factually existent actuality and also accept it as it presents itself to me as factually existing. No doubt about or rejection of data belonging to the natural world alters in any respect the general positing that characterizes the natural attitude. "The" world is always there as an actuality. (*Id I* 52–3)

[31] Heidegger's response to skepticism is very different, as we shall see in Chapter 4.

Years later, in the lecture notes published under the title *Experience and Judgment*, Husserl puts the point more directly:

> an actual *world* always precedes cognitive activity as its universal ground; and this means first of all a ground of universal passive belief in being, which every particular cognitive action presupposes. . . .
>
> It is this *universal ground of belief in a world* that all practice presupposes, the practice of life no less than the theoretical practice of cognition. The being of the world as a whole is the obviousness (*Selbstverständlichkeit*) that is never doubted and that is not first acquired through acts of judgment, but rather already forms the presupposition for all judgment. *Consciousness of the world is consciousness in the mode of certainty of belief.*[32]

In our most basic consciousness of things, Husserl says, "we already believe 'before we know it'" (*Id I* 236). All modifications of original protodoxic positings "refer back . . . to primal believings and their primal reason" (*Id I* 289–90). Moreover, "the problems of reason in the doxic sphere must take precedence over those of axiological and practical reason" (*Id I* 291).

The Natural Attitude and the "Paradox of Subjectivity"

In the first division of *Being and Time*, but even more explicitly in his lectures prior to its publication, Heidegger rejects the notion that everyday experience or understanding rests on (doxic) positing acts of consciousness in which we suppose or take for granted the existence or presence of objects. As early as 1919, Heidegger criticizes what he calls the "general hegemony of the theoretical" and insists that "the experience of an environment involves no *theoretical positing* at all."[33] And in 1925, more obviously in reference to Husserl, he states:

> nothing exists in our relation to the world that provides a basis for the phenomenon of belief in the world. I have not yet been able to find this phenomenon of belief, rather the curious thing is just that the world is "there" *prior to* all belief. It is never experienced in the manner of

[32] Husserl, *Erfahrung und Urteil*, §7: 24–5.
[33] Heidegger, *Zur Bestimmung der Philosophie*, 87, 93. 'Theoretical,' as the term was then used, did not mean hypothetical, abstract, or explanatory, but, after the Greek *theōria*, contemplative or observational. The contrast is not with ordinary or intuitive, that is, but with practical. In *Ideas I*, for example, Husserl refers to the natural attitude as the "natural theoretical attitude" and later wonders in a marginal note about its possible counterpart, "And the natural practical attitude?" *Id I* 7.

being believed ... moreover any purported belief in it is a theoretically
motivated misunderstanding. (*PGZ* 295–6)

In addition to denying that our primitive attitude toward the world is
one of belief, even prepredicative, "primal belief," Heidegger rejects
Husserl's description of the "natural attitude" of everyday life as one
in which we apprehend ourselves as objects among objects. The world,
Husserl writes, "is continually 'occurrent' (*vorhanden*) for me, and I myself am a member of it" (*Id I* 50). "As something occurrent, I continually
find the one spatiotemporal actuality to which I belong like all other
human beings who are to be found in it and who are related to it as I
am" (*Id I* 52). In short, "I, the actual human being, am a real object like
others in the natural world" (*Id I* 58).

For Heidegger, this description of the natural attitude as a (doxic)
positing apprehension of occurrent objects misrepresents our pretheoretical, prereflective understanding of useful things as "available"
(*zuhanden*), and of our ourselves as being-in-the-world. Quoting Husserl
directly, Heidegger comments in his 1925 lectures: "How am I given in
the natural attitude in Husserl's description? I am a 'real object like others in the natural world,' that is, like houses, tables, trees, mountains.
Human beings thus occur *realiter* in the world, among them I myself"
(*PGZ* 131). But at a primitive level we do not encounter things, least
of all ourselves, in this blandly objective way. Instead, we make use of
things, we work with them, we rely on them, we avail ourselves of them;
they attend and assist our efforts, but without standing over against us as
mere objects of awareness. Husserl's account of the "natural" attitude
is in truth, at best, the description of a kind of reflective standpoint
we can adopt by stepping back from our ordinary involvements with
things, coming to regard them as objects standing over against ourselves as epistemic subjects.

We will return to Heidegger's alternative conception of everyday understanding in later chapters. Suffice it here to note that Husserl seems
to conflate two rather different senses of 'natural' in his description of
the natural attitude. On the one hand, 'natural' can mean ordinary,
spontaneous, unreflective. But it can also refer to objective nature, in
which case it means external, public, impersonal. Husserl equivocates
between these two senses of the word in assuming that our unreflective,
everyday understanding is fixed on things as parts of nature, that is, as
objective components of an objective world. Hence he assumes that in
the natural attitude I must regard myself as "a real object like others
in the natural world." Further, for Husserl, the "positive sciences" are

mere extensions of the "general positing that characterizes the natural attitude" (*Id I* 53).

But even if we can and do adopt such an attitude, whether in naive reflection or in science, Husserl's account is hardly a compelling description of our spontaneous use of and reliance on things in the course of everyday life, not to mention the way in which we conduct and coordinate ourselves among them. After subjecting Husserl's description of the intentional acts to an extensive critique in his 1925 lectures, Heidegger remarks:

> the basic difficulty in this determination of the reality of acts lies already in its point of departure. What is here fixed as the given in the natural attitude, namely that man is given as a living creature, as a zoological object, is this [very] attitude that is called natural. Is it the natural mode of reflection, for man's form of experience vis-à-vis others and himself, to experience himself as *zōon*, as a living creature, as a natural object in the widest sense, which occurs in the world? In his natural experience, does man experience himself, in a word, zoologically? Is this attitude a *natural attitude*, or is it not?

"It is an experience that is *not at all* natural, but harbors a definite theoretical stance, for which all entities are grasped a priori as a law-governed order of events in the spatiotemporal manifold of the world" (*PGZ* 155–6). The natural attitude with which Husserl begins, then, is natural not in the sense of being ordinary and familiar, but rather in virtue of its theoretically detached, *naturalistic* orientation.

This fundamental difference between Husserl's and Heidegger's conceptions of intentionality became fully evident in 1927, if it was not already, in their failed collaboration on an introductory article on phenomenology for the *Encyclopaedia Britannica*.[34] In his marginal notes on one of the several different drafts of the text, Heidegger takes issue with Husserl's notion of being as position, or positedness. In a typical passage Husserl remarks that "everything and anything real for us is all the while 'occurrent' (*vorhanden*)" (*Hu* IX 271; *PTP* 124 n66), including our own psychological states, for "it is part of the habituality of the psychological attitude, which we call its positivity, that with each step

[34] The final German text, which Husserl composed alone, appears in *Hu* IX. The translations that follow are my own, though I have also included page citations to the English edition of Sheehan and Palmer (*PTP*), which contains all of Husserl's drafts of the article, together with an exhaustive account of Heidegger's involvement in their various stages of composition and revision. See also Walter Biemel, "Husserl's *Encyclopaedia Britannica* Article and Heidegger's Remarks Thereon."

the world of apperception, though it remains latent, is put forward ever anew" (*Hu* IX 274; *PTP* 129). Alongside the latter sentence Heidegger writes: "Something occurrent! But human Dasein 'is' in such a way that, although it is an entity, it is never merely occurrent" (*Hu* IX 274 n2; *PTP* 129).

The disagreement was this. For Husserl, consciousness is a temporally enduring psychological phenomenon that occurs in the world, yet at the same time it stands outside the world in virtue of having an intentional relation to things in the world, including itself. So, although he explicitly repudiates the substance dualism of Descartes[35] and Spinozistic dual-aspect theories, such as Wilhelm Wundt's (*Krisis* 67, 235), Husserl nevertheless describes the peculiar dual status of consciousness at once inside and outside the world, as it were, as the "paradox of human subjectivity" (*Krisis* §53). He therefore hesitates to identify the psychophysical empirical self with what he calls the "transcendental subjectivity" of consciousness understood in its intentional relation to objects. Bracketing the world external to consciousness in the transcendental reduction, and now regarding myself as pure transcendental subjectivity, Husserl writes,

> the momentous fact is that I and my life, in the validity of my being, remain untouched, however things stand with the being or nonbeing of the world, whatever I might decide about it. This I and its ego-life, which necessarily endures for me in virtue of such an *epochē*, is not a piece of the world, and if it says, "I am, *ego cogito*," this no longer means: I, this human being, am. No longer am I the one who finds himself in the natural experience of himself as a human being.

The transcendental I, which remains intact after the reduction, is not the naturally existing human being, that is, the psychophysical ego. Husserl therefore repeats, "the reduced I is not a piece of the world."[36]

Similarly, in the *Encyclopaedia Britannica* article, Husserl argues that, following the reduction: "I am then not a human I" (*Hu* IX 275; *PTP* 130). At this point in the text Heidegger responds, "Or perhaps *precisely* that, in its ownmost 'wondrous' possibility of existence. Cf. p. 27 below, where you speak of a 'kind of transformation of the form of life' " (*Hu* IX 275 n1; *PTP* 131 n89). The phrase in question in Husserl's text

---

[35] In *Krisis* Husserl not only argues convincingly that the Cartesian notion of a substantial soul is a derivative construction based on a prior conception of physical bodies and of mathematical natural science, he also comments on the "absurdity" of "this centuries-old prejudice." *Krisis* §60 (216); cf. §64 (224), §66 (232).

[36] Husserl, *Cartesian Meditations*, §11.

reads: "thus the transcendental reduction is a kind of transformation of the entire form of life, which goes completely beyond all previous life-experience, and because of its absolute foreignness is difficult to grasp in its possibility and actuality" (*Hu* IX 276–7; *PTP* 133–4). Here Heidegger writes: "Ascendance (going beyond) that yet remains 'immanent,' i.e. a *human possibility*, in which the human being comes precisely to *itself*" (*Hu* IX 276 n1; *PTP* 134 n101). Heidegger then adds a second, more critical note to Husserl's phrase, "I am then not a human I." He asks:

> Why not? Is this deed not a possibility for human beings, though precisely because they are never occurrent, is it not a kind of *comportment*, i.e. a mode of being that apprehends itself in its own quarters, and thus never belongs to the positivity of the occurrent? (*Hu* IX 275 n1; *PTP* 130 n89)

For Heidegger, that is, the putative paradox of subjectivity, the transcendental-empirical duality in our conception of ourselves, reveals Husserl's failure to articulate a unified and coherent conception of human existence as being-in-the-world. Heidegger therefore rejects both elements in the equation: the "worldless" transcendental subject (*SZ* 211)[37] and the conception of human beings as occurrent objects. So, when Husserl refers to the "concrete *ego*, which is the absolute presupposition of all transcendence valid for 'me.' Evidently it is in fact, in its reduced ownness, ultimately positable" (*Hu* IX 275, 604; *PTP* 131), Heidegger responds, "*positum*! Something positive! But what kind of *positing* is this? In what sense *is* this something *posited*, if it is not *nothing*, but is rather in a certain sense supposed to be everything?" (*Hu* IX 604; *PTP* 131 n91).

Again, Husserl is not a substance dualist. For him, the unity and identity of the subject is a primitive structure of all consciousness. Indeed, in the *Encyclopaedia* article, he simply stipulates the identity of the empirical and transcendental I:

> My transcendental I is thus evidently "different" from my natural I, but in no way as a second, as one *separate* from it in the natural sense of the word, nor on the other hand in any way bound up or intertwined with it, in the natural sense. It is simply the field of transcendental self-experience (conceived in full concreteness), which in every case can, *through mere alteration of attitude*, be changed into psychological self-experience. In this transition, an identity of the I is necessarily brought about. (*Hu* IX 294; *PTP* 173)

---

[37] Cf. *SZ* 55, 110–11, 188, 192, 206, 315–16, 366, 388.

It is sometimes supposed that Heidegger has simply failed to acknowledge this stipulation of the identity of the subject across the shift from the empirical to the transcendental attitude. But Heidegger's objection is not that Husserl posits two selves instead of one; it is rather that the operative notion of the I's identity is no more than an empty stipulation, an ad hoc device intended to preserve the integrity of the empirical–transcendental distinction itself. But without some further clarification of human existence as a single coherent phenomenon, the very idea of a double-aspect subject, at once positing and posited, remains obscure.

In a letter to Husserl of 22 October 1927, Heidegger asks for just such a clarification: "What is the mode of being of this absolute ego – in what sense is it *the same* as the factical I; in what sense *not* the same? What is the character of the positing in which the absolute ego is something *posited*? To what extent is there no positivity (positedness) here?" (*Hu* IX 602; *PTP* 139). Moreover, Heidegger explains that his own existential analytic of Dasein is a response to precisely this obscure conception of subjectivity, which is of course not Husserl's invention, but has defined modern philosophy since Descartes:

> We agree that the entity in the sense of what you call "world" cannot be elucidated in its transcendental constitution by appealing back to entities with the same mode of being. But this is not to say that that which takes the place of the transcendental is not an entity at all – rather it raises precisely the *problem:* what is the mode of being of the entity in which the "world" is constituted? This is the central problem of *Being and Time* – i.e. a fundamental ontology of Dasein. It aims to show that the mode of being of human Dasein is totally different from that of all other entities and that, as such, it harbors within itself the very possibility of transcendental constitution. (*Hu* IX 601; *PTP* 138)

Heidegger therefore rejects Husserl's complementary notions of an objectively positing natural attitude and a worldless transcendental subject, and with it the supposed paradox of subjectivity itself, in favor of a conception of "factical," that is, practically situated being-in-the-world. Dasein's being-in-the-world, which is neither subjective nor objective in any traditional sense, bears within it an understanding of being and is the condition of the very intelligibility of all positivity as such:

> Transcendental constitution is a central possibility of existence of the factical self. This, the concrete human being as such – as an entity, is never a "real worldly fact" because the human being is never merely occurrent but exists. And what is "wondrous" is the fact that the existential

constitution of Dasein makes possible the transcendental constitution of everything positive. (*Hu* IX 601–2; *PTP* 138)

But to say that Dasein itself is not a posited or positable object is not to say that it has no interpretable mode of being, and it is precisely the question concerning the mode of being of the entity that has an understanding of being that Heidegger charges Husserl with having neglected: "That which does the constituting is not nothing, and is thus something, something being – though not in the sense of something positive. The question concerning the mode of being of that which itself does the constituting cannot be sidestepped" (*Hu* IX 602; *PTP* 138).

The deep philosophical disagreements that arose in the course of Husserl's and Heidegger's attempted collaboration soon revealed the hopelessness of formulating an introductory account of phenomenology faithful to their respective aims and assumptions simultaneously, and Husserl eventually completed the article on his own, leaving little or no trace of Heidegger's critical intervention. Understanding the impasse they reached is crucial for an appreciation of the radical critique to which Heidegger had already been subjecting the fundamental aims and methods of Husserl's enterprise in his lectures.

The Eidetic and Transcendental Reductions

Specifically, Heidegger's dissatisfaction with Husserl's insistence on the primacy of (doxic) positing attitudes helps makes sense of his rejection of the "reductions," the "eidetic" and the phenomenological or "transcendental," which lie at the very heart of Husserl's doctrine and method.[38]

The eidetic reduction consists in abstracting from "real" (concrete, temporal) particulars and focusing instead on "ideal" (abstract, atemporal) properties. So, for example, one can abstract from all the other features of roses and fire trucks and grasp the redness instantiated in both. Husserl calls such general properties "essences," hence "eidetic," from the Greek *eidos* (Plato's "form"). In phenomenological reflection on consciousness, then, we abstract from real concrete mental

---

[38] In addition to *Id I*, which I rely on in what follows, accounts of the various reductions, under various names, can be found in Husserl's fourth version of the *Encyclopaedia Britannica* article, §§3–5 and 9, and in the ultimate reworking of that text in his 1928 Amsterdam Lectures on "Phenomenological Psychology," §§6, 8, 13. Both texts appear in *Hu* IX and *PTP*.

episodes occurring in time and concentrate on their ideal structures and contents – for example, the distinction between the act-quality and the act-matter, or the positing character and the noematic sense, of an intentional state. What matters to phenomenology is not particular experiential episodes as such, but the general essences those particulars instantiate. Husserl can therefore insist that

> a phenomenological doctrine of essence is no more interested in the methods by which the phenomenologist might ascertain the *existence* of some experiences . . . than geometry is interested in how the existence of the figures on the board or the models on the shelf might be methodically confirmed. (*Id I* 153)

Bracketing its existence in order to focus on its essence, Heidegger says, the eidetic reduction methodically ignores the *that* of intentionality in favor of its *what*:

> in the contemplation and elaboration of pure consciousness, only the *what-content* is brought out, without inquiring into the being of the acts, in the sense of their existence. In the reductions, the transcendental as well as the eidetic, not only is this question not posed, but *it gets lost precisely through them*. From the what, I never experience anything about the meaning and the manner of the that. (*PGZ* 151–2)

According to Heidegger, however, the very fact of our existence is itself constitutive of our self-understanding, so the eidetic reduction effectively suppresses and obscures what is most essential to the structure of intentional comportment itself:

> this notion of ideation as disregarding real individuation thrives on the belief that the what of any entity is to be defined by disregarding its existence. But if there were an entity *whose what is precisely to be and nothing but to be,* then this ideative contemplation of such an entity would on the contrary amount to a fundamental misunderstanding. It will turn out that this misunderstanding is dominant in phenomenology, and moreover dominates because of the dominance of the tradition. (*PGZ* 152)

Here Heidegger might sound as if he is simply reasserting the primacy of (doxic) positing attitudes after all, since he insists that existence is constitutive of our self-understanding and so cannot be bracketed or set aside, as the eidetic reduction requires. But Husserl's conception of positing is tied to a specific interpretation of being as objective presence, or occurrentness. And it is precisely because Heidegger is critical of that undifferentiated notion of being that he can claim that Husserl and the tradition have failed to grasp the specific mode of existence that constitutes intentional comportment and is hence eidetically irreducible. It is not objective presence or occurrentness, but rather situated, "factical" *Existenz*, or being-in-the-world, that cannot be coherently subtracted from our primitive self-understanding. Dasein has no *what* at all distinct from its *that;* rather, it has an identity, or a *who* (*SZ* §25), which is inextricably bound up with its temporal, worldly existence as "thrown projection" (*geworfener Entwurf*). The scholastic notions of *essentia* and *existentia* are therefore fundamentally unsuited to Dasein, whose peculiar identity cannot be understood except as being, and as understanding itself in its being.[39]

So, far from insisting that the eidetic reduction is untenable because we just cannot help positing ourselves as objectively present, Heidegger is saying just the opposite, namely, that because Husserl has mistaken human being-in-the-world for objective occurrentness, he has wrongly supppsed that the reduction reveals the essence of intentionality apart from any assumption of its existence. If human existence is fundamentally different from occurrentness, we are left with no reason to assume that our *what* can be carved off and separated from our *that*. We cannot claim to have discovered the essence of intentionality by first presupposing and then ignoring the mode of being peculiar to intentional comportment.

Even more central to Heidegger's critique of Husserl than his denial of the primacy of positing or his rejection of the eidetic reduction, however, is his repudiation of the phenomenodogical *epochē*, or transcendental reduction (*Id I* §§31–4, §§56–64). The *epochē* consists in bracketing or abstracting from all objects transcendent to consciousness in order to reflect on the contents immanent within it, contents in virtue of which we are aware of things transcendent.[40] An object is "transcendent," in Husserl's sense, if only one side or aspect of it can be immediately present to us at any one time; such objects are given to us perspectivally, or in "adumbrations" (*Abschattungen*). An object is "immanent" if it is given to consciousness all at once, transparently, so that no perspectival variation mediates our apprehension of it. Physical bodies and worldly states of affairs are transcendent objects, for

---

[39] Again, see Heidegger's criticism of Sartre for having simply reversed the priority of the traditional terms, failing to recognize their fundamental inappropriateness to Dasein as being-in-the-world. *Wegmarken*, 159.

[40] The reduction is called "transcendental" in virtue of the alternative standpoint on consciousness that it affords, not because it happens to exclude things "transcendent."

example, and so too are the abstract entities of mathematics and formal ontology (*Id I* §§59–60). The contents of consciousness are immanent, by contrast, since we each have immediate, transparent access to our own (current) thoughts and experiences.

The transcendental reduction therefore consists in methodically turning away from everything external to consciousness and focusing instead on what is internal to it. The reduction thus amounts to a special kind of reflection in which the ordinary objects of our intentional attitudes drop out of sight, while the immanent contents of those attitudes become the new objects of our attention. The inward reflection of the *epochē* first presents a mental state as a concrete particular, or *noesis,* and the eidetic reduction then brackets its concrete actuality with a view to the ideal intentional structures and contents it instantiates. Those ideal structures and contents constitute the *noema* of the intentional state, which includes a "core" of representational content or "sense" (*Sinn*) as well as the "positing character" (*Setzungscharakter*) in which that sense is put forward in one's mind as either perceived, judged, remembered, anticipated, imagined, or wished for. The two reductions taken together therefore reveal the *noema* as a whole, in effect "fixing the noematic sense by distinguishing it sharply from the object *simpliciter* and recognizing it as something belonging inseparably to the [pure] psychological essence of the intentional experience" (*Id I* 184).[41]

As we have seen, Heidegger thinks that the idealizing effect of the eidetic reduction blinds us to the way in which the *what* of Dasein necessarily makes reference to its *that,* its concrete existence as being-in-the-world. But he considers the transcendental reduction equally if not more problematic in its assumption of a rigorous distinction between the inner and the outer, the immanent and the transcendent. "An essential difference thus emerges between *being qua experience* and *being qua thing*" (*Id I* 76), Husserl writes, and "Therein the fundamental distinction among modes of being, the most cardinal that there is, reveals itself: that between *consciousness* and *reality*" (*Id I* 77). Husserl even insists on "the fundamental detachability (*Ablösbarkeit*) of the entire natural world from the domains of consciousness, the sphere of being of experiences" (*Id I* 87). Husserl is not suggesting that consciousness and the transcendent world are simply two things existing alongside each

---

[41] See Føllesdal, "Husserl's Notion of *Noema,*" and Izchak Miller, *Husserl, Perception, and Temporal Awareness.*

other within the world: "consciousness (experience) and real being are anything but coordinate kinds of being that dwell peaceably side by side and occasionally become 'related to' or 'connected with' one another" (*Id I* §49: 92). His point is rather that consciousness and the world are radically distinct, and that our concept of the latter is essentially tied to our concept of the former.

For Husserl, then, the actual world and all possible worlds are conceivable only as "correlates" of consciousness: "One must therefore not let oneself be deceived by talk of the transcendence of the thing over against consciousness, or of its 'being-in-itself'" (*Id I* 89). Although he rejects the notion of mind-independent things in themselves, he insists that both physical and abstract objects "transcend" consciousness in the aforementioned sense, so that "Between consciousness and reality there yawns a veritable abyss of meaning " (*Id I* 93). The immanence of transcendental subjectivity occupies an altogether different sphere of existence from anything natural or positive: "Everything that is purely immanent to experience . . . is separated from all nature and physics, and no less from all psychology, by abysses – and even this image, as naturalistic, is not strong enough to indicate the difference" (*Id I* 184).

On closer inspection, then, notwithstanding his appeal to the primacy of positing attitudes, it turns out that Husserl himself is in principle a kind of skeptic. For although he thinks no argument for the existence of the external world can have more authority than the doxic positing already built into the natural attitude itself, he nonetheless accepts the possibility that there could fail to be a world transcendent to consciousness at all:

> no conceivable proofs gathered from experiential considerations of the world could make the existence of the world certain for us with an absolute assurance. The world is dubitable not in the sense that rational motives are present to be taken into consideration over against the tremendous force of harmonious experiences, but rather in the sense that a doubt is *conceivable* because, of essential necessity, the possibility of the nonbeing of the world is never excluded. (*Id I* 87)

Further: "it is quite conceivable that experience, because of conflict, might dissolve into illusion . . . in short, that there might no longer be any world." Given "the possibility of the nonbeing of everything physically transcendent," Husserl goes so far as to suggest that "while the being of consciousness . . . would indeed necessarily be modified by an annihilation of the world of physical things, its own existence would not be touched" (*Id I* 91). "Consequently," he continues, "no real being, no being that is presented and legitimated in consciousness by appearances, is necessary to the being of consciousness itself." Appealing to Descartes' definition of a substance as "a thing which exists in such a way as to depend on no other thing for its existence,"[42] Husserl writes, "Immanent being is thus undoubtedly absolute being in the sense that it fundamentally *nulla 're' indiget ad existendum*" (*Id I* 92).[43] The two reductions taken together thus specify the domain of transcendental subjectivity as both immanent and ideal.

Husserl's Internalism

Ernst Tugendhat has argued that the project of *Being and Time* is compatible with the phenomenological reductions inasmuch as it focuses on being (*Sein*) rather than entities (*Seiende*). Tugendhat thinks that, like Husserl, Heidegger assumes something like a "transcendental standpoint," and indeed that his notion of being-in-the-world is effectively equivalent to Husserl's own concept of transcendental subjectivity. "If by 'being-in-the-world' Heidegger meant no more than that consciousness is essentially directed to something," he observes, "there could hardly be a philosopher worth taking seriously who would not agree with him, least of all Husserl." Indeed, according to Tugendhat, fundamental ontology is not only compatible with but presupposes the transcendental reduction, or *epochē*, for "In the transcendental reduction Husserl goes back not to a 'worldless subject,' but 'to the transcendental phenomenon, world' (*Krisis* 155).... Precisely by means of the *epochē*, then, Husserl enters the dimension of Heidegger's

---

[42] Descartes, *Principles of Philosophy* §51, in *Selected Philosophical Writings*, 177.

[43] Herman Philipse reads these passages as implying a radical version of what he calls "Transcendental Idealism," in his essay by that title, according to which not just "intentional objects," by which Husserl often simply means noematic contents, but indeed "the existence of the material world depends on consciousness" (256). Unfortunately, Philipse obscures the issue by conflating Kantian and Berkeleyan idealism, arguing that "Husserl's transcendental idealism is closer to traditional idealist positions such as Berkeley's or Kant's than is commonly thought" (242). Husserl is indeed a Kantian transcendental idealist, but that position is meant to include an "empirical realism," that is, a commitment to the mind-independence of objects that we can know only because of their conformity to epistemic conditions peculiar to us. Neither Kant nor Husserl supposed that, absent consciousness, entities would cease to exist. It is implausible, then, to equate Husserl's position with Berkeleyan phenomenalism, or "empirical idealism," as Philipse does.

being-in-the-world." "Heidegger is mistaken," Tugendhat concludes, "when he claims to have overcome the problem of epistemology with [his notion of] 'being-in-the-world' (*SZ* §13, §43a)."[44]

Is Tugendhat right? Was Heidegger mistaken in regarding his own conception of being-in-the-world as a genuine break with Husserl's notion of intentionality in terms of transcendental subjectivity? By insisting on a continuity between Husserl and Heidegger, it seems to me, Tugendhat loses sight of what is distinctive in each. Above all, he underestimates the subjectivism, more importantly the *internalism,* that is crucial to Husserl's view. For the transcendental reduction is essentially a statement of what Carnap called "methodological solipsism," the idea that, as Jerry Fodor puts it, "how the world is makes no difference to one's mental states."[45] Internalism lies at the heart of the skeptical arguments at the beginning of Descartes' *Meditations,* and it forms the substance of the *epoché,* which assumes that consciousness can be described in total abstraction from the real being of its purported objects.

But what do its purported objects amount to? Tugendhat is right that the only objects Husserl had in mind, at least initially, in introducing the reductions, hence the only objects falling under the scope of the *epoché* as he conceived it, were the objects of "objectifying positing" acts, that is, objects of theoretical attitudes. What Tugendhat therefore infers, however, is that the reduction in no way brackets or excludes *the world,* in the distinctive sense to which Heidegger would appeal in his conception of Dasein as being-in-the-world. If Heidegger rejects the reduction with respect to the world in that existential sense, Tugendhat suggests, he is not thereby disputing anything Husserl ever actually asserts:

> That Heidegger no longer goes along with the *epoché* is therefore not, as Husserl thought (*Ideen III,* 140), a lapse from the transcendental phenomenological problematic, but rather its proper radicalization. The necessity of the *epoché* is relative to Husserl's exclusive assumption of an objective world; in other words, it relates to his conception of all human comportment as "intentionality," which is to say as objectifying positing. This is the point where Heidegger's critique enters in. Only objectifying positing can be "bracketed," and only where comportment as a whole is

44 Tugendhat, *Der Wahrheitsbegriff bei Husserl und Heidegger,* 263.
45 Fodor, "Methodological Solipsism Considered as a Research Strategy in Cognitive Psychology," 280.

understood as objective positing can and must a universal *epochē* be the decisive move in staking out a philosophical position.[46]

But Tugendhat has told only half of the story of the *epochē*. For the transcendental reduction does not merely bracket the objects of theoretical, objectifying acts; it is also meant to direct our attention exclusively to consciousness and its supposedly immanent intentional contents. It is precisely this privileging of consciousness that is the target of Heidegger's critique, over and beyond his rejection of Husserl's impoverished conception of the character of everyday experience. Tugendhat thus misrepresents the aim of the reduction and so fails to appreciate how radically Heidegger departs from it. What the transcendental reduction abstracts from is not just the objectivity of experience, but all "transcendencies" as such, as Husserl insists (*Id I* §42, §§56–62).[47] If it was never Husserl's intention to bracket what Heidegger calls the "worldliness of the world" (*die Weltlichkeit der Welt*), the reason is that the concept of worldliness was never at his disposal, certainly not when he introduced the idea of the reduction in 1905.[48] But this cannot imply, as Tugendhat seems to suggest, that Heidegger's description of the everyday world and mundane practice simply agrees with Husserl's view. For the very substance of that view involves a failure to recognize the way in which subjects and objects, consciousness and reality, are intelligible only against a background of being-in-the-world.

Heidegger makes the point in his 1925 lectures in discussing Husserl's remark that "the perception of a physical thing ... *lacks any essential unity with it*" (*Id I* 69). Paraphrasing Husserl, Heidegger continues: "Every thing, that is, every real object, indeed the entire material

---

[46] Tugendhat, *Wahrheitsbegriff*, 263–4.

[47] Maurice Merleau-Ponty seems to appropriate the transcendental reduction for his own purposes in the Preface to *Phenomenology of Perception*, but only because he misconstrues Husserl's argument in the same way Tugendhat does, that is, as putting in brackets the objectivity, but not the externality or transcendence, of the world.

[48] According to J. N. Mohanty, Husserl's first reference to the reduction occurs in the so-called *Seefelder Blätter*, written in the summer of 1905. Mohanty, "The Development of Husserl's Thought." The internalism that made the reduction possible, however, was arguably already present in spirit in *Logical Investigations* of 1900–1. For an argument to this effect, see Jacques Derrida's *Speech and Phenomena*. Husserl's later celebrated concept of the "lifeworld" (*Lebenswelt*), elaborated especially in the mid-1930s in *The Crisis of European Sciences*, is admittedly much closer to Heidegger's notion of worldliness. Yet the fundamental difference is still unmistakable, since Husserl attributes the meaningful structures of the lifeworld itself to the immanence of transcendental subjectivity, while Heidegger sees it embodied concretely in external social practice.

world, is closed off (*ausgeschlossen*) from this stream of experience as a self-contained (*in sich geschlossen*) totality. Over against the region of experience, the material world is alien, other" (*PGZ* 133). Intentionality consists in the "self-contained totality" of experience, "closed off" from an external world that is essentially "alien" to it. Heidegger describes Husserl's position in these terms by way of introducing his own "immanent critique," and indeed, it is hard to imagine a conception of intentionality more radically removed from Heidegger's conception of human existence as being-in-the-world.

What Tugendhat quotes Husserl referring to as the "transcendental phenomenon, world," then, is emphatically *not* worldliness in Heidegger's sense. The Husserlian "phenomenon, world" is not the concrete social-practical world in which we find ourselves among others, availing ourselves of useful things in the pursuit of often unconceptualized ends, nor is it even the domain of objects we are conscious of in the natural attitude. For the reduction consists precisely in an *epoché*, a turning away from the world itself in order to reflect on transcendental subjectivity in its pure givenness. Husserl's "phenomenon, world" is immanent in consciousness. So, in spite of its objectivity qua intentional content, the given world is in another sense radically subjective inasmuch as it falls wholly on the subject side of the "abyss" that, Husserl insists, divides consciousness from all external reality. Surely no philosophical approach to intentionality could be further from both the spirit and the letter of the existential analytic in *Being and Time*.

Unlike phenomena as Husserl conceives them, the hermeneutic conditions uncovered by Heidegger's analytic of Dasein do not reside in the subjectivity of consciousness. As we shall see, the worldliness of the world is outside ourselves in the circumstances of practical life, not internal to consciousness or the subject. It is the intentional structure of absorbed practical behavior or "comportment" (*Verhalten*) that makes possible our very perception and cognition of objects as transcendent to our subjective states. Indeed, contrary to Husserl, who takes for granted the "diversity between consciousness and reality" (*Id I* 77), and for whom subjects and objects are essentially separated by an "abyss" (*Id I* 93, 184), Heidegger insists that "For Dasein there is no outside, which is why it is also nonsensical to talk about an inside" (*GP* 93).

Of course, Heidegger would not disagree with Husserl that, conceptually speaking, human beings are distinguished from nonhuman beings by something like an abyss in the sense that our understanding of ourselves draws on fundamentally different hermeneutic resources from those conditioning our understanding of mere objects. He would also clearly share Husserl's misgivings about the "naturalistic image" of an abyss, which, perhaps contrary to Husserl's own intentions, does indeed suggest something like "coordinate kinds of being that dwell peaceably side by side" (*Id I* 92–3). Yet Husserl's argument is not that our understanding of human beings and our understanding of objects demand fundamentally different hermeneutic or ontological frameworks, but that human beings are themselves divided between the immanence of their consciousness and the transcendence of their bodies. For Husserl, that is, the boundary in question runs not between human and nonhuman entities, but between consciousness and *the world*. Intentionality is internal, the world is external, and the transcendental reduction focuses on the former to the exclusion of the latter.

Heidegger's Immanent Critique

If it is not already evident from the text of *Being and Time* itself that fundamental ontology is deeply at odds with Husserl's central methods and assumptions, Heidegger himself makes it clear enough in the 1925 lectures in which he advances what he calls an "immanent critique" of Husserlian phenomenology by way of motivating the question of being. In setting out to articulate "a more radical definition of the task of phenomenological research," he says, "The immanent critique of the course of phenomenological research itself allows the question of being to arise" (*PGZ* 124).

He begins by posing the question, "How is the fundamental and explicit elaboration of the thematic field of phenomenology carried out by Husserl?" More precisely, "Can intentionality in its a priori be singled out as its own region, as the possible field of a science?" (*PGZ* 129). Whereas, he says, Brentano and the early Husserl analyzed intentionality with almost exclusive reference to logic and psychology, Heidegger's own discussion

> has to do with the connection between the phenomenological field to be secured and the field with which we begin, i.e. it deals with the concrete individuation of intentionality, of comportments, of experiences; it now has to do with a determination of the field in which comportments become accessible in the first place.... The question is: How do comportments, from which the structure of intentionality is to be read off, become accessible? How is anything like intentionality, the structure of

experience, experience [itself] initially given? Initially given, that means: given for the so-called *natural attitude*. (*PGZ* 130–1)

Heidegger's question, I want to suggest, is a transcendental question concerning hermeneutic conditions. That is, he is asking what renders intentionality intelligible and interpretable to us at all in our ordinary understanding, and hence to the phenomenological standpoint as Husserl conceives it, given that it is instantiated in a concrete entity existing "out" in the world:

> We will have to ask more precisely: how is it possible at all that this sphere of absolute position, pure consciousness, which is supposed to be separated by an absolute gulf (*Kluft*) from all transcendence, is at the same time united with reality in the unity of a real human being that itself occurs as a real object in the world? How is it possible that experiences make up an absolutely pure region of being and at the same time occur in the transcendence of the world? (*PGZ* 139)

This transcendental question concerning the interpretability of our own intentionality thus already raises the question Heidegger would pose to Husserl two years later in their collaboration on the *Encyclopaedia Britannica* article, namely, "What is the mode of being of the entity in which the 'world' is constituted?" Heidegger calls this "the central problem of *Being and Time* – i.e., a fundamental ontology of Dasein" (*Hu* IX 601; *PTP* 138). We are now in a position to see why this question is not just tangential or complementary to Husserl's inquiry, but is indeed a problem in the most pressing sense.

Of Husserl's description of pure consciousness as transcendental subjectivity, Heidegger asks, "Does this elaboration of the thematic field of phenomenology, the field of intentionality, raise the question of the *being of this region*, of the *being of consciousness?*" (*PGZ* 140). Husserl himself never considered Heidegger's question of being essential, or even relevant, to phenomenological research. Indeed, as we have seen, he invoked the eidetic reduction precisely in order to abstract from the real being of consciousness and focus instead on its ideal semantic structure. If the question of being turns out to be crucial to the very coherence of the phenomenological enterprise, Heidegger maintains, then Husserl's account of intentionality will prove to be not just ontologically but indeed "phenomenologically inadequate" (*PGZ* 140). For in that case, far from having overcome or circumvented the question, Husserl will have simply presupposed an answer, tacitly forcing the phenomena into traditionally preconceived, critically unexamined ontological categories.

Heidegger therefore wants to know what Husserl's theory says, or assumes, about the being of consciousness itself. Lest this appear to beg the question against Husserl, who meant his own descriptions of consciousness to be regarded as ontologically neutral, remember that Heidegger conceives of being in terms of hermeneutic conditions, that is, conditions of the interpretability of entities. Husserl takes it for granted that consciousness is transparently accessible to itself, and Heidegger wants to know what he thinks makes such transparency possible. To ask what Husserl's theory of intentionality tells us about the being of consciousness, then, is not to impose some extraneous metaphysical burden on an otherwise free-standing, metaphysically innocent description of the phenomena understood as pure appearance. Rather, it is to ask what such a description presupposes about the conditions of the intelligibility of reflective consciousness to begin with.

Heidegger finds four putative hermeneutic conditions implicit in Husserl's description of pure consciousness: its immanence, its absolute givenness, its self-sufficiency, and its "purity," or ideality. "Of these four determinations of being," Heidegger asks, "Are they such as to emerge from a regard for the thing itself (*die Sache selbst*)? Are they determinations of being drawn from consciousness and from the entity intended by this term?" (*PGZ* 142). Heidegger's answer is *no*. Instead, he says, they issue from the Cartesian tradition in which Husserl's thought is firmly entrenched, specifically from the idea of an "absolute science," that is, a methodical procedure or discipline yielding certain knowledge and objective results, independent of historical or cultural context and free of any interpretive indeterminacy. Heidegger had always rejected that scientific ideal as normative for phenomenology. As we shall see, however, it was not until his lectures of 1929–30 that he would explicitly repudiate Husserl's notion of "philosophy as a rigorous science" as a fundamental misunderstanding of the nature of philosophy.

Heidegger begins by pointing out that Husserl's notion of "immanence" merely specifies the inclusion or inherence of one thing inside another. It describes a relation among things but says nothing at all about what kinds of things they *are*. It thus describes entities in relation to one another, but not in their mode of being as such, that is, not *as* entities:

> This relation is characterized as a *real* [being-] *in-one-another*, but nothing at all is said about the being of this being-in-one-another, about realness

(*Reellität*), about entities as a whole in this region. A relation of being among entities, not being as such, is defined here. (*PGZ* 142)

Similarly, the "absolute givenness" of consciousness merely describes the status of one experience in relation to another within the same immanent region; it says nothing about the mode of being of those experiences as such:

> With the first characteristic, immanence, a relation of being between acts of the same region was identified, now it is the particular mode of being-an-object that one entity in the region of experience can have for another. Once again, not the entity in itself, but rather the entity insofar as it is a possible object of reflection, becomes the theme. (*PGZ* 143)

Husserl has therefore obscured the being of experience itself by taking for granted a particular conception of our access to it, namely, the mental reflection that supposedly reveals it as "absolutely given" in consciousness.

But all this says is that one experience affords complete and transparent access to another; it says nothing about the conditions of our making sense of ourselves as subjects of such experiences in the first place. Appealing to the "absolute givenness" of one experience within and to another tells us no more about the *being* of experience, that is, the conditions of its interpretability, than the circular definition of a word informs us of its meaning. Just as a circular definition takes for granted our prior understanding of a word's meaning, so too Husserl's conception of the absolute givenness of consciousness to itself presupposes that we already know what consciousness *is,* that we have already made sense of it in a wider hermeneutic context. Yet Husserl tells us nothing at all about that wider context.

Heidegger then turns to Husserl's assumption of the self-sufficiency of pure consciousness vis-à-vis the world, that is, his internalism. He refers to Husserl's description of the sphere of immanence in terms of the Cartesian definition of substance, and to Husserl's notorious remark that the existence of consciousness as such could in principle survive an annihiliation of the physical world. For Husserl, Heidegger explains, "Consciousness is the earlier, the a priori, in the Cartesian and Kantian sense." What the "absolute being" of consciousness amounts to is "the priority of subjectivity over every objectivity." Consequently,

> This third determination – absolute being – is once again not one that defines entities themselves in their being, but one that grasps

the region of consciousness in the order of constitution and grants it
a formal priority in that order before everything objective. This determination and conception of consciousness is at the same time the
point where idealism and the idealistic problematic, more precisely
idealism in the sense of neo-Kantianism, enter into phenomenology.
Accordingly, this determination of being is also not an original one.
(*PGZ* 145)

Husserl's insistence on the self-sufficiency of consciousness is drawn
not from an open inquiry into "the things themselves" (*die Sachen
selbst*), but from an immersion in a philosophical tradition that regarded the subject and subjectivity as the intrinsically intelligible starting point for philosophical inquiry. The tradition begins with Descartes,
of course, but continues in the work of Husserl's contemporaries, the
neo-Kantians Rickert, Natorp, and Cassirer.

Finally, Heidegger considers Husserl's commitment to the "pure
being" of consciousness, that is, the ideality of intentional content
as revealed by the eidetic reduction, over against the real flux of
temporal experience isolated by the transcendental reduction. In
Part Four of *Ideas I,* "Reason and Actuality," Husserl defines intentional contents in abstraction from the acts realizing them in order
to secure the phenomenological field and to draw "a distinction between two realms of being that are radically opposed and yet essentially related to one another," so that "consciousness taken universally
must be accepted as a proper region of being." As a result, Husserl
says,

> we notice that while objects simpliciter (understood in the unmodified
> sense) stand under fundamentally different highest genera, all object-
> senses and all *noemata* taken completely, no matter how different they
> may be otherwise, are of essential necessity of one single highest genus.
> (*Id I* 265)[49]

Notwithstanding the multiplicity and variety of psychological phenomena regarded as real events in time, ideal intentional contents constitute an ordered whole and exhibit an overall rational
structure.

As we have seen, Heidegger objects to Husserl's fixation on
ideal essences or abstract structures at the expense of the concrete

---

[49] Cf. *LU* II/2, §§30–5, 102–27.

entities instantiating them, especially in the case of human beings, whose *that* is not detachable, even in principle, from their *what*. Consequently,

> With this characteristic of being, consciousness as pure, it becomes especially clear that it concerns not the characteristics of the being of the intentional, but the determination of the being of intentionality; not the determination of the entity that has the structure of intentionality, but the determination of the being of the structure itself as in itself detached. (*PGZ* 146)

In *Being and Time* Heidegger also refers disparagingly to "the ontologically unclarified separation of the real and the ideal" (*SZ* 217).[50] Heidegger is here taking aim at the Platonic tradition at large, but the immediate allusion is clearly to Husserl, who inherited the dichotomy from Bolzano's distinctions between subjective and objective "ideas" (*Vorstellungen*), and between spoken and mental propositions, on the one hand, and "propositions in themselves" (*Sätze an sich*) on the other, and possibly from Frege's critique of psychologism.[51]

Husserl acknowledges the influence of Bolzano on his own early theory of meaning in *Logical Investigations* and on his later concepts of *noesis* and *noema,* but he distances himself from both Bolzano and Frege by insisting on a strict isomorphism, and hence a purely internal relation, between ideal intentional contents and real intentional acts. For Husserl, that is, ideal contents have no "separate" existence à la Platonic forms. Frege compares grasping a thought in one's mind with grasping an object in one's hand, where the thought and the object are extrinsic, unlike subjective ideas, which reside "in" the mind in the same sense in which bones and muscles reside in the hand.[52] Husserl, by contrast, treats ideal contents as dependent on the acts realizing them: "the essences, *noema* and *noesis,* are inseparable from one another: *infima species* on the noematic side eidetically point back to

---

[50] Cf. *SZ* 156 and 229.

[51] Bolzano, *Wissenschaftslehre,* §§48–9. Bolzano anticipates Frege's distinction between subjective psychological phenomena and objective concepts and thoughts, though Frege denied any direct influence. Husserl criticizes Bolzano's Platonism at *Id I* 196 n38, but he does not reject the real–ideal distinction as such, which is the real object of Heidegger's criticism.

[52] Frege, "Thoughts," in *Collected Papers.*

infima species on the noetic side" (*Id I* 265).[53] The *noema* is so far from being a separate Platonic entity, in fact, that Husserl insists that "Its *esse* consists exclusively in its '*percipi*' " (*Id I* 206).

But to disavow the strict Platonism of Bolzano and Frege in this way by insisting on an internal relation between real acts and ideal contents is in no way to disavow the conceptual distinction between reality and ideality itself, and it is that distinction that Heidegger rejects as ontologically obscure. To ground the distinction phenomenologically, to show that it belongs to the "things themselves," as he is committed to doing, Husserl needs to say more about just what makes it possible for us to draw the distinction in the first place. Heidegger considers the distinction "obscure" in the absence of any such account, not because he finds it contradictory or incoherent. He does not say that the distinction is unintelligible, only that Husserl offers no phenomenological account of the conditions of its intelligibility.

As Heidegger sees it, then, Husserl's description of consciousness, at once motivated by and motivating the transcendental and eidetic reductions, is itself phenomenologically groundless: "All four determinations of the being of the phenomenological region," he concludes, "are in no way drawn from the entity itself" (*PGZ* 146). The source of Husserl's description of consciousness does not lie in the phenomena at all, but in the Cartesian ideal of rational scientific certainty: "All of these determinations of being are in fact derived with a view to working out the *experiential context as a region of absolute scientific contemplation*" (*PGZ* 147).

> Husserl's primary question is simply not concerned with the character of the being of consciousness, instead he is led by the following concern: *How can consciousness become the possible object of an absolute science?* The primary concern guiding him is the *idea of an absolute science.* This idea, *that consciousness should be the region of an absolute science,* is not simply invented, rather it is the idea that has occupied *modern* philosophy since Descartes. The elaboration of pure consciousness as the thematic field of phenomenology is *not derived phenomenologically by going back to the things themselves,* but by going back to a traditional idea of philosophy. For this reason, none of the defined characteristics put forward as determinations

---

[53] Cf. Husserl's insistence in *Logical Investigations* that ideal meanings would exist whether anyone ever thought them or not, though he adds that "all metaphysical hypostatizations would be absurd." For an illuminating account of the development of Husserl's conception of meaning, see Peter Simons, "Meaning and Language," in *The Cambridge Companion to Husserl.*

of the being of experiences is primordial. . . . [T]he four characteristics of being that are given for consciousness are not derived from consciousness itself. (*PGZ* 147)

"In the fundamental task of determining its proper field," Heidegger concludes, "phenomenology is *unphenomenological!*" (*PGZ* 178). As he writes in *Being and Time* itself, "The idea of a '*pure I*' and a 'consciousness in general' contain so little of the a priori of 'actual' (*wirklich*) subjectivity that they pass over, or do not even recognize, the ontological characteristics of facticity and the constitution of the being of Dasein" (*SZ* 229).

Is Philosophy a Rigorous Science?

One might reply that Heidegger's critique of Husserl is surely misguided, since it was never the purpose of the phenomenological reductions or the description of pure consciousness to raise the question of *being* in the first place. Indeed, it was precisely the point of the eidetic reduction to bracket that question in favor of an examination of the structure of intentionality, quite apart from its manifestation in concrete psychological episodes. Heidegger's critique is tendentious and irrelevant in attending to the putative ontological prejudices underlying Husserl's account, one might argue, since pure phenomenology is ontologically neutral. Perhaps Heidegger's "immanent critique" is not immanent at all, then, but wholly external to the interests animating Husserl's theory.

Heidegger himself considers this response in the course of his lectures. Having concluded that Husserl's description of consciousness is not in fact motivated by genuine phenomenological considerations at all, but by a preconceived scientific ideal of objective theoretical knowledge, he remarks, "Perhaps precisely here one should not ask about the being of the entity" (*PGZ* 147). After all,

> the mathematician can circumscribe the mathematical field . . . without thereby necessarily raising the question concerning the mode of being of mathematical objects. In the same way, one can with some justification initially grant that here it is just the region of phenomenology that is circumscribed by these four characteristics, without thereby necessarily asking about the being of that which belongs in this region. Perhaps the being of consciousness should not be asked about at all. (*PGZ* 149)

But it is hard to see how Husserl could enlist any such analogy with mathematical knowledge in defense of his own project, since mathematics makes no pretense of describing anything concrete. Mathematical structures may be more or less imperfectly exhibited in concrete phenomena, but such instantiation is irrelevant to the study of mathematics. The whole point of phenomenology, by contrast, is to describe intentionality as it is given in our concrete lived experience itself, not just as we might conceive of it in abstract terms. The aim of the reductions is precisely to detach intentionality from its real embodiment in concrete experience, and it is that detachment that Heidegger challenges by pressing the question concerning the being of consciousness itself:

> The point of the reduction is precisely to make no use of the reality of the intentional . . . to dismiss the reality of consciousness as such. Consequently, in accord with its methodological significance as a disregarding, the reduction is fundamentally unsuited to a positive determination of the being of consciousness. The sense of the reduction is precisely to give up the ground on which alone the being of the intentional could be asked about (of course with a view to first determining the very sense of this reality from out of the region now secured). But here all that is in question is whether the reduction as such yields anything for the determination of the being of the intentional. Of course, one must be careful here, since Husserl would reply: It is precisely the point of the reduction *at first* to disregard reality precisely in order then to be able to view it as reality as it manifests itself in pure consciousness, which I secure through the reduction. (*PGZ* 150)

Heidegger responds, as we have seen, by insisting that the being of intentionality – both its *what* and its *that* – is fundamentally different from the being of mere objects, and so cannot be analyzed in the way one can analyze the essence and the existence of something purely occurrent. Dasein understands itself not as a mere *what*, specifiable apart from its *that*, but as a *who*, whose nature and existence are inseparably constitutive of its very intelligibility to itself as such.

What does Husserl purport to discover by means of the reductions, whose methodological legitimacy is supposed to stand on its own, quite apart from any presuppositions concerning the outcome of the inquiry they make possible? The immanent sphere of consciousness and its ideal contents. But such a discovery is no discovery at all, since it rests on a prior interpretation of the very conditions of the possibility of the reductions themselves, namely, the distinction – indeed, the abyss – between immanence and transcendence, the inner and the outer, consciousness and reality.

Husserl's findings are not findings at all, then, but metaphysical prejudices regarding the being of human beings. As Heidegger put the point in a letter to Husserl himself, "The 'purely mental' in no way arises in light of the ontology of the whole human being, i.e. not in regard to a psychology – rather it springs, since Descartes, from prior *epistemological* considerations" (*Hu* IX 602; *PTP* 138). "In the fundamental task of determining its proper field," then, "phenomenology is *unphenomenological!*" (*PGZ* 178). Husserl's uncritical appropriation of the Cartesian tradition prevents him from asking the radical question to which phenomenology initially seems to lend itself. For just as Descartes pretends to subject his entire self-understanding to a systematic doubt, only to have taken for granted all the ontological notions crucial to his description of subjects and objects as substances with properties, so too Husserl performs the reductions precisely by ignoring the fundamental question concerning the being of the entity endowed with intentionality to begin with. As Heidegger puts it in his lectures of 1929–30,

> This semblance and this ambiguity of a critical stance runs straight through all of modern philosophy, right up to the present day. It is, at most, a scientifically critical, not a philosophically critical stance.... A fundamental Cartesian stance in philosophy cannot in principle put the Dasein of man in question at all; it would thereby destroy itself at the outset in its ownmost sense.[54] It, and with it all philosophizing of the modern age since Descartes, puts nothing at all at stake. On the contrary, the fundamental Cartesian stance already knows in advance, or thinks it knows, that everything can be absolutely rigorously and purely demonstrated and justified.... So long as we take such a stand on ourselves and things, we stand outside philosophy. (*GM* 30–1)

Heidegger's rejection of Husserlian phenomenology consequently entails a reconsideration of the very nature of philosophy itself. It had always been Husserl's ambition, as it had been Kant's before him, to set philosophical inquiry on the secure path of genuine scientific progress.

---

[54] The phrase 'the Dasein of man' makes it clear that by this time, just a few years after the publication of *Being and Time*, Heidegger had begun to use the term 'Dasein' in a fundamentally new sense. Here it no longer denotes the human being or man as such, but rather that entity's mode of being. As I read it, then, 'Dasein' thereby becomes roughly synonymous with '*Existenz*' and 'being-in-the-world,' while 'man' (*Mensch*) reoccupies its traditional semantic role in referring to us as entities.

Strangely, given his explicit repudiation of the reductions, Heidegger echoes Husserl's rhetoric concerning the disciplinary ambitions of phenomenology in his own lectures throughout most of the 1920s. As late as the summer of 1927, for instance, Heidegger could be heard referring to "Philosophy as a science (*Wissenschaft*) of being" (*GP* §3). His central concern at the time was to follow Husserl in distinguishing philosophy from the mere construction or expression of *Weltanschauungen*, a term made fashionable in part by Dilthey and Jaspers.[55] Heidegger tries to make the distinction between philosophy and *Weltanschauungen* his own by grounding it in the ontological difference between being and entities, for whereas the latter are merely ontical in their orientation toward entities, the former is ontological in its concern with the question of being: "philosophy is not a *science of* entities, but of *being*, or as the Greek expression has it, *ontology*" (*GP* 15). And already in *Being and Time* he states, "In terms of its subject matter, phenomenology is the science of the being of entities – ontology" (*SZ* 37). Heidegger even goes so far as to describe his own digression from entities to being as a kind of "phenomenological reduction," though he immediately explains, "We are thus adopting a central term of Husserl's phenomenology in its literal expression, though not in its substantive intent" (*GP* 29). However, Heidegger goes on to say,

> The distinction between scientific philosophy and *Weltanschauung* philosophy is invalid ... since the concept of a *Weltanschauung* philosophy is not even a coherent concept.... To anyone who has even the slightest understanding of the concept of philosophy and its history, the notion of a *Weltanschauung* philosophy is an oxymoron (*hölzeres Eisen*). If one of the terms of the distinction between scientific philosophy and *Weltanschauung* philosophy is a nonconcept, then the other must also be ill defined. If one sees that *Weltanschauung* philosophy, if it is to be philosophy, is fundamentally impossible, then the distinguishing adjective "scientific" is no longer needed to characterize philosophy. That it is that, lies in its concept. (*GP* 16)

If the expression '*Weltanschauung* philosophy' is an oxymoron, it seems, the expression 'scientific philosophy' is objectionable only in being redundant.[56]

---

[55] Heidegger was already critical of the notion in his 1919 "Review of Jaspers's *Psychologie der Weltanschauungen*," reprinted in *Wegmarken*.

[56] In *Being and Time* Heidegger also objects to the expression 'philosophy of life' (*Lebensphilosophie*) on the grounds of its redundancy, quite apart from its misleading

Within a few years, in his lectures of 1929–30, Heidegger's conception of philosophy takes a subtle but radical turn. His still resists any characterization of philosophy in terms either of science or of *Weltanschauung*, not simply because the idea of a scientific philosophy is somehow redundant, but because it is a profound, indeed catastrophic, mistake. Heidegger opens his lectures with a rhetorical question: "What if it were a *prejudice* that metaphysics is a fixed and secure discipline, and an *illusion* that philosophy is a science that can be taught and learned?" Having reiterated the familiar observation that modern philosophy has failed to establish any decisive results since its inception with Descartes, Heidegger asks,

> Or is all this talk of philosophy being the absolute science a delusion? Not just because the individual or some school never achieves this end, but because positing the end is itself fundamentally an error and a misunderstanding of the innermost essence of philosophy. Philosophy as absolute science – a lofty, unsurpassable ideal. So it seems. And yet perhaps even judging philosophy according to the idea of science is the most disastrous debasement of its innermost essence. (*GM* 2)[57]

Heidegger still insists, of course, that "the interpretation of philosophy as the propagation of a *Weltanschauung* involves the same mendacity as characterizing it as science." In the end, he suggests, philosophy is *"determinable only in terms of itself and as itself – comparable to nothing* in terms of which it could be positively defined. In that case philosophy is something *original and autonomous (Eigenständiges)*, something *ultimate"* (*GM* 3). In any case, philosophy "is something totally different from science" (*GM* 15), not just because it has failed to achieve genuinely scientific results, but because philosophical truth is other than and incommensurable with scientific, particularly mathematical, truth:

> We do not deny philosophy the character of absolute science because it has never yet attained it, but because this idea of the philosophical essence is attributed to philosophy on the basis of its ambiguity, and because this

biological connotations, since for him all philosophy is essentially related to Dasein's being-in-the-world (*SZ* 46).

57 Especially in light of his earlier sneering references to "the medicine men of contemporary philosophy," it is hard not to read the following caricature of academic philosophers as an allusion to Husserl and the pseudotechnical jargon of Husslerian phenomenology: "And the teacher – what can he not prove, what a forest of concepts and terminology he moves about in, wielding some scientific apparatus, so that the poor listener is scared away. He enters in, as if with him philosophy has come to the world as absolute science for the first time" *GM* 18.

idea undermines the essence of philosophy at its core.... Although it
objectively comprises a great wealth, mathematical knowledge is in itself,
in terms of its content, the emptiest knowledge that can be conceived,
and as such is at the same time the least binding for human beings. (*GM*
24–5)

For this reason, "mathematical knowledge cannot be advanced as the
ideal of philosophical knowledge" (*GM* 25).

By the winter semester of 1929–30, then, Heidegger's conception
of philosophy had finally broken free of its lingering ambivalent loy-
alties to Husserl's vision of phenomenology as a rigorous and purely
descriptive discipline. The consistency that emerged suddenly in Heidegger's view in 1929 was due in part, no doubt, to the professional
and intellectual autonomy he now enjoyed, having taken over the chair
of philosophy at Freiburg upon Husserl's retirement, and apparently
having severed all personal and social ties with his former friend and
mentor. In hindsight, then, we can see more clearly the unresolved ambiguity that marks *Being and Time* itself, in which Heidegger still refers
to his own enterprise as a "science *of being as such*" (*SZ* 230). But if I
am right that Heidegger's critique of Husserl rests on a recognition
of the importance of hermeneutic conditions for our understanding of
phenomenological inquiry, then his repudiation of Husserl's notion of
"philosophy as a rigorous science" is already implied by his hermeneutic
conception of phenomenology itself. For Heidegger, that is, "the meaning of phenomenological description lies in interpretation" (*SZ* 37),
and "By showing how all sight is primarily grounded in understanding,
we have robbed pure intuition of its privilege" (*SZ* 147).

This methodological innovation, moreover, brings with it a new
and original concept of *phenomenon*. Remarking that the word
'phenomenon' is ambiguous "between *appearing* and *that which appears*,"
Husserl insists that the term be "used primarily for the appearing itself,
the subjective phenomenon,"[58] that is, for the contents *of* or *in* consciousness, not for the transcendent objects appearing *to* consciousness.
Heidegger, by contrast, treats the term as a purely formal indicator referring simply to "that which shows itself, the manifest" (*SZ* 28), a notion
that "has in the first instance nothing whatever to do with what one
calls 'appearance,' or indeed 'mere appearance'" (*SZ* 29). For Heidegger, then, phenomena are nothing essentially subjective; in particular,

---

[58] Husserl, *Die Idee der Phänomenologie,* 14.

they are not the immanently or self-evidently *appearing* contents of consciousness that, according to Husserl, stand in representational or referential relations to transcendent objects that make their *appearance* in or through them. Heidegger, that is, refuses to define phenomenology from the outset in terms of its domain of application: "The word only informs us of the *how* of the way of showing and treating *what* is to be dealt with in this science" (*SZ* 34–5); it does not yet specify the *what*, or subject matter, itself. Heidegger's redefinition of phenomenology is thus inextricably bound up with his repudiation of the representationalism, the internalism, and the mentalism informing Husserl's project.

In addition to the merely formal notion of phenomenon, of course, Heidegger offers a substantive, or what he calls the specifically "phenomenological," conception. Taken formally, a phenomenon is just anything that manifests itself, as opposed to merely appearing in or through some representational or referential intermediary. Substantively, though, not every aspect of what manifests itself is "given" in the sense of being self-evident or fully open to direct inspection. Indeed, "what is to become phenomenon can be hidden. And it is precisely because phenomena are first and for the most part *not* given that there is a need for phenomenology" (*SZ* 36). A phenomenon in the substantive phenomenological sense, then, is

> something that first and for the most part precisely does *not* show itself, something that, in contrast to what first and for the most part shows itself, is *hidden*, but is at the same time something that essentially belongs to that which first and for the most part shows itself, and belongs to it in such a way as to constitute its meaning and ground. (*SZ* 35)

The task of phenomenology is therefore not to give a purely descriptive report of something self-evidently given, but to let the ordinarily hidden aspects of what shows itself *show themselves* or make themselves manifest. Moreover, as we shall see, since Heidegger interprets *logos* as a "letting something be seen" (*SZ* 33), he takes the interpretive work of the phenomenologist to lie in drawing out, evoking, and uncovering what is covered up and buried over in what ordinarily shows itself in our everyday understanding.

Heidegger agrees, then, that phenomenology is a descriptive, rather than a hypothetical or explanatory, enterprise, let alone an exact science. But Husserl understood the work of phenomenology on analogy with descriptive natural sciences like botany. Geometry, for all its exactness, Husserl says, lacks the resources for morphological descriptions of natural phenomena as, for example, "'serrated,' 'notched,' 'lens-shaped,' 'umbellate,' and the like" (*Id I* 138). For Husserl, then, phenomenology amounts to "a systematic and eidetic morphology" (*Id I* 302). Heidegger, too, regards phenomenology as a descriptive undertaking; he even refers to "the at bottom tautological expression 'descriptive phenomenology.' " Perhaps with the preceding passages in mind, however, he goes on to say, "'Description' here does not mean a procedure in the manner of, say, botanical morphology" (*SZ* 35). Rather, "the meaning of phenomenological description as a method is *interpretation*," so that "The phenomenology of Dasein is a *hermeneutic*" (*SZ* 37). "Interpretation is never a presuppositionless apprehension of something pregiven" (*SZ* 150), Heidegger insists. Indeed, the "hermeneutic situation" in which fundamental ontology finds itself consists precisely in the presuppositions that situate any such inquiry as a matter of principle (see *SZ* 232).

3

INTERPRETING INTENTIONALITY

*You have to have found a thing, if
you want to know where it lies.*

Goethe

Husserl's theory of intentionality is uncritical and incoherent, I have
argued, owing to its disregard of its own hermeneutic conditions, that
is, the conditions underwriting its own intelligibility as philosophical discourse. Heidegger's existential analytic, by contrast, offers an account
of the conditions of interpretation in order to set out a fundamental ontology from within which we can understand how intentionality
manages to be intelligible to us at all as such. The hermeneutic phenomenology in *Being and Time*, then, rests on a radical repudiation of the
very idea of a rigorous discipline of pure description and embraces instead an unabashedly interpretive conception of phenomenology itself.
Heidegger's fundamental ontology can thus in no way be understood
as a mere amendment or continuation of the Husserlian program, as
some critics, particularly those who sympathize with Husserl's views,
would have it.

Husserl, however, is by no means alone in his critical neglect of the intelligibility conditions of his own philosophical claims. Indeed, more recent theories of intentionality persist in a peculiarly unreflective mode,
both methodologically and ontologically, and Heidegger's analytic of
Dasein can be read as an extended reminder of the existential conditions of the intelligibility of philosophical discourse itself and the distinctions philosophers habitually draw between subjectivity and objectivity, internal and external, mind and world. Contemporary theories of
mind and agency in particular tend to slide uncritically into one of two

dogmatic positions, taking one or the other term of such distinctions as primitive and then trying to construct or explain the other with reference to it. In addition to all the specific problems inevitably facing those theories, I want to suggest, the strategies underlying them rest on a more fundamental error, or more precisely a fatal omission, in taking the conceptual distinctions themselves for granted and ignoring the conditions in which they arise meaningfully in our philosophical understanding in the first place. Heidegger's analytic, being a general account of hermeneutic conditions, is at once an account of the conditions of philosophical intelligibility, and he introduces his notion of being-in-the-world (*In-der-Welt-sein*) as an account of human existence prior to the emergence of any distinction between an agent's point of view and facts or values external to it, between the inner and the outer, between subjective experience and objective reality.

In this chapter I want to present Heidegger's alternative account of human action and experience to forestall the conceptual slide into one or another of those philosophical reconstructions of the ordinary understanding we have of ourselves prior to the abstract distinctions that make that ordinary understanding look either impossible or incoherent in retrospect. I shall begin by contrasting Heidegger's notion of being-in-the-world with some contemporary theories of subjectivity and intentionality, paying special attention to the assumptions they make regarding our mode of being and the relation in which we stand to the worldly context in which things show up for us at all, whether as objects or as subjects. For recent debates in the philosophy of mind tend to recapitulate assumptions about intentionality with which Heidegger was already familiar, and which he explicitly criticized both in *Being and Time* and in his lectures of the 1920s.

As we have seen, Heidegger rejects the subjectivism and internalism of Descartes and Husserl, which rest on an uncritical bifurcation of human agents from the social and equipmental contexts in which they make sense of themselves, and which impose on our mundane existence a needlessly paradoxical conception of subjectivity and objectivity as exclusive, exhaustive, and ultimately incommensurable categories. But Heidegger also rejects scientific naturalism and reductionism, which proceed by assimilating our everyday self-understanding to the explanatory and predictive goals peculiar to the natural sciences. What fundamental ontology seeks, and what so many contemporary theories of mind neglect, is an account of the conditions rendering intentionality intelligible as such for the entity whose intentionality it is. The question systematically obscured by both naturalism and subjectivism, that is, has to do with the *being* of the entity that is able to understand itself in terms of subjective experience and objective behavior alike, for to inquire into the conditions of the intelligibility of intentionality in its subjective and objective aspects is in effect to ask what intentionality *is*. How are we to understand the *being* of entities capable of intentional attitudes and behaviors? How are we interpretable to ourselves as subjects of experience, as having a world? As we have seen, this is how Heidegger understood his project, and it is how he explained it to Husserl in 1927. What he was concerned with, he said, and what he evidently felt Husserl had neglected, was "the *problem*: What is the mode of being of the entity in which the 'world' is constituted? This is the central problem of *Being and Time* – i.e. a fundamental ontology of Dasein" (*Hu* IX 601; *PTP* 138).

Subjective and Objective

Heidegger's notion of being-in-the-world, then, amounts to a rejection of traditional metaphysical distinctions philosophers have been tempted to draw between ourselves and the world, distinctions, for instance, between the mind and the body, the inner and the outer, "consciousness and reality" (*Id I* 77), subjective and objective. In his 1927 lectures Heidegger likewise refers to "two persistent misinterpretations of intentionality," its "false objectification" and its "false subjectification." On the one hand, he points out, intentionality is not a mere objective relation between two things, a subject and an object, but rather "a structure that makes up the *relational character* of Dasein's comportment as such." Intentionality is not just a feature of events and states of affairs, that is, but essentially involves agency, meaningful behavior or "comportment" (*Verhalten*).[1] On the other hand,

> the intentional structure of comportments is not something immanent to the so-called subject and that would first of all be in need of transcendence, rather the intentional constitution of Dasein's comportments is precisely the *ontological condition of the possibility of every and any transcendence*. (*GP* 91)

---

[1] The German word *Verhalten* just means conduct or behavior; indeed, 'behavior' would have been a good translation had the term not become so closely associated with behavior*ism,* so that, in philosophical contexts anyway, it tends to suggest mere bodily movement, devoid of intentionality. Interestingly, applications of the word to nonhuman events and processes may be relatively recent in English, there being only one such entry in the *Oxford English Dictionary* dating from before the mid-nineteenth century.

That is, intentionality is not something internal to the mind, but rather describes the prior practical conditions for the particular intentional attitudes that might strike us as philosophically mysterious or problematic, for example memories, perceptions, and purposive actions. Intentionality cannot be abstracted from agency and discovered in events and states of affairs objectively described, nor is it something mental residing in the inner realm of subjective experience. "Intentionality is neither objective nor subjective in the usual sense" (*GP* 91).

Yet the temptation to fit it into the one category or the other can be nearly irresistible. As we have seen, Husserl's phenomenology prides itself on upholding and maintaining a categorical distinction between subjective and objective, in addition to the distinction between the concrete reality of psychological processes and the timeless ideality of meaning and intentional content. Husserl conceived of his own phenomenology as a variation on Kant's critique of the subjective conditions of objective knowledge, the conditions within us of the apparent objectivity of the world outside us. But whereas the Kantian enterprise embarked on a transcendental construction of the knowable world in the impersonal terms of Euclidean geometry and Newtonian physics, Husserl sought to give a purely intuitive, descriptive account of the conditions of prescientific, pretheoretical commonsense experience. The world whose subjective conditions Husserl sought to exhibit was not the world of the natural sciences, but what he came to call the "lifeworld" (*Lebenswelt*), the commonsense world of everyday life, which includes values, ends, and practical interests no less than objects, properties, and relations. Thus, in his last great work, *The Crisis of European Sciences and Transcendental Phenomenology* (written between 1935 and 1937), Husserl describes the way in which the idealized spatiotemporal manifold taken for granted by the physical sciences since the time of Galileo continually presupposes a world given to us under personal and practical descriptions. Like the Gestalt psychologists influenced by him, Husserl conceives of perception in terms of a unity of figure and ground, every given object appearing only in the context of the "inner horizons" peculiar to it and the "outer horizons" situating it in the world.[2] So, for instance, we do not infer from subjective sense data that objects have back sides and persist in time beyond the present moment, nor do we typically judge that some event is the cause or effect of another. Rather, we perceive objects *as* three-dimensional things with back sides and *as*

---

[2] Husserl, *Cartesian Meditations*, §19: 82.

temporally enduring, just as the perception of one event does not just cause but rather *motivates* an anticipation of another.[3]

And yet precisely because in its most primitive aspect the world presents itself to the transcendental subject as so many bare objects, or what Husserl calls "original substrates,"[4] the subject cannot itself be given to itself as a mere object in the world. There will always be a kind of phenomenological gap between transcendental subjectivity and the embodied psychophysical ego in the objective world with which it must be identical. "Between consciousness and reality," Husserl writes, "there yawns a veritable abyss of meaning" (*Id I* 93). As we saw in Chapter 2, this radical incommensurability of our subjective point of view with the objective world is what Husserl calls "the paradox of human subjectivity," the fact of our being both objects *in* the world and at the same time subjects intentionally cognizant *of* it (*Krisis* §53).

This radical diversity and incommensurability of the subjective and the objective points of view remains a familiar theme among contemporary analytic philosophers, notably Thomas Nagel. In *The View from Nowhere,* for example, Nagel offers a synoptic view of the central defining concerns of philosophy as derivative of what Husserl called the "paradox of subjectivity." The problem, as Nagel sees it, is "how to combine the perspective of a particular person inside the world with an objective view of that same world, the person and his viewpoint included." It is the problem of reconciling what he calls "the internal and external standpoints." The worry is no mere scholastic exercise, however, Nagel insists, for the roots of the problem reach deep into the soil of common sense: "It is a problem that faces every creature with the impulse and the capacity to transcend its particular point of view and to conceive of the world as a whole." It is therefore not just a puzzle for philosophers: "The difficulty of reconciling the two standpoints arises in the conduct of life as well as in thought."[5] Moreover, "there is probably no area of philosophy in which it doesn't play a significant role."[6]

---

[3] See the First Logical Investigation, §§2–3 (*LU* I, 24–8). For a closer critical evaluation of Husserl's concept of motivation, and its influence on Merleau-Ponty's account of perception and embodiment in *Phenomenology of Perception*, see my "The Body in Husserl and Merleau-Ponty."

[4] Husserl, *Experience and Judgment*, §5: 26. Cf. *Formal and Transcendental Logic*, §83: 181.

[5] Nagel, *The View from Nowhere*, 3. Cf. "Subjective and Objective," chapter 14 of *Mortal Questions*.

[6] *The View from Nowhere*, 6.

Nagel's global, and I believe artificially sharp, distinction between the subjective and the objective standpoints provides perhaps the clearest and most systematic example of the kind of phenomenological amnesia that Heidegger's notion of being-in-the-world is meant to treat. For what Nagel's emphasis on the apparent conflict of the two standpoints obscures is precisely the ways in which they derive from a single source that is itself neither subjective nor objective. Nagel acknowledges that "the distinction between more subjective and more objective views is really a matter of degree, and it covers a wide spectrum."[7] But to concede that the distinction is gradual is not to recognize either its hermeneutic contingency or its failure to capture so much of our ordinary understanding of ourselves and the world. To describe our various views of the world as simply subjective or objective, though in varying degrees, is like describing human beings as ethnically either black or white, though in varying degrees. It would be absurd to try to defend such a schema by adding that between the two extremes there may be many shades of gray. For even supposing that there are uncontroversial cases of black and white, it does not follow that every anomaly must be some intermediate between the two. Indeed, trying to account for the anomalies simply by filling in the middle of the spectrum is a way of refusing to acknowledge the poverty of the categories defining the distinction to begin with. Similarly, while some views of the world may be plainly subjective and others objective, even in varying degrees, positing subjectivity and objectivity as fundamental categories at the outset does violence to the phenomena by flattening them out along a single dimension, and this can yield another kind of incoherence, short of downright contradiction.

Consider, for example, the context of everyday social practice that Heidegger takes as his point of departure in his account of Dasein's everyday "worldliness" (*Weltlichkeit*) in *Being and Time*.[8] Is our everyday practical world and its mundane intelligibility something subjective or

---

[7] *View from Nowhere*, 5.

[8] Heidegger clearly intends his notion of "worldliness" to resonate with the Christian conception of an overall sense of orientation or disorientation in life. In the 1928 essay "On the Essence of Ground," for instance, he writes, "It is no accident that in connection with the new ontic understanding of existence that arose in Christianity the relation between *kosmos* and human Dasein, and with it the concept of world in general, became sharper and clearer" *Wegmarken* 39. Since Heidegger countenances no contrasting unworldly or otherworldly condition, however, for him the terms 'world' and 'worldly' carry none of the pejorative connotations they have in religious discourse.

objective? Is it internal or external to us and our point of view? Take economic value as a case in point. It is plainly neither an objective physical property of anything nor merely a function of the isolated subjective attitudes of individuals. Like many collective practices and institutions, economic exchange is in one sense something perfectly objective, though it is constituted by our shared dispositions and attitudes and relies entirely on the durability of a vast network of interconnected social phenomena. Any attempt to construct an ontology of economic value by taking physical properties and subjective attitudes as primitive notions is therefore likely to run aground on its own inability to describe the phenomenon in adequate terms and in sufficiently rich phenomenological detail at the outset. Will such a scheme do justice, for example, to the notoriously context-sensitive norms governing practices of barter, not to mention the sense of propriety and impropriety informing affective attitudes such as desire, gratitude, and resentment? Even the institution of money, whose function is defined in part by perfectly explicit rules and legal institutions, is also constituted by noninstitutionalized social phenomena such as ambition, competition, envy, class consciousness, and customs prescribing appropriate and inappropriate attitudes about saving and spending, about the prestige of wealth and the shame of poverty.[9] Or consider, at a more primitive level, our ordinary understanding of the human body as the locus of human agency and experience. Is my experience of my own body something subjective or objective? Is my body internal or external to me and my understanding of myself? And what of my experience and understanding of the bodies of others? Do I know them as subjects or as objects? No answer seems quite right; indeed, the concepts of subjective, objective, inner, and outer simply seem out of place here.

Leaving such preconceived categories aside, then, Heidegger enlists his notion of worldly intelligibility in an effort to undermine the metaphysical distinctions that have led philosophers like Husserl and Nagel to conclude that our conceptual grip on ourselves and the world is somehow necessarily paradoxical, even incoherent – ordinary understanding

[9] See, by contrast, John Searle's theory social institutions in terms of collective intentionality in *The Construction of Social Reality*. In his account of money, for example, Searle brackets from consideration, and so ignores as irrelevant, the entire preinstitutionalized background of social intelligibility such as I have very briefly described. Relying as he does on a preconceived schema of subjectivity and objectivity, I shall argue later, Searle leaves no room for the prethematic normativity that informs our worldly understanding in everyday life.

to the contrary notwithstanding. Subjectivists like Husserl and Nagel are no doubt right to insist that a purely third-person or wholly external point of view leaves questions concerning our experience and understanding of ourselves from the first-person point of view untouched. But what such theorists go on to say about consciousness and subjectivity in turn affords little insight into the conditions of the intelligibility of that first-person perspective itself, to itself. If consciousness is transcendentally subjective, how can it be understood to be identical with something empirically objective? How do we manage to acquire a coherent understanding of ourselves so effortlessly in our daily lives if the only conceptual resources available to us are in fact as thin and abstract as such philosophers suppose?

In what follows, I want to say more precisely what I take to be philosophically inadequate in two contemporary theories of intentionality that adopt uncritical attitudes about their own essential categories and interpretive standpoints. The point of doing so will be to situate Heidegger's interpretation of human existence as being-in-the-world in what I take to be the largely uninhabited middle ground between first- and third-person approaches to intentionality, between its "false objectification" in the hands of naturalists and reductionists, on the one hand, and its "false subjectification" in the hands of Cartesian theorists of consciousness, on the other (GP 91). More or less reductive forms of materialism currently hold sway as a kind of reigning, if somewhat inchoate, orthodoxy in the philosophy of mind, often promising an analysis or explanation of intentional phenomena in terms of nonintentional events, sometimes striving even to "eliminate" intentionality altogether in favor of some purely physicalistic description of the brain.[10] Daniel Dennett is representative of prevailing opinion when he candidly states his allegiance to the philosophical presuppositions of explanatory scientific inquiry: "I declare my starting point to be the objective, materialistic, third-person world of the physical sciences," he writes, adding correctly that "This is the orthodox choice today in the English-speaking philosophical world." Naturalism, physicalism – indeed, scientism – is Dennett's point of departure because, like Quine, he conceives of philosophy itself as essentially "allied with, and indeed continuous with, the physical sciences."[11]

[10] For example, Rorty, *Philosophy and the Mirror of Nature*, chapter 2, and Churchland, "Eliminative Materialism and the Propositional Attitudes."

[11] Dennett, *The Intentional Stance*, 5.

Philosophers such as Colin McGinn, Thomas Nagel, and John Searle, by contrast, have in different ways insisted on the irreducibility of the subjective point of view and the intrinsic or original intentionality of consciousness.[12] For Searle, intentionality is strictly speaking of two sorts. Words and pictures derive their representational function from human beings who interpret them *as* representational, that is, as representations *of* something. The intentionality of consciousness, by contrast, is original to or inherent in it, independently of anyone's interpretation of it as intentional. Consciousness stands in no need of an interpreter construing it as intentional in order to be intentional, whereas even the most sophisticated digital computer is not even really *computing* in the absence of some conscious mind to interpret its states and processes as computational. Searle therefore proposes a "connection principle," according to which mental states in general can be conceived as intentional only in virtue of their potential explicitness, so that, for example, "all unconscious intentional states are in principle accessible to consciousness."[13] Nagel makes even stronger claims for the intrinsic and irreducible subjectivity of conscious experience when he insists:

> There are things about the world and life and ourselves that cannot be adequately understood from a maximally objective standpoint . . . and the attempt to give a complete account of the world in objective terms . . . inevitably leads to false reductions or to outright denial that certain patently real phenomena exist at all.[14]

There are in fact two different issues at play in the current debate: one purely metaphysical, the other more broadly methodological in nature. On the one hand, the traditional mind–body problem remains the primary force driving discussions concerning the reducibility or irreducibility of the mental to purely physical states and processes. On the other hand, there is a prior, arguably deeper, question about how to conceive of intentionality in the first place. For example, should

---

[12] See McGinn, *The Problem of Consciousness*; the last four essays in Nagel's collection, *Mortal Questions*; and Searle, *The Rediscovery of the Mind*. Their views differ in many respects, but they share a critical view of the reductionism-cum-eliminativism of Dennett, Rorty, and Churchland.

[13] Searle, *The Rediscovery of the Mind*, 156.

[14] Nagel, *The View from Nowhere*, 7. For an example of outright denial of the sort Nagel deplores, see Dennett's observation that "strictly speaking, ontologically speaking, there are no such things as beliefs, desires, or other intentional phenomena." Dennett, *The Intentional Stance*, 342.

efforts at reduction have in view purely individual or also contextual correlates of cognition? Is intentionality realized in states of the brain and the nervous system alone, or in the body taken as a whole, or in the interactions between an organism and its environment?

Both issues arguably fall within the domain of phenomenology, which strives to describe our ordinary understanding of intentionality and its relation to the world in the face of philosophical, theological, and scientific traditions that have continually distorted it in favor of their own theoretical constructions and reconstructions. Heidegger's fundamental ontology itself proceeds phenomenologically and ought therefore to speak to the contemporary antagonism between subjectivism and reductionism in the philosophy of mind. For all resolutely first- and third-person approaches to intentionality are parallel lines destined never to converge if the surface on which they are drawn is really as flat as it appears. The spirit of phenomenology is to resist all such Euclidean idealizations in philosophy and to remind ourselves of the uneven surface of everyday understanding on which our concepts are originally inscribed.

From a Heideggerian point of view, then, what the contemporary debate lacks is some critical account of the conditions of the very *interpretability* of subjectivity and objectivity, that is, of the first- and third-person points of view themselves, which so much contemporary philosophical discussion simply takes for granted. For Heidegger, intentionality is neither an objective phenomenon in the "third-person world of the physical sciences" nor an inner, intrinsic property of the subject, as Nagel and Searle assume. In short, intentionality can be "neither subjective nor objective in the usual sense" (*GP* 91), as Heidegger says, precisely because it is what our understanding of both subjects and objects continually presupposes.

What *Is* the "Intentional Stance"?[15]

The drive to conceive of intentionality in wholly objective and external terms has led Dennett to regard it as nothing more than an artifact of the theoretical attitude we adopt in our explanations of behavior. Dennett therefore traces intentionality itself back to what he calls the "intentional stance," that is, the framework or perspective of the theoretical observer to whom the behavior of an organism or system

---

[15] Portions of this section appeared in my paper "What Is Intentionality? Heidegger's *via media.*"

is rationally explicable and predictable in intentional terms. Like all theoretical attitudes, the intentional stance is not imposed on us by things, but on things by us, by way of rendering them intelligible. Like any "stance" worthy of the name, the intentional stance is not compulsory, and nothing in principle prevents our eventually eliminating intentionality from our ontology altogether, however improbable such a change may be in fact. The notion of a person, for example, Dennett has said, "has a relatively vulnerable and impermanent place in our conceptual scheme, and could in principle be rendered 'obsolete' if some day we ceased to *treat* anything . . . as an Intentional system."[16] As long as we continue to adopt the intentional stance, of course, intentionality is here to stay, and in that case it is as much a part of the world as abstract particulars such as centers of gravity, constellations, and the equator.[17]

Dennett's notions of a physical, a design, and an intentional stance have struck some readers as reminiscent of Heidegger's account of Dasein's understandings of objects as occurrent, of equipment as available for use, and of itself as being-in-the-world. Each category constitutes a way in which entities are intelligible as the entities they are. Each carves out a horizon or framework of intelligibility for entities of a definite kind, what Husserl would call a "regional eidetic" or "regional ontology" (*Id I* 9–10). John Haugeland thus sees a convergence of interests and commitments between Heidegger's fundamental ontology and Dennett's conception of the intentional stance. "Daniel Dennett's landmark 'Real Patterns' (1991) is an essay in *ontology*: its topic is the being of entities," Haugeland writes. In it, "the issue is not intentionality at all, except in passing, but rather *being*."[18]

---

[16] Dennett, *Content and Consciousness*, 190.

[17] Although Dennett insists that he is not denying the existence of intentional phenomena understood as *abstracta*, he is clearly insisting on their theory-dependence, which is what interests me here. See "Three Kinds of Intentional Psychology," *The Intentional Stance*, chapter 3. Elsewhere, as we shall see, he comes closer to denying their existence altogether.

[18] Haugeland, "Pattern and Being," 53. Though he does not actually mention Heidegger's name in the present context, the language and the substance of Haugeland's argument make the allusion clear enough. I do not assume that he would attribute to Heidegger everything he attributes to Dennett, only that he finds significant convergence between Heidegger's notion of an understanding of being and Dennett's conception of a stance. Dennett, it should be noted, rejects Haugeland's ontological construal of stances, according to which what a thing *is* is constituted by what it is recognized to be according to a stance. Dennett opts instead for a kind of reductionism, or what he calls "the conservative default ontology: patterns are patterns of prior elements, even if you don't know what those elements are (yet)." Dennett, "Back from the Drawing Board," 214.

But the analogy between Heidegger's ontological categories and existentials and Dennett's explanatory stances runs aground precisely on the question What *is* a stance? What makes possible the intelligibility of a stance qua stance? Heidegger's existential analytic of Dasein draws its inspiration from this transcendental question concerning the possibility of anything like a stance making sense as a stance to the entity whose stance it is. Dennett, as we have seen, does not concern himself with that question, but opts instead for what he describes as the "orthodox choice" among contemporary theorists of mind, namely, reductive physicalism. Of course, orthodox choices always enjoy a spurious sort of obviousness and inevitability for those who embrace them, in this case owing in large part to the de facto cultural authority of the natural sciences, which no doubt explains why so many philosophers since Quine have come to view philosophy as of a piece with science. Heidegger, by contrast, like Kant and Wittgenstein before him, regards philosophy as something radically different from any positive science, so for him it still makes sense to ask, indeed one *must* ask, about the conditions of our taking up anything like the "objective, materialistic, third-person" perspective that so many philosophers now simply take for granted. What makes it possible for us to have or take up anything like a stance? No adequate answer to that question, it seems to me, can afford to regard itself simply as a naive product of the kind of stance whose conditions it wants to comprehend.

Dennett's appeal to the notion of an intentional stance, then, ignores the question What *is* a stance? Obviously, a stance is an intentional attitude, or rather a complex system of intentional attitudes that make up a theoretical framework or explanatory strategy. In any case, a stance is something intentional. So, what does Dennett's construal of intentionality as an artifact of the intentional stance have to say about the intentional stance itself? Of course, we can tell ourselves a story, from the intentional stance, about the causal history of our capacity to ascribe beliefs and desires, that is, to adopt the intentional stance with regard to ourselves and others. Perhaps this story will be illuminating, or perhaps it will stumble on some step in its account of the transition from mindless mechanisms to adaptive biological traits, to intelligent behavior, to full-fledged self-conscious agency. But the story need not be mysterious in principle, so let us grant that the developmental story is plausible and that the evolution we are asked to imagine is entirely and evidently nonmiraculous.

All this is fine by way of an empirical theory of the evolution of intentionality, but it leaves the philosophical question, the transcendental question, untouched. Namely, how are we to understand our own intentional stance, and all the attitudes making it up, *from our own situated point of view?* What are its conditions of intelligibility internal to our understanding of ourselves? Notice that this question is fundamentally different from the questions How did intentionality evolve in biological history? and How do infants (or fetuses) come to acquire it in the course of their psychological development? The transcendental question is not about the origins of intentionality, but about its current intelligibility to itself, its subjects, those of us who *have* it. The question is not Where did intentionality come from? but What *is* it? What can we say about intentionality, including the intentional stance itself, from our own point of view *within* it – over and beyond the tautological claim that ascribing intentionality to ourselves presupposes that we take up the intentional stance? For to say that intentionality presupposes itself is either to admit that there is something in the phenomenon that we have not yet come to terms with philosophically after all, something no amount of further empirical detail and thick causal description will eliminate, or it is to say nothing.

Dennett's theory of intentionality as an artifact of the intentional stance simply fails to recognize, let alone answer, that transcendental question. In a sense, the theory is not a philosophical account of intentionality at all, since it tells us nothing about the phenomenon except that it presupposes itself. It is understandable, then, that Dennett finds himself equivocating about the ontological status of intentional phenomena, at times insisting that they are as real as any "patterns" discoverable and describable in the world,[19] but more often lapsing into the eliminativism that his theory arguably ultimately demands. "*There seems to be phenomenology,*" he writes at one point. "But it does not follow from this undeniable, universally attested fact that *there really is* phenomenology."[20] Dennett allows that we may legitimately include the speech acts subjects make (seemingly) about their own experience in the stockpile of behavioral evidence to be interpreted from a third-person (what he calls the "heterophenomenological") point of view, tentatively treating what they say as a kind of fictional text, with no presumption of truth. But when his imaginary interlocutor goes on

---

[19] See Dennett, "Real Patterns."   [20] Dennett, *Consciousness Explained,* 366.

to ask, "But what about the *actual* phenomenology?" Dennett replies, "There is no such thing."[21] It might appear, then, that the theory can be vindicated only by denying the reality of what it purports to be a theory of.

But this can hardly be a welcome result, since it implies that the intentional stance that seems to be doing all the work in the theory is itself just a fiction. One fiction explains another, Dennett might reply, and perhaps he believes that spinning webs of fiction in large enough hermeneutic circles is the best we can hope to do, philosophically speaking. Perhaps the idea that there is anything more to be said about intentionality over and beyond the role the concept plays in our best explanations of physical behaviors is just an illusion brought on by some unsatisfied religious craving still smoldering in our philosophical imagination, in spite of the cold water Darwin threw on it nearly a century and a half ago.[22] Indeed, one might object, how is it even possible for a Heideggerian to criticize Dennett from the standpoint of hermeneutic phenomenology, which itself insists on the irreducible circularity of our interpretations of ourselves and our intentional attitudes? Is Haugeland right, after all, that Dennett's appeal to the intentional stance draws its inspiration from the same antifoundationalist insight as Heidegger's fundamental ontology, that his account of intentionality as an interpretable pattern of things in the world is just another version of Heidegger's conception of the ontological constitution of entities correlative with Dasein's understanding of being, albeit in a different philosophical idiom?

The reason this cannot be so, the reason Dennett's evidently question-begging theory cannot easily be reconciled with the interpretive circularity of hermeneutic phenomenology, is simply that Dennett refuses to engage with interpretations of the *phenomena* at all. For Dennett, it seems, the intentional stance *as such* is not a subject fit for serious philosophical reflection on its own terms, but merely a theoretical

---

[21] Ibid., 365. By 'phenomenology' Dennett does not mean the philosophical method, but something like real phenomenal *seemings*, distinct from our beliefs and *judgments about* how things seem to us. The clear implication, however, is that there can be no philosophical discipline of phenomenology, relying as it must on some unabashed first-person description of experience, "from the inside" as it were. What Dennett calls the "method of heterophenomenology," by contrast, takes its cue from "objective physical science and its insistence on the third-person point of view," and so promises to do justice to our crude intuitions "while never abandoning the methodological scruples of science." *Consciousness Explained*, 72. See also Dennett, "On the Absence of Phenomenology."

[22] For more in this vein see Dennett's *Darwin's Dangerous Idea*.

lens through which to view physical behavior as – or *as if* – driven by attitudes of belief and desire. But the very idea of an intentional stance, regarded as an aspect of our understanding of ourselves, from our own point of view, is apparently not up for discussion. It is simply an explanatory tool to be wheeled out in the service of an empirical theory. Genuine hermeneutic engagement with intentional phenomena à la fundamental ontology would mean taking seriously our own understanding – or our own pretheoretical, prescientific point of view – as something worthy of philosophical interpretation in its own right, rather than just so much loose folk-psychological talk.

The circularity of hermeneutic phenomenology and the circularity of Dennett's theory of intentionality are therefore two entirely different kinds of circles, and Dennett can no more be said to have taken up a critical perspective on the hermeneutic conditions of his own discourse than Husserl did in underwriting his quite different substantive claims by referring us back to pure consciousness and transcendental subjectivity. Of course, Dennett admits this by openly declaring that the only philosophical court of appeal he is willing to recognize is the philosophically naive standpoint of the physical sciences.

What *Is* the "Background"?[23]

One way of answering the question concerning the nature and conditions of stances, of course, is to revert to the first-person, internalist conception of intentionality as an intrinsic property of consciousness. For internalists like Husserl and Searle, mental states are not individuated by their connections with the external world at all, but instead have representational content specifying what Searle calls "conditions of satisfaction," whether the world in fact satisfies those conditions or not.[24] What Dennett calls a stance thus consists in intentional attitudes, and intentional attitudes are states intrinsic to consciousness.

On closer inspection, however, it turns out that such a subjectivist approach to intentionality is no more an answer to Heidegger's transcendental question than Dennett's blunt appeal to the impersonal perspective of natural science and its curiously free-floating explanatory frameworks. From the first-person point of view, that is, the question

---

[23] Portions of this section appeared in my paper "Normativity and Social Skill in Searle and Bourdieu."

[24] Searle, *Intentionality*, chapter 1.

concerning hermeneutic conditions cannot even be framed, since the internalist simply stipulates that the intentional content of consciousness is intrinsic to it and therefore, at least in principle, transparently intelligible to its owner. It is important to recognize that the internalist thesis is not so much a psychological observation or the conclusion of a reasoned argument as a refusal to entertain the question concerning the conditions of the interpretation of mental content. In the previous chapter, I argued that Heidegger rejects Husserl's phenomenological reductions as a sophisticated means of evading the question, and that his fundamental ontology is hermeneutical precisely in its recognition of the role and significance of hermeneutic conditions in human understanding.

Searle's theory of intentionality bears a striking resemblance to Husserl's phenomenology, yet Searle goes beyond Husserl in a number of interesting ways. In particular, though he has always insisted that intentionality is intrinsic to consciousness, he goes on to offer an account of what he takes to be its biological and social conditions, which he refers to as "the Background."[25] Searle's concept of the Background might at first glance seem to coincide with Heidegger's notion of engaged, practical being-in-the-world. But Searle equivocates in his treatment of the bodily and social conditions of intentionality, in effect conflating merely causal with what I have called hermeneutic conditions. As a result, I shall argue, his position is incoherent in a way that Heidegger's is not.

Like Husserl, Searle conceives of intentionality in terms of representation. Unlike Husserl, however, he observes further that mental representation presupposes "the capacities, abilities, and general know-how that enable our mental states to function." According to Searle, "intentional phenomena only determine conditions of satisfaction relative to a set of capacities that are not themselves intentional."[26] Since intentional content is representational and "not, so to speak, self-interpreting,"[27] Searle concludes, "Even if you spell out all contents of the mind as a set of conscious rules, thoughts, beliefs, etc., you still require a set of Background capacities for their interpretation."[28] Searle's conception of nonintentional skills and capacities underlying

---

[25] See *Intentionality,* chapter 5; *The Rediscovery of the Mind,* chapter 8; and *The Construction of Social Reality,* chapter 6.

[26] Searle, *The Rediscovery of the Mind,* 175.   [27] Ibid., 176.

[28] Ibid., 189–90.

our intentional states seems to echo Heidegger's claim in *Being and Time* that knowledge or cognition is parasitic on practical understanding and is therefore, as he says, a "founded mode" of being-in (*SZ* §13).

But Searle's conception of the Background is fatally ambiguous and poses a general dilemma for his subjectivist theory of intentionality. Whereas Dennett defines intentionality in terms of an interpretive stance taken up by a theoretical observer, effectively begging the question concerning the intelligibility conditions of stances, Searle simply insists that intentionality is intrinsic to consciousness, but then goes on to anchor it in the biologically and culturally determined background capacities that make it possible. But what kinds of things *are* those background capacities, and what sorts of "conditions" do they constitute?

Searle insists that the Background is nonintentional, and he refers to its capacities as "contingently existing biological and cultural facts about human beings."[29] It would therefore seem that such capacities are simply causal, or Heidegger would say "ontic,"[30] conditions of intentionality, conditions such as the circulation of blood and a steady supply of oxygen to the brain. At the same time, such a reading would seem to trivialize Searle's point, for in fact he presents his argument as an extension of Wittgenstein's observation of an infinite regress in theoretical and commonsense accounts of rule-following. For it turns out that, like the words, gestures, and color samples Wittgenstein discusses, intentional contents themselves, according to Searle, stand in need of interpretation in order to determine conditions of satisfaction, that is, to mean what they do. Indeed, Searle frequently helps himself to intentional characterizations of the Background, describing it at one point as "an inductively based set of expectations."[31] The "capacities" constituting the Background therefore cannot just consist in the causal conditions that, like gravity and air pressure, allow our minds to function as they do, but must evidently have *normative* import in guiding and informing our interpretation of the contents of our own minds.

---

[29] Ibid., 191.

[30] Heidegger distinguishes between ontic and ontological priority, or what I have called causal and hermeneutic conditions, when he writes, " 'there is' something available, after all, only on the basis of the occurrent. But does it follow from this – granting this claim for the moment – that availability is founded on occurrentness ontologically?" (*SZ* 71). That is, although the causal structure of occurrent *entities* conditions the instrumental character of things available, availability as a mode of *being* conditions the interpretability of objects as occurrent.

[31] *The Rediscovery of the Mind*, 182.

Searle has also enlisted his notion of the Background in support of a theory of social reality, specifically of the normative structure of social institutions, extending and building on the theories of linguistic practice and intentionality in his earlier works. His "General Theory of Institutional Facts"[32] draws crucially on two prominent features of mental life: collective intentionality, which he maintains is biologically primitive and intrinsic to individual consciousness, and our imposition of "observer-relative" functions on mere physical phenomena.[33] Institutional facts are social facts, Searle argues, inasmuch as they depend on collective intentionality, unlike natural or "brute" facts, which do not. Further, institutional facts (but not all social facts) consist in assignments of function, in particular what he calls "status functions," which rest on constitutive rules of the form "X counts as Y in C."[34] That is, something with certain intrinsic properties (say, a piece of paper) counts as something with a certain functional status (money) in certain (in this case economic) conditions.

I do not want to analyze the nuts and bolts of Searle's theory here. Instead, I want to consider the specific way in which he tries to ground public norms in the abilities and attitudes of individual agents. It is Searle's mentalism that interests me, but not because I think it renders too much of the social world subjective, though it may in fact do so. What I want to point out is that Searle's social ontology commits him to a kind of objectivism inasmuch as he supposes that the normativity of social institutions is *exhausted* by the rules that a detached observer could in principle articulate in *describing* them. He writes: "the institutional structure is a structure of rules, and the actual rules that we specify in *describing* the institution will *determine* those aspects under which the system is normative."[35]

Of course, constitutive rules must *govern,* not merely *describe,* the institutions they constitute. Yet, as Searle points out, it is not as if we are typically aware of all the rules that inform even the most familiar and trivial institutions of daily life. Searle must therefore account for the efficacy of constitutive rules as they operate beneath the threshold of any conscious awareness on the part of the agents themselves. He

---

[32] Searle, *The Construction of Social Reality,* chapters 4 and 5.

[33] Ibid., 18.

[34] Ibid., 28, 40–4. Searle points out that not all constitutive rules are strictly speaking conventional, if 'conventional' means arbitrary. I take he means they are not revisable without essential revisions in the institutions they constitute. See ibid., 28.

[35] Ibid., 146–7, emphasis added.

does so not by positing some form of explicit but in principle unconscious rule-following, à la Noam Chomsky and Jerry Fodor, and I think he is right to dismiss that hypothesis as ad hoc at best, incoherent at worst.[36] Rather, he wants to ground the normativity of social practice in the Background abilities of individual agents. Searle's social ontology therefore rests on a conception of social skill, as any plausible account must.

On closer inspection, however, it turns out that Searle has no positive account of social skill as distinct from nonnormative causal mechanism on the one hand, and conscious rule-following on the other. Searle sometimes suggests an analogy between his own notion of the Background and Pierre Bourdieu's concept of *habitus,* that is, our embodied, precognitive understanding that consists in "systems of durable, transposable dispositions" for social behavior.[37] The two notions are superficially similar, but they differ crucially. Indeed, Bourdieu enlists his concept in part in the service of a critique of Lévi-Strauss and structural anthropology, which, like Searle's theory of institutional facts, seeks to reduce the *practical* intelligibility of social behavior to the explicit rules describable by an idealized *theoretical* observer.[38]

Interestingly, in elaborating his theory of social reality Searle settles on a purely causal account of the Background after all, which he again defines as "the set of nonintentional or preintentional capacities that enable intentional states of [*sic*] function." He goes on to explain, "By *capacities* I mean . . . *causal structures generally*. It is important to see that when we talk about the Background we are talking about a certain category of neurophysiological causation."[39] The Background enables mental states to function, and "*Enabling* is meant," he says, "to be a causal notion." What we are talking about is "neurophysiological structures that function causally in the production of certain sorts of intentional phenomena."[40]

How then do such neurophysiological capacities figure into an account of rule-governed social institutions? What Searle proposes, in

---

[36] See ibid., 128

[37] Bourdieu, *The Logic of Practice,* 53. See Searle, *The Rediscovery of the Mind,* 177; *The Construction of Social Reality,* 132.

[38] See Bourdieu, ibid., Book I, chapter 1.

[39] Searle, *The Construction of Social Reality,* 129.

[40] Ibid., 130. Searle appeals to Wittgenstein's notion of "an ungrounded way of acting," but such an appeal assumes a Humean interpretation of Wittgenstein. See *The Construction of Social Reality,* 140; and Wittgenstein, *Philosophical Investigations,* Part I, §§324ff.

short, is that, where conscious awareness of rules leaves off, neuro-physiological capacities enter in to take up the slack: "One develops skills and abilities that are, so to speak, functionally equivalent to the system of rules."[41] We don't typically think through the constitutive rules governing a social institution. "Rather, we develop skills that are responsive to that particular institutional structure."[42] How does this happen? Searle explains the process by analogy with natural selection in evolutionary biology. "First," he says, "the person behaves the way he does, because he has a structure that disposes him to behave that way; and second...he has come to be disposed to behave that way, because that's the way that conforms to the rules of the institution."[43] In short, "we evolve a set of dispositions that are sensitive to the rule structure";[44] "an undifferentiated mechanism that happens to look as if it were rule structured... *has evolved precisely so that it will be sensitive to the rules.*"[45]

But how can a set of neurophysiological capacities and dispositions be sensitive to *rules*? How can a mere "undifferentiated mechanism" be responsive to rules *governing* what we do? Is the Background mechanism sensitive to the rules *as rules* or merely as patterns or regularities in the environment? Since the mechanism is not strictly speaking rule-structured or rule-governed, it remains obscure, on Searle's account, how it can conform to a system of rules that is not merely descriptive, but *normative*. I take it that what Searle means is that our Background capacities conform to, or are shaped by, the material and social conditions that *instantiate* or *satisfy* the constitutive rules governing our institutions. But this leaves the theory with two parallel explanatory lines that never converge. On the one hand, we are sometimes consciously aware of and responsive to explicit rules governing what we do, presumably in virtue of our awareness of them, as for example when we deliberate and make a move in a game of chess. On the other hand, we inherit and acquire bodily capacities that are biologically and socially selected precisely because they mesh causally with our environment. As Searle puts it, "The man at home in his society is as comfortable as the fish in the sea or the eyeball in its socket."[46]

---

[41] Searle, *The Construction of Social Reality*, 142.
[42] Ibid., 143.　　　　　　　　　　[43] Ibid., 144.
[44] Ibid., 145.　　　　　　　　　　[45] Ibid., 146.
[46] Ibid., 147.

But in that case it is misleading at best, false at worst, to say that what Background capacities are responsive to is *rules*. For it is not strictly speaking the rules governing our social institutions that impinge on us causally; it is the physical and cultural environment itself. The Background therefore cannot be responsive to governing rules *qua governing* or to the normative structure of institutions *qua normative*. Strictly speaking, the Background is no more sensitive or responsive to the rules of social conduct than racehorses are to the rules of gambling. Like them, we are simply adapted to an environment that can be described with reference to rules that, for quite different reasons, also function as governing rules.

Searle's theory is not so much inconsistent as incomplete. What it leaves out of account is, among other things, the phenomenon of embodied social skill as such, which is arguably neither full-blown conscious obedience to explicit rules nor mere blind neurophysiological capacities and dispositions. Between the mental and the physical levels of description, customarily understood, that is, there is an intermediary phenomenon of practical understanding, anchored in the bodily abilities that orient us meaningfully in our physical and social environment. What is an ability? Not a mere causal capacity, but a skill, a competence, a know-how – indeed, if we take the expression 'know-how' seriously, a kind of knowledge. Searle has gone much further than Dennett in describing the conditions under which subjective attitudes can have genuine intentional directedness to the world. But his theories of intentionality and social practice stand in need of some further account of the embodied practical understanding that makes thoughts and institutions intelligible. Searle's conception of the Background fails to supply that desideratum, however, since it forgoes an account of the hermeneutic conditions of intentionality and institutional meaning in favor of a mere reminder of their causal conditions.

The Primacy of Being-in

Heidegger's interpretation of human being as being-in-the-world is part of an effort to resist the temptation to construe mundane intentional phenomena in either exclusively subjective or exclusively objective terms. Heidegger does not want to deny that minds and objects figure into our understanding of ourselves and the world at all, but he insists that we understand them only with reference to the background milieu or situation in which they show up for us. Minds, for example, are intelligible to us above all as the minds *of* human beings, and human beings we understand as situated agents inhabiting practically structured worlds. Similarly, mere objects are things abstracted from pragmatic contexts, stripped of the instrumental significance under which we may encounter them. Self-sufficient minds and isolated objects are not primitive notions, then, but abstractions, dependent moments of something more basic that gives them meaning, namely, our understanding of *the world*.

What is a world? In Heidegger's language, what does the "worldliness" (*Weltlichkeit*) of the world consist in? And what does it mean for us to *be in* a world? What notion of "being-in" (*In-sein*) describes our relation to the world? These are the questions around which Heidegger frames the analytic of Dasein. What is crucial to note at this point, however, is that we lose sight of the phenomena of being-in and worldliness if we try to assimilate them to the subjective and the objective, or the internal and the external, as Nagel does. What we encounter prior to abstracting to the "worldless subject" (*SZ* 211) arguably presupposed by Descartes, Husserl, and Searle, and to "the objective, materialistic, third-person world of the physical sciences" taken for granted equally uncritically by materialists like Dennett, is the normatively structured, publicly shared space of practical life. It is a mistake to reduce situated agency to something subjective, just as it is a mistake to reduce the normative structure of the practical situation itself to a value-free manifold of objective facts. Heidegger insists, in short, that no sharp metaphysical distinction can be drawn between ourselves and the world, and that the world has an irreducible normative dimension. Subjectivists are wrong to begin by positing the mind and the world, or "consciousness and reality" as Husserl has it (*Id I* 77), as separately intelligible entities, just as reductionists are wrong to suppose that the decontextualized objects and states of affairs posited by the natural sciences can in turn explain, or explain away, the prior background meanings against which they were originally, privatively defined.

Heidegger's existential analytic of Dasein thus amounts to a form of *nonreductive externalism*. It is externalist in insisting that our intentional relations to the world are constituted by our orientation in the public domain, not by our private possession of internal mental states. And it is nonreductive in accepting normative structure as an ontologically primitive aspect of worlds, neither analyzable in terms of brute natural facts nor construed as mere functions of explicit

subjective attitudes, whether individual or collective. I shall consider
these two aspects of Heidegger's analytic in this and the following section, respectively.

According to Heidegger, intentionality is not indifferent with respect to its worldly context, as the logic of some intentional verbs
might lead us to believe; rather, it has to do with our concrete practical "dealing" (*Umgang*) with things. He accordingly defines intentional
directedness not in terms of the representational content of subjective attitudes like belief and desire, but in terms of our competent
"comportment" (*Verhalten*) in everyday life, which includes such things
as "having to do with something, producing something, taking care of
and tending to something, making use of something, giving something
up and letting it go, undertaking, accomplishing, evincing, asking, considering, discussing, determining" (*SZ* 56). These forms of practical
comportment differ from intentional phenomena traditionally conceived above all in that they are not specifically psychological phenomena. Nor do they invite the *narrow* interpretation favored by internalist
conceptions of intentionality. Instead, almost all of the expressions on
Heidegger's list are defined *widely* in terms of the environment in which
they occur. According to the logic of a success verb like 'see,' for example, if the thing does not exist, you do not *see* it. Likewise, if a thing
is not part of the everyday practical environment, you can't have to do
with it, produce it, take care of it, tend to it, make use of it, give it up,
let it go, and so on. The intentional phenomenon Heidegger regards
as basic is what he calls "concern" (*Besorgen*) (*SZ* 57), and its specific
instances are always defined in terms of our embeddedness in concrete
practices.

Heidegger thus makes it clear that he does not intend his notions of
being-in and worldliness simply to reiterate traditional metaphysical distinctions between self and world. As he says, "subject and object do not
coincide with Dasein and world" (*SZ* 60). Chapters 2 and 3 of Division
I of *Being and Time* nonetheless proceed programmatically as accounts
of being-in and worldliness, respectively, understood as formally
distinct but ontologically inseparable elements of the a priori structure
of being-in-the-world. "This a priori [element] of the interpretation
of Dasein is not a pieced-together determination, but a primordial
and constant unitary structure," Heidegger says. We can distinguish
formally among its "constituting moments," but only as derivative
aspects of the phenomenon taken as a whole, so that "By keeping the

prior totality of this structure constantly in view, these moments may be made to stand out" (*SZ* 41). 'Being-in-the-world' therefore cannot be understood as a mere summation of its constituent terms:

> The compound expression "being-in-the-world" indicates in its very coinage that what is meant by it is a *unitary* phenomenon. This primary datum must be seen as a whole. Its indissolubility into component parts that could be pieced together does not rule out a manifold of constitutive structural moments in its makeup. (*SZ* 53)

Heidegger's programmatic account of being-in and worldliness, then, understood as formally distinct aspects of being-in-the-world, must not mislead us to construe them as ontologically discrete, independently intelligible phenomena in their own right. They are rather two sides of the same coin.

Nor can being-in or worldliness be understood as *properties* of Dasein and the world, any more than being can be understood as a property of entities generally. All talk of entities and their properties and relations remains ontic, not "ontological" in Heidegger's sense. Traditional ontology has typically tried to account for the intelligibility of entities with recourse to more or different entities, whether mundane or esoteric, for example ideal forms, self-sufficient substances, autonomous agents, or creative willing. Fundamental ontology, by contrast, takes up and radicalizes Kant's denial that being is a "real predicate" and inquires instead into the conditions of the interpretability of entities as entities.[47] Such hermeneutic conditions cannot themselves just be so many entities or properties on pain of regress, since we would then have to ask how those entities, those hermeneutic conditions themselves, are intelligible to us as such, and so on.

What then is being-in if it is neither an entity nor the property of an entity? One might be tempted to say that it consists in *having* a world, except that this invites the question, What does it mean to "have"

---

[47] At the same time, Heidegger remarks that in denying that being is a real predicate, Kant "is merely repeating Descartes's proposition" that substance itself is empirically inaccessible, since its mere existence cannot affect us as such (*SZ* 94; see Descartes, *The Principles of Philosophy*, §52, in *The Philosophical Writings of Descartes*, Vol. 1). In his 1927 lectures, too, immediately following the publication of *Being and Time*, Heidegger argues that Kant's notion of being as *absolute position* is still essentially the concept of occurrentness (*GP* 36). Nevertheless, it is plain that Kant's thesis is at least in part what inspires Heidegger's distinction between being and entities, which he here for the first time formally dubs the "ontological difference."

something in the salient sense?[48] Being-in, or having a world in the proper sense, means having a meaningful practical orientation among entities in virtue of our understanding of them as entities. Being-in makes epistemic states such as perception and cognition intelligible as such. Heidegger calls such epistemic states "founded modes" of being-in (*SZ* §13), since we can make sense of them only as occurring in the wider context of human existence, or being-in-the-world, whereas we cannot in turn analyze being-in in terms of some prior and independent conception of those states. Heidegger inherits the notion of "founding" (*Fundieren*) from Husserl, who defines it in the third *Logical Investigation* as a relation of formal-ontological dependence: To say that A founds B, or that B is founded on A, is to say that B depends for its existence on A. One entity can therefore found another without in turn being founded on it. For example, objects often found, but are not themselves founded on, their properties and relations. Similarly, two entities or properties can found each other, such as for example the interior and exterior of an object or the two sides of a coin. Husserl's concept of founding relations is thus central to his generally mereological approach to formal ontology.

Heidegger, by contrast, is offering a fundamental, not a formal, ontology, so his own notion of founding rests not on abstract metaphysical intuitions, but on a concrete account of the conditions of interpretation. Consistent with Husserl's notion of founding, then, to say that cognition is a founded mode of being-in is to say, first, that cognition is itself a kind of being-in, so that there could be no cognition without being-in, and second, that being-in does not in turn depend on cognition. Unlike Husserl, Heidegger does not ground his claim in any putative "intuition of essences"; indeed, his practical conception of understanding is meant to supplant all such lingering Platonic prejudices:

> By showing how all sight is primarily grounded in understanding, we have robbed pure intuition of its privilege, which corresponds noetically to the traditional ontological privileging of the occurrent. "Intuition" and

[48] Heidegger therefore rejects the locution as unhelpful: "The expression so often used today, 'man has his environment,' says nothing ontologically as long as this 'having' remains undefined. The possibility of this 'having' is founded on the existential constitution of being-in. As essentially this kind of entity, Dasein can explicitly uncover entities it encounters environmentally, know about them, avail itself of them, and *have* a 'world.' The ontically trivial talk of 'having an environment' is a problem ontologically. Solving it requires nothing less than first defining the being of Dasein in an ontologically adequate way" (*SZ* 57–8).

> "thinking" are both rather distant derivatives of understanding. Even the phenomenological "intuition of essences" (*Wesensschau*) is grounded in existential understanding. (*SZ* 147)

Far from appealing to brute, reifying intuitions, Heidegger's conception of cognition as a founded mode of being-in amounts to a recognition that our practical orientation in the world is a condition of the very interpretability of our own cognition *as* cognition. For all theories of cognition inevitably presuppose and draw on some understanding, however tacit, of our being-in, which they can never in turn exhaust. Again, this is not to insist that all organisms must have an understanding of being in order to have intentional states, only that *our* having the cognitive states *we* have is intelligible to us solely in virtue of our understanding of being, which includes our understanding of ourselves as oriented agents with practical projects and concrete histories. Again, as I suggested in Chapter 1, Heidegger is not interested in the conditions of intentionality generally, but in the practical conditions of our interpretation of intentional attitudes, our own or those of animals, *as* intentional.

Heidegger's insistence on the primacy of being-in is one of his most radical departures from the metaphysical and epistemological tradition. The idea that cognitive attitudes are parasitic on concrete practical understanding goes against the mentalism and internalism that have defined that tradition since the seventeenth century. Philosophers from Descartes to Husserl have conceived of consciousness as a kind of inner sanctum of transparent subjective content, self-sufficient vis-à-vis the world outside. Heidegger's description of human existence as being-in-the-world, as temporally ecstatic "thrown projection," is a repudiation of the subjectivism that lies at the heart of modern philosophy. As he puts it,

> The more unequivocally one maintains that cognition (*Erkennen*) is primarily and genuinely "inside" (*drinnen*), and indeed has nothing at all like the kind of being of a physical or mental entity, the more one believes one is proceeding without presuppositions in the question concerning the essence of cognition and the clarification of the relation between subject and object. For only then can a problem first arise, namely the question: How does the knowing subject come out from its inner "sphere" into one that is "other and external," how can cognition have an object at all, how must the object itself be conceived, so that in the end the subject knows it, without needing to venture a leap into another sphere? (*SZ* 60)

What looks like progress to a phenomenologist like Husserl, to whom the passage alludes, Heidegger regards instead as an ontological step backward. For with the invocation of the problem of skepticism and mere "wonder" at the fact that there is such a thing as intentionality at all,[49] "the question concerning the mode of being of this subject comes to a complete standstill" (SZ 60). The very idea of a bare, disembodied epistemological subject rests on a forgetfulness (one is tempted to say a willful forgetfulness) of the existential context that conditions our interpretation of ourselves *as* subjects.

Moreover, notwithstanding the genuine innovations that distinguish his direct realism from the indirect representational theories of perception that have dominated the tradition, Husserl's conception of transcendental subjectivity as a region of pure "immanence" is no less obscure ontologically than the Cartesian *res cogitans*. As Heidegger observes,

> Of course, one is always assured that the inside and the "inner sphere" of the subject is certainly not conceived as a "box" or a "cabinet." What the "inside" of immanence, in which cognition is first of all contained, means in a positive sense, though, and how the ontological character (*Seinscharakter*) of this "being inside" of cognition is grounded in the mode of being of the subject, remains shrouded in silence. (SZ 60)

What the tradition has forgotten, in a word, is that "cognition is a mode of the being of Dasein as being-in-the-world" (SZ 61). By placing Dasein's epistemic situation back in its proper existential setting, Heidegger is in effect advancing a form of practical externalism:

> In directing itself toward something and grasping it, Dasein does not somehow first get out of an inner sphere in which it has first been encapsulated, rather its primary kind of being is such that it is always "outside" with entities that it encounters and that belong to an already discovered world. Nor is any inner sphere abandoned when Dasein dwells with the entity to be known, and determines its character; rather even in this "being-outside" amidst the object, Dasein is still "inside" as being-in-the-world that knows. And furthermore perceiving what is known is not a matter of

[49] Husserl refers frequently to the philosophical "wonder" of the very fact of intentionality or pure consciousness. For example, "The wonder of all wonders is the pure I and pure consciousness" (*Id III*, 75). Cf. *Erste Philosophie*, I: 27; *Hu* IX 174; *Analysen zur passiven Synthesis*, 13, 21, 213.

returning with one's booty to the "cabinet" of consciousness after one has gone out and grasped it; even in perceiving, retaining, and preserving, the knowing Dasein, *as Dasein, remains outside.* (*SZ* 62)

Similarly, in his 1927 lectures he says,

the intentional structure of comportments is not something that is immanent to the so-called subject, and which would first of all stand in need of transcendence, rather the intentional constitution of Dasein's comportments is precisely the *ontological condition of the possibility of every and any transcendence.* (*GP* 91)

Strictly speaking, rejecting the notion of a subjective "inside" suggests a corresponding rejection of any parasitic notion of an "outside," which thrives only on a contrast with the interiority of the subject. As Heidegger says, "For Dasein there is no outside, which is why it is also nonsensical to talk about an inside" (*GP* 93). This should not prevent us from understanding Heidegger's position as a kind of externalism, however, since the salient sense of externality is clear enough with reference to the putative interiority of subjective experience as the locus of intentionality. Like any philosophical view, Heidegger's makes sense only in relation to the competing alternatives. Of course, it makes sense to talk about externalism only in a conceptual space that includes internalism as a contrasting account of the phenomena. But such is the conceptual space we inhabit. We could in principle describe Heidegger's conception of being-in absent any reference to internalist theories of mind, in which case we would no longer be entitled to refer to the world as "external" to anything. Indeed, if 'inner' and 'outer' are supposed to describe the modes of being of Dasein and the world, understood as two entities subsisting side by side as subject and object, then Heidegger rejects the distinction. For it is just as misleading to regard the world as somehow outside us as to conceive of ourselves as somehow inside some private subjective sphere.

Worldliness, Reality, and the Real

What then is the meaning of the word 'world' in the expression 'being-in-the-world'? Is it nothing beyond the correlative structure associated with whatever practical and theoretical attitudes and interests Dasein happens to have? No, for to insist that cognition is founded on being-in is not to say that objects perceived and conceived by us are dependent on our perceptions and conceptions of them. So, as we shall see in Chapter 4, although "the worldliness of the world" is, like being-in, part of the ontological structure of Dasein's being-in-the-world, occurrent entities themselves are not. To appreciate this point, it is necessary to distinguish the notion of worldliness from three other distinct senses of the word 'world,' as Heidegger does in *Being and Time*.

Of the four senses Heidegger identifies, two are ontic, two onto-logical. The "world" in the first, *ontic* sense is simply a notion of the sum total of all objects, properties, and relations, or as Heidegger puts it, "the totality of entities that can be occurrent within the world" (*SZ* 64). This concept of world is indifferent with respect to the being or ontological status of various kinds of entities, in particular Dasein, which Heidegger in fact insists "can never be taken ontologically as a case or instance of a species of entities as something occurrent" (*SZ* 42).[50] It is this ontic-categorial concept of world that has dominated the meta-physical tradition, and in *Being and Time* Heidegger refers to it variously as "nature" (*SZ* 65)[51] and "the real" (*das Reale*) (*SZ* 212).

The second, this time *ontological,* sense of the word refers to the do-mains in which, or the schemes or frameworks according to which, entities of various kinds can be said to *be*. Husserl distinguishes in much the same way various "regional eidetics" or "regional ontologies" appro-priate to essentially different kinds of entities (*Id I* 9–10).[52] 'World' in

---

[50] A few pages later, however, Heidegger writes, "even entities that are not worldless, e.g. Dasein itself, are occurrent 'in' the world, or more precisely put, *can* with a certain right and within certain limits be *taken* (*aufgefaßt*) as something merely occurrent. For this it is necessary to disregard completely, or not see, the existential constitution of being-in" (*SZ* 55). Does this admission undermine Heidegger's distinction between Dasein and occurrent entities altogether? No, but it suggests that Heidegger has done fairly little to resolve, let alone address, the mind–body problem. William Blattner is right, it seems to me, to say that regarding Dasein in an "abstracted" way as something merely occurrent "is not to consider Dasein properly" (*Heidegger's Temporal Idealism*, 37, 85). But does this commit Heidegger to a kind of "dualism," as Blattner suggests? I am tempted to say that Heidegger is a pluralist about entities and their ontological kinds, and that the mind–body problem thrives largely on our impoverished phenomenological descriptions of the ways in which fundamentally different kinds of entities figure into our understanding at large. In any case, in forgoing any account of the human body (*SZ* 108), Heidegger in effect evades the problem.

[51] Heidegger adds, however, that "The 'nature' that 'surrounds' us is indeed an intraworldly entity, but it exhibits neither the mode of being of the available nor of the occurrent in the sense of 'natural materiality' (*Naturdinglichkeit*)" (*SZ* 211).

[52] Interestingly, Heidegger rejects Husserl's talk of ontological "regions" as confined to a strictly categorial understanding of entities, to the exclusion of our existential under-standing of ourselves. Already around 1920, in his "Comments on Karl Jaspers's *Psychology*

this sense, Heidegger says, "functions as an ontological term and means the being of the entities cited in number 1," that is, in the foregoing ontic sense (*SZ* 64), so that, for example, "in talking about the 'world' of the mathematician, 'world' means the region of possible objects of mathematics" (*SZ* 64–5).[53] As an example of this understanding of world Heidegger refers to the ancient Greek concept of *kosmos*, which he interprets to mean the general order or intelligible condition of all things as they hang together in a coherent whole, so that *kosmos* "does not mean anything like all entities together; it does not at all mean entities themselves; it is not a name for them. Rather, *kosmos* means 'condition' (*Zustand*); *kosmos* is the term for the *mode of being*, not for entities themselves" (*MAL* 219).[54] So too, as we have just seen, whereas Heidegger refers to the totality of occurrent entities as "the real," he reserves the term 'reality' (*Realität*) for the mode of being of the real: "If we grant this word its traditional[55] significance, then it means being in the sense of the pure occurrentness of a [mere] thing (*pure*

of Worldviews," for example, Heidegger says of "the authentically enacted fundamental experience of the 'I am'" that "Holding purely to this enactment of experience reveals the specific foreignness of the 'I' to regions and objective domains" (*Weg/GA* 9, 29). "*Hence the need for a radical suspicion . . . of all regionally objectifying preconceptions (Vorgriffe)*" (*Weg/GA* 9, 30). Heidegger's rejection of Husserl's conception of ontological regions is also clearly tied to his notion that Dasein cannot understand itself merely as the token instantiation of a general type, as the eidetic reduction seems to require: "The factical experience of life itself . . . is nothing like a region in which I stand, or a universal whose individuation would be the self" (*Weg/GA* 9, 32).

53   It is unclear whether Heidegger regards mathematical objects as genuinely occurrent things. In fact, he has almost nothing to say about the being of abstract entities. Of course, the thesis of *Being and Time* itself – that time is "the possible horizon of any understanding of being at all" (*SZ* 1) and that "the central problematic of all ontology is rooted in the phenomenon of time, properly viewed and properly explained" (*SZ* 18) – is hardly hospitable to Platonism. But neither does it necessarily entail that Platonism is false, for it says only that (so-called) "atemporal" entities are intelligible to us solely in virtue of their relation to temporality, even if that relation is wholly negative. If Platonism maintains, as Plato himself seems to have maintained, not just that some entities exist outside of time, but that they are intelligible to us, to our "mind's eye," as it were, without any reference to time at all, that is, if Platonism is not just a metaphysical thesis about abstract entities, but a claim about the hermeneutic conditions associated with them, then Heidegger rejects Platonism. If Platonism merely insists that there are such things, however, then Heidegger's position seems to be one of neutrality, or perhaps indifference (see *SZ* 18).

54   Hence the origin of the word 'cosmetic,' which has to do with the overall coherence of aspect, for example the appearance of a face. Heidegger refers here to Karl Reinhardt, *Parmenides und die Geschichte der griechischen Philosophie*.

55   In the margins of his copy of the text, Heidegger has replaced 'traditional' with 'contemporary' (*heutige*).

Dingvorhandenheit)" (*SZ* 211). Consequently, although reality as an ontological category is dependent on Dasein's understanding of being, the real is not. Again, "That reality is grounded ontologically in the being of Dasein cannot mean that the real could only be, as what it is in itself, if and as long as Dasein exists" (*SZ* 211–12).

This ontological conception of world is also not unlike Carnap's notion of theoretical systems or linguistic frameworks presupposed by sentences about entities of some kind, abstract or concrete. Questions about entities are either internal or external to the frameworks in which we refer to them, so that a claim that *there are* entities of a certain kind – physical objects, numbers, propositions, properties – will either be internal to a system and therefore analytically true, or else external and so just a practical matter of the utility of the system itself. Carnap intended this approach to do away with general metaphysical questions about entities altogether, since such questions purport to be neither internal and simply analytic nor mere external matters of linguistic policy.[56] Yet the very idea that languages can constitute systems or frameworks is itself a metaphysical idea, and Heidegger would say that a discourse like Carnap's, referring freely as it does to such systems or frameworks, is a discourse about worlds in precisely this ontological sense.

The ontological notion of world has even more in common with Thomas Kuhn's account of practical and theoretical "paradigms" in the history of science. Kuhn's use of the term 'paradigm' in *The Structure of Scientific Revolutions* is notoriously ambiguous; indeed, as we shall see, his notion applies more directly to Heidegger's third sense of 'world.' What concerns us here, however, is his idea that frameworks or norms of understanding are not just integral to the practice of science, but "are constitutive of nature as well."[57] There is a sense, that is, in which fundamental changes in the normative standards of scientific practice do not just effect transformations in science itself, but can also be said to "transform the world."[58] For Kuhn, "paradigm changes do cause scientists to see the world differently. Insofar as their only recourse to that world is through what they see and do, we may want to say that after a revolution scientists are responding to a different world." Scientific training is not just the accumulation of knowledge, but involves coming

---

[56] Carnap, "Empiricism, Semantics, and Ontology."
[57] Kuhn, *The Structure of Scientific Revolutions*, 110.
[58] Ibid., 106.

to see things differently, and "Only after a number of such transformations of vision does the student become an inhabitant of the scientist's
world."[59]

But such gestalt transformations of worlds do not necessarily amount
to alterations or substitutions of entities. The sense of 'world' Kuhn
has in mind in these passages, then, is clearly not the ontic sense, that
is, the mere sum total of entities. Indeed, he invokes the ontic notion
later, though without making the distinction explicit, when he writes,
"changes of this sort are never total. Whatever he may then see, the
scientist after a revolution is still looking at *the same world*."[60] The ontic
world, the world of entities, remains the same, Heidegger would say;
the ontological world, the world understood as the intelligible ordering
of those entities as the kinds of entities they are, has changed.

'World' has a third, once again *ontic* sense, referring not just to occurrent or theoretical entities, but to "that 'wherein' a factical Dasein,
as Dasein, 'lives.' 'World' here has a preontological, existentiel meaning," Heidegger says, since it captures our ordinary notion of the practical worlds in which people live their lives. It therefore has an ontic
significance since it refers to concrete particulars, though of a distinctively human sort, for example "the 'public' we-world or one's 'own'
most familiar (domestic) environment (*Umwelt*)" (*SZ* 65). Were one
to speak of the world of the mathematician in this "existentiel" sense,
then, one would be referring not to a domain of possible abstract entities like numbers and figures, but to such things as offices, colleagues,
jobs, and journals. Again, taking science as an example, an existentiel world is much like a Kuhnian paradigm understood as a "disciplinary matrix" consisting of "symbolic generalizations, models, and
exemplars," that is, the familiar practical and cognitive tools of scientific
practice.[61]

Of course, human beings typically occupy more than one existentiel world, depending on the complexity and variety of their practical occupations and social identities. In modernity, as Heidegger
says, we all typically occupy at least two: the world of our own private lives on the one hand, and the public sphere on the other.
But the list could be extended indefinitely, perhaps arbitrarily, to
include all manner of more or less stable and enduring institutions

---

[59] Ibid., 111.   [60] Ibid., 129 (emphasis added).
[61] Kuhn, *The Essential Tension*, 297.

that shape our identities, such as academia, the art world, the business world, the entertainment industry, the media, the political arena, and so on.

The fourth and final sense of 'world,' like the third, has to do with the structure of human practices but is again *ontological,* not merely ontic – in Heidegger's terminology, existenti*al* as opposed to existenti*el.* This final sense thus constitutes "the ontological-existential concept of *worldliness*" (*SZ* 65). Ontic-existentiel worlds vary widely, as anthropologists know, according to the particular character of the lives that at once shape and are shaped by them, Dasein at once projecting in and being thrown into them. But while worlds vary culturally and historically, worldliness is the invariant ontological structure common to them all, and so "contains in itself the a priori" in virtue of which any particular world, in either of the ontic senses described previously, *is* a world, rather than a mere collection of entities (*SZ* 65). The worldliness of the world is what constitutes the essential intelligibility, hence interpretability, of entities as such in any particular cultural or historical context. It thus consists in the practical circumstances "wherein" (*das Wobei, das Worin*) human activity is always meaningfully situated, the useful things "with-which" (*das Womit*) we carry out our tasks, the "in-order-to" (*Um-zu*) or "wherefore" (*Wozu*) of the activity, which we ordinarily do not represent to ourselves explicitly, and finally the point or "for-the-sake-of" (*das Worumwillen*) that finally makes sense of pursuing some ends and not others (see *SZ* 68, 78, 85–7).[62] In short, the worldliness of the world is the ontological structure of the preconceptual practical intelligibility of things, in virtue of which we can find our way about in any particular world, make use of things, and act in a way that has both purpose and point.[63] It is essential to our existence as Dasein that

---

[62] In his lectures in the summer of 1928 Heidegger says, "The for-the-sake-of-which, as the primary character of the world, i.e. of transcendence, is the *primordial phenomenon* (*Urphänomen*) *of ground in general*" (*MAL* 276); it is therefore constitutive of Dasein's "metaphysical I-ness" or "ontological selfhood," which he says is "the basic character of existence" (*MAL* 243).

[63] It is important to distinguish between the purpose and the point of an action, or what Heidegger calls the "in-order-to" and the "for-the-sake-of" that constitute the structure of practical significance. For I can know my purpose perfectly well without feeling that there is any point in pursuing it, just as I can have a sense of the ultimate point of my commitments without knowing exactly what I ought to be doing in light of them. Examples of pointless purposes are abundant: I aim to get rich and retire young, but I come to see the emptiness of idle wealth. Examples of purposeless points are less obvious

our being is a being-in-the-world in this ontological-existential sense: "Worldliness itself is an *existentiale*" (*SZ* 64).

The real and worldliness, then, correspond to the first and the last of these four concepts of world: the sum total of occurrent entities on the one hand, and the intelligible structure of practical significance peculiar to Dasein on the other. To say that Heidegger is an *ontic realist*, then, is to say that, although he maintains that cognition is founded on being-in, and that occurrent reality is interpretable for us only against the horizon of our own worldliness, which constitutes a practical context of hermeneutic conditions, occurrent entities themselves nevertheless do not depend on Dasein's being-in-the-world. Heidegger therefore refers to the "independence of being, not of entities, on the under-standing of being, that is, the dependence of reality, not of the real, on care" (*SZ* 212). Readers of *Being and Time* often suppose that, be-cause reality understood as the mode of being of the real depends on Dasein's being-in-the-world, Dasein's understanding itself therefore somehow constitutes the real, so that it is only in virtue of the structure of cognition that objects themselves can be said to exist at all, and to be the things they are. But such antirealist or nonrealist claims are either trivial, if they mean that we must employ concepts in order to assert or believe in the existence of objects, or false if they mean that objects would not exist or be real in the absence of cognition. If Heidegger is not an antirealist, how does he conceive of the relation between cogni-tion and the real?

He discusses the relation between "Worldliness and Reality" explicitly in §43. Referring back to his earlier discussion of Descartes' concep-tion of world as *res extensa* (*SZ* 89, 100), Heidegger says that in Cartesian ontology "*being in general* acquires the sense of *reality*. The concept of reality thus has a peculiar privilege in the ontological problematic," so that "the other modes of being are defined negatively and privatively in relation to reality" (*SZ* 201). The traditional "problem of reality," as Heidegger describes it, poses four questions: Are there any entities "transcendent to consciousness"? Can the reality of the "external world" be proved? Can what is real be known "in itself"? And finally, what does it mean to understand the world in terms of the concept of reality?[64]

---

but still not hard to imagine: I want to be a good father, but I don't know what actions or projects constitute good parenting.

[64] These questions are partially overlapping allusions to Descartes, Kant, Hegel, and Husserl, among others.

Rather than confront these problems directly, Heidegger turns his attention instead to questions concerning reality, understood as the being of the real, which is to say our understanding of occurrent entities as such, the epistemological problem of proving the existence of the external world, and finally the relation between reality and "care" (*Sorge*), Heidegger's central term marking his ontological interpretation of the meaning of human existence.

It is in the context of his discussion of worldliness that Heidegger introduces his celebrated distinction between the "availability" (*Zuhandenheit*) of useful things or equipment (*Zeug*) and the mere "occurrentness" (*Vorhandenheit*) of objects. Heidegger seems to use the term '*Zeug*' to refer primarily to produced goods or artifacts, but in fact availability is the mode of being of natural entities, too, insofar as they figure functionally in our everyday practices. The salient distinction, then, is not between objects and produced artifacts, but between mere objects and anything at all defined essentially by its functional role in the context of human practices. Notwithstanding Heidegger's own well-worn example, then, it is not just hammers and nails, but also wind, sand, and stars that are available. "The wood is a forest, the mountain a quarry, the river is water power, the wind is wind 'in the sails' " (*SZ* 70). So too, the sun is available in its "distinctive, circumspectly discovered places: sunrise, midday, sunset, midnight" (*SZ* 103).

We are liable to misunderstand Heidegger's ontological categories, too, if we take for granted that they describe two ways in which Dasein can encounter or relate to things. The term '*zuhanden*' does make essential reference to the human practices in which things can figure as available for use, but the term '*vorhanden*' does not. Occurrentness, that is, is not a relation between objects and the observers or knowers to whom they appear. Both terms have literal roots in the word 'hand,' and Macquarrie and Robinson try to preserve the allusion in their renderings, "ready-to-hand" and "present-at-hand." But the German words are ordinary enough that any connotation of an actual relation to human hands is arguably a dead metaphor and so potentially misleading. '*Vorhanden*' just means present, and although we can talk about the presence of something *to us,* we can as easily say that a thing exists just by being present at some place at some time. I believe this latter concept of mere spatiotemporal presence is what Heidegger has in mind with his category of occurrentness, though of course he introduces the category in the course of his phenomenological account of the conditions of our interpretation of entities as occurrent. That phenomenology consequently refers to the Dasein who understands occurrentness and things occurrent.

What Dasein understands in understanding entities as occurrent, however, is *not* just their possible relations to its own understanding, but precisely their existence apart from and independent of itself and its understanding of them. To read Heidegger's account of occurrentness as a description of nothing more than Dasein's encounter with things standing over against it as objects is to conflate the conditions of the intelligibility of the category with the content of the category itself. If the category of occurrentness made reference only to Dasein's actual perceptual and epistemic relations to objects, then Dasein's own naive realism about such entities would remain an unjustified epistemological leap beyond the bounds of its own experience. Dasein's commonsense belief in the independent existence of occurrent entities would then be a problematic and embarrassing projection beyond anything Heidegger could plausibly claim to be shedding light on phenomenologically in his account of everydayness.

But while it is true that nothing in our experience could prove to us that objects exist outside of or independent of that experience, neither does anything in our experience tell us that our ontological categories are or ought to be grounded in experience. And indeed, the category of occurrentness is not grounded in but grounds our experience of objects. It is an a priori category of the understanding, and its content is precisely the content of Dasein's naive realism about objects as existing independently of us and our understanding. This may seem paradoxical, but it is not. It would be paradoxical if there were any reason to suppose with the empiricists that we are somehow not entitled to a priori categories of that kind, but Heidegger is not an empiricist of that sort. His phenomenology is an account of the categories by which we do in fact make sense of things, so his account of our interpretations of entities as occurrent is precisely an account of our understanding of them as existing independently of that understanding. This fidelity to a kind of metaphysical common sense is at the heart of what I shall call Heidegger's *ontic realism,* and I shall have more to say in defense of its coherence against critics of realism in Chapter 4.

"The One" (*das Man*) and the Articulation of Significance

I have said that Heidegger is an externalist, but it is important to notice that his view differs crucially from some externalist theories of meaning and mental content advanced more recently by Anglo-American philosophers such as Hilary Putnam, Saul Kripke, and Tyler Burge.[65] Simply put, on my reading, Heidegger is a social externalist, not a physical externalist. That is, although he locates the constitutive conditions of intentionality out in the world, rather than in our heads, he does not take for granted any specialized descriptions of the external world drawn from the natural sciences. Instead, on his account, the world that has authority over the contents of our intentional attitudes is not the physical world itself, but the social world, that is, the world of human customs and institutions made accessible to us by our ordinary shared normative standards of intelligibility.[66]

When we see Dasein in its "average everydayness," Heidegger suggests, we see that what situates us in a world most fundamentally is not our subjective experiences or mental states, but our externally situated social skills and practices. So too, as we have seen, the entities we typically encounter and concern ourselves with in our everyday practical activity present themselves not as merely occurrent objects, but as transparently available equipment, which we rely on and take for granted in going about our daily business. When I grasp a doorknob or wield a hammer, I am neither perceiving nor thinking about it as

---

[65] See Putnam, "The Meaning of 'Meaning'"; Kripke, *Naming and Necessity*; Burge, "Individualism and the Mental," inter alia.

[66] Burge, who accepts both physical and social externalism, has observed a curious division of intuitions between Anglo-Americans, who often find the former plausible and the latter not, and Europeans, who tend to favor the social thesis over the physical. The European view, as it were, strikes me as correct, since social externalism arguably subsumes and explains our intuition that scientifically established facts about the world have authority over the contents of naive attitudes and the objects of pretheoretical kind terms. For such intuitions are fueled by an aspect of our sociability, namely, our readiness to defer to knowledgeable opinion. What is doing the real work in externalist theories of meaning and mental content, that is, is our own social deference, not physical fact as such. Expertise is not always scientific expertise, of course. We might take it on faith from an art historian, for example, that what connoisseurs of nineteenth-century French history painting liked was kitsch, even if we concede that the connoisseurs themselves would not have, indeed could not have, understood their own preferences under that description. Yet that is what they liked. Arguments for physical externalism are consequently much less convincing when they cannot appeal to some de facto scientific discovery. For example, are we really to suppose that the contents of our current thoughts and the objects of our naive kind terms are determined by *all* facts (if such a notion even makes sense) about natural kinds that now, and may forever, lie hidden from us? Is it not more plausible to say, on the contrary, that the intuitions that seem to speak in favor of physical externalism have simply turned up an interesting social fact about us, namely, willingness to revise our ascriptions of content and to interpret anyone's use of kind terms in deference to our own esteemed authorities?

an object with properties, but rather availing myself of it unthinkingly, skillfully treating it as a handy element in the overall purposive structure of the situation. Moreover, individual pieces of equipment do not just occur alongside one another in objective space and time, but instead form an organized "equipmental totality" (*Zeugganzheit*), which holistically assigns each item its specific practical significance (*SZ* 68ff).

That equipmental totality is in turn implicated in a broader intelligible network of pragmatic relations assigning tools to contexts, to tasks, to goals, and to the ultimate underlying point of what we are doing, our "for-the-sake-of-which." Heidegger describes these practical relations as "signifying" (*be-deuten*) and calls the entire intelligible network of signifying relations "significance" (*Bedeutsamkeit*) (*SZ* 87). As we shall see in greater detail in Chapter 5, the pragmatic structure of significance is a condition of the possibility of linguistic meaning and mental content, both of which occur only against a background of practical understanding. More generally, our being-in-the-world consists precisely in our primordial familiarity with such a structure of significance. For being-in consists not in possessing cognitive attitudes, but in being competently oriented and involved in practically intelligible situations. Similarly, as we have seen, the "worldliness" of the world is not just a sum total of objects, properties, and relations, but a meaningfully structured domain of practices and institutions.

Heidegger refers to the socially constituted normative framework of Dasein's understanding as "*das Man*," a nominalization of the impersonal pronoun '*man*,' which literally means *one*, as in anyone, but no one in particular.[67] What is "the one"? It is not an entity, let alone some person or group of persons, but the impersonal normative authority underwriting the social practices that make things intelligible on a mundane level, in Dasein's "everydayness" and "averageness" (*SZ* 43). The one is therefore neither Dasein nor an entity distinct from Dasein, but a general structural feature of our being-in-the-world. More specifically, it is the "who" of everyday Dasein, "the 'subject' of everydayness" (*SZ* 114), a kind of shared normative common sense, prior to and distinct from

---

[67] Because it is a personal rather than an impersonal pronoun, the standard translation of *das Man* as 'the they,' though it alludes fittingly to colloquial appeals to "what they say," nevertheless gives the appearance of referring exclusively to others, whereas Heidegger clearly means it to include ourselves, both collectively and individually. The word 'one' is therefore preferable.

any authentic individual identity we might acquire or achieve in the course of our lives: "The self of everyday Dasein is the *one-self,* which we distinguish the *authentic self,* that is, the self grasped as its own (*eigens ergriffen*). As the one-self, the particular Dasein is *dispersed* into the one and must first find itself." What is given to us in our everyday understanding, then, is not fully individualized selves, each understood as its own, but rather selves as conforming appropriately to anonymously instituted social norms: "I am 'given' to my 'self' in the first instance in terms of, and as, the one" (*SZ* 129).

In what follows, I want to say how Heidegger's appeal to the normativity of social practice grounds his account of the intentionality of understanding. I will return later to the phenomenon of the one in order to indicate the positive and negative constraints it imposes on Dasein's existing as its own or not its own, that is, as authentic (*eigentlich*) or inauthentic (*uneigentlich*). Because our understanding of being is subject to the pressure of social norms, Heidegger argues, Dasein has a structural tendency, rooted in its very being, to lapse into banal, inauthentic interpretations of itself. Here, however, I want to focus on the positive role the one plays in normatively structuring our practices and thereby constituting the intentionality of our everyday understanding.

Heidegger's account of the one, especially in Chapter 4 of Division I and throughout Division II of *Being and Time,* has been widely misunderstood in several ways. For example, Heidegger is often charged with simply repeating in a different terminology Kierkegaard's critique of what he calls the "present age." Heidegger's notion is also frequently dismissed as so much warmed-over *Kulturkritik,* symptomatic of the unhealthy pessimism and antidemocratic sentiment of reactionary German intellectuals of the Weimar era. There is admittedly some truth in each of these charges, but they tend to divert attention from what is philosophically important and original in Heidegger's account. I shall consider the first of these two interpretations presently. The second, more crudely reductive sociological reading is obviously less susceptible to direct refutation, being less responsive to the text in the first place.

In *A Literary Review* Kierkegaard describes the insidious normalizing effects of what he calls "the public," the disembodied authority of common sense and received opinion, whose tacit judgments undermine individuality and personal subjective commitments. Kierkegaard refuses to identify the public with any concrete person or group: "The public is not a people, a generation, one's era, nor a religious community, a society, nor such and such particular people, for all these are what they are only by virtue of what is concrete."[68]

What he infers from this, however, is that *there is no public,* though in the present age people think, talk, and live their lives more and more *as if* there is. For Kierkegaard, the public is a myth, an artifact of reflection, whose effects include the increasing normalization of behavior and the inculcation of an unprecedented degree of conformism and self-consciousness, a process he calls "leveling." The myth of the public thus functions in the service of the leveling process:

> For leveling really to come about a phantom must first be provided, its spirit, a monstrous abstraction, an all-encompassing something that is nothing, a mirage – this phantom is *the public.* Only a passionless but re-flective age can spin this phantom out, with the help of the press when the press itself becomes an abstraction. In spirited times, times of pas-sionate upheaval... there is no public; there are parties and there is concreteness.... [But] a passionless, sedentary, reflective age ... will spin out this phantom. The public is leveling's real master, for when leveling is only approximate there is something it levels with, while the public is a monstrous nothing.[69]

Consequently, for Kierkegaard, the public, being an artifact of the ob-jectivity and spiritlessness of bourgeois society, "is a concept that cannot possibly occur in antiquity."[70]

When he introduces his concept of the one in his 1925 lectures (*PGZ* §26b), Heidegger's debt to Kierkegaard is plain. In its everydayness, Heidegger says, "Dasein as being-with *is lived* by the Dasein-with (*Mitdasein*) of others and by the world that concerns it thus and such. Precisely in its ownmost everyday pursuits Dasein, as being-with with others, is not itself, rather it is others who live one's own Dasein" (*PGZ* 337). This loss of self is apparently just the kind of depersonal-ized social anonymity that Kierkegaard diagnosed some eighty years earlier:

> This being-with-one-another dissolves one's own Dasein wholly in the mode of being of others; it lets itself be carried along by others in such a way that the others vanish ever more in their distinctiveness. In the sphere

[68] Kierkegaard, *A Literary Review,* 82–3.   [69] Ibid., 80–1.
[70] Ibid., 81.

of its possibilities of being, each is wholly the other. Here the peculiar
"subject" of everydayness – the *one* – first has its total dominance. Public
being-with-one-another is lived wholly in terms of this one. *One* enjoys
and amuses oneself as *one* does, and we read and judge literature as *one*
judges; we hear music as *one* hears music; we speak about something as
one speaks.

   This one, which is no one in particular, and which "all" are, though not
in their being, dictates (*diktiert*) the mode of being of everyday Dasein.
(*PGZ* 338)

Unlike the tyranny of the public in the present age, as conceived by
Kierkegaard, however, this dictation, or indeed "dictatorship" (*Diktatur*)
of the one, as Heidegger puts it in *Being and Time* (*SZ* 126), is not just
some contingent historical development of modernity. Instead, "publicness" is an essential ontological dimension of any shared human world
as such:

   The one, as that which forms everyday being-with-one-another in these,
   its modes of being, constitutes that which we call *publicness* in the genuine
   sense. What this means is that the world is always already given primarily
   as the common world, and it is not as if there are first, on the one hand,
   individual subjects, indeed individual subjects who each have their own
   world, and that now the problem arises of putting together, by means of
   some kind of arrangement, the different respective environments of the
   individuals and of agreeing how it is that one has a common world. This
   is how philosophers imagine things when they ask about the constitution
   of the intersubjective world. We say: what is first, what is given, is the
   common world – the one – i.e. the world in which Dasein is absorbed
   such that it has not yet come to itself, as it can constantly be without
   having to come to itself. (*PGZ* 339)

For Heidegger, then, the one is no mere ontic contingency, but a universal ontological structure of human existence: "*The one is an existential
and belongs as a primordial phenomenon to the positive constitution of Dasein.*"
Moreover, the normativity of the one is responsible for carving out
or "articulating" the pragmatic structure of Dasein's everyday world:
"the one-self, for the sake of which Dasein is from day to day, articulates (*artikuliert*)[71] the referential context of significance" (*SZ* 129).
It is not an extraneous or coercive force interfering with Dasein's

---

[71] See Chapter 5, footnotes 38 and 42, on Heidegger's (in my view indistinguishable) uses
   of the words '*Gliederung*' and '*Artikulation*.'

understanding from without; rather, "The one prescribes a disposed-ness (*Befindlichkeit*); it determines what and how one 'sees'" (*SZ* 170).

Moreover, as we shall see in Chapter 5, just as everyday intelligibility is at once projected in understanding and articulated in what Heidegger calls "discourse" (*Rede*), so too the common, average world Dasein inhabits and takes for granted in its everyday practices is articulated in a common, average form of discourse called "idle talk" (*Gerede*). Idle talk is, in a word, the discourse of the one, appropriate for anyone and everyone, consequently distinctive of no one in particular. What is said in idle talk is what one says, what it is sensible and proper to say. Idle talk thus consists not just in talking normally, but in repeating what one hears, or as Heidegger puts it, "*gossiping* and *passing the word along* (*Weiter- und Nachreden*)*.*" In this way, however, idle talk makes a genuine sharing of meanings and understandings possible not as some special achievement or after some deliberate effort, as traditional epistemological assumptions either implicitly or explicitly maintained, but as a matter of course: "one means *the same,* since one understands what is said in common, in *the same* averageness" (*SZ* 168). Indeed, for better as well as for worse, "The groundlessness of idle talk does not block its access to publicness, but encourages it. Idle talk is the possibility of understanding everything without any prior appropriation of the matter (*Sache*)" (*SZ* 169). Of course, the more one seems to understand everything, the less one in fact understands anything. Consequently, just as it affords us access to public meanings and understandings generally, idle talk at once levels things off by way of rendering them generically intelligible. As idle talk, discourse becomes capable

> not so much of holding being-in-the-world open in an articulated understanding, but of closing it off and concealing intraworldly entities.... Something's being said groundlessly, and then being repeated further, amounts to disclosing (*Erschließen*) reverting to a closing off (*Verschließen*).... Idle talk is thus inherently a closing off, in virtue of its own *failing* to go back to the ground of what is talked about. (*SZ* 169)

At this point, of course, Heidegger's own rhetorical tone has made idle talk appear thoroughly debased and despicable. Yet that rhetorical effect is directly at odds with at least part of his avowed philosophical purpose. For just as the one is not itself a mere contingent modification of some prior authentic understanding, neither is idle talk a mere distortion or degradation of authentic discourse. Indeed, in the very first sentence in §35 Heidegger warns, "The expression 'idle talk' is not to be used here in a pejorative sense." His point is that all discourse, including but not exclusively linguistic practice, is governed by common, anonymously sanctioned norms of intelligibility. "Language," he says, "harbors in itself a way in which Dasein's understanding has been interpreted" (*SZ* 167). There is an understanding "already lodged in expressedness (*Ausgesprochenheit*)," an "average intelligibility that already lies in the expression (*Sichaussprechen*) of spoken language" (*SZ* 168). Eschewing idle talk altogether, then, is no more possible, or desirable for that matter, than being rid of the one, for both are just aspects of the mundane authority of normality and the normal. Dasein cannot escape the influence of the one and understand itself in fully autonomous terms, untouched by the normative authority structuring its everyday world: "This common world, which is there primarily, and into which every maturing Dasein first grows up, governs, qua public, all interpretation of the world and of Dasein" (*PGZ* 340); "Dasein is never able to extricate itself from this everyday interpretedness that it has grown into in the first place. In it and out of it and against it all genuine understanding, interpretation and communication, rediscovery and renewed appropriation take place" (*SZ* 169).

Consequently, for Heidegger, as we shall see in Chapter 6, existing authentically does not consist simply in freeing oneself from all entanglements with the one, but rather in taking up a new, distinctive relation to the social norms always already governing one's concrete possibilities: "Authentic existentiel understanding is so far from escaping its inherited interpretedness that it always grasps its chosen possibility in its resolution in terms of it and against it and once again for it" (*SZ* 383). That is, "*Authentic being-oneself* does not rest on some exceptional condition of the subject, detached from the one, rather *it is an existentiel modification of the one as an essential existential*" (*SZ* 130).[72]

To see how the anonymous social normativity of the one conditions Dasein's intentionality, then, consider the form intentional attitudes ordinarily take in everyday life. One standard criterion of intentionality (with a *t*) is to be found in the intensionality (with an *s*) of sentences describing it. If a sentence describing a putative attitude passes the text of extensionality, that is, permitting the substitution of coextensive terms *salva veritate*, then the attitude is not genuinely intentional. It is not hard

---

[72] As we shall see in Chapter 6, Heidegger says the same things about "falling" (*Verfallen*), which is also an essential structure of being-in-the-world, not just some unfortunate accident.

to demonstrate the intensionality of sentences describing the practical understanding or know-how underlying our cognitive states, for such sentences regularly fail tests of extensionality by being opaque to the substitution of coextensive terms. Cognitivists can just as easily grant the intentionality of practical understanding or know-how, however, by insisting that it must be parasitic on full-blown cognitive attitudes, whose intentionality is uncontroversial. For example, from *I understood her anger* and *Her anger was what he found insulting*, it does not follow that *I understood what he found insulting*. Similarly, from *He knows how to make small talk* and *Making small talk bores me*, it does not follow that *He knows how to bore me*. I choose these examples because, it seems to me, understanding emotions and knowing how to engage in conversation are in large part, though of course not entirely, noncognitive abilities. Their intentionality is therefore arguably not just a function of the intentionality of the beliefs and desires also typically at play in such situations.

Nevertheless, one might reasonably worry that such verbal references to *understanding* and *knowing how* are in effect sneaking propositional attitudes into these cases through the back door, as it were, so it would be nice to find an example that focuses on practical skills as such, an example we can describe without invoking verb phrases that might lend themselves to a purely cognitive interpretation. So, consider this. From *I can restore and refinish the cabinet* and *The cabinet is a priceless antique*, it does not follow that *I can restore and refinish the priceless antique*. I can, of course, do to the priceless antique what I have done to other pieces of ordinary furniture, but that might well count not so much as restoring and refinishing the thing as ruining it. My *ability* to restore and refinish furniture competently is intentional, then, since the skills it involves are aspectual in the same way in which intentional attitudes at large are aspectual. For the way I treat things is selective and responsive to the kinds of things they are, and my skills may be sensitive or insensitive to them across a spectrum of understandings of them as junk, as ordinary furniture, as museum pieces, or as cultural treasures.

Someone might object at this point that a machine to which no one was tempted to attribute intentional attitudes could in principle do to cabinets what I, competently albeit inexpertly, do to them. Does this mean that the machine, too, has intentional skills? No. For to say in all seriousness that the machine "can" refinish furniture, that it is "able" to do so, is already to start down the treacherous path of anthropomorphism, just as when we say the vending machine "gives" me the soft drink or that the computer "wants" me to insert the disk into the floppy drive. That this isolated ability of mine is a genuinely intentional competence, a kind of understanding, is rooted in the vast background of all my other situated practical and discursive skills. What we might call the mere *event*-doings of vending machines and computers are of a fundamentally different ontological kind than the skillful *agent*-doings of human beings. And just as we confess to speaking metaphorically in attributing mental attitudes to mindless devices, so too we ought to confess to speaking metaphorically in attributing genuinely skillful competences to designed or programmed machines. Indeed, as artificial intelligence researchers have discovered, such machines always turn out to be shockingly inflexible and incompetent when their supposed skills are put to real-life tests. What is at stake, then, both in mental states and in practical skills, is a kind of intentionality.

Both in the competent cabinet-refinishing case and more generally, then, what makes skills the skills they are, what constitutes their specific sensitivity to certain aspects of the environment and not others, even when several among those alternative aspects coincide extensionally, is their *appropriateness* in a given situation. The proper refinishing job for the ordinary piece of furniture is not the proper refinishing job for the priceless antique. Social norms specify proper comportments and constitutive standards governing the intelligibility of equipment and its availability in a practical environment. There are any number of different instrumentally effective ways of getting food into your mouth, only some of which will be socially correct and hence intelligible as *having a meal.* There are appropriate and inappropriate ways of sitting down at the dinner table, using silverware, serving and being served, and so on, and such proprieties and improprieties are what make dining *dining,* as opposed to mere consumption and digestion.

Heidegger's account of the one in *Being and Time,* then, is an account of the socially constituted normative standards that make our practices intelligible as the practices they are, and so render our behavior sensitive in distinctive ways to salient aspects of our practical world. The intentionality of practice does not derive from some more basic form of intentionality intrinsic to consciousness or cognition. It is instead a function of the normativity inherent in our practical understanding of what it makes sense to do and of what entities *are.* Socially articulated proprieties and improprieties constitute what it is to have a conversation, what it is *to be* angry or offended or bored, and what it is *to be* a cabinet, an antique, a living room, or a museum. Heidegger's account of the anonymous normativity of social life can figure in his fundamental ontology at all only because he maintains that social norms define entities according to what is primitively right and wrong, appropriate and inappropriate, with respect to them. This is what Heidegger means when he says it is the "one-self," not the authentic self, that "articulates the referential context of significance" (*SZ* 129). Social norms of intelligibility constitute the *being* of things in Dasein's average everyday world.

It is true that Heidegger's rhetoric in *Being and Time* is symptomatic of a general anxiety in the face of the increasing normalization and banality of modern life and the threat this seems to pose to Dasein's ability to own up to itself and live authentically. Nevertheless, and more importantly, it is clear that his account of the one is not merely a comment on social conformism and superficiality, but marks an essential element in his conception of human existence as being-in-the-world. Being-in-the-world, thanks to the normative structure of social practice, provides Heidegger with an alternative to the conceptual ruts of subjectivism and objectivism, internalism and reductionism, that philosophical theories of intentionality have habitually fallen into since Descartes.

Was Heidegger a Social Externalist?

Mark Wrathall has recently leveled a powerful attack both on social externalism itself and on the social externalist reading of *Being and Time* that others, including myself, have favored. Wrathall argues that those, like Dreyfus and myself, who would assimilate Heidegger's account of the social conditions of intelligibility to the semantic and psychological claims of Hilary Putnam or Tyler Burge[73] are in part reading implausible theories back into *Being and Time,* and moreover rendering those theories even more implausible by fixing discursive content not to the practice of knowledgeable experts, but to the one – which is to say anyone and everyone. This kind of communitarianism strikes Wrathall as

---

[73] Putnam's claim about linguistic meaning, as opposed to what he calls "narrow" psychological content, is that it "just ain't in the head." Putnam, "The Meaning of 'Meaning,'" 227. Burge holds the more radical view that all intentional content, not just linguistic meaning, is externally determined: "Theories of vision, of belief formation, of memory, learning, decision-making, categorization, and perhaps even reasoning all attribute states that are subject to practical and semantic evaluation *by reference to standards partly set by a wider environment.*" In fact, he adds, "I doubt that all biological, including physiological, processes and states in a person's body are individualistically individuated." Burge, "Individualism and Psychology," 25, 35n.

a tyranny of the majority in which individual intentions are held hostage to average understanding and common usage, however debased or misinformed.

Drawing on Donald Davidson's objections to Burge,[74] Wrathall maintains that arguments for externalism illicitly overgeneralize from special cases in which it may be reasonable to defer to expert opinion in fleshing out the contents of the attitudes of individuals who are ignorant, confused, or linguistically incompetent. He proposes, however, that it is unreasonable and counterintuitive to relativize all meanings and intentional contents to the generally shared linguistic practices of experts and nonexperts alike: "From the fact that we are not conversant with everything we can talk about, it does not follow that we can only intend to say what anyone and everyone is capable of understanding." Wrathall argues, moreover, that Heidegger never intended his concepts of the one and of idle talk to imply that the attitudes of individuals are themselves defined or individuated, as opposed to being merely socially and psychologically conditioned, by external circumstances. According to Wrathall, that is, Heidegger simply insists that "what we can mean is always shaped (but not determined) by the people and things around us."[75]

Wrathall makes an interesting and challenging case, but I believe he is wrong about social externalism itself and about the substance and implications of Heidegger's accounts of the one and of idle talk. To begin with, it seems to me that Burge is right that individualism imposes implausible, theoretically motivated restrictions on our ordinary understanding of our intentional attitudes, and that the descriptions of our experience invoked to support it are often little more than, as he says at one point with reference to internalist accounts of perceptual content, "over-intellectualized philosophers' conceits."[76] It seems to me, moreover, that Wrathall's reading threatens to trivialize the notion of being-in-the-world generally as implying no more than that individuals are profoundly influenced by their environments – an interesting and important idea, to be sure, but hardly startling news by the time Heidegger was writing *Being and Time* in the 1920s. I shall take these two points, the systematic and the exegetical, in turn.

---

[74] See Davidson, "Knowing One's Own Mind" and "Epistemology Externalized," in *Subjective, Intersubjective, Objective,* and "The Social Aspect of Language."

[75] Wrathall, "Social Constraints on Conversational Content: Heidegger on *Rede* and *Gerede*," 44.

[76] Burge, "Individualism and Psychology," 37.

First, the systematic issue. Wrathall maintains that arguments for so-cial externalism typically blur a crucial distinction between what an in-dividual knows about matters of fact and what he knows about how others use language. He therefore draws what strikes me as an im-plausibly sharp – and moreover *un*-Heideggerian – distinction between the contents of a person's attitudes on the one hand, and the social norms governing the expression of those attitudes on the other. So, for example, Burge asks us to consider a man who comes to believe that he has arthritis in his thigh. In the actual world, this is not only not the case but impossible, since 'arthritis' refers only to an inflammation of the joints. His belief is thus necessarily false. Holding constant every-thing with respect to the man himself, however, we can easily imagine a counterfactual world in which 'arthritis' also refers to ailments in other parts of the body, not just the joints. In that case, the man's belief that he has arthritis in his thigh may well be true. But the same belief can-not be both necessarily false and possibly true about one and the same physical ailment. It therefore follows that the contents of his belief are themselves relative to the external linguistic practices of his surround-ing community: "[A] person's thought *content* is not fixed by what goes on in him, or by what is accessible to him simply by careful reflection."[77] Wrathall objects that this story fails to distinguish between what the man believes about arthritis itself and what he believes about how people re-fer to it. Getting clear about that distinction, he suggests, will allow us to carve off the real contents of a person's attitudes from extraneous matters having to do with how people generally think such attitudes ought to be expressed.

Insisting on such a distinction a priori as a matter of principle, how-ever, seems to beg the question in favor of individualism. The anti-individualist thesis, after all, is precisely that the content of an attitude is itself in part a function of external conditions, in this case collec-tive linguistic conventions governing the use of a word. Why should we draw a rigid distinction between content and context in the way Wrathall proposes? Consider his own alternative story. Wrathall confesses that he once thought the word 'gable' referred to a peaked roof rather than the triangular portion of wall supporting the roof. It would have been incorrect and unfair, he says, to take him to be referring to a gable when he said "gable" if this means ascribing to him an obviously false belief

---

[77] Burge, "Individualism and the Mental," 104.

about the thing, such as that it is covered with asphalt shingles instead of being made of brick:

> it would have been manifestly wrong, before I got clear about how other speakers use the term, to say of me: "Wrathall thinks that gable there is covered with asphalt shingles, but anyone can see it is made of brick." The right thing to say would be: "Wrathall says the gable is covered with asphalt shingles, but he thinks a gable is a gable roof."[78]

But what does this show? Wrathall constructs the example so as to expose his confusion about gables by pointing out that an interpretation of his actions or words according to conventional norms would entail an absurdity, for example that he thinks bricks are shingles, or perhaps that he is blind or insane. Wrathall, the protagonist, apparently has a nonstandard but otherwise coherent and serviceable conception of a gable as a kind of roof. We can therefore painlessly exchange the standard concept of gable for his idiosyncratic conception by way of rendering his actions and words more intelligible. He can also presumably spell out his concept for us by pointing to the roof and telling us that *that* is what he takes the word 'gable' to refer to. It is more reasonable, then, he argues, to interpret him according to his own peculiar conception than in conformity with standard linguistic practice.

True, but only because it would be grossly uncharitable to interpret him as believing that bricks are shingles, or that the shingles that he insists are on the gable are invisible, or some such absurdity. In short, what Wrathall has described is a breakdown case of a very peculiar sort, one from which nothing much can be inferred concerning the practice of content-ascription in the normal course of events. Moreover, nothing Wrathall says about the example suggests that the content of his understanding of *gable roofs* was not itself already defined relative to the community's practices with respect to *them*. Deviant cases of individualistically definable content, such as Wrathall describes, that is, are arguably isolated islands surrounded by a vast ocean of community practices defining most of the rest of what we say and do. The fact that we sometimes suspend the ordinary rules of interpretation in order to reconstruct a person's apparently peculiar or idiosyncratic understanding does nothing to show that interpretation is individualistic in general.

---

[78] Wrathall, "Social Constraints," 32.

To see that this is the case, consider the following hypothetical elaboration of Wrathall's story, which brings it back in line with the arguments of Putnam and Burge. Suppose our protagonist is unaware that there is a difference between a gable roof, which is symmetrical, and the saltbox style, which is otherwise similar but asymmetrical. Now imagine that in his neighborhood most of the houses have gable roofs but a few are saltboxes. He inspects them and reports that they all have gable roofs. I think it is obvious that we *would* say, and indeed *should* say, that he is wrong about this. And wrong not just in the weak sense that he has uttered a false sentence, or misused words, or that he somehow *meant* something false while nevertheless *thinking* something true, but wrong in the strong sense that he has *false beliefs* about the roofs in his neighborhood. Individualism implausibly asks us to indulge him in his idiosyncratic conception of gable roofs, so that his belief will turn out to be true, provided that, according to his peculiar conception, asymmetrical roofs atop triangular wall segments just *are* gable roofs.

Does he have a clear opinion about asymmetrical roofs counting as gable roofs or does he simply fail to appreciate the difference between them as a significant difference? If the difference simply never struck him as important, then so much the worse for our being able or willing to interpret him according to his own idiosyncratic concepts, since those concepts will be so impoverished or vague as to frustrate our sincere efforts to know what he really thinks. What are the extensions of his concepts? But even if he does have an explicit belief that asymmetrical roofs atop triangular wall segments must be considered gable roofs, that hardly justifies extending the principle of charity so far as to acquit him of being wrong about the roofs themselves. We will still say he is wrong about the roofs precisely because he does not know very much about roofs, gable roofs in particular.

Or consider again the sort of counterfactual scenario Burge invokes against individualism. In the actual world, I am wrong about the roofs in my neighborhood owing to my confusion about gables and gable roofs. But now imagine another world, one in which we hold everything constant with respect to my person, but in which no one else in fact distinguishes between symmetrical and asymmetrical roofs on triangular walls, so that no one has a concept of the saltbox style as distinct from the gable. Suppose, that is, that in that counterfactual world the extension of 'gable' were wider than it is in our world so as to include what we call saltbox roofs. In that world I would be *right* that all the roofs in my neighborhood were gable roofs. But if I am wrong about the roofs in the first world and right in the second, without there being any difference in the roofs themselves from one world to the other, this can only be because the content of my belief is not the same in the two cases. And if the content of my belief is different in the two worlds, though everything about my person is held constant, then individualism is false.

Wrathall's objection to social externalism, but even more his resistance to reading Heidegger as an anti-individualist, rests on his reluctance to generalize from our deference to expert opinion in fixing the meanings of the words we use. For example, Wrathall points out, many of us ask for more RAM in our computers without having any very clear understanding of what RAM is, yet we ourselves intend others to understand us to mean by that term what those who do know what it is mean by it. Expert opinion fleshes out the meanings of the terms we use and so in part determines what we say.[79] But why should we defer to anyone's and everyone's understanding of things, Wrathall asks, over and beyond those who know what they're talking about? He therefore maintains that Dreyfus and I "see Heidegger as an anti-Putnam – as holding that the meaning of what we say is determined not by the experts, but by the lowest common denominator of a linguistic community." Why be so recklessly democratic? That is, "what justifies the assumption that what is said in language must be available to everyone?"[80]

I would certainly never insist that linguistic meaning or intentional content be determined by universal consensus, or that average intelligibility puts absolute limits on what any one individual can say or think. Such a view would not be communitarian but totalitarian. But neither do I think it possible to draw a very sharp distinction between generally received opinion and expert opinion. There are clear cases of each, of course, but there is also a large gray area between the two. Is it specialists or just plain folk, for instance, who know the difference between a gable roof and a saltbox roof, or between a birch and an elm, or between the salad fork and the dinner fork? How expert must experts be before we admit their authority in the individuation of our attitudes? Or conversely, how debased and confused can collective opinion become

---

[79] Wrathall, ibid., 31–3. Wrathall seems to concede Putnam's point about the social determination of semantic content, but I think he regards it as contingent on the individuals themselves intending that their words should be so understood. Burge's view, like Heidegger's, is stronger, namely, that external conditions are already authoritative in the individuation of content and so stand in no need of the individual's explicit endorsement.

[80] Wrathall, ibid., 43.

before it no longer gets any grip on the meanings of our words and the contents of our attitudes? Common understanding, not specialized expertise, it seems to me, is what governs what is reasonable and unreasonable in our interpretations of others, and even of ourselves, in ordinary circumstances. Of course, deviant cases like the one Wrathall describes, in which it turns out that an individual was in fact saying or thinking something intelligible but crucially different from what any ordinary interpreter would have supposed, are always possible, but they are special cases and require special pleading. The principle of charity can always make particular exceptions to any general rule of interpretation as a kind of courtesy, but it cannot support all interpretation in every case or even the bulk of it in the normal course of events.

More to our present purpose, though, is the exegetical issue, namely, Wrathall's plausible, but I think mistaken, claim that Heidegger's discussions of the one and of idle talk imply nothing like the kind of externalism at issue in contemporary debates in the philosophy of mind and language. Heidegger is not interested in the determination or individuation of the contents of our understanding, he argues, but with "the difference between linguistic understanding and a practical conversance with a matter" and the frequent "divergence" of the former from the latter.[81] Idle talk pulls us away from concrete context and fine detail, which is why it amounts to a closing off rather than a disclosing.

I believe Wrathall is largely right about this, but that the negative point he emphasizes neither exhausts Heidegger's account nor conflicts with the kind of externalism he rejects. Of course, no simple distinction between practical familiarity and linguistic understanding will do, since many contexts of familiarity are themselves essentially linguistic. It is not language as such that pulls Dasein away from an authentic engagement with things and people, but what I have elsewhere called the "generic drift" of discourse, that is, its essential tendency toward common intelligibility, which draws Dasein away from the particularity of its own concrete situation. There is no tension at all, it seems to

---

[81] Wrathall, ibid., 41. 'Conversation' and 'conversance' are Wrathall's renderings of Heidegger's term *Rede,* which is ordinarily translated 'discourse.' As will become clear in Chapter 5, I favor the standard translation, not because I think discourse is necessarily linguistic, but because Heidegger understands it as a kind of expressive and communicative comportment fundamentally distinct from, but equiprimordial with disposedness and understanding (*SZ* 133, 161). Wrathall's account of *Rede* in *Being and Time,* by contrast, conforms to the "pragmatic model" advanced and defended by Dreyfus, Haugeland, and Blattner.

me, between language itself and what Heidegger calls the "reticence" (*Verschwiegenheit*) of authentic discourse (*SZ* 277), since even the most authentic understanding admits of some articulation and expression or other, however subtle or indirect. Reticence is not just saying nothing, after all, but refraining from merely saying what "one" says, assimilating every situation into already familiar tropes and preconceived categories. It is mere talkativeness, which is to say *idle* talk, not language itself, which renders discourse inauthentic.[82]

It is possible to regard the one and idle talk as constitutive conditions of intelligibility, that is, while at the same time admitting that discourse itself exhibits an inherent tendency toward relatively generic and superficial forms of expression. Indeed, what I think Wrathall underestimates is the way in which social practices and institutions constitute not just causal but *hermeneutic conditions* of meaningful expression and mutual understanding. No doubt our practices condition what we are likely to be able to think or say. But the norms governing the practices into which we find ourselves thrown are not just antecedent ontic conditions of intelligibility; they are contemporary ontological conditions or constitutive criteria governing the significance of what we do, both discursively and nondiscursively. As Heidegger says, "The one-self, for the sake of which Dasein is [in an] everyday [manner], articulates the referential context of significance" (*SZ* 129). Everything Dasein says and does, linguistically or otherwise, is saturated with the kind of public significance that philosophers like Putnam and Burge have more recently, and with far greater analytical precision, located in our practices of individuating linguistic meanings and intentional contents.

To revert to an individualistic theory of interpretation guided wholly or primarily by the principle of charity, it seems to me, in effect undermines the force of Heidegger's insistence that it is the commonly intelligible world that "governs, qua public, *all* interpretation of the

---

[82] See my "Must We Be Inauthentic?" My view thus differs from that of Dreyfus, whom Wrathall also criticizes. Dreyfus, that is, countenances a kind of reticence that is entirely and unproblematically free of any of the leveling forces of a publicly shared language, as if it were the language itself that produced the banality. See his "Reply to Taylor Carman," *Heidegger, Authenticity, and Modernity*, 308. What this ignores is that, for Heidegger, *reticence is itself a mode of discourse*. So, if I am right that discourse always exhibits a generic drift away from the concrete situation, however subtle, the syndrome is no less in effect in authentic discourse than in idle talk. The mistake, it seems to me, is to suppose that if you are subject to the generic drift of discourse, you are *eo ipso* inauthentic. But that is as wrong as supposing that if you are subject to the force of gravity, you are *eo ipso* on the ground.

world and of Dasein" (*PGZ* 340, emphasis added); that "Dasein is *never* able to extricate itself from this everyday interpretedness"; rather, "In it and out of it and against it *all* genuine understanding, interpretation and communication, rediscovery and renewed appropriation take place" (*SZ* 169, emphasis added). Average everyday understanding constitutes the permanent background of all interpretation, a background that does not merely inform the reasonable individualistic interpretation of idiosyncratic speakers, but already constitutes the semantic and intentional contexts within which individuals can enter into discursive practice at all. Social practice provides hermeneutic, not just causal, conditions of interpretation, which in turn render implausible any form of individualism purporting to offer a general account of meaning and understanding, over and beyond parasitic cases deviating from normal usage and so calling for special charitable hermeneutic measures.

HEIDEGGER'S REALISM

*Let us therefore know our limit. We are
something, and we are not everything.*

Pascal

My reading of fundamental ontology is a Kantian reading inasmuch as
it recognizes the analogy Heidegger clearly had in mind between the
existential analytic of Dasein in *Being and Time* and the transcendental
analytic of the understanding in the *Critique of Pure Reason*. But whereas
Kant offers a subjectivist and intellectualist account of the conditions
of conceptually articulated knowledge, Heidegger is concerned more
broadly with the practical and mundane conditions of interpretation,
or explicit practical understanding. Kant and Heidegger are both interested in the transcendental conditions of the intelligibility of entities to
finite human understanding. Yet notwithstanding the formal analogy
between their respective projects, Heidegger's fundamental ontology
is not just a pragmatic reiteration of the Kantian critique of the mind
and its cognitive faculties. For the kind of conceptual knowledge that
Kant considered definitive of human understanding, whether overtly
expressed in the form of assertions or silently cognized in the form
of judgments, is just one instance of a more general phenomenon,
namely, interpretation, that is, understanding or knowing how to cope
with something explicitly *as* something. The analytic of Dasein can plausibly claim priority not just to epistemology, then, but to all philosophies
of mind that forgo any phenomenological account of the ways in which
intentionality or mental content itself becomes intelligible to us to begin with. Heidegger is engaged in a kind of transcendental enterprise,
then, and he draws philosophical inspiration from Kant, as he does

from Husserl, yet his guiding question is of a wholly different order from theirs.

More specifically, Heidegger refuses to take on board Kant's transcendental idealism, which Husserl seems to have embraced in some form, at least in his later works.[1] Scholars often take it for granted that Heidegger must have been as hostile to realism as Kant and Husserl were before him,[2] but I think all nonrealist readings of *Being and Time* are mistaken. In *Contributions to Philosophy,* which dates from the mid-1930s, for instance, Heidegger explicitly rejects any ascription of "idealism," according to which entities become dependent on the subject, as among "the crudest misinterpretations" of *Being and Time* (*Beiträge* 259). Indeed, I believe Heidegger's conception of human existence as being-in-the-world stands opposed not just to transcendental idealism, but to contemporary varieties of antirealism, and even to what is sometimes simply called "nonrealism," or "deflationary realism," which seeks a neutral middle ground between realism and idealism, both of which it rejects as metaphysical excrescences. From Heidegger's point of view, I want to suggest, all such views threaten to conflate the ontic structure of occurrent (*vorhanden*) entities with the ontological modes, or hermeneutic conditions, that render those entities intelligible to us as such.[3]

---

[1] See Husserl, *Formal and Transcendental Logic,* the 1930 Postscript to *Ideas I, Cartesian Meditations,* and *Crisis of the European Sciences.*

[2] Idealist readings of Heidegger can be found in A. de Waelhens, *La philosophie de Martin Heidegger,* 316; William Blattner's "Is Heidegger a Kantian Idealist?" and *Heidegger's Temporal Idealism*; Cristina Lafont's *Linguistic Turn in Hermeneutic Philosophy* and *Heidegger, Language, and World-Disclosure*; and Frederick Olafson's *Heidegger and the Philosophy of Mind,* 11. For more on Olafson's rejection of realist readings of *Being and Time,* see the later discussion in this chapter.

[3] Of course, Kant rightly insisted on calling himself an "empirical realist," just as Husserl could with some justification protest that no "realist" had ever been more deserving of the title than himself. See Chapter 1, footnote 34. Yet the realism that Kant and Husserl embraced was essentially epistemological, that is, a denial of the skeptical challenge that we can have no genuine noninferential knowledge of objects in space and time. Kant often sounds like a realist in another sense, of course, inasmuch as he seems to regard things in themselves as constituents of a kind of ultimate reality that exists independently of human cognition, notwithstanding the fact that "reality" and "existence" are themselves mere categories of the understanding. Moreover, as students of the first *Critique* are invariably somewhat perplexed to discover, Kant regards space and time themselves as the merely subjective form of our sensibility, not properties of things in themselves. Husserl makes no such claim since he rejects the very concept of things in themselves as "absurd." In any case, Harrison Hall is right to attribute to Husserl a purely epistemological form of realism in his essay "Was Husserl a Realist or an Idealist?"

Neither Kant nor Husserl nor more recent critics of realism, that is, anticipate what I shall call Heidegger's *ontic realism* in *Being and Time*. By 'ontic realism' I mean the claim that occurrent entities exist and have a determinate spatiotemporal structure independently of us and our understanding of them. In spite of what Heidegger regards as "the necessary connection between being and understanding," he insists that "Entities *are*, quite independently of the experience in which they are disclosed, the acquaintance in which they are uncovered, and the grasping in which their nature is ascertained" (*SZ* 183). Being is internal to, and thus in a sense dependent on, Dasein's understanding of being,[4] but entities are not: "In the order of ontological founding relations (*Fundierungszusammenhänge*) and of possible categorial and existential identification, *reality is referred back to the phenomenon of care*" (*SZ* 211). However, "That reality is grounded ontologically in the being of Dasein cannot mean that the real could only be, as what it is in itself, if and as long as Dasein exists" (*SZ* 211–12). Similarly, in his 1927 lectures, Heidegger insists that our understanding of nature in its being is precisely an understanding of an entity existing independently of us and our encounter with it:

> This entity is intraworldly. But innerworldliness nonetheless does not belong to its being, rather in dealing with this entity, nature in the widest sense, we understand that this entity *is* as something occurrent, as an entity that we run up against, to which we are given over, that for its own part always already is. It is, without our uncovering it, i.e. without our encountering it in our world. Innerworldliness *devolves upon* this entity only when it is *uncovered* as an entity. (*GP* 240)

And in his lectures of 1927–8 on Kant's *Critique of Pure Reason*, he says,

> Physical nature can only occur as intraworldly when world, i.e. Dasein, exists. Nature can, however, very well be in its own way without occurring as intraworldly, without human Dasein, and hence a world, existing; and it is only because nature is *by itself* occurrent that it can also confront Dasein within a world.[5]

---

[4] In fact, I argue later that it is at best misleading to say that being "depends on" Dasein's understanding of being, since being is not an entity and so cannot strictly speaking stand in dependence or independence relations with other entities. What I mean here is simply that being *consists in* or is *constituted by* our understanding. See my discussion of Olafson in the last section of this chapter.

[5] Heidegger, *Phänomenologische Interpretation von Kant Kritik der reinen Vernunft*, 19.

So, although it makes no sense to talk about *being* subsisting or obtaining outside or independently of Dasein's understanding of being, Heidegger is very clear that occurrent entities, for example nature, can perfectly well *be* independently of us and our understanding of them and their being. Indeed, their independent existence is part of what we understand about them in their being when we encounter them within our world. His insistence that *being* is internal to Dasein's understanding of being, then, in no way commits Heidegger to transcendental idealism or antirealism about occurrent *entities*.

Readers have often supposed that Heidegger's notion of the "worldliness of the world" (*die Weltlichkeit der Welt*) entails some form of antirealism with regard to the entities posited in common sense and by the natural sciences, citing as evidence his claim that the ontological category of occurrentness (*Vorhandenheit*) is hermeneutically parasitic on that of availability (*Zuhandenheit*). But to ascribe hermeneutic primacy to availability is not to say that, like available things, occurrent entities are themselves constituted by the practices and interpretations in which we make sense of them. Reading the description of worldliness in *Being and Time* as an account of hermeneutic conditions suggests instead that Heidegger considers available and occurrent entities themselves equally primitive ontically, and that he would reject antirealist arguments purporting to show that occurrent entities are somehow constituted by, hence dependent on, Dasein's being-in-the-world.

As Heidegger sees it, metaphysical and epistemological problems about reality and our knowledge of objects cannot be made sense of without some preliminary interpretation of the general structures of our existence: "Only in some definite mode of its own being-in-the-world can Dasein discover entities as nature" (*SZ* 65). Existential phenomenology reminds us that we can make sense of entities as entities only within the horizon or framework of our finite understanding of being, and moreover that that finite understanding of being is itself an essential aspect of our own being. Knowledge of entities rests on an understanding of being, then, which is in turn definitive of the kind of entity we ourselves are. Cognition itself, Heidegger says, is a "founded mode of being-in" (*SZ* §13). This fact, that human knowledge is intelligible only as an aspect of human existence, is what I shall call the *existential groundedness of cognition*. There is no such thing as knowledge that is not tied in some way to a definite mode of being-in-the-world. There is no God's Eye point of view, or "view from nowhere," as Nagel puts it. The phrase itself is an oxymoron. A view from nowhere would not be a view. Every view is a view from somewhere.

The fact that every view is a view from somewhere does not, how-ever, entail that it is impossible to know, at least in part, how things are independently of *any view from anywhere*. The existential groundedness of cognition, that is, presents no obstacle in principle to the discovery or "uncovering" (*Entdeckung*) of entities as they transcend the finite conditions of any of our interpretations of them. Contrary to Kant's prohibition, that is, there is no good reason to deny that we can and do have knowledge of things as they are in themselves.[6] Resistance to realism among readers of *Being and Time* seems to be driven by the suspicion that it must be incompatible with Heidegger's insistence on the existential groundedness of cognition. On the contrary, I shall ar-gue, the two commitments are compatible; indeed, they are mutually reinforcing elements in a fundamental ontology.

Heidegger is a realist, then, in the sense that he takes occurrent enti-ties to exist and to have a determinate causal structure independently of the conditions of our interpreting or making sense of them. In order to appreciate the status and relative priority of Heidegger's categories, and so the nature and scope of his realism, however, it is necessary to remind ourselves just how widely the analytic of Dasein departs from traditional metaphysical and epistemological interpretations of the world and our relation to it. For Heidegger claims to have overcome the epistemolog-ical paradigm altogether, and with it the very notion of a "worldless" subject standing over against purely occurrent substances, properties, and relations (*SZ* 211). Because he rejects that epistemological scheme as a profoundly mistaken conception of human existence, he also dis-misses skepticism about the external world as deeply misguided, even incoherent.

Principled philosophical arguments against skepticism, however, typ-ically go hand in hand with a rejection of realism, since the indiffer-ence of entities to our understanding of them is often precisely what motivates the idea of possible global epistemic failure. It will there-fore be necessary to explain how the analytic of Dasein manages to bypass the epistemological problem of skepticism while at the same time embracing a realist conception of physical nature as occurrent and independent of Dasein and Dasein's understanding of being.

---

[6] At the very least, it seems to me, there is no good reason to accept what Ameriks has iden-tified more precisely as Reinhold's prohibition, if not Kant's, which rules out knowledge of things in themselves analytically owing to the putative incoherence of the very idea of a representation of a thing in itself. See Ameriks, *Kant and the Fate of Autonomy*, chapters 2 and 3.

The Incoherence of Skepticism

Heidegger marshals his notion of being-in-the-world against the epistemological interpretation of human beings as knowing subjects, and since that epistemological interpretation is what drives the problem of skepticism, at least in modern philosophy, Heidegger dismisses skepticism as incoherent. What are the grounds for his rejection of skepticism, and are they consistent with his realism about occurrent entities?

Realism and skepticism have been closely allied since at least the seventeenth century, when the new mechanical conception of nature seemed to demand a more rigorous account of the possibility of objective knowledge. If nature can be fully described without any reference to our beliefs, then surely we can be (and often have been) massively mistaken about the nature of things, perhaps even mistaken that there *are* any of the kinds of things we think there are. Indeed, in his Copernican revolution, Kant defends the possibility of knowledge precisely by rejecting what he calls "transcendental realism," the assumption that our knowledge is, or could be, a knowledge of things as they are in themselves. Of course, Kant insists that his own transcendental idealism is tantamount to "empirical realism," which, while barring us from epistemic access to things in themselves, still affords perfectly objective knowledge of things as they appear to us.[7]

How then can Heidegger reject skepticism as incoherent and yet embrace precisely the kind of realism that seems to motivate it? Doesn't a commitment to the independent reality of occurrent entities plainly beg the skeptical question? If such entities have a fixed, determinate structure, independent of all our practices and interpretations, must we not take seriously the possibility, at least in principle, that our beliefs may be wildly mistaken, even that we lack empirical knowledge altogether?

Heidegger's response to this challenge is implicit in his rejection of the conception of knowledge that has driven both skepticism and realism throughout the modern tradition, for both have failed to appreciate the embeddedness of human knowledge in the existential structures of being-in-the-world. Making realism safe for fundamental ontology will therefore mean disentangling it from the epistemological and metaphysical distortions that have customarily attended it. Before examining

---

[7] Hillary Putnam defends essentially the same view under the title "internal" or "pragmatic realism." *Reason, Truth and History*, 54; *The Many Faces of Realism*, 17.

exactly what his realism amounts to, then, we should consider first why he thinks skepticism itself is philosophically nonsensical.

Heidegger advances two distinct arguments against skepticism. First, much like Carnap and Wittgenstein,[8] he tries to undercut skeptical arguments at the outset by simply denying that we have the beliefs the skeptic purports to call into question. The skeptic is fighting shadows, for "The reality of the external world is exempt from any proof of it *or belief in it*" (*PGZ* 293, emphasis added).

> nothing exists in our relationship to the world that provides a basis for the phenomenon of belief in the world. I have not yet been able to find this phenomenon of belief. Rather, the peculiar thing is precisely that the world is "there" *before* all belief.... [A]ny putative belief in it is a theoretically motivated misunderstanding. (*PGZ* 295–6)

It is doubtful that such an explicit belief ever even occurred to anyone, that is, before the first skeptic purported to call it into question. Consequently, "The true solution to the problem of the reality of the external world lies in the insight that it is not a problem at all but an absurdity."[9]

Second, Heidegger argues that skepticism is incoherent because it systematically ignores and obscures the conditions of its own intelligibility, namely, Dasein's being-in-the-world. Every expression of skepticism, that is, tacitly relies on an understanding of the very worldliness that it pretends to challenge. Thus, to Kant's remark that "it always remains a scandal of philosophy and universal human reason" that no proof has yet been given for the existence of the external world (*KRV* Bxxxix, note), Heidegger replies,

> The "scandal of philosophy" is not that this proof has yet to be given, but *that such proofs are expected and attempted again and again.* . . . If Dasein is understood correctly, it defies such proofs because in its being it already *is* what subsequent proofs deem necessary to demonstrate for it. (*SZ* 205)

> The "problem of reality," in the sense of the question whether an external world is occurrent and whether it can be proved, turns out to be an impossible one, not because its consequences lead to inextricable aporias, but because the very entity that serves as its theme as it were rules out any such problematic. (*SZ* 206)

---

[8] See Carnap, "Empiricism, Semantics, and Ontology," and Wittgenstein, *On Certainty*.
[9] Heidegger, *Zur Bestimmung der Philosophie*, 92.

Moreover, the epistemological skepticism with which Descartes begins his *Meditations* necessarily leaves our preontological understanding of ourselves intact precisely by thematizing problems about knowledge, representation, and the subject–object relation. As Heidegger says in his lectures of 1929–30,

> Here philosophizing begins with *doubt,* and it seems as though everything is put into question. But it only seems so. Dasein, the I (the *ego*), is not put into question at all.... What is put into question – or still less, what is left open and never taken up – is always only knowledge, consciousness of things, of objects or even of subjects, and this only in order to make the anticipated certainty more urgent – *but Dasein itself is never put into question.* A fundamental Cartesian stance in philosophy cannot in principle put the Dasein of man into question at all, for it would thereby destroy itself at the outset in its most proper intention. (*GM* 30)

The plausibility of skepticism is vitiated from the outset, that is, by the truncated and distorted conception of the human being as a mere epistemological subject, for only a human being intelligible to itself as being-in-the-world is ever in a position to entertain anything like a skeptical doubt in the first place. In short, "The question whether there is a world at all, and whether its being can be proved, is without meaning as a question raised by *Dasein* as being-in-the-world – and who else would raise it?" (*SZ* 202).

Epistemological skepticism has proved itself an extraordinarily resilient idea, however, and I think Heidegger cannot be said to have refuted it once and for all. For it always remains open to the skeptic to reject Heidegger's phenomenological account of Dasein's existence as begging the question simply by building the notion of worldliness into his very conception of the skeptic himself as being-in-the-world. So, even if Heidegger's interpretation of the skeptic's predicament as being-in-the-world effectively renders skepticism absurd or incoherent, there is nothing in that interpretation itself to compel the skeptic to embrace it in place of his skepticism. Similarly, there is nothing in Kant's conception of the transcendental conditions of the possibility of knowledge that forces the skeptic to admit that knowledge is not just *possible* but *actual.*

Still, one way to sustain the charge that skepticism is absurd after all, notwithstanding its astonishing dialectical resilience, is to remind ourselves just how radically underdeveloped and necessarily inarticulate it is as an interpretation of ourselves and our attitudes. Even if we cannot show it to be demonstrably self-undermining or in conflict with the conditions of its own intelligibility, we can still plausibly maintain that it is incoherent in a weaker sense, namely, that it fails to hang together as a viable interpretation, and so in some sense lacks determinate content. This is not to say that skeptical propositions, such as that no one has knowledge of the external world, are strictly speaking meaningless, only that it remains profoundly obscure what philosophical interpretation of the human condition could possibly sustain or motivate such a proposition. Even if it is semantically intelligible, then, skepticism remains in a deep sense pragmatically empty and as a matter of cognitive fact untenable, for its apparent unassailability turns crucially on its peculiar dimensionlessness as an interpretive standpoint:

> A skeptic can no more be refuted than the being of truth can be "proved." The skeptic, if he factically *is,* in the mode of negating truth, does *not* even *need* to be refuted. Insofar as he *is* and has understood himself in this being, he has obliterated Dasein, and with it truth, in the despair of suicide. Truth in its necessity does not admit of proof, since Dasein cannot for itself first of all be subjected to proof. Just as it has never been demonstrated that there are "eternal truths," neither has it been demonstrated – as the refutations of skepticism at bottom believe, in spite of what they undertake to do – that there has ever "really" "been" a skeptic. (*SZ* 229) [10]

No one really *is* a skeptic, except as a purely formal intellectual exercise (or as psychosis). So, although we may understand it in the abstract, we can never really engage meaningfully with the skeptic's blunt, phenomenologically unmotivated denial of the possibility of knowledge. Indeed, such a vanishingly small target is arguably no target at all, but the mere semblance of one.

Skepticism is not logically contradictory, then, but incoherent in a weaker sense, since it rests on a hopelessly distorted picture of Dasein

---

[10] This paragraph is very confusing since Heidegger concludes with a sentence that seems to contradict the one immediately preceding it. Having said that it has never been established that anyone ever really was a skeptic, he then says, "Perhaps [skeptics have been] more frequent than the formal-dialectical surprise attacks launched against skepticism, in their innocence, would like to believe" (ibid.). What Heidegger means, I suppose, is that refutations of skepticism, for example Hegel's in the Introduction to the *Phenomenology of Spirit*, are no less ontologically misguided than their intended targets, and that clever antiskeptical arguments by themselves somehow fail to take the putative skeptic seriously as a real possibility. But what is that possibility supposed to amount to?

as a worldless subject. It makes no sense to suppose that our actual cognitive attitudes might fail completely to hook up with the world, that is, if Heidegger is right that the world is in the first instance the practical context in terms of which mental states themselves show up for us as intentionally directed to putative objects of knowledge. Knowledge, on Heidegger's account, is a founded mode of being-in, and our attitudes claim cognitive significance only in the worldly settings in which we are in fact able to interpret ourselves as epistemic subjects.

What Is Realism?

'Ontic realism' is my term, not Heidegger's. Heidegger's own explicit remarks in *Being and Time* about what he calls "realism" are, by contrast, pretty uniformly negative. Frederick Olafson therefore dismisses realist interpretations of fundamental ontology in view of what he calls Heidegger's "explicit repudiation of any characterization of his philosophy as a form of realism."[11] But the textual evidence is misleading, since Heidegger identifies realism with a number of different philosophical views, none of them identical with the ontic realism I am ascribing to him.

Heidegger rejects realism because he understands it as one of two things: the naive idea that skepticism can be proved false, or any reductive naturalistic conception of intelligibility in the absence of a phenomenological account of hermeneutic conditions. In the first sense, realism is the idea that the existence of the external world can be rationally demonstrated: Realism, he says, "holds that the reality of the 'world' is not only in need of proof, but also can be proved" (*SZ* 207). In the second sense, realism amounts to a failure to appreciate that the problem of intelligibility is not a *factual* matter at all, but a *transcendental* problem concerning the conditions of our interpretation of entities in their being. Realism, that is, fails to distinguish occurrent entities themselves from the conditions of their interpretability for us: "[E]very realism is right in attempting to capture Dasein's natural consciousness of the occurrentness of its world; but it goes wrong immediately in attempting to explain this reality by appeal to the real itself, i.e. in believing that it can clarify reality by appeal to a causal process" (*PGZ* 306).

In these narrow, perhaps by now antiquated, senses of the word, then, Heidegger is certainly no realist. Indeed, as Heidegger himself says, if

---

[11] Olafson, *Heidegger and the Philosophy of Mind,* 11.

idealism is just a commitment to an account of hermeneutic conditions, then he is an idealist – but in that case, so was Aristotle:

> If the term idealism just means an understanding that being is never explicable in terms of entities, but is instead always already what is "transcendental" for every entity, then the only genuine possibility of a philosophical problematic lies in idealism. Then Aristotle was no less an idealist than Kant. (*SZ* 208)

Similarly, though, if realism just means a commitment to the independent reality of occurrent entities, or what I have called ontic realism, then the existential analytic is a form of realism:

> Along with Dasein as being-in-the-world, intraworldly entities are always already disclosed. This existential-ontological assertion seems to accord with the thesis of *realism* that the external world is really occurrent. To the extent that the existential assertion does not deny the being-occurrent of intraworldly entities, it agrees in effect – doxagraphically, as it were – with the thesis of realism. (*SZ* 207)

The existential analytic does not, however, suppose that the reality of occurrent entities either warrants or admits of rational demonstration: "It distinguishes itself from realism fundamentally, however, in that the latter takes the reality of the 'world' to be in need of proof, and moreover provable. The existential assertion directly negates both" (*SZ* 207).

What Heidegger rejects, then, is the kind of metaphysical realism that collapses the ontological difference by attempting to derive the very intelligibility of entities as entities from their mere ontic structure, for example their causal interactions. The existential analytic, by contrast, is precisely an attempt to direct our philosophical attention away from entities themselves, back to being as such. Consequently, "What distinguishes it completely from realism is the latter's ontological incomprehension. For realism tries to explain reality ontically in terms of real interconnections among real [things]." Idealism at least appears to avoid such reductionism:

> If idealism stresses that being and reality are only "in consciousness," this expresses the understanding that being cannot be explained in terms of entities. But to the extent that it remains unclarified *that* an understanding of being occurs here and *what* this understanding of being itself means ontologically, how it is possible, and that it belongs to the constitution of the being of Dasein, idealism renders its interpretation of reality vacuous. (*SZ* 207)

On this page in his own copy of *Being and Time* Husserl wrote – with an
almost audible sigh of despair – "Heidegger's realism," followed a few
lines later by a question mark, then an exclamation point (*PPT* 351–2).
Husserl was predictably exasperated. For, as we have seen, Heidegger
is never willing to bracket the question of being from questions concerning the internal structure of our understanding of entities, as the
phenomenological reductions demand, not just because he insists that
every interpretation of entities presupposes some understanding of being, but also because he insists that our understanding of being is not
just a free-floating system of essences in transcendental consciousness,
but constitutes the concrete structures of our existence. What Husserl
seems to be lamenting, then, is at least in part Heidegger's rejection of
the eidetic and transcendental reductions, as we saw in Chapter 2. In
turning against idealism, however, Heidegger is also simply insisting on
the irreducibility of the ontological to the ontic. Or, as Kant or Husserl
might prefer to say, mere facts about entities can never account for the
normative structure of our understanding of them.

But what more specifically does Heidegger's realism amount to? Is it
incompatible with idealism or antirealism? To understand Heidegger's
ontic realism, it will help first to get clear about what it is not. Hilary
Putnam has challenged the "externalist perspective" presupposed by
what he calls "metaphysical realism," according to which "the world
consists of some fixed totality of mind-independent objects. There is
exactly one true and complete description of 'the way the world is.'
Truth involves some sort of correspondence relation between words or
thought-signs and external things and sets of things."[12] If metaphysical
realism entails commitment to each of these three distinct claims, then
Heidegger is no metaphysical realist. To begin with, he has no interest
in defending the correspondence theory of truth, though, as we shall
see in Chapter 5, he accepts the notion of adequation or agreement
as a benign metaphor at home in our preontological common sense.
Second, he categorically rejects the reductionist thesis that there is just
one correct and complete description of the world. Instead, he is a
thoroughgoing pluralist, and so believes that there are many possible
true descriptions of the world and that no particular class of descriptions
has any special privilege or authority a priori.

Putnam's alternative to metaphysical realism is what he has called "internal" or "pragmatic realism," according to which "'objects' themselves

---

[12] Putnam, *Reason, Truth and History*, 49.

are as much made as discovered, as much products of our conceptual invention as of the 'objective' factor in experience."[13] Internal realism is in many ways a reiteration of Kant's empirical realism, and indeed Putnam supports his case historically by appealing to what he takes to be Kant's rejection of the correspondence theory of truth in the *Critique of Pure Reason*.[14] Putnam is certainly right to see the Kantian revolution in epistemology as a radical rejection of any God's-Eye point of view against which to measure the adequacy of human knowledge. To accept such an external or transcendent epistemic standard is to assume that our knowledge is genuine just in case, and precisely to the extent that, it approximates a complete and perfect knowledge, a divine omniscience, of things in themselves.[15]

If realism is understood so as to entail commitment to some such absolute and authoritative perspective, a God's-Eye point of view, a view from nowhere, then I believe Heidegger is no more a realist than Kant. But then, no one ought to be a realist in that strong sense, if not because, as Nietzsche famously declared, God is dead, then at least because the expression 'view from nowhere' is a contradiction in terms. We can reject the notion of a unique, ideal, exhaustive view of the real as incoherent, that is, without rejecting the notion that occurrent entities exist and have a determinate structure in the absence of any and all views, period. This more austere ontic realism with respect to occurrent entities, I want to suggest, is coherent and plausible quite apart from any commitment to reductionism or the correspondence theory of truth.

Heidegger is an ontic realist, then, in that he believes in the occurrent existence of, in Putnam's words, "some fixed totality of mind-independent objects."[16] Of course, such a belief immediately raises at least three questions: What are objects? What is the mind? and finally, What kind of independence do the former enjoy vis-à-vis the latter? In a single remarkable paragraph that has come to be regarded as the locus classicus of his complex and perhaps ambivalent attitude toward both

---

[13] Ibid., 54.

[14] Interestingly, like Brentano, Heidegger reads Kant as embracing the correspondence theory of truth as philosophically unobjectionable. For Kant, of course, the correspondence in question is purely formal and empty and cannot be said to obtain between our representations and things in themselves.

[15] See Allison, *Kant's Transcendental Idealism*, 19–25.

[16] Hartry Field, too, has pointed out that one need embrace neither the correspondence theory of truth nor the notion that there is a single true and complete description of the way the world is in order to be a realist in this minimal sense. See his "Realism and Relativism," 553–4.

realism and idealism, Heidegger insists that although *being* depends on Dasein's understanding of being, *entities* do not:

> Of course only as long as Dasein – that is, the ontic possibility of the understanding of being – *is*, "is there" (*gibt es*) being. If Dasein does not exist, then "independence," too, "is" not, nor "is" there an "in itself." Any such thing is then neither intelligible nor unintelligible. Then innerwordly entities are neither discoverable nor can they lie hidden. *Then* it can be said neither that entities are nor that they are not. It can indeed be said *now,* as long as there is an understanding of being, and with it an understanding of occurrentness, that *then* there will continue to be entities. (*SZ* 212)

Since Heidegger understands being as the conditions of the intelligibility of entities as entities, one could also say that occurrent entities exist independently of Dasein and Dasein's understanding of being, though their intelligibility as entities does not. As he puts the point in his lectures of 1931,

> The independence of occurrent things from us human beings is not vitiated by the fact that this independence as such is only possible if human beings exist. The being-in-itself of things becomes not just inexplicable but completely senseless without the existence of man; *which is not to say that the things themselves are dependent on man.*[17]

Is Heidegger a "Temporal Idealist"?[18]

William Blattner has read the foregoing paragraph from *Being and Time* as an expression of what he calls Heidegger's "ontological idealism," a view he is supposed to have inferred from his prior commitment to "temporal idealism," the thesis that time depends on human beings. Temporal idealism is in turn the conclusion of an argument in *Being and Time* purporting to explain the sequential structure of time itself, ordinarily conceived as a pure succession of empty instants, by tracing it back first to what Heidegger calls "world-time" – the series of enduring, significant times, or pragmatic nows, appropriate for this or that worldly activity: time to get up, time to eat, and so on – and then further back to the primordial or "originary" (*ursprünglich*) temporality, which

---

[17] Heidegger, *Aristoteles, Metaphysik Θ 1–3: Vom Wesen und Wirklichkeit der Kraft,* 202, emphasis added.

[18] Portions of this section appeared in my review of William Blattner's book *Heidegger's Temporal Idealism.*

makes up the basic structure of human existence, or being-in-the-world. Blattner offers a clear and compelling account of originary temporality as a nonsequential structure of past, present, and future, which make sense, respectively, in terms of Dasein's facticity, its falling, and its projection into possibilities. According to Heidegger, originary temporality is the basis or "origin" of world-time, which in turn underlies the "ordinary" (*vulgär*) concept of time as merely a continuous, unending succession of qualitatively indistinguishable nows.

Blattner argues, however, that Heidegger fails to explain the sequentiality of world-time in terms of primordial temporality, as he set out to do, and so fails to derive the ordinary concept of time from the existential structure of being-in-the-world. If Heidegger's putative explanation of time in terms of the structure of human existence fails, then he is not entitled to the claim that time in general depends on us. Moreover, the collapse of temporal idealism brings with it in turn the collapse of ontological idealism, hence a crisis at the foundations of Heidegger's project. Heidegger subsequently traded the idealism of fundamental ontology for the mystical posture of his later works, Blattner concludes, which no longer assert the dependence of being on human being, but instead treat being as something essentially mysterious and inexplicable. I believe Blattner's reconstruction of Heidegger's project is flawed in two ways, substantively and methodologically. Substantively, I think Heidegger was not a temporal idealist; methodologically, I think he was not trying to construct an *explanation* of the sequentiality of time.

Temporal idealism, as Blattner defines it, is the thesis that "*If Dasein did not exist, time would not obtain.*"[19] Heidegger could not have embraced temporal idealism in this form, it seems to me, since doing so would rob him of the realism that Blattner agrees he maintains with respect to entities. Blattner acknowledges, for example, Heidegger's assertion of "the dependence of being, *not of entities,* on the understanding of being" (*SZ* 212).[20] He tries to soften such claims, however, by assimilating them to Kant's "empirical realism," though he also admits that "Kant, but not Heidegger, is an 'ontic idealist' – one who regards entities ... as dependent on Dasein/the subject."[21] But if Heidegger is, like Kant, a temporal idealist, it is hard to see how he can avoid ontic idealism, too. If dinosaurs and meteorites, say, are (or were) genuinely

[19] Blattner, *Heidegger's Temporal Idealism,* 232.
[20] Quoted in Blattner, ibid., 242, 251 (his emphasis).
[21] Ibid., 245n.

Dasein-independent, surely some of them preceded others of them *in time.*

Blattner tries to preserve Heidegger's realism by ascribing to him a version of Kant's distinction between a "human" and a "transcendental" standpoint (*KRV* A26/B42), not unlike Putnam, who contrasts his own internal, pragmatic perspective with the naive externalism of the metaphysical realist. According to Blattner, Heidegger would like to carve off a transcendental perspective from Dasein's mundane understanding of being – as indicated by the first occurrence of the word 'then,' and by the 'now' and the second 'then,' respectively. Thus, from the empirical or human standpoint it makes sense to talk about objects existing before and after we do, causally independent of us. From the transcendental – or, for Heidegger, Blattner says, "phenomenological" – point of view, however, questions about the dependence or independence of entities relative to Dasein are supposed to be "senseless," or more precisely "unanswerable" in principle,[22] since they rest on the false presupposition of Dasein's nonexistence. From within our understanding of being, that is, we can say that objects exist independently of us, while from the transcendental standpoint such assertions fail to have any truth value at all.[23] This is Blattner's ingenious gloss on Heidegger's remark that "If Dasein does not exist ... [*t*]*hen* it can be said neither that entities are, nor that they are not" (*SZ* 212).[24]

I agree with Blattner, of course, that there is an unmistakable Kantian element in the analytic of Dasein in *Being and Time,* but I think he is wrong to read Heidegger as a transcendental idealist.[25] More specifically, the distinction between a human and a transcendental standpoint strikes me as insupportable within the context of existential phenomenology. Of what philosophical use is a transcendental perspective if all it does is generate senseless questions? Kant can embrace a distinction between an empirical and a transcendental standpoint only because the latter purports to tell us something about things in themselves abstracted from the sensible conditions of our knowledge,

---

[22] Blattner, ibid., 248, 242ff.

[23] Blattner takes Kant to be committed to the claim that, from the transcendental standpoint, assertions about things in themselves lack truth value. If this were the case, though, he could hardly maintain, as he does, that things in themselves are nonspatiotemporal and unknowable. Also, Blattner denies that Kant asserts the existence of things in themselves, yet Kant writes: "The understanding ... by assuming appearances, grants the existence of things in themselves also." *Prolegomena,* 314–15.

[24] Blattner, ibid., 238, 240.   [25] Ibid., 233–54.

for instance that they exist outside space and time, and so outside the scope of human knowledge. Even on an Allisonian double-aspect construal of the phenomena–noumena distinction, the very notion of a transcendental standpoint is doing work in the first *Critique* precisely because there is something philosophically substantive to say about things in themselves as failing to conform to the sensible, though not the intellectual, conditions of knowledge. The spirit of fundamental ontology, by contrast, is to stand fast in the human standpoint of our being-in-the-world, and so to reject the very idea of an alternative transcendental point of view from the start, even as stating merely negatively that things in themselves are nonspatiotemporal and therefore unknowable. For Heidegger, the human standpoint is the only one it makes sense to talk about, and his attempt in the preceding passage to deflect metaphysical questions purporting to abstract from our being-in-the-world is not an endorsement but a repudiation of any such Kantian distinction.

I therefore read the paragraph in *Being and Time* differently. Heidegger is not echoing Kant, nor for that matter anticipating Putnam, by juxtaposing two incommensurable but separately coherent perspectives. Instead, he is trying to point out the vacuity and futility of all efforts to stake out a distinct transcendental standpoint from which to engage such issues. It makes no sense to insist that meaningful claims concerning the ontological status of occurrent entities must somehow lack truth value in abstraction from Dasein's understanding of being. For such an assertion is itself either false or trivial: false if it means that we cannot coherently say, as Heidegger himself says, that occurrent entities exist independently of Dasein and Dasein's understanding of being; trivial if it just means that if we deprive ourselves of all possible hermeneutic resources, we will literally find ourselves unable to say anything.

There is an equivocation, that is, in the form of abstraction invoked by the transcendental standpoint. If, on the one hand, it is a straightforward abstraction from Heidegger's conception of Dasein as "the ontic possibility of the understanding of being," then nothing blocks the assertion of ontic realism: Occurrent entities exist independently of Dasein. What supports or authorizes such an assertion? The understanding of being that we actually have. If, on the other hand, the abstraction has a reflexive relation to the very vocabulary within which we are conducting the discussion, then of course anything we try to say will be trivially self-defeating. It is of course a tautology that the sky cannot literally be *said* to be blue if we systematically disallow all references to the sky and to the color blue.

Heidegger's point, then, is simply that in the absence of our own ontological framework or vocabulary, we can say and think nothing at all. That should not be surprising, but neither is it trivial, thanks to the peculiar and persistent illusion that there is, or could be, a speculative theoretical standpoint from which to say something intelligible about our relation to entities, quite apart from the conditions constituting our own finite existence. But there is no such standpoint. The only standpoint it makes sense for us to entertain philosophically is the one we occupy in virtue of our preontological understanding of being. Do occurrent entities exist independently of Dasein? In the absence of any coherent notion of a transcendental position from which to reject the question as critically unsophisticated or self-defeating, there is no better answer than *yes*.

Apart from such considerations, is there textual evidence to support Blattner's contention that Heidegger was a temporal idealist? In 1924 Heidegger does indeed say that "Dasein, conceived in its extreme possibility of being, *is time itself,* not *in* time,"[26] and in 1925–6 that "time is not only and not primarily the schema for determining the ordering of changes, but rather is actually Dasein itself."[27] In 1927 he says, "There is no nature-time, inasmuch as all time belongs essentially to Dasein" (*GP* 370).[28] The question is, which of his own several notions of time is Heidegger here denying to nature and attributing to, or equating with, Dasein? World-time and originary temporality no doubt belong to Dasein exclusively, but what about the ordinary or vulgar concept of time as mere succession? That concept is naively realistic, since the endlessness of the sequence of instants necessarily transcends Dasein's finitude. And Blattner acknowledges Heidegger's view that the traditional conception of time "is not just an illusion. The tradition has not just made a mistake."[29] Indeed, in *Being and Time* Heidegger writes, "The thesis of the primordial finitude of temporality does not deny that 'time goes on,' rather it simply holds fast to the phenomenal character of primordial temporality, which shows itself in what is projected in Dasein's primordial existential projection" (*SZ* 330). Consequently,

[26] Heidegger, *Der Begriff der Zeit*, 19.
[27] Heidegger, *Logik: Die Frage nach der Wahrheit*, 205. Quoted in Blattner, *Heidegger's Temporal Idealism*, 230.
[28] Quoted in Blattner, ibid., 217, 231.   [29] Ibid., 185.

"*The ordinary representation of time has its natural right,*" which it loses only "if it claims to supply the 'true' concept of time and to be able to present the only possible horizon for the Interpretation of time" (*SZ* 426).[30] I am not convinced, then, that Heidegger regarded time in that ordinary sense as anything dependent on Dasein, as Blattner's ascription of temporal idealism suggests.

The passage to which Blattner calls special attention is from the *Introduction to Metaphysics,* the text of Heidegger's lectures of the summer of 1935. Heidegger writes:

> There indeed was a time when humans were not. But strictly speaking, we cannot say: there was a time when humans *were* not. In every *time,* humans were and are and will be, because time only temporalizes itself insofar as humans are. There is no time in which humans were not, not because humans are from eternity and to eternity, but rather because time is not eternity, and time only temporalizes itself in each case in every time as human-historical.[31]

Blattner remarks, "Heidegger could not put the stronger thesis – that all time depends on Dasein – more clearly that this"; here, "Heidegger states clearly that he is a temporal idealist."[32]

But there is another way of reading this seemingly paradoxical text. In insisting that there was a time when there were no human beings, though "strictly speaking" there was no *time* when human beings were not, Heidegger seems to be suggesting that time *in one sense* depends on human beings and *in another sense* does not. One plausible reading of the passage would suggest that Heidegger believes that in the absence of human beings there is no *time* – that is, no present, no *now* – even though events do indeed occur earlier and later than one another, prior and posterior to human existence, with or without us. Blattner is right when he says that McTaggart's distinction between an "*A* series" (past-present-future) and a "*B* series" (earlier and later), between a tensed and a tenseless view of time, does not capture Heidegger's own notions of originary temporality, world-time, and the ordinary conception.[33] Nevertheless, it seems to me, the distinction does offer a plausible reconstruction of his point in this case: Events occur earlier and later in time independently of Dasein, but only thanks to Dasein

---

[30] Quoted in Blattner, ibid., 213.
[31] Heidegger, *Einführung in die Metaphysik,* 64. Quoted in Blattner, ibid., 231.
[32] Blattner, ibid., 217, 231. [33] Ibid., 125.

is there a time in the sense of an abiding present with past and future
horizons.

Indeed, this is precisely what Heidegger says in the very last sentence
of the published version of his lectures of 1925: "The movements of
nature, which we define spatiotemporally, these movements do not run
off or elapse (*ablaufen*) 'in time,' as 'in' a hinge (*Scharnier*); they are,
as such, completely *time-free;* they are encountered only 'in' time to
the extent that their being is uncovered as pure nature" (*PGZ* 442).
Natural events do not flow or pass by in time, except with respect to
Dasein's ecstatic temporality, which differentiates past, present, and
future. Consequently, there is a *B* series, an earlier and a later, in such
events, but no *A* series, no *time* in the sense of temporal flow to and
from a privileged *now:* no approaching future, no present, no receding
past. Even in the absence of Dasein and its temporal horizons, though,
there are indeed "movements of nature," and they do indeed occur in
space and time. Blattner rejects this naively realistic interpretation as
too naturalistic for Heidegger, but it strikes me as no more so in that
regard than, and is indeed arguably required by, the ontic realism that
Blattner himself wants to preserve.

A more serious difficulty about this text, however, is the late date of
its composition. Blattner's argument is that the failure of the derivation
of world-time, and so of the ordinary conception, from originary temporality led Heidegger to abandon temporal idealism in favor of the
"mystical" orientation of his later works. But Blattner also tells us that
Heidegger had already begun to lose confidence in the viability of fundamental ontology as early as "January 1927, before the extant portion
of *Being and Time* was even in print."[34] If Blattner is right that the failure
of temporal idealism is what prompted that sudden loss of confidence,
why would he still be propounding the theory eight years later?

Perhaps even more original and problematic than Blattner's substantive thesis, however, is his methodological claim that "at its core
Heidegger's enterprise is explanatory." Temporal idealism, he argues,
amounts to a two-step explanatory thesis "that ordinary time … can
be explained by world-time"[35] and that "*World-time depends explanato-
rily upon originary temporality.*"[36] Such an approach might be innocuous
given a bland enough gloss on explanation. But Blattner appears to

[34] Ibid., xvi, 2 n2.   [35] Ibid., 19.
[36] Ibid., 165.

embrace a robust notion of explanation as an account not just of *necessary* but of *sufficient conditions,* and I think he is certainly right that *Being and Time* fails to supply such a desideratum. Since world-time is sequential and originary temporality is not, an explanation of world-time boils down to an explanation of its *necessary* sequentiality. World-time is "what comes of originary temporality, if its features are sequential. But why should those features be sequential?"[37] Heidegger's account of time reckoning seems to *assume* temporal succession, Blattner observes, whereas "it is precisely the successiveness of time that we are trying to explain."[38]

I think Heidegger was not trying to explain the sequentiality of time. And if he was, it is hard to imagine what could count as an adequate explanation. More generally, I think Heidegger's phenomenological project was not explanatory at all in any nontrivial sense of the word. Here, as elsewhere in *Being and Time,* it seems to me, what Heidegger offers is an account not of sufficient explanatory conditions, but of hermeneutic conditions. His argument has to do with the understanding constitutive of Dasein's being-in-the-world; it is not in competition with traditional metaphysical theories of time, nor does it entail temporal idealism. I think Blattner unfortunately obscures the distinction between this kind of hermeneutic phenomenology and metaphysics, between fundamental and traditional ontology, by frequently substituting the term 'ordinary time' for Heidegger's locution 'ordinary *concept of* time.' *Being and Time* does not aspire to an explanatory theory of *ordinary time* itself; it offers a hermeneutic account of the conditions informing our *ordinary understanding* of time.

Neither Realism nor Antirealism?

Like Blattner, Joseph Rouse reads Heidegger as a critic of realism, for whom "the possibility of [there] being something merely present-at-hand was ultimately dependent upon the being of equipment and the in-order-to-for-the-sake-of configuration within which it was intelligible."[39] More precisely, Rouse attempts to enlist the fundamental ontology of *Being and Time* in support of a conception of scientific practice that is strictly speaking neither realist nor constructivist, but

---

[37] Ibid., 173.   [38] Ibid., 175.
[39] Rouse, *Knowledge and Power,* 158.

that instead rejects the representationalist presuppositions underlying both. It is not uncommon to say that Heidegger is neither a realist nor an antirealist, since realism and antirealism are misconceived alternatives sharing some problematic or incoherent presuppositions in common. It is tempting to take up such a position above the battle or to find a *via media* between the opposing parties. And as I have said, Heidegger does reject realisms committed to the idea of a single privileged description of the world or to the correspondence theory of truth, just as he rejects idealisms committed to relativizing entities of all kinds to the representational capacities of thinking subjects. Rouse's strategy is therefore appealing in principle, but I think it cannot do justice to the ontic realism Heidegger does embrace.

As Rouse defines the terms of the debate, realists are committed to "the mind- and language-independence of the world and the explanatory power of truth and reference,"[40] while constructivists maintain that, in the words of Steve Woolgar, "the objects of the natural world are constituted in virtue of representation."[41] Rouse would dispense with both realism and constructivism by rejecting the representationalism or "semantic realism" that each view takes for granted. On the one hand, he cautions, representationalism leads inexorably to idealism: "Once it is presumed that language and knowledge are representational, then we inevitably discover ourselves trapped within our representations."[42] On the other hand, representationalism is incoherent to begin with since, as Davidson argues, semantic content and the world can be defined only in relation to each other, never in isolation. According to Rouse, then, the problem with realism is that "Realists believe that scientific theories say something definite *apart* from their many practical interconnections with the world and that the world has a preferred description prior to those same interactions with language users."[43]

But must an ontic realist like Heidegger embrace a representationalist theory of meaning? Should we abandon ontic realism's commitment to the mind- and language-independence of the world and conclude that Heidegger has also abandoned it by insisting that human cognition is hermeneutically dependent on and relative to Dasein's being-in? No. Heidegger's ontic realism requires no assumption concerning the explanatory power of truth or reference, nor does it imply that the world itself has any "preferred description" apart from our practices,

[40] Rouse, *Engaging Science*, 222.
[41] Woolgar, quoted by Rouse, ibid., 206
[42] Rouse, ibid.
[43] Ibid., 222.

except in the straightforward sense that some descriptions are true and some false, thanks in part to the structure of occurrent entities.

But neither is there any reason to suppose that occurrent entities are therefore ontologically dependent on us and our practices. On my reading, Heidegger would agree with Rouse that theories have meaning, and that entities themselves are interpretable, only in the context of our practices. Indeed, many of the things Rouse describes as "practical interconnections" between theories and the world are what I would call hermeneutic conditions. The difference is that Rouse conceives of the real itself as a constituent of human practices, whereas Heidegger does not. Rouse therefore objects to the concepts of practice in Wittgenstein and Winch, Sellars and Brandom, and in Dreyfus's reading of Heidegger, all of which, he says, "insist on both metaphysical and epistemological distinctions between the domain of practices and the domain of 'nature' that is susceptible to causal explanation." Such accounts, he thinks, presuppose "underlying dualisms between nature and practices."[44] For Rouse, by contrast, "practices are not just patterns of action, but the meaningful configuration of the world within which actions can take place intelligibly, and thus practices incorporate the objects that they are enacted with and on and the settings in which they are enacted."[45]

But Rouse's gloss on realism is ambiguous in light of Heidegger's distinction among four different notions of world. If, on the one hand, Rouse means 'world' in either of the two ontological senses, or in the ontic-existentiel sense, then Heidegger would agree that practices must be defined in terms of, and are thus constituted by, the worlds and objects that condition them. But the structures and contents of such worlds tell us little or nothing about the status of the real as such. If, on the other hand, Rouse means 'world' in the ontic-categorial sense, that is, as the sum total of occurrent entities, then his argument diverges sharply from Heidegger's. Occurrent objects and states of affairs obviously make up the causal conditions of human behavior. But, as I argued in Chapter 1, causal conditions are not hermeneutic conditions, and only the latter can be said to constitute the phenomena they condition, so that an understanding of those phenomena must presuppose some understanding of the conditions rendering them intelligible. And whereas interpretation always presupposes some familiarity with the whereins, with-whiches, in-order-tos, and for-the-sakes-of-which that

44 Ibid., 134.   45 Ibid., 135.

make up the worldliness of the world, little or no specific theoretical knowledge of the objective causal structure of physical events and human behavior necessarily figures into our everyday interpretation of ourselves as practical agents.

So, Heidegger is not a realist about the world in either of the two ontological senses of the word 'world,' namely, the meaningful horizon or framework rendering intelligible the totality of occurrent entities as such, or the worldliness of the various existentiel worlds constituted by Dasein's practices. These two ontological senses of 'world' refer not to entities, but to being, and being is not an entity about which one could be a realist or an antirealist. Nor is there any reason to be a realist about worlds in the ontic-existentiel sense, which are by definition constituted by, hence dependent on, Dasein's practices. It is perfectly reasonable, however, to be a realist about the world in the first of the four senses, namely, the world understood as the fixed totality of occurrent entities. Indeed, the idea of purely occurrent entities is precisely the idea of entities abstracted from their pragmatic relations to Dasein and Dasein's practices.

The fact that our mundane practices condition our interpretations of entities, including our interpretations of occurrent entities as occurrent, in no way implies that those entities are not after all occurrent independently of our practices and interpretations. Indeed, precisely by distinguishing as he does among the four distinct notions of world, Heidegger is able to accept the premises and yet reject the conclusions of antirealist and nonrealist arguments like Blattner's and Rouse's. It is uncontroversial (or ought to be) that as an empirical matter of fact, most physical states of the universe are not causally dependent on our knowledge of them. It is also trivially true that we cannot make assertions or have beliefs at all absent the practices and interpretations that constitute the content of those assertions and beliefs. But opponents of realism often incline toward a further, stronger claim about the existence and occurrent structure of objects themselves depending on our practices of describing and interpreting them. They want, that is, to resist as either false or incoherent a third claim, intermediate between the first two, namely, that facts describable by us, in virtue of our practices and interpretations, really do obtain in the world independently of the practical and hermeneutic resources by means of which we come to know them. But the internal dependence of knowledge on practice and interpretation gives us no reason to deny that our knowledge uncovers things as they are in themselves.

Does Heidegger's ontic realism then go beyond Kant's empirical realism or Putnam's internal realism? The minimal point of agreement between realists and antirealists is what Arthur Fine calls the "core position" or the "natural ontological attitude" (NOA, pronounced "Noah"), the idea that our senses are more or less reliable and that in addition to ordinary perceptible physical objects there are molecules and atoms (maybe even quarks), just as scientists say there are. Not unlike Rouse, Fine argues that we ought to embrace this "homely line" by itself and dispense with both realism and antirealism, for the assertion of realism adds nothing to the core position beyond

> a desk-thumping, foot-stamping shout of "Really!" So, when the realist and antirealist agree, say, that there really are electrons and that they really carry a unit negative charge and really do have a small mass (of about 9.1×10^{-28} grams), what the realist wants to add is the emphasis that all this is really so. "There really are electrons, really!"

For Fine, this additional emphatic "Really!" is no more than "an arresting foot-thump and, logically speaking, of no more force." The best position, he concludes, is "the core position itself, *and all by itself*."[46]

But consider the following comparison. The planet Earth is a (roughly) spherical object with a diameter of (roughly) 7,900 miles, and it exists independently of our practices and attitudes. Of course, miles as units of measurement have been instituted by our practices, and no one supposes that that institution has itself had any causal effect on the actual diameter of the Earth. Nevertheless, some find it tempting to say that in the absence of that institution, although the Earth would still have the same diameter, it would not strictly speaking be (even roughly) 7,900 *miles*, since *miles* are conventional, hence dependent on us and our practices. But this is a confusion. Of course, if I omit the word 'miles' from my vocabulary, I can no longer *say*, "The Earth has a diameter of (roughly) 7,900 miles." Still, it is perfectly reasonable to insist that the Earth *does have* a diameter of (roughly) 7,900 miles, whether I or anyone says so or not, independently of our practices of measurement, including the institution of miles as units of measurement.

---

[46] Fine, *The Shaky Game*, 129. Fine argues in chapter 8, "And Not Antirealism Either," that antirealism, too, errs in trying to add something metaphysically extraneous to the core position itself.

But now let us consider the instruments by which we measure things by miles or kilometers. Unlike the Earth, regarded as a mere object, measuring devices are not occurrent but available for use. They are what they are, that is, in virtue of the functional roles they play in our practices. Again, to say that something is available is not necessarily to say that we have produced it or even that our practices exert any causal influence on it. The wind in the sails and the stars in the sky are available for the purposes of navigation, but we neither produce nor control them. Heidegger's point is just that it is our practices that constitute their availability, effectively bringing them into being as the things they are, for in the absence of our practices of measurement, disturbances in the atmosphere and balls of fire in outer space would not *be* the west wind or a constellation, just as pieces of wood and strips of tape would not *be* measuring instruments. Unlike the diameter of the planet, navigational conditions and equipment are constituted by, hence hermeneutically dependent on, us and our practices. It therefore makes no sense to be an ontic realist about available settings and artifacts; indeed, it seems to me that many arguments against realism are compelling precisely – but only – with reference to pragmatically constituted equipment such as landmarks, instruments, and devices.

Over and beyond the core position of Fine's NOA, then, Heidegger's ontic realism offers something more substantial than a mere stamp of the foot, namely, the recognition that both in science and in everyday experience we can come to know things as they really are independently of our practices and attitudes. And the 'really' in that sentence is more than an empty gesture, since the available things we make use of in our practices are emphatically *not* independent of the practices that render them intelligible. Hammers and nails are hammers and nails, but only in virtue of our practices of hammering and nailing. Money is money, but only in virtue of buying and selling. Without builders and buyers and sellers, there would be no hammers, no nails, no money.

The situation is quite different when it comes to natural objects like galaxies, planets, plants, animals, molecules, atoms, and quarks (if there are any), for there are no human practices or interpretations in virtue of which such things *are*. They are, and they are what they are whether we interpret them or not. Fine's NOA does not rise to the level of ontic realism precisely because there is no sense in being a realist about entities whose mode of being makes essential reference to us and our practices, whereas occurrent entities are precisely those things we understand to exist and to be what they are independently of us and our practices.

Far from a merely emphatic but inarticulate sound, then, the 'really' in realism is a perfectly legitimate way of distinguishing independently existing objects and states of affairs from entities constituted by our uses and interpretations of them. We should therefore resist the reduction of 'real' and 'really' to mere endorsements of truth, for it is no less *really true* that there are hammers and nails and money than that $f = ma$ or that $E = mc^2$.[47]

There is, and perhaps always will be, a temptation to read the features of our interpretations back into the objects we interpret. But that is a mundane, in principle avoidable, mistake. Any interpretation that gets it right about some independently existing objects or states of affairs will have some features that do not mirror those objects or states of affairs themselves. Linguistic and nonlinguistic representations can serve as a conventional means of saying something true or false about things as they exist independently of those conventions. It is a confusion bordering on superstition to suppose that all our linguistic and conceptual conventions somehow lie hidden in objects, simply waiting to be reflected in our discourse. I may truly assert that it is $32\,°F$ one day, $64\,°F$ the next. If I insist that the temperature has really doubled as a matter of objective fact, however, I am confusing the temperature itself with an artifact of my system of measurement. But there is no reason to continue down that slippery slope and infer that all projections from our discursive practices to the structure of occurrent entities are on the same footing, or that that there is no way in principle to distinguish the structure of objects from the structure of concepts and utterances.

How then does Heidegger's position stand in relation to transcendental idealism? The answer to that question will depend, of course, on

---

[47] This distinction between Dasein-constituted and Dasein-independent entities is similar to, but not the same as, Searle's distinction between "institutional" and "brute" facts. The principal differences lie, first, in the way Searle and Heidegger conceive of the order of intelligibility between what is ontologically dependent on us and what is not, and second, what they think the normativity of social practice consists in. On the first point, Searle writes as if the knowledge individual agents have of brute natural objects is not just a causal but what I have called a hermeneutic condition of the collective attitudes that figure into their normative practices. For Heidegger, conversely, it is objective knowledge that presupposes as a hermeneutic condition our competent participation in normative social practices. On the second point, as we saw in Chapter 3, whereas Heidegger believes that explicit rules are parasitic on linguistically unarticulated background practices, Searle maintains that the normativity of institutions is exhausted by the explicit rules that a detached observer could in principle articulate in describing them. See Searle, *The Construction of Social Reality*, 146–7.

how we understand Kant. It seems to me that Kant's empirical realism is too weak to support the claims Heidegger makes concerning the independent status of occurrent entities as objects of knowledge. At least on one reading, Kant conceives of things "as they appear to us" and "as they are in themselves" in such a way as to rule out a priori the possibility of their coinciding – except perhaps in a thin indexical sense of their being the same things. Heidegger, by contrast, appears to accept that we can have knowledge of things as they are independently of the conditions of our knowing them. Even on a double-aspect construal of appearances and things in themselves, that is, transcendental idealism denies genuine independence to objects *as* they figure in our knowledge of them, even if it grants such an independent status to those same things under a different description. Heidegger's ontic realism requires the further possibility that things can in principle appear to us as they are in themselves. Of course, no knowledge is complete or exhaustive, so appearances will always only be partial and selective. Nevertheless, it is perfectly possible, in Heidegger's view, that appearances will sometimes coincide with at least parts or aspects of the structure of occurrent entities in themselves. Again, it is only apparently paradoxical to insist that we can know things as they are, independently of the conditions of our knowing them, in the same way that it is only apparently paradoxical to claim that a planet can be (roughly) 7,900 miles in diameter, independent of the institution of miles as units of measurement. For from the fact that we cannot specify the size of anything without relying on our own conventions of measurement, it does not follow that nothing can be said to have any determinate size independently of those conventions. Similarly, although it is trivially true that we cannot know anything independently of the conditions of our knowing them, it is plausible to insist that we can know things as they are, independent of our knowing them.

Heidegger does not, then, relegate occurrent entities to a metaphysically secondary status in relation to available things and human practices. His argument is rather that our interpretation of occurrent things in their occurrentness is parasitic on our understanding of available things in their availability. Interpretation is crucially dependent on the worldly structure of Dasein's understanding, which is constituted in part by our use of things available. Cognitive attitudes, for instance, are possible only as modifications of the skilled understanding that guides our everyday activities. Indeed, "For cognition to be possible as an observation and determination of what is occurrent, there must first be a *deficiency* in concern and having to do with the world" (*SZ* 61). The primacy Heidegger attributes to availability, then, has to do specifically with its role as a hermeneutic condition. Occurrentness plays no such role, since descriptions of the world in ideally objective terms could never stand in for our everyday understandings of things as available, of actions as appropriate or reasonable, of ends as worthwhile, or of Dasein itself as being-in-the-world.

A Phenomenological Argument for "Robust Realism"?

Drawing on Heidegger, Hubert Dreyfus and Charles Spinosa have criticized what they call the "deflationary realism" of philosophers like Rouse and Fine, according to whom "the objects studied by science are just as real as the baseballs, stones, and trees we encounter with our everyday practices."[48] Deflationists regard any further claim for the independence of things relative to our minds and our practices as either groundless or incoherent.[49] Donald Davidson is a deflationary realist, for example, since he maintains that we cannot conceive separately of entities as a whole, and of our thoughts and practices as a whole, in order then to ask whether the former depend or do not depend on the latter. We cannot assert with realists that things exist independently of us and our thoughts, but neither can we assert with idealists that thoughts and things are by definition just two sides of the same coin. As Davidson puts it, "The conceptual connections between our knowledge of our own minds and our knowledge of the world of nature are not definitional but holistic."[50]

Dreyfus and Spinosa enlist Heidegger in a defense of the intelligibility of what they call "robust realism" against its deflationary critics.[51] They also offer what they call a "phenomenological argument" for

---

[48] Dreyfus and Spinosa, "Coping with Things-in-Themselves: A Practice-Based Phenomenological Argument for Realism," 49.

[49] Fine, for his part, considers realism not incoherent, but fanciful and rationally unmotivated: "I have long felt that belief in realism involves a profound leap of faith, not at all dissimilar from the faith that animates deep religious convictions." All such religious and metaphysical constructions, of course, will strike nonbelievers like himself as so many "wonder-full castles in the air." *The Shaky Game*, 116 n4.

[50] Davidson, "Three Varieties of Knowledge." *Subjective, Intersubjective, Objective*, 214.

[51] Their argument therefore departs from Dreyfus's own earlier interpretation of Heidegger's position as a kind of "minimal hermeneutic realism," which he at one time took to coincide with Fine's NOA and Davidson's holism. See *Being-in-the-World*, 253–4, 262–3.

realism, intending to show that there are reasons to be robust, as opposed to merely deflationary, realists. I want to say briefly how their conception of robust realism differs from the ontic realism I attribute to Heidegger and why I think their positive phenomenological argument for realism fails. In short, on the one hand, I think Fine is right that philosophical arguments for realism can no more convince the metaphysical agnostic than theological arguments can convince the religious skeptic, and Dreyfus's and Spinosa's argument strikes me as no exception. On the other hand, I think realism needs no special argument, since I believe we are all ontic realists outside philosophy class anyway, and arguably ought to remain so until convinced otherwise.

What I shall suggest, then, is that although realism can be defended against charges of incoherence, it cannot bear the burden of proof. What arguably requires special pleading, on the contrary, is any view that departs from the realism we all embrace and take for granted just in being confronted by, perceiving, and forming beliefs about occurrent entities existing independently of us and our practices. Of course, critics of realism cannot be refuted simply by dogmatic appeal to the putative authority of our customary conception of occurrent reality; indeed, Davidson's argument from holism is a powerful philosophical challenge to what I take to be our ordinary ontological understanding. If the argument is compelling, we ought to abandon the ontic realism that informs our mundane understanding of entities and our relation to them. But we will need to be convinced. It is not enough to point out that realism has no additional rational basis over and beyond our ordinary understanding of reality. That ordinary understanding will be enough to defend realism against its cultured despisers, unless they can positively demonstrate its incoherence.

The robust realism Dreyfus and Spinosa ascribe to Heidegger brings with it a radical ontological pluralism about natural kinds. They deny that "the universe has a single order"[52] and insist instead that "the universe can function in a finite number of different ways, each having its own components or kinds." This view, which they call "multiple realism," goes beyond traditional nominalism, they say, since it insists "that the independent stuff to which we have access has a determinate structure and specific causal powers."[53] But that structure and those powers can

[52] Dreyfus and Spinosa, "Coping with Things-in-Themselves," 49.
[53] Ibid., 50.

appear to us under incommensurable aspects or interpretations, which is to say, the same entities can occupy distinct and conceptually incompatible worlds: "two partially incommensurate worlds...enable a person to encounter the same thing under contradictory descriptions."[54]

Dreyfus and Spinosa ask us to consider as an example someone effectively occupying two worlds: one constituted by the concepts and values of Christianity, the other by those of clinical psychology. The "bi-worldly" Christian psychologist regards people now as saints or sinners, now as mentally healthy or mentally ill, but she cannot reconcile the two interpretive schemes in a single coherent understanding. Like Kuhnian paradigms in science, that is, the Christian and the psychological worlds are not just incomparable, but inconsistent, incompatible, and contradictory, and "Nothing requires the existence of any third world in terms of which this contradiction can be resolved."[55] Genuine conflict between interpretive frameworks is possible because, although different systems of kinds may rule out any identification of a type in one world with a type in another, tokens may yet be identifiable across worlds. Even where translation is impossible from one language to another, that is, we might still be able to pick out particulars to which each makes reference in its own terms. The Christian psychologist, for example, regards one and the same person as either saintly or sinful *and* as either normal or pathological; it is not as if the diagnosis and the religious judgment constitute two distinct objects and so only appear to conflict.

The possibility of this kind of conflict of incommensurable worlds, together with a defamiliarized experience of the radical strangeness of things as going beyond *all* our attempts to make sense of them, provides Dreyfus and Spinosa with their argument for the intelligibility of robust realism. When things confront us as utterly incomprehensible, they say, we can come to regard them as existing independently of any of our ways of interpreting them. Our scientific practices can then plausibly purport to discover the real essences of entities we had previously identified only according to their contingent properties, so robust realism about the essential properties and causal powers of those entities makes sense: "*In sum,* the *strangeness* of things as they appear to us when defamiliarized, the *contingency* of our everyday practices in helping us make the strange thing intelligible, and the practice of *rigid*

---

[54] Ibid., 59.　　　　[55] Ibid., 61.

designation make intelligible the claim that we can have access to things-in-themselves."[56]

Dreyfus's and Spinosa's phenomenology of defamiliarization and rigid designation of natural kinds strikes me as plausible as an account of at least one of the ways in which we experience entities as radically independent of our understanding of them, yet as knowable in themselves.[57] However, I believe their radical pluralism about natural kinds is incoherent and that their phenomenology does nothing to make realism any more coherent or plausible than it already was. The problem with multiple realism, as Mark Wrathall has pointed out in his reply to Dreyfus and Spinosa, is that it defies the law of noncontradiction.[58] Even if we accept a plurality of practically defined worlds, as Heidegger does, that is, we can hardly accept that contradictions between one form of understanding and another reflect contradictory features really instantiated in things in themselves. Two contradictory descriptions of the world cannot both be true: Either one is true and the other is false, or both are true, but only relative to distinct frameworks of understanding, in which case they are not true of things *in themselves*. Wrathall therefore suggests that we ought to distinguish between logical contradiction and practical incompatibility, so that for example the spiritual veneration and the clinical diagnosis of someone who seems at once saintly and neurotic will not commit us to attributions of genuinely contradictory properties, even though the two interpretations are mutually exclusive from a practical point of view, since we cannot act on both interpretations at once.

Wrathall's proposal seems to draw a sharp distinction between cognitive and practical attitudes, and for this reason I think Dreyfus and Spinosa are right not to embrace it as it stands.[59] There is an important difference between beliefs and logical inferences on the one hand, and practically meaningful ways of dealing with things on the other, to

[56] Ibid., 66.

[57] As I said in Chapter 3, footnote 64, I accept Kripke's account of rigid designation only in a modified form as a function of our willingness to defer to informed opinion about the identities of individuals and natural kinds. It is thus the social structure of authority, it seems to me, not the physical structure of reality, that determines the reference of names and kind terms. If we, as it were, let the world decide the extension of a term, it is only in virtue of the social sanction endorsing one of the indefinitely many different ways of doing so.

[58] Wrathall, "Practical Incommensurability and the Phenomenological Basis of Robust Realism."

[59] Dreyfus and Spinosa, "Robus Intelligibility: Response to Our Critics," 182.

be sure, but the difference is gradual and complex, mediated by non-conceptual, nonpropositional forms of interpretation. Consequently, we can draw no very sharp distinction between cognitive and practical attitudes even in principle. At the same time, I think no very sharp distinction is necessary in order to vindicate our abhorrence of contradictions and so reject out of hand the idea of multiple *contradictory* natural orders in reality itself. I think Dreyfus and Spinosa are not wrong when they reply that acknowledging limits on the application of the principle of noncontradiction often affords a better account of the way human beings make sense of things, since some ways of making sense of things fall outside the bounds of logical thought. This is not to reject, or per impossibile contradict, the principle of noncontradiction, but to recognize constraints on the reasonableness of insisting on it as an unconditional demand in all hermeneutic situations.

That is, the effort to resolve contradictions and rationalize our understanding may be reasonable as a matter of general principle, but it may not always be our highest priority. Like Gloucester in *King Lear*, we might at times concede with a sigh, "And that's true too."[60] But the *sigh* is crucial. The sigh means that our situation is not fully intelligible as it stands. If things are bad enough, of course (as they apparently are for Gloucester), the situation might become even more senseless and intolerable if we force ourselves simply to affirm one proposition and deny the other. But none of this requires us to say that two genuinely contradictory propositions can both be true. Indeed, it is virtually the definition of a contradiction that they cannot be, for there is no way of identifying two propositions as contradictory other than precisely refusing to accept that they might both be true. It is not, after all, as if the law of noncontradiction just asserts itself out of the blue, at which point we might reasonably ask whether or not it is justified. Rather, 'contradiction' is just our name for the relation between any two propositions that we ourselves unconditionally insist *cannot* both be true. The "law," that is, expresses our practice of refusing to accept both propositions as true in such cases. If multiple realism requires us to believe that they can be, the theory is doomed.

There is a further question, which I will only mention here, concerning the plausibility of Dreyfus's and Spinosa's suggestion that nonscientific as well as scientific interpretations of entities posit systems

---

[60] Shakespeare, *King Lear*, 5.2.11. Quoted by Dreyfus and Spinosa, ibid., 181.

of natural kinds at all. They write, "It is crucial to recognize that, for the Christian, saints are as much natural kinds in God's creation as are lions and maples. Likewise for the psychologist, the various dysfunctions are natural kinds."[61] I think there are enough examples of apparent incommensurability among scientific approaches to nature, between Aristotelian and Newtonian physics for example, that Dreyfus and Spinosa do not need to widen their argument to include ethical and religious interpretations of the world. Indeed, it seems to me that doing so blurs an essential difference between scientific and nonscientific forms of understanding. Saints and sinners may be *kinds* for the Christian, but what makes them *natural* kinds? The point of scientific systems of classification is to discover entities whose existence and character are not tied essentially to our ways of interpreting them. Indeed, the notable failure to identify natural kinds of normality and pathology is a perennial embarrassment to psychology precisely because its classifications always turn out to be so sensitive to the normative attitudes that hold sway locally in different cultures and generations. Religious categories are not typically vulnerable to that kind of theoretical embarrassment, since, though they fluctuate across time and place, they make no pretense of uncovering natural kinds as such, so there is no task of empirical confirmation or disconfirmation haunting them to begin with. It therefore strikes me as anachronistic, not to say scientistic, to read explicitly normative modes of discourse in ethical and religious contexts as positing natural kinds of the sort chemists and physicists purport to discover in nature.

Apart from the relevance of natural kinds to nonscientific forms of discourse and the intelligibility of multiple conflicting natural orders, however, I think Dreyfus's and Spinosa's positive argument for the intelligibility of realism is unnecessary, since, as I have said, I believe realism is already intelligible, with or without the plurality of worlds. All Dreyfus and Spinosa want to defend, after all, is the *intelligibility* of realism. But either realism is intelligible or it is not. If the deflationists are right and realism is incoherent, then no argument from the incompatibility of worlds and confrontation with the strange is likely to redeem it. Incommensurability and strangeness by themselves prove nothing, and it is hard to see how such arguments could render intelligible an otherwise unintelligible idea. If realism were prima facie incoherent on other grounds, then the appearance of incoherence would stand

---

[61] Dreyfus and Spinosa, "Coping with Things-in-Themselves," 60.

as an objection to any subsequent argument purporting to vindicate it. That is, any argument Dreyfus and Spinosa advance would have to address the specific flaws deflationists purport to find in realism at the outset. But if Dreyfus and Spinosa are right that realism is intelligible, as I believe they are, then their subsequent argument from incommensurability and strangeness is not necessary. If an idea is coherent, it does not become more coherent with further thick description of its original phenomenological motivation in our experience and understanding. And if it is already demonstrably incoherent, no additional phenomenological pleading will help.

But although I believe their positive argument for robust realism fails, I do think Dreyfus and Spinosa make a deep and important point when they suggest that, while it may be that no purely cognitive or intellectual encounter with entities could ever by itself show that those entities exist independently of our conceptual scheme, nevertheless "practices do allow us to have an experience that reveals that they and the meanings they provide are contingent."[62] Indeed, the contingency of our practices vis-à-vis the occurrent entities to which they afford us access is itself part of what we understand about ourselves and our relation to the world in our encounter with those entities. It is a striking fact about our understanding of things that we can, as it were, see past the contingency of our practices in a way Cartesian and Kantian subjects arguably would not be able to see past their ideas, their rational faculties, and the pure categories of their understanding. For unlike mere mental representations and cognitive faculties, our practices manifestly uncover things precisely as abstractable from our purely cognitive relation to them, remaining minimally intelligible as purely occurrent, "deworlded," and so, as Heidegger will say, "unintelligible" (*PGZ* 298) with reference to any of Dasein's practical interests or purposes. It is hard to see how it could ever even occur to purely epistemological subjects that the entities apparent and intelligible to them might exist independently of the categories of their experience. The thought might well cross their minds, but what would make it seem even remotely plausible or compelling to them, as it seems to us? If cognition is the ground floor of our experience and understanding, then arguably no experience or understanding could afford a glimpse of things as they are, independently of the categories of our cognition.

[62] Ibid., 61.

And yet, even if realism were to remain as unmotivated an idea for such subjects as it seems to be in fact to critics like Arthur Fine, I believe Fine is right that it would still not be an incoherent idea. What Dreyfus and Spinosa have provided, then, is neither a demonstration of the truth of realism nor even a novel defense of its intelligibility, but rather a thick phenomenological description of the way in which practical understanding, defamiliarization, and abstraction to pure occurrentness together *motivate* realism and make it more than the vacuous gesture or gratuitous leap of faith that critics like Fine see in it.

Fundamental Moods and the Primacy of the Available

The pure occurrentness of entities therefore cannot be exhausted by the kind of objectivity constituted in cognition and theory or assertoric interpretation (SZ §§33, 44b). If our concepts and propositions were essential to our understanding of occurrent entities in the way buying and selling are essential to our concept of monetary value, then we might be as little inclined to conceive of those entities as distinct from and independent of the contingencies of our conceptual categories as we are to suppose that money retains its value outside the domain of our economic practices.

But in fact, we understand occurrent entities and socially constituted artifacts in fundamentally different ways, and our phenomenology ought to reflect that difference. Heidegger's analytic is sensitive to the difference in denying that cognition, or assertoric interpretation, has a monopoly on our understanding of the occurrent. Again, if it did, we would be in no position to suppose that the entities uncovered in those interpretations themselves lie outside the sphere of ontological structures or hermeneutic conditions constitutive of Dasein's being-in-the-world. And yet this is precisely what Heidegger's ontic realism asserts: *Occurrent entities exist independently of the conditions constitutive of our interpretation of them as occurrent.* Such a notion of occurrent reality would find no place in our understanding if we had no experience of the occurrentness of entities apart from our conceptual and propositional attitudes about them. But we do. Indeed, as Heidegger says, not only is cognition a founded mode of being-in (SZ §13), it is also a founded mode of access to brute physical nature: "[T]he primary mode of access to the real must be ascertained by deciding the question whether cognition can take over this function at all." The result of the existential analytic, Heidegger reports, is that it cannot: "Cognition

(*Erkennen*) is a *founded* mode of access to the real" (*SZ* 202). Upon what more fundamental mode of access to the real is cognition founded?

One might suppose that what Heidegger means here is not that we have some more basic access to the real qua real, that is, to occurrent entities *as* occurrent, but simply that we have practical access to those same things understood as available, as embedded in the referential context of significance. But I think this is not what he means. Consider the fact that water shows up for us as snow, as ice, as steam, and as something to drink. But do skiing, skating, bathing in a sauna, and quenching our thirst give us "access" (*Zugang*) to H_2O molecules? Do those practices by themselves uncover *nature* or *the real*? No. In *Being and Time* Heidegger seems to suggest that nature confronts us as something available, but he puts the word 'nature' in scarequotes: "In equipment that is used, 'nature' is uncovered along with it (*mitentdeckt*) through that use, 'nature' in the light of natural products." Moreover, he then immediately proceeds to distinguish this sense of 'nature' from the sense in which we understand nature as an occurrent entity, or object of inquiry, and from the sense of nature as a kind of sublime force:

> Nature, however, must here not be understood as what is merely occur-
> rent – nor as the *power of nature*. The wood is a forest, the mountain a
> quarry, the river is water power, the wind is wind "in the sails." With the
> "environment" uncovered, we encounter "nature" so uncovered. Disre-
> garding its mode of being as available, we can uncover and define it by
> itself simply in its pure occurrentness. Nor in this uncovering of nature,
> however, does nature remain that which "stirs and strives" (*webt und strebt*),
> assails us, captivates us as a landscape, hidden. The botanist's plants are
> not the blossoms at the hedge, the geographically fixed "source" of a
> river is not the "spring in the ground soil." (*SZ* 70)

Which is to say, we must be careful not to conflate these three different senses of the word. In the 1929 essay, "On the Essence of Ground," for example, Heidegger explicitly reserves the word 'nature' for what is merely occurrent, or real, in contrast to the things we encounter in the context of our practices. Moreover, he denies that nature in this sense shows up in our mundane practices as a matter of course: "[N]ature is encountered neither within the circumference of the en-vironment nor in general primarily as something *to which* we *comport* ourselves" (*Wegmarken* 52).

What it means to say that cognition is a founded mode of access to the real, then, is not just that real things show up in our practices *as*

available, but that some experiences uncover the real neither as embedded in the practical-purposive structure of significance nor as sub-
sumed under explicit concepts and propositions. We have a preconceptual, precognitive access to the real *as such,* an access that is mediated
neither by our familiar practices nor by conceptual or theoretical content, but rather in virtue of our disposedness (*Befindlichkeit*) or mood
(*Stimmung*). Disposedness or mood is the disclosure of Dasein's thrownness (*Geworfenheit*), which establishes our primordial temporal sense
of pastness or "having been" (*Gewesenheit*). Thrownness is the companion concept to projection, which is to say our understanding of
the possibilities that carve out the temporal horizon of the future.
Along with the abiding present or "now" in which we encounter intraworldly entities, those two ecstases constitute Dasein's temporal structure as "thrown projection." More specifically, moods make it possible
for things to "matter" (*angehen*) (*SZ* 137) to us, or not, over and beyond
their specific pragmatic intelligibility within the referential context of
significance.

Moreover, some moods, what Heidegger calls "fundamental moods"
(*Grundstimmungen*), have special ontological significance inasmuch as
they reveal entities as a whole in their being, pure and simple. In some
moods, Heidegger says, "the pure 'that it is' shows itself" (*SZ* 134). In
Being and Time (§40) and the essay "What Is Metaphysics?" Heidegger
pays special attention to anxiety (*Angst*), which discloses not just the
bare *something* of entities, as it were, but also "the nothing" (*das Nichts*)
alongside it.[63] In the latter essay he also mentions boredom and joy as
uncovering entities in their totality, as a whole, as such. In 1929–30, too,
he lectures at length about boredom as a fundamental mood indicative
of the structure of Dasein's worldliness (*GM* §§18c–41).

What a fundamental mood like anxiety reveals will differ for ontologically different kinds of entities. In the case of Dasein, for instance,

---

[63] It is important to understand that the distinction Heidegger draws in "What Is Metaphysics?" is not between nothing and *being,* but between nothing and *something,* that is,
entities. Indeed, since nothing is literally *no thing,* Heidegger can concede that Hegel
is formally "correct" in the *Science of Logic* in equating pure being and pure nothing.
Ontically speaking, that is, from the point of view of entities, being is nothing. Being
and nothing, however, "belong together" not just negatively, not because they are merely
empty or self-evident concepts, but because they condition our understanding of entities *as entities.* The experience of the nothing in anxiety is thus intimately tied to the
dawning of wonder and the question of being: "Only because the nothing is manifest in
the ground of Dasein can the utter strangeness of entities overwhelm us. Only when the
strangeness of entities oppresses us does it awaken and evoke wonder." *Wegmarken,* 18.

what anxiety uncovers is our radical thrown projection, our personal and shared histories always already irrevocably slipping away as we push on – sometimes blindly, helplessly – into future possibilities. Heidegger emphasizes this existential dimension of anxiety in §40 of *Being and Time*. In the case of non-Dasein, or categorially defined entities, by contrast, what anxiety uncovers is their intrinsic irrelevance to our projects. Things show up for us in anxiety as radically unfamiliar, cut off from the pragmatic context of our everyday activities. Thus, in "What Is Metaphysics?" Heidegger writes, "anxiety finds itself precisely in utter impotence over against entities as a whole," so that "the nothing (*das Nichts*) manifests itself at once along with and in entities slipping away from one as a whole." It is not that entities vanish or that we negate them in thought, for "the explicit act of a negating assertion is foreign to anxiety as such." Instead, famously, "the nothing noths" (*das Nichts nichtet*), which is to say, we have a primitive affective sense of the totality of things as radically indifferent to our everyday context of significance. The nihilating of the nothing, Heidegger writes,

is not just some contingent occurrence, rather, as a repelling reference to entities as a whole, slipping away, it makes manifest those entities in their full, hitherto concealed strangeness as radically other – over against the nothing.

In the clear night of the nothing of anxiety the primordial openness of what is as such first arises: that they are entities – and not nothing. (*Wegmarken* 11)

As a fundamental mood, that is, anxiety constitutes a primitive element in our understanding of being, revealing entities as radically indifferent to us and our practices. As he puts it in *Being and Time,*

we encounter that in the face of which we have anxiety not as some determinate matter of concern. The threat comes not from the available and the occurrent, but rather precisely from the fact that all things available and occurrent no longer "say" anything to us at all. They no longer have any relevant connection (*Bewandtnis*) with surrounding entities. The world in which I exist has sunk into insignificance, and the world so disclosed can free entities only as irrelevant. The nothing of the world, in the face of which anxiety is anxious, means... the intraworldly occurrent... must be encountered in such a way as to have *no relevance at all* and to show itself in an empty mercilessness. (*SZ* 343)

Again, this "slipping away" of things into strangeness, insignificance, and irrelevance will be different for available and occurrent entities, though Heidegger does not explicitly spell out the difference. When available artifacts and equipment become defamiliarized in anxiety, it seems wrong to say that the mood simply transforms them into utterly meaningless objects. Rather, it is precisely their utility, their normal and appropriate use, that we feel pulling away from us, as if slipping through our fingers. We still know perfectly well how to use telephones and subways, but that ordinary use now seems somehow alien to us, even if we can still go through the motions of our daily business perfectly skillfully.

But what kind of strangeness and radical otherness do *occurrent* entities exhibit in anxiety? Here it seems to me that Heidegger's description invites a realist interpretation.[64] The brute fact that occurrent entities are *something* and not *nothing,* the sense that they are slipping away from us as a whole, standing apart from the familiarity of our practices in their radical otherness – it is hard to read this account of the fundamental mood of anxiety as anything other than a phenomenological description of our primitive, though in a sense perfectly ordinary, understanding of the fixed structure of real occurrent entities. Indeed, the previously mentioned remark from "On the Essence of Ground" occurs in the context of an argument that nature as such is disclosed to Dasein only in the primacy of disposedness or mood, a point that does not arise explicitly in *Being and Time* itself:

> If nature appears to be absent in the [environment-] oriented analytic of Dasein – not only nature as an object of natural science, but also nature in a primordial sense (cf. *SZ* 65ff) – there are reasons for this. The decisive one lies in the fact that nature is encountered neither within the circumference of the environment nor in general primarily as something *to which* we *comport* ourselves. Nature is manifest primordially in Dasein because Dasein exists as attuned (*befindlich-gestimmtes*) *in the midst of* entities. Since disposedness (throwness) belongs to the essence of Dasein and is expressed in the unity of the full concept of *care,* however, it is

---

[64] Piotr Hoffman has recently made this same point. Like Dreyfus and Spinosa, however, he takes Heidegger's phenomenology of the disposedness that motivates realism as an argument in support of realism: "[A]t least as far as the issue of idealism is concerned," he writes, "it is precisely our knowledge of the overwhelming which carries the day in favor of realism." Hoffman, "Heidegger and the Problem of Idealism," 410. I think critics of realism could reasonably reply that noncognitive moods by themselves provide no argument one way or the other for or against idealism, except insofar as they remind us that in our ordinary understanding of being we are not in fact idealists.

here alone that the *basis* for the *problem* of nature can first be attained. (*Wegmarken* 52).

Anxiety thus reveals what Dasein always already understands about occurrent reality, namely, that it is radically, stubbornly, awesomely independent of us and our abilities, our hopes, our fears, indeed the very conditions of our interpretations of things at large. Nature as such, that is, stands beyond the bounds of the mundane hermeneutic conditions it is the task of the analytic of Dasein to elucidate:

> [I]n dealing with this entity, nature in the widest sense, we understand that this entity *is* as something occurrent, as an entity that we run up against, to which we are given over, that for its own part always already is. It is, without our uncovering it, i.e. without our encountering it in our world. (*GP* 240)

Or again, "Nature can . . . very well be in its own way without occurring as intraworldly, without human Dasein, and hence a world, existing; and it is only because nature is *by itself* occurrent that it can also confront Dasein within a world."[65]

Joseph Fell has drawn attention to Heidegger's conception of nature as "indifferent to all praxis and meaning,"[66] and from it he infers that "the presentness-at-hand, which in section 18 of *Being and Time* is secondary, reached only by 'going through' the ready-to-hand, is not the fundamental or original disclosure of the present-at-hand."[67] Drawing on Heidegger's discussion of mood, he observes that "The priorities or sequences of disclosure in anxiety and in average everydayness are not the same." Fell therefore suggests that "both anxiety-disclosure and everyday-disclosure are *partial* disclosures of the being of beings and of the relation of Dasein to these beings. . . . Thus one can speak of no absolute categorial priority in the early Heidegger. One can speak only of *relative* priorities."[68]

Fell's argument is subtle and persuasive, and I think he is right to deny that there is any absolute explanatory or metaphysical ordering

---

[65] Heidegger, *Phänomenologische Interpretation von Kant Kritik der reinen Vernunft*, 19.

[66] Fell, "The Familiar and the Strange: On the Limits of Praxis in the Early Heidegger," *Heidegger: A Critical Reader*, 78.

[67] Ibid., 70–1. Note that Fell is translating *Vorhandenheit* as 'presentness-at-hand,' *Zuhandenheit* as 'readiness-to-hand.' When I am not quoting him, I will continue to use 'occurrentness' and 'availability.'

[68] Ibid., 76.

among the ontological categories in Heidegger's view.[69] As he correctly points out, "Heidegger never says that readiness-to-hand is 'primordial'; it is the kind of being that is experienced 'first and for the most part' in 'average everydayness.' "[70] How then can we account for the appearance of a general categorial priority of the available in *Being and Time*? Why does Heidegger lay such stress on our ordinary skillful manipulation of equipment? In part, his phenomenological description of the equipmental context is meant to draw our attention to the structure of worldliness, which is surely "primordial" if anything is. But is that all? On Fell's account, the priority of availability seems to be no more than chronological, that is, priority in the order of discovery: "In the order of everyday practice, readiness-to-hand has priority, and presentness-at-hand is derived from it."[71] What this leaves out of account, I want to suggest, is that our familiarity with available things does not just show up *earlier* in our experience than any anxious or cognitive encounter with the occurrent; rather, it serves Heidegger's analytic as a *hermeneutic condition,* a condition of our interpretation of entities *as* having some definite, specifiable character, for example, as cognizable objects with determinate properties standing in objective relations.

We should therefore abandon the widespread view that Heidegger simply subordinates occurrentness to availability *tout court* in favor of the more subtle argument that he conceives of *interpretation* as having its constitutive conditions in the referential structure of practical significance, which of course includes equipment and its availability. Fell's analysis makes the negative point that Heidegger's categories stand in no fixed metaphysical order by themselves. What needs to be said in addition, however, is that the priority thesis unmistakably running throughout *Being and Time,* the thesis that animates the bulk of Heidegger's remarks concerning availability and occurrentness, posits the *hermeneutic priority* of the existential structures of worldliness at large relative to *interpretation* and its further derivative modes, assertion and cognition. Were it not for Heidegger's parallel account of disposedness and fundamental moods, there would be no good reason to suppose that he took the occurrentness of nature to be any more than the

---

[69] Stephen Mulhall makes the same, much underappreciated, point: "Readiness-to-hand is not metaphysically prior to presence-at-hand." *Routledge Guidebook to Heidegger and "Being and Time,"* 42.

[70] Fell, op. cit., 67.   [71] Ibid., 72.

intelligible objectivity constructed in and by our assertions, thoughts, and theories.

The hermeneutic primacy of availability is crucial, for example, to Heidegger's insistence that, although we can describe occurrent objects privatively in relation to available things, we cannot construct or reconstruct our practical understanding of the available from any conception of decontextualized objects and their objective properties and relations. Again, of nature, he says, "Disregarding its mode of being as available, we can uncover and define it by itself simply in its pure occurrentness" (*SZ* 70). Later, however, following his interpretation and critique of Descartes' ontology of substance, he writes: "The critical question now arises: Does this ontology of the 'world' get at (*sucht*) the phenomenon of world at all, and if not, does it at least define intra-worldly entities to the extent that their worldly character can be made visible along with them? *To both questions we must answer, No*" (*SZ* 95).

Real, occurrent entities, their properties and structures, that is, whether conceived by Descartes as substances with properties or by contemporary physicists as particles in fields of force, constitute *causal* but not *hermeneutic* conditions. Occurrentness is nonetheless a fundamental mode of being in which nature confronts us as radically independent of our practices, going beyond the hermeneutic conditions constitutive of Dasein's being-in-the-world. Heidegger therefore describes occurrent entities as fundamentally lacking meaning and as strictly speaking unintelligible: "*[O]nly Dasein can be meaningful (sinnvoll) or meaningless (sinnlos)*.... [A]ll entities whose mode of being is not that of Dasein must be conceived as without meaning (*unsinnig*), as essentially devoid of any meaning at all." And only what is so lacking in meaning can confront us as senseless or absurd (*widersinnig*), as for example "violent and destructive natural events" (*SZ* 151–2). Nature as such, however, extends beyond the domain of interpretation:

> *Nature is what is in principle explainable and to be explained* because it is in principle unintelligible (*unverständlich*); it is *the unintelligible pure and simple*, and it is the unintelligible because it is the *deworlded world*, if we take nature in this extreme sense of entities as they are uncovered in physics. (*PGZ* 298)

I take this to mean that we need not strictly speaking *interpret* physical nature as occurrent in order to *apprehend* and even *understand* it as occurrent; rather, its minimal ontological intelligibility consists precisely in its being disclosed to us as radically independent of us and as indifferent to any of our ways of *interpreting* it, which is to say understanding it *explicitly*.

So, although it is true that interpretation is possible only on the basis of practical competence guided by social norms, it is not the case that occurrent entities are accessible and intelligible to us only as constructions or modifications of things already domesticated within the existential conditions of interpretation. Although our encounters with nature always as a matter of fact occur against a background of cultural practices, nature as such is minimally accessible to us precisely as extending beyond the hermeneutic conditions peculiar to us and our familiar worlds.

Such an understanding of nature is, for all that, an understanding of ours, to be sure, and as such it will find us wholly embedded in our own existential situation, as we must be. And yet, though we are essentially situated in a cultural world of some kind, we are also capable of understanding that in our absence, nothing is intelligible. Without Dasein, that is, nothing could be beautiful or expensive or noble or disturbing, for having any such significance can only mean showing up for someone as having it. This point should not be confused with the incoherent idea that without Dasein things would somehow *fail* to make sense, if failing to make sense means coming in conflict with some understanding of how things ought to be. Nor should it be confused with the truism that we cannot think of entities except from the point of view of our own situated understanding of being, just as we cannot see except with our own eyes or hear except with our own ears. Having to understand entities only from our own existential situation in no way rules out the possibility of anxiously apprehending the real as "devoid of meaning," as "the unintelligible pure and simple"; indeed, such an apprehension is part of our understanding of being. Nor is it the case that our minimal ontological understanding of nature as intrinsically unintelligible is itself just one more interpretive elaboration of the prior practical intelligibility of things, that is, just another explicit assertion or thought or theory. It is rather a primitive form of attuned ontological understanding, an understanding we cannot comfortably assimilate among the indefinitely many possible interpretations of things we might articulate.

Availability and occurrentness may therefore be said to be equiprimordial in the disclosure of entities, at least in principle, but only the former plays the distinctive role of a hermeneutic condition. The category of occurrentness offers nothing by way of an objective reconstruction of the structure of everyday significance. On the other hand, neither does the category of availability by itself offer any essential insight into the brute presence of meaningless objects. At best, it is the "unavailability" of things, for instance when they malfunction or are missing or obtrusive, that forges a link between everyday practical activity and the contemplation of things as occurrent. In any case, we should not conclude that since availability cannot be reduced to or derived from occurrentness, occurrentness must therefore be fully reducible to or derivative of availability.

Could There *Be* Entities without Being?

One last point. As we have seen, Heidegger maintains that being consists in, and in that sense "depends on," Dasein's understanding of being. But surely entities are themselves constituted by, and so depend on, their own being, in which case it follows that entities do indeed depend on Dasein. Without Dasein, no being – and surely without being, no entities! It appears, then, that either Heidegger is equivocating on the meaning of the word 'being,' or else fundamental ontology must be tantamount to idealism after all, inasmuch as it reduces entities themselves to the intelligibility immanent in our understanding of them.

With something like this dilemma in mind, Frederick Olafson has argued that whereas according to our ordinary notion, "being must *always* characterize entities if they are to be entities at all," Heidegger defines it instead in terms of "something like *taking* them as entities." As Olafson observes, however, the latter conception, "unlike the first construal, would not rule out the possibility that there could be entities without being."[72] Commenting on the same paragraph from *Being and Time* that I discussed earlier (*SZ* 212), Olafson writes:

> Ordinarily, the concepts of being and of entity – both of them nominalizations of the verb "to be" – are linked with one another in such a way that anything that *is* – any entity – would also be said to have being as that by virtue of which it is an entity at all. What Heidegger is doing in linking his concept of being to understanding and hence to *Dasein* is breaking its linkage with the concept of entity.

[72] Olafson, *Heidegger and the Philosophy of Mind*, 136. See Chapter 1, footnote 23, this volume.

"That this is a revisionary use of the concept of being seems beyond dispute," he remarks. Moreover, "those who, like Heidegger, use it in this way must use it in an implicit pairing with a concept of being that is *not* tied to understanding or to *Dasein* and is in fact applicable to anything that can be described as an entity."[73] Thus:

> there are *two* concepts of being – one familiar and the other new, at least as a concept – at work in typical Heideggerian uses of this term. The first is pretty much taken for granted; the second is the one on which he focuses attention, and for which the term itself is officially reserved.[74]

Since he thinks Heidegger equivocates between an ordinary and a novel, technical sense of the word, Olafson regards explicit statements of ontic realism in *Being and Time* as textual evidence of Heidegger's implicitly abandoning his own revisionist notion of being and falling back on the standard conception instead.

Olafson makes an important point. Indeed, he has put his finger on a nagging problem that I am sure has occurred to many readers of *Being and Time,* but which scholars have rarely, or only recently, confronted directly. When they do, some willingly embrace the discourse of fundamental ontology as they would any other fruitful but otherwise unfamiliar language game, while others, following Carnap, rally to the defense of traditional grammatical and philosophical conventions and reject Heidegger's language as nonsense.[75]

But is Heidegger's notion of being really in conflict with our ordinary understanding, as Olafson suggests? Not necessarily, and to see why not, think again of what Heidegger calls the "ontological difference" between being and entities. Though we may often remind ourselves in the abstract that being is not an entity, it can be quite difficult to keep in mind the implications of the difference in the heat of the philosophical moment. Olafson, it seems to me, elides the difference at the outset by asking whether and under what conditions being "characterizes" entities, as if it were a characteristic, property, or feature that entities might possess, instantiate, exhibit, or not. But being is not a property of entities. Olafson is surely right to insist that for anything to lack being is simply for it not to be an entity, but I think he lapses into an incoherent

---

[73] Ibid., 140.   [74] Ibid., 141.

[75] Carnap, "The Elimination of Metaphysics Through Logical Analysis of Language." Following in this tradition, for example, Herman Philipse concludes that "Heidegger's question of being and nothingness is nonsensical because it is ruled out by the principle of noncontradiction." *Heidegger's Philosophy of Being,* 13.

locution when he says explicitly, "being *exists.*" Being does not, indeed cannot, exist. Only entities exist, and being is not an entity. Strictly speaking, then, it makes no sense to assert, as Olafson does, that "being exists only if *Dasein* does."[76] For being is not an entity and so cannot strictly speaking be said to exist or not exist.

Rather, being consists in the *meaning* of being. Being is *what it means to be.* Our understanding of our own being, for instance, is an understanding of what it means to be a human being. Our understanding of occurrentness is an understanding of what it means for an entity to be a mere object. In the absence of Dasein's understanding of being, however, there is no such thing as *what it means to be* anything, and in that sense there is no being. But *what it means to be* is neither an entity nor a property or feature of entities, so there is no problem about entities existing in its absence. In Dasein's absence, and so in the absence of any *understanding* of being, and likewise in the absence of its *meaning* anything to be an entity, entities would still *be.* Without Dasein, there would still be occurrent entities; indeed, they would have much (or at least more or less) the same ontic structure we find in them in our everyday encounters and in scientific inquiry. Occurrent entities would remain as they are, only there would be nothing to be understood about what it means to be such an entity. Without Dasein, nothing would mean anything. In the absence of any understanding of occurrentness, there would still be occurrent entities, but there would be nothing intelligible either in there being such entities or in their having the specific ontic structure they would have.

---

[76] Olafson, *Heidegger and the Philosophy of Mind,* 138. Olafson compounds the problem when he suggests that Heidegger's much discussed reversal or "turn" (*Kehre*) amounts to an assertion of the independence of being vis-à-vis Dasein: "What Heidegger appears to be most concerned about in his later writings is . . . establishing that being . . . is in some vitally important sense prior to and independent of human beings." Ibid., 159. But this is incorrect. Indeed, Heidegger insists in all his works, early and late, that being is inextricably bound up with and dependent upon human being. In *Introduction to Metaphysics* he refers, approvingly I think (though admittedly this is not always obvious in Heidegger's readings of other thinkers), to Parmenides' understanding of "the belonging-together of being and the human essence." *Einführung in die Metaphysik,* 108. And in *Beiträge zur Philosophie* he writes, "belongingness to being holds sway only because being in its uniqueness needs Da-sein and man, who is grounded in and grounds it" (317). In one of the latter portions of the *Nietzsche* volumes dating from the mid-1940s, he writes: "Being is . . . needful in relating to an abode that essentially occurs as the essence to which man belongs, man being the one who is needed." *Nietzsche IV,* 244. Finally, in the essay "The Turning," he says, "being's coming to presence needs the coming to presence of man." *Die Technik und die Kehre,* 38.

In *Being and Time* Heidegger is careful to put the verb 'to be' in scarequotes when he applies it to being, since it is not literally true that being *is*. As he says later in the "Letter on 'Humanism,'"

> *Being and Time* (212) purposely and cautiously says... "there is" (*es gibt*) being.... [T]he "it" that "gives" here is being itself.... "[T]here is" is used first of all in order to avoid the locution, "being is"; for "is" is ordinarily said of something that is. Such a thing we call an entity. But being "is" precisely not "an entity." (*Wegmarken* 165)

We should not let that locution – "'*es gibt*' *Sein*" – fool us into conceiving of being itself as if it were an entity whose own being must somehow be posited along with that of entities in general. Being is not an entity, and the notion of *being* itself literally existing or not existing is incoherent. This is why Heidegger cautions against reading *Being and Time* as if it maintained that human understanding produces or causes being the way one entity creates or brings about another:

> But does not *Being and Time* (212), where the "there is" (*es gibt*) comes to language, say: "Only as long as Dasein is, is there being"? Of course. That means: only as long as the clearing (*Lichtung*) of being happens (*sich ereignet*) does being deliver itself over (*übereignet sich*) to man.... The sentence, however, does not mean: the existence (*Dasein*) of man in the traditional sense of *existentia,* and thought in modernity as the actuality (*Wirklichkeit*) of the *ego cogito,* is the entity through which being is first created. The sentence does not say that being is a product of man. The Introduction of *Being and Time* (38) says simply and clearly, even in italics, "being is the *transendens* pure and simple." (*Wegmarken* 167)

Being is incommensurable with entities as a whole, and is in that sense like the *transcendens* of Aquinas. At the same time, being is the transcendental condition of entities making sense *as* entities. Being is thus inextricably bound up with Dasein's understanding of the intelligibility of entities as entities, but it is emphatically not an entity brought into existence by Dasein. Without Dasein there would "be" no *being*, which is to say there would be no understanding of being, so that *that* and *what* entities *are* would add up to nothing intelligible. But occurrent entities would still be, nonetheless.

Heidegger appears to equivocate about the meaning of the word 'being,' it seems to me, only because we are prone to conflate the *expression of* our understanding of being with *references to* being itself, so understood. To say that entities exist independently of us is not to assert the being or existence of anything like being or existence, as if it too were a kind of entity, that is, something that *is* alongside or in addition to the entities themselves. It is consistent, then, to say that although being consists solely in our understanding of being, occurrent entities *are* independently of us and our understanding. For although the claim that entities exist independently of us invokes and presupposes our notion of being, it asserts nothing about being itself, only about entities. Again, as Kant says, being is not a "real predicate," so to invoke or express a notion of being in referring to entities is not to attribute existence to things as if existence itself were a kind of property. We cannot avoid relying on or making use of our understanding of being in saying or thinking that things exist, but that does not literally entail the existence of something else called *being* in addition to entities. The seemingly (but only seemingly) paradoxical conclusion, then, is that there can *be* entities without there literally "being" anything like the *being* of entities, as if it too were an entity. This would not mean that entities *are not*, only that there would be nothing intelligible to be understood by Dasein concerning what it *means* for entities to be.

The ambiguity lies not in Heidegger's position, then, but in the peculiar proposition, *Entities can be without being.* On the one hand, the proposition can be understood in such a way as to be straightforwardly contradictory, analogous with, *He can walk without walking.* On the other hand, it can mean something perfectly coherent and consistent with both ontic realism and common sense, namely, that there would still be entities even in the absence of the entity that has an understanding of what it means to be, that is, for whom alone it is meaningful or significant in some way *that* entities are, and moreover that they are *what* they are. Again, in order for occurrent entities *to be,* it is not necessary for it to *mean* anything, or for it to be intelligible, *that* anything is.

5

DISCOURSE, EXPRESSION, TRUTH

What if I should ask you what walking is,
and you were then to get up and do it?

St. Augustine

In spite of the recent growing interest in Heidegger, there is in the existing secondary literature, with only a few exceptions, surprisingly little sustained discussion of the account of discourse (*Rede*) in *Being and Time*. Moreover, when commentators do examine the concept in any detail, they often all too quickly assimilate it to some notion of language or language use, even while acknowledging that Heidegger intended the notion to describe a wider range of phenomena than just words and speech acts. '*Rede*' is admittedly a common German word meaning speech or talk, and Heidegger does say that the constitutive elements of discourse "first make anything like language possible ontologically" (*SZ* 163). Both the ordinary meaning of the word and Heidegger's explicit reliance on linguistic examples in his account have therefore led readers to suppose that discourse is no more than a practical prefiguration or anticipation of the structure of fully linguistic artifacts and behaviors. Other interpreters incline in the opposite direction by in effect divorcing the concept of discourse from anything even remotely tied to gesture, expression, or communication. But neither of these two approaches can do justice to all the things Heidegger says about discourse in *Being and Time*. More importantly, both readings obscure the role discourse plays as a condition of interpretation in the overall argument of the analytic of Dasein.

Much of the confusion about the nature of discourse and its place in fundamental ontology, it must be said, is due to Heidegger himself.

For two distinct strands run throughout his account of discourse in *Being and Time,* only one of them tying it very closely to language and linguistic practice. I shall here try to disentangle the two strands, not in order to bifurcate the concept, but rather to show how the two aspects of discourse converge in a single phenomenon and how that phenomenon constitutes a crucial hermeneutic condition in its own right. What I want to suggest is that Heidegger includes his account of discourse in the analytic of Dasein precisely because of the indispensable role he thinks it plays as a condition of explicit understanding. Indeed, what has hitherto eluded even very discerning readers, in part because it never becomes fully explicit in the text, is the very close conceptual and phenomenological connections between discourse and interpretation, as Heidegger understands them.

In this chapter, then, I shall say what I think discourse is and why I believe it occupies a privileged place among the conditions of the explicitness of understanding. In a word, discourse is the expressive-communicative dimension of practice, broadly conceived, language being just one of its concrete manifestations. More particularly, discourse constitutes a kind of public space of expressive possibilities, a domain of expressive comportments that it makes sense to engage in, in some local world.[1] For just as our pragmatic ends are sketched out in advance in the projection of our understanding, so too our expressive possibilities are articulated in advance by the discursive intelligibility of the social world in which we live.

Discourse is therefore neither identical with nor merely an aspect of the purposive structure of intelligibility as such. Instead, it is constitutive of a kind of meaning (*Sinn*) that is distinct from, but no less basic than, practical significance (*Bedeutsamkeit*): "Discourse," Heidegger says, "underlies interpretation and assertion. What can be articulated in interpretation, thus even more primordially in discourse, we have called meaning (*Sinn*)." Discourse underlies and is more primordial than interpretation precisely because it is a condition of interpretation, a hermeneutic condition. Indeed, Heidegger regards discourse as a primitive element in Dasein's disclosedness: "*Discourse is existentially equiprimordial with disposedness and understanding.*" Moreover, it is essential to Dasein: "As [part of] the existential constitution of Dasein's disclosedness, discourse is constitutive for its existence" (*SZ* 161). Discourse is a

---

[1] I mean 'world' in the ontic-existentiel sense, that is, the third of the four senses Heidegger distinguishes (*SZ* 65). See Chapter 4.

fundamental feature of being-in-the-world, reducible neither to the disposedness that orients us in our given situation nor to the understanding in which we project ourselves into future possibilities.[2] Discourse is a primitive way in which entities show up and are intelligible for us; it is a basic structure of being-in-the-world.[3]

What then is discourse? It is, in short, the way in which our world is coherently articulated, not just pragmatically or teleologically in terms of ends and activities, but expressively and communicatively, that is, in terms of how it makes sense to express our understanding and convey it to others, and indeed to ourselves. To say, as Heidegger does, that discourse is "equiprimordial" with understanding is to insist that meaningful expressive-communicative practice is something conceptually and phenomenologically distinct from the mere purposive intelligibility of practices that individual agents might in principle perform in isolation, or in mere strategic coordination with one another. The expressive-communicative dimension of being-in-the-world is irreducible to purposive understanding, though the two are always in fact

---

[2] Heidegger equivocates with respect to the systematic place of discourse in the structure of Dasein's disclosedness. Chapter 5 (Part A) of Division I identifies discourse as the third of three basic elements of disclosedness, along with disposedness and understanding (see *SZ* 133). Similarly, in Division II (§60), having described the anxious mood and the self-understanding constituting Dasein's "wanting to have a conscience," Heidegger continues, "The third essential moment of disclosedness is *discourse*" (*SZ* 296). Later in the text, however, falling (*Verfallen*) replaces discourse as the third element of disclosedness, corresponding to the temporal ecstasis of the present, and discourse comes to occupy a more general role in articulating disclosedness as a whole (see §68d). And yet, apparently because discourse manifests itself here and now in concrete linguistic practice, Heidegger still seems to want to tie it to the present: "The full disclosedness of the there (*das Da*), constituted by understanding, disposedness, and falling, maintains its articulation through discourse. Discourse therefore does not temporalize itself primarily in any definite ecstasis. However, since, factically, discourse expresses itself for the most part in language, and first of all speaks in the manner of a concerned-discursive addressing the 'environment,' *making-present* (*Gegenwärtigen*) nonetheless has a *privileged* constitutive function" (*SZ* 349). The specific association of discourse with the temporal present strikes me as problematic, but I will not pursue the point here.

[3] Heidegger's ambivalence with regard to the systematic role of discourse (see footnote 2) leads Dreyfus to equivocate in his commentary on *Being and Time* about whether or not discourse is indeed a primitive feature of disclosedness. For although he affirms Heidegger's claim that discourse is "equiprimordial" with disposedness and understanding, he seems to take it back by adding that discourse "is not on a par with the other two aspects of Dasein's openness." Dreyfus, *Being-in-the-World*, 217. The challenge facing any interpretation of Heidegger's notion of discourse is to say how it can indeed be on a par with disposedness and understanding while not just collapsing into either of them, even if it is specific to no single temporal ecstasis.

interwoven, running orthogonally across one another, each moving, as it were, along a different axis of intelligibility.[4]

Disposedness, understanding, and discourse are thus three equally basic but distinct conditions of interpretation. In order to see more specifically how discourse functions as a hermeneutic condition, we must consider again what interpretation itself is and what exactly its "explicitness" consists in.

Interpretation as Demonstrative Practice

As we saw in Chapter 1, "interpretation" (*Auslegung*), in Heidegger's sense of the word, just means understanding made "explicit" (*ausdrücklich*). Again, Heidegger conceives of understanding in practical terms. Understanding in his sense therefore includes, but is by no means restricted to, cognitive and intellectual capacities, since those capacities are essentially grounded in the competent performance of practical tasks. This is not merely to say that practical competence is a causal condition of cognition, but that cognition is itself constituted by the practical performances that count as its overt manifestations. We ought not to conceive of understanding as a physical or psychological event that occurs in the brain or mind, then, any more than we ought to conceive of talking as something that happens in the tongue or walking in the feet. Understanding is instead the way we make sense of entities by dealing with things available for use in everyday practical activity. Understanding means *knowing how,* and it precedes and makes possible cognition, or *knowing that.* Heidegger says, "In speaking ontically we sometimes use the expression 'to understand something' in the sense of 'managing (*vorstehen*) an affair,' 'being up to it,' 'being able to'" (*SZ* 143). The mundane or merely ontic sense of the word, then, provides the basis for the existential concept of understanding:

---

[4] Putting it this way makes it sound reminiscent of Jürgen Habermas's distinction between communicative and instrumental rationality. But Heidegger's point, as I understand it, is quite different. For whereas Habermas invites us to imagine approximating an "ideal speech situation" by abstracting from our merely "strategic" practical interests, Heidegger regards *all* human interaction as constituted by both instrumental and discursive structures, which do not typically figure in our practices as exclusive and competing interests. Habermas, that is, draws a sharp distinction between communicative and strategic rationality at the outset. As a result, his ethical concept of discourse is arguably tied to just the sort of "worldless" conception of the subject that Heidegger criticizes in *Being and Time* and elsewhere. See Habermas, "Wahrheitstheorien" and *The Theory of Communicative Action,* Vol. 1.

"understanding oneself in the being of one's ownmost ability to be is the primordial existential concept of understanding. Its terminological meaning harkens back to common linguistic usage when we say: someone can manage (*vorstehen*) an affair, i.e. he has an understanding of it (*versteht sich darauf*)" (*GP* 391–2).

What then is understanding "made explicit"? What we understand explicitly in interpretation, Heidegger says, "has the structure of *something as something.* . . . The 'as' makes up the structure of the explicitness of something understood; it constitutes interpretation" (*SZ* 149). Understanding precedes and conditions interpretation; interpretation presupposes understanding. Dasein always already has an understanding of some sort, nor is understanding a mere product or effect of interpretation, as if interpretation could proceed blindly in the absence of understanding.

I have suggested, too, that Heidegger is interested in the explicitness definitive of interpretation precisely because what he calls the "*as*-structure" of interpretation is at bottom the structure of the intelligibility of *being*, that is, the intelligibility of entities *as entities*. The *as*-structure of interpretation, then, is the structure of our understanding of being, even though that understanding is itself not always explicit or thematic. This is why Heidegger insists that interpretation is not just some random modification or inessential by-product of understanding, as if Dasein's understanding could remain insulated from and unaffected by its own explicit manifestation in interpretation. On the contrary, our understanding is the understanding it is, at least in part, precisely because of the way it becomes explicit in interpretation. As Heidegger says, in interpretation "understanding does not become something different, it becomes itself" (*SZ* 148).

Indeed, Heidegger insists that Dasein is never without some explicit interpretation of being, of itself, and of the entities in its environment. The fact that Dasein has an understanding of being at all, he says, "in turn means that Dasein understands itself in its being in some particular way *and to some extent explicitly* (*in irgendeiner Weise und Ausdrücklichkeit*)" (*SZ* 12, emphasis added); "it belongs to its ownmost being to have an understanding of that being and to comport itself *in each case as already interpreted* in some particular way in its being" (*SZ* 15, emphasis added).[5] Heidegger does not argue a priori that interpretative activity is a necessary condition for Dasein to understand anything, but he does say that

---

[5] See Chapter 1, footnote 26.

as a matter of fact Dasein interprets entities. Indeed, although I know of no knock-down argument demonstrating the dependence of Dasein's understanding on its occasional interpretive explicitness, I think it is undeniable that the kind of understanding distinctive of human beings is unimaginable in the absence of an enormous amount of explicit interpretation of entities *as* the entities they are. More specifically, as I shall argue in Chapter 6, I believe authenticity and inauthenticity, as Heidegger conceives them, are possible modes of existence only for entities that are, like us, capable of expressing and entertaining explicit competing interpretations of themselves.

But if interpretation is understanding made explicit, what does its *explicitness* amount to? It is often supposed that the kind of explicitness Heidegger has in mind just consists in some kind of mentality or consciousness. Perhaps the best textual evidence in apparent support of this assumption is Heidegger's repeated claim that our ordinary perceptual awareness of things is itself interpretive. Knowledge or cognition (*Erkennen*), Heidegger says, rests on a mere "looking at" (*Hinsehen*) things:

> In this kind of "*sojourn*" (*Aufenthalt*) – a holding oneself back from any handling and use [of things] – *perception* of the occurrent takes place. Perception is carried out in *addressing* (*Ansprechen*) and *discussing* (*Besprechen*) something as something. On the basis of this *interpretation* in the broadest sense, perception becomes a *determining* (*Bestimmen*). (*SZ* 61–2)

Interpretation, then, "in the broadest sense" of determining "something as something," already informs our most basic perceptual experience. Similarly, Heidegger later in the text refers to "The circumspective-interpretive dealing with what is environmentally available, which 'sees' this *as* a table, a door, a car, a bridge." Indeed, "All prepredicative simple seeing of the available is in itself already understanding-interpreting." Even in the case of "a pure perception of something," he insists, "The seeing of this sight is already understanding-interpreting" (*SZ* 149). The explicitness of interpretation, it would seem, is just our explicit conscious awareness of the things we deal with in our everyday experience *as* the things they are.

But I think this interpretation cannot be right. To begin with, as I said in Chapter 3, there is almost no mention of consciousness in *Being and Time* at all, and the foregoing passages in fact attribute very little importance to consciousness as such. For notice that when Heidegger writes that our "circumspective-interpretive dealing with what is environmentally available . . . 'sees' this *as* a table," the perceptual verb occurs in scarequotes: Heidegger is not referring literally to visual awareness, but to our practical dealing with things, which "has its own kind of sight (*Sicht*)," namely, "circumspection (*Umsicht*)" (*SZ* 69). Of course, practical circumspection does typically involve some form of perceptual awareness, but the two are not identical: Not all circumspection is perceptual, and not all perception is circumspective. When Heidegger does refer to "a pure perception of something," his point is that it *depends on* something else, something more basic, namely, our practical "circumspective-interpretive dealing" with things.

I do not deny that Heidegger takes conscious perceptual experience itself to be a form of interpretive comportment. My point is just that to insist that perception is always interpretive is not to *define* the explicitness of interpretation in terms of some prior, ontologically unproblematic notion of consciousness, perceptual or nonperceptual. Heidegger's claim that perception itself is "already understanding-interpreting" is not part of a stipulative definition of the term 'interpretation'; it is a substantive claim about the nature of perceptual awareness itself, namely, that its intentional content is derivative of the content of our understanding as it becomes explicit in interpretive *practice*. So, granted that the intentional content of perceptual awareness is parasitic on interpretive practice, it remains to say, apart from any reference to consciousness or subjectivity, what the explicitness of understanding in interpretation consists in. What does the *practical explicitness* of understanding amount to?

An adequate account of the explicitness of interpretation, it seems to me, must be an account of the distinctive nature of interpretive *comportment,* in contrast to the prethematic form of understanding that characterizes the bulk of our practical activity. We must therefore cash out the proper existential notion of explicitness in practical, not mental, terms. We ought to ask not, What is the *experience* of explicitness *like* subjectively, psychologically? but rather, What does it mean to *make* something explicit? What are we *doing* when we do that? What I want to propose is this: If understanding in Heidegger's sense consists in *knowing how,* then interpretation – the explicitation of that understanding – must consist in manifesting, demonstrating, or *showing* the *how* that we know in understanding. If understanding is *knowing how,* interpretation must be a kind of *showing how*. By 'showing how' I do not mean specifically instructive or didactic behavior, but rather *demonstrative* practice, where 'demonstrative' means indicating, manifesting, showing.

For example, as we shall see, assertion, which Heidegger calls "a derivative mode of interpretation" (§33), shows *how* things are, which is revealed (though not necessarily determined) by *how* we understand them: "Assertion communicates entities in the how (*im Wie*) of their uncoveredness" (*SZ* 224). As we shall see, this conception of assertion as interpretive uncovering of the *how* of understanding is closely tied to Heidegger's existential conception of truth (*alētheia*) as the "uncoveredness" of entities, which he also glosses as "entities in the how of their uncoveredness" (*SZ* 219). What I am proposing, then, is that interpretation is the demonstration, the making manifest, of what is understood in understanding, that is, the *how* of our practical comportment. The German word for interpretation, *Auslegung,* literally means *laying out,* as in displaying or setting something down in plain view, opening it up for inspection. Interpretation, as Heidegger intends it, then, is literally a kind of *exhibiting* or *showing.*

The kind of exhibiting or *showing how* that is constitutive of interpretation must therefore be understood not as a kind of mental state or subjective attitude, but as a mode of practical comportment. Interpretation lies not just in our thoughts or experiences, but in our overtly demonstrative practices. To make an understanding explicit, to show the *how* known in know-how, is not just to think or to have a special kind of inner subjective awareness, but to *do* something. The explicitness that constitutes interpretation, then, is a practical and public explicitness. What is "explicit," for Heidegger, is what is *expressed,* or manifest in some manner of expression. '*Ausdrücklich*' (explicit) is of course cognate with '*Ausdruck*' (expression), and in English, too, 'express' and 'expressly' are near synonyms with 'explicit' and 'explicitly.' Of course, we describe as explicit some things that are not expressions at all, for example, mental episodes such as memories or expectations. But again, Heidegger wants to trace the intentional contents of such mental phenomena back to the concrete pragmatic contexts originally rendering them intelligible to us. The intelligibility of mental states, he insists, is parasitic on the pragmatic intelligibility of Dasein's worldly comportment. Similarly, Heidegger breaks from his phenomenological and neo-Kantian contemporaries by replacing the theory of *judgment* with an account of *assertion* as a mode of practical comportment, a doing. So, even if we describe some of our unexpressed mental states as explicit, Heidegger regards those psychological forms of explicitness as parasitic on the public explicitness of concrete expressive comportments, for example the bodily postures and facial expressions that capture and convey our prelinguistic understanding of ourselves and our situations.

If interpretation is essentially expressive, what then is an expression? The concept of expression we must rely on here is extremely broad, though not so broad as to apply equally well to everything we do (in which case the notion would be vacuous). To begin with, expressions are not necessarily linguistic, nor must they figure in any *system* of signs or symbols. Thus, bodily postures and facial expressions are expressions in the wide sense since they show and convey something intelligible about us, our attitudes, and the situations we find ourselves in. Indeed, what facial expressions typically exhibit or demonstrate is something we already have some prior understanding of, or else something already manifest in our disposedness. They thus afford an almost ideal example of what I think Heidegger has in mind when he defines "interpretation" as the "development" or "cultivation" (*Ausbildung*) of understanding (*SZ* 148) and as "the working-out (*Ausarbeiten*) and appropriation (*Zueignen*) of an understanding" (*SZ* 231). When I shrug my shoulders or wrinkle my nose, I make my attitude manifest and intelligible to anyone who sees my reaction, provided of course that we share the same general background understanding of the situation to begin with. Bodily postures and facial expressions are primitive instances of the elaboration and appropriation of understanding in overt demonstrative form, for they point up something understood *as* so understood.[6]

The Structure of the "*As*"

How then does interpretation arise out of understanding? The *as*-structure of interpretation, Heidegger says, presupposes the "fore-structure" of understanding, which he further analyzes into three components: "fore-having" (*Vorhabe*), "fore-sight" (*Vorsicht*), and "fore-conception" (*Vorgriff*).[7] These three aspects of understanding are

[6] Charles Taylor uses the example of facial expressions in his account of the expressive, in contrast to the designative, dimension of meaning. Expressions, he says, echoing Heidegger, "make our feelings manifest; they put us in the presence of people's feelings. Expression makes something manifest by embodying it." Taylor adds, however, that "What expression manifests can *only* be manifested in expression," whereas it seems likely that expressions, "interpretations" in Heidegger's sense, frequently capture something already intelligible in nonexpressive form. Taylor is surely right, however, that many forms of expressive significance are intelligible only expressively. See Taylor, "Language and Human Nature," in *Human Agency and Language,* 219.

[7] As often happens, the English terms sounds far more awkward and artificial than the original German. '*Vorhabe*', '*Vorsicht*,' and '*Vorgriff*' are fairly ordinary words meaning something like prior plan or intention, caution or circumspection, and anticipation, respectively. Somewhat stilted literal renderings are necessary here, however, since Heidegger is

hermeneutic conditions, conditions of interpretation. But it is not clear that each is an aspect of all understanding at all times, independent of its being made explicit in interpretation. Rather, I take it that the three elements in the fore-structure of understanding constitute a continuum extending from tacit understanding to explicit interpretation, and in this way describe a gradual transition from the one to the other. "Fore-having," for instance, is just the background understanding we already *have* in advance of any particular development or explicitation:

> The available is always already understood in terms of a totality of involve-
> ments (*Bewandtnisganzheit*). This [totality of involvements] need not be
> grasped explicitly by any thematic interpretation. Even if it has under-
> gone such an interpretation, it recedes again into an unobtrusive under-
> standing. And it is precisely in this mode that it is the essential foundation
> of everyday circumspective interpretation. Interpretation is in every case
> grounded in a *fore-having*. It proceeds as the appropriation of understand-
> ing in an understanding being toward an already understood totality of
> involvements. (*SZ* 150)

Understanding is not all background, of course. Often, if not always, there is foreground, too. But foreground implies something like per-spective, selectivity, partiality, a particular *take* on things over against an otherwise undifferentiated background. We approach situations with an eye to what we want to pay specific attention to; we zero in on this or that. This selective cut we take into the totality of involvements is what Heidegger calls our "fore-sight":

> The appropriation of what is understood, but still veiled, brings about
> an unveiling always under the guidance of a point of view (*Hinsicht*) that
> fixes that in view of which (*im Hinblick worauf*) what is understood is to
> be interpreted. Interpretation is in every case grounded in a *fore-sight* that
> "cuts" into what has been taken in fore-having in terms of a definite way
> it can be interpreted. (*SZ* 150)

We can plausibly suppose so far that these two aspects of understand-ing – figure and ground: specific focus or interest on the one hand, background context on the other – are general aspects of understand-ing at large, prior to any explicit interpretation. These two notions already make it clear, however, that the eventual emergence of inter-pretation is no mere accident or aberration. Understanding becomes

---

relying chiefly on the linguistically embedded metaphors of having, seeing, and grasping. Of course, 'fore-sight' is not the same as, though it might conceivably include, foresight ordinarily understood, that is, anticipating future events.

explicit precisely by zeroing in and focusing on one aspect of things rather than another. The possibility of interpretation is therefore inherent in the structure of understanding, and this is why Heidegger remarks that in interpretation "understanding does not become something different, it becomes itself" (SZ 148).

The third element in the fore-structure, by contrast, what Heidegger calls our "fore-conception," looks less like a prior condition of interpretation and more like one of its own proper features:

> What is held in fore-having and viewed "fore-sightedly" becomes conceivable through interpretation. Interpretation can draw the conceivability belonging to the entity being interpreted from the entity itself, or it can force it into concepts to which the entity is opposed according to its kind of being. In either case, interpretation has always decided definitively or tentatively in favor of a particular conceivability; it is grounded in a *fore-conception*. (SZ 150)

Unlike the first two moments in the fore-structure, fore-conception seems to belong to interpretation itself, not just to the understanding that makes it possible. Interpretation always involves preconceptions, already prescribed ways in which things are to be rendered explicitly intelligible. There is in this loose sense, then, always something a priori taken for granted in our interpretations.[8] Saying this much, however, does not tell us what a conception or fore-conception is, as distinct from background fore-havings and foreground fore-sights. What does the fore-conceptual aspect of interpretation consist in?

Fore-conception in Heidegger's sense, it seems to me, involves nothing like fully articulated concepts, that is, recurring and reidentifiable constituents of propositional contents. For example, Heidegger nowhere says that fore-conceptual aspects of interpretation correspond to particular linguistic terms. Indeed, subjects and predicates appear only in his account of assertion, which he calls "a derivative mode of interpretation" (SZ §33). Not all interpretation is assertoric, but interpretation apparently always involves preconceptions of some kind. However, although fore-conception is something more primitive than full-fledged conceptual content, I believe it must nevertheless be tied in

---

[8] Needless to say, "the character of this 'fore-'," which Heidegger also refers to here as a kind of "formal 'a priori'" (SZ 150), is not that of the pure forms of intuition and understanding in Kant. Heidegger appropriates the familiar Latin term for anything falling under the existential structure of thrownness (*Geworfenheit*), only some of which will be a priori in the Kantian sense, that is, nonempirical.

some way to the concrete gestural repertoire of demonstrative comportments that constitute our interpretive practice. The kind of grasping or preconceiving that Heidegger has in mind, I believe, is part of our mastery of a way of expressing what we understand from some particular point of view. Prior to the conceptual regimentation of discrete linguistic subjects and predicates, that is, we have a kind of shared vocabulary of expressive gestures that we can recognize in a rough and ready way across a wide variety of disparate situations and contexts. I have in mind such gestures as raising one's eyebrows in curiosity or doubt, wrinkling one's nose in distaste, shrugging one's shoulders in indifference or irritation, waving one's hand dismissively, and so on. These expressive comportments are not conceptual or linguistic, but they introduce and foreshadow the kind of generality and iterability essential to language, predication, and concepts proper.

How then are we to conceive of the emergence of interpretation in contexts constituted by mere practical understanding? How does a practice become an expressive or demonstrative practice? How does its defining aspect become explicit? A full answer to this question would require an entire chapter (or book) of its own, but suffice it to say that interpretation involves practical norms at two distinct levels: first, in the practical intelligibility – the *how* – being made explicit itself; second, in the comportment effecting the explicitation. Interpretive activity, that is, makes manifest normative aspects of everyday intelligibility in a way that is itself sensitive to norms, in this case the norms governing *how* things are to be made properly manifest or explicit. Expressive gestures are parasitic on the norms they uncover in our everyday practical world, but they are also subject to norms of their own. There is a *how* in the very way we make manifest the *how* of things when we interpret them. Interpretation emerges, then, when these two levels of normativity govern and make intelligible what we do: first, norms governing some given domain of practices; second, norms governing how to comport oneself so as to highlight salient aspects of those practices. This twofold normativity constitutes what we might call an existential condition of semantic meaning and intentional content as the tradition prior to Heidegger conceived it, that is, as distinct in principle from its objects or referents. For it is only because we can understand something explicitly *as* something in interpretation that we can make sense of the contents of our understanding as systematically distinct from the objects they describe. For example, it is only because we can regard the planet Venus *as* the morning star or *as* the evening star that we can then be in a position to draw a general theoretical distinction between the planet itself and any of the descriptions under which we view it. Only because there are socially normal and appropriate ways of expressing and interpreting, then, can expressions and interpretations serve to highlight aspects of what we already understand prior to their being made explicit.

Indeed, as I shall argue, what makes an expression an expression at all is its public intelligibility in communication, not the private intentions of the person whose expression it is. For example, our bodily gestures frequently express our understanding in spite of ourselves, indeed often in spite of our best efforts to conceal our attitudes. My expressive comportments are not expressive because I intend them to be, then, any more than I can determine the meanings of the words I utter or dictate the monetary value of the coins in my pocket. It is precisely because interpretation is essentially public and social that it must have its roots in discourse, as Heidegger insists it does. For discourse is essentially communicative, and it is the communicative dimension of everyday intelligibility that makes expressive comportment intelligible as such, as expressive *of* something. Discourse, that is, underlies and makes possible the *as*-structure in virtue of which interpretive expressions demonstrate or make manifest our understanding of something *as* something – at bottom, entities *as* entities.

As a result, Heidegger's accounts of discourse, of interpretation, and of language all conspire against the *assertoric paradigm* that has dominated theories of meaning since Aristotle.[9] Philosophers, linguists, and speech-act theorists have often privileged assertions and propositions in their accounts of language, since it is these units of discourse that express complete judgments or thoughts, and since it has seemed obvious to many that the essential function of language lies in the articulation and expression of thought. Even when they turn their attention to sentences and utterances other than declaratives and assertions, such theorists often take it for granted that speech itself is meaningful only in virtue of its propositional content.[10] Wilfrid Sellars, for example, has extended the assertoric model into the domain of sensory experience itself by arguing that perception must be understood as involving a

---

[9] In §4 of *De Interpretatione* Aristotle defines a sentence (*logos*) as a meaningful unit of speech and an assertion or proposition (*apophansis*) as the kind of sentence that can be true or false. He thereby privileges what Heidegger insists is a special case of discursive intelligibility and passes over the phenomenon at large.

[10] See Searle, *Speech Acts*, §2.4.

"propositional claim" admitting of truth or falsity. *Seeing* proper is *seeing that* such and such; to call an experience an experience of seeing, he insists, is "to apply the semantical concept of truth to that experience."[11]

Heidegger, by contrast, wants to avoid any surreptitious reading of the structures and contents of propositionally articulated thought back into the preconceptual skills and attitudes of everyday practical understanding. He therefore denies assertions and their propositional contents any privileged place in his account of discourse and interpretation. "Asserting is an *intentional comportment of Dasein*," he says (*GP* 295). As such, it must be understood in the context of all the other kinds of comportment that go toward making it intelligible. Most of our understanding and interpretation of things, Heidegger insists, involves no assertoric component at all: "Circumspective-interpretive dealing with what is environmentally available, in which we 'see' this *as* a table, a door, a car, a bridge, needn't necessarily also lay down in a determining *assertion* what is circumspectively interpreted" (*SZ* 149). Assertion is not a primitive or self-sufficient mode of interpretation, nor does interpretation typically take the form of assertion:

> Assertion is not a free-floating comportment that could in and of itself disclose entities in a primary way, rather it always already rests on the basis of being-in-the-world. What was shown earlier[12] in connection with cognition of the world (*Welterkennen*) holds of assertion as well. It requires a fore-having of what is disclosed generally, which [latter] it points out in the manner of determination. (*SZ* 156–7)

It seems obvious that not everything Dasein does involves even an implicit making of assertions, so it would be disappointing if that is all Heidegger means to say. In fact, I think he is saying something more subtle and more interesting, namely, that we should not mistake the intentional contents of actions and attitudes that may admit of various kinds of rightness and wrongness for the fully propositional contents of assertions, which can be literally true or false. Intentional attitudes and experiences do not, it seems to me – *pace* Sellars – typically contain propositional claims, even if we can evaluate them as appropriate or inappropriate, successful or unsuccessful by their own lights, in relation to the practical environment.

---

[11] Sellars, *Empiricism and the Philosophy of Mind*, §16.

[12] Heidegger's refers here to *SZ* §13: "Being-in exemplified in a founded mode. Cognition of the world (*Welterkennen*)."

Rather, genuine propositions are artifacts of a refinement and articulation of such attitudes, specifically in linguistic assertion. Judgment, whose content is propositional, is therefore a product, not a condition, of assertion. To analyze assertion in terms of the judgments supposedly underlying and giving rise to them is to put the cart before the horse. Consequently, in *Being and Time* Heidegger intends to supplant the tradition of philosophical theories of judgment with an existential account of assertion.[13] If we take the Greek notion of *logos* to mean assertion in the sense of judgment, he says,

> this seemingly legitimate translation can still miss the fundamental meaning, especially if judgment is conceived in the sense of contemporary "theory of judgment." *Logos* does not mean judgment, not primarily anyway, if by that one means "binding" or "taking a stand" (accepting, rejecting). (*SZ* 32)

There are forms of understanding, indeed forms of discourse, whose content is neither explicitly nor implicitly propositional. *Logos* is more than just logic, then, and "The task of *liberating* grammar from logic requires *beforehand* a *positive* understanding of the basic a priori structure of discourse in general as an existential" (*SZ* 165). Rational norms governing evidence and inference among propositions, that is, are rooted in and dependent on the normativity of preassertoric forms of discursive practice.

Heidegger therefore distinguishes the derivative "apophantic *as*" of assertion (*apophansis*) from the "hermeneutic *as*" of interpretation generally. At the same time, he appeals to what he takes to be the more literal and more primordial meaning of *apophansis,* according to which "the function of *logos* as *apophansis* lies in letting something be seen by pointing it out (*aufweisenden Sehenlassen*)" (*SZ* 33). It is crucial to recognize, then, that Heidegger is helping himself to both a broader and a narrower sense of the term. Broadly speaking, *letting something be seen in itself* is the "apophantic" or disclosive function of discourse generally: "Assertion means primarily *pointing out (Aufzeigen)*. We thereby capture the primordial sense of *logos* as *apophansis:* letting an entity be seen from itself" (*SZ* 154). More narrowly, however, the term 'apophantic' refers to the specific function to assertion,

---

[13] Heidegger's own earliest philosophical work, in particular his dissertation of 1913, *Die Lehre vom Urteil im Psychologismus,* reprinted in *Frühe Schiften,* belongs to the tradition he would soon be attempting to overthrow.

in contrast to the disclosive power of discourse and interpretation generally.

The indicative function of assertion is tied to the phenomenon of predication. In assertion, "A 'predicate' is 'asserted' of a 'subject'; the latter is *determined* by the former" (*SZ* 154). Predication is not a general feature of discourse at large but is the hallmark of specifically assertoric modes of interpretation. Nor is predication the mere combination or "binding" of two disparate elements, a subject term and a predicate (*SZ* 32). Rather, specification of a predicate consists in a "narrowing" (*Verengung*) of hermeneutic content, an "explicit *restriction* (*Einschränkung*) of view" in which

> "positing a subject" dims the entity down . . . in order, by means of this dimming down, to let what is manifest be seen *in* its determinable determination. Positing a subject and positing a predicate, positing both together, are through and through 'apophantic' in the strict sense of the word. (*SZ* 154)

Predicative assertions, that is, *let things be seen* in a specific light, *as* this or that. Dimming down and so letting things be seen is not so much a constructive or synthetic procedure, a piecing together of discrete logical or semantic elements, as a kind of abstraction or decontextualization against a background of prior practical familiarity. Propositional content itself therefore derives from a kind of privation, or perhaps a refinement or distillation, of practical interpretive meanings. Indeed, "leveling down" the interpreted intelligibility of entities of all kinds to mere determinations of occurrent objects is "the specialty of the assertion" (*Aussage*) (*SZ* 158).

Heidegger asks, "*Through what existential-ontological modifications does assertion arise from circumspective interpretation?*" (*SZ* 157). And again, later in the text, "In what way can assertion be carried out through a variation of interpretation?" (*SZ* 443). What is the difference between preassertoric interpretation and assertion, and how does the former make the latter possible? The difference obviously lies not just in linguistic articulation, since not all language use involves making assertions. Nevertheless, there is a kind of articulation that is distinctive of assertions, namely, the differentiation of subject terms referring to discrete entities on the one hand, and predicates selecting and describing aspects or properties on the other. The semantic contents of assertions must be sufficiently well defined to stand in determinate evidential and inferential relations with nonlinguistic entities and with one another, so that any particular assertion will occupy a unique place in logical and discursive space.

Heidegger has no very well worked-out theory of assertion, then, except to say that its structure is intelligible only against a background of less finely articulated and individuated interpretive meanings embedded in what he calls the "referential totality" or "referential context" of practical significance (*SZ* 70, 87–8, 123, 129). It is important to keep in mind that by 'reference' (*Verweisung*) Heidegger does not mean semantic reference, but pragmatic intelligibility. Tools "refer" in this sense just by fitting into some context of practical activity. Heidegger's terms for semantic reference are 'showing' (*Zeigen*) in the case of signs (*SZ* §17), and 'pointing-out' (*Aufzeigen*) in the case of assertions (*SZ* §33). Semantically referring linguistic terms, then, are refined modifications of preassertoric interpretive gestures whose communicative function is to highlight salient expressible aspects of the world as it is already intelligible in practice. It remains to say more concretely how to understand the existential structure of discourse as it conditions the possibility of interpretation generally. What is discourse?

The Linguistic Model

Interpretation, I have suggested, amounts to *showing how*, or demonstrative practice. The explicitness of interpretation, that is, must be understood in practical, *expressive* terms. Interpretation is in this sense already a discursive notion. But although discourse and interpretation are indeed closely interrelated, they are not identical, for not all discourse is explicit. Discourse, Heidegger says, "*underlies* interpretation and assertion" (*SZ* 161, emphasis added), and nothing can very easily underlie itself, or what it coincides with. There must therefore be a kind of discourse that is not already explicit or manifest in interpretive practice, that is, in overt expressive comportment. What then *is* discourse if it can fall beneath the threshold of interpretive explicitness and thus fail to manifest itself even in our most primitive forms of expressive behavior?

Whatever else it may be, discourse is clearly the expressive dimension of our practices that makes linguistic phenomena – words, sentences, overt speech acts – intelligible. Indeed, Heidegger writes, "*The existential-ontological foundation of language is discourse*" (*SZ* 160). He even seems to equate discourse with language when he says, "Carried out concretely, discoursing (letting be seen) has the character of speaking, of vocal proclamation in words" (*SZ* 32); "Discourse for the most part expresses itself (*spricht sich aus*) and has always already spoken out (*sich ausgesprochen*). It is language" (*SZ* 167); "factically, discourse expresses itself for the most part in language" (*SZ* 349). It is tempting, then, to say the least, to understand discourse as something very closely bound up, if not indeed identical, with language. And such an approach, what I shall call the *linguistic model*, finds considerable support in *Being and Time*. Heidegger already draws a close association between discourse and language in the title of §34, for instance: "Being-there and discourse. Language." In this section of the text, Heidegger tells us, "language *now* becomes our theme *for the first time*" (*SZ* 160). Moreover, "The overt expression (*Hisausgesprochenheit*) of discourse is language," indeed, "Discourse is language [considered] existentially" (*SZ* 161).

Does Heidegger mean to say that *all* overt expressions of discourse are somehow linguistic, that discourse just *is* language, viewed ontologically? Charles Guignon advances an interpretation of *Being and Time* along these lines when he attributes to Heidegger, albeit with some reservations, what he calls a "constitutive," as opposed to a merely "instrumentalist," view of language:

> On the constitutive view, language generates and first makes possible our full-blown sense of the world. The constitutivist maintains that the mastery of the field of significance of a *world* (as opposed to, say, an animal's dexterity in its natural environment) presupposes some prior mastery of the articulate structure of language. . . . Here there is no way to identify a nonsemantic field of meaning which can be grasped independently of the language that serves to constitute it.[14]

Guignon approvingly quotes Hans-Georg Gadamer, who has written, "Language is not just one of man's possessions in the world; rather, on it depends the fact that man has a *world* at all."[15] Guignon concludes that "For Heidegger, Dasein's everyday preontological understanding and its thrownness are constituted by language." In short, "human existence is possible only within language"; language is "a medium in which we can first *become* Dasein."[16]

Guignon admits that Heidegger seems to oscillate between an instrumentalist and a constitutive view of language in *Being and Time*, but he thinks there is enough evidence of the constitutive view to prefer it in

[14] Guignon, *Heidegger and the Problem of Knowledge*, 118.
[15] Gadamer, *Wahrheit und Methode*, 419; *Truth and Method*, 443.
[16] Guignon, ibid., 125.

his assessment of Heidegger's early position taken as a whole. I believe this is a mistake. As Guignon says, Heidegger settled unequivocally on a constitutive conception of language in his later writings, at least by the mid-1930s.[17] In *Being and Time,* however, Heidegger does not make the strong claims for the constitutive status of language that Guignon makes on his behalf. In fact, as Guignon concedes, he seems to reject the constitutive view when he suggests that "words accrue to significations (*Bedeutungen*)" (*SZ* 161), which are themselves constituted by a kind of practical "signifying" (*be-deuten*) that renders things intelligible in the everyday context of significance (*Bedeutsamkeit*) (*SZ* 87). Significance, signifying, and signification, as Heidegger deploys these notions in *Being and Time,* very clearly constitute a form of prelinguistic, or at any rate *non*linguistic, practical meaning. Indeed, Heidegger's hostility to autonomous theories of language, abstracted from any phenomenological grasp of the wider context of everyday intelligibility, is evident in §34: "Philosophical research," he declares there, "will have to dispense with the 'philosophy of language' in order to inquire into 'the things themselves' " (*SZ* 165–6). As Guignon points out, Heidegger later repudiated this view. In the margins of his own copy of *Being and Time,* next to a sentence claiming that practical significations "in turn found the possible being of words and language" (*SZ* 87), Heidegger later wrote, "Not true. Language is not built up, rather it *is* the primordial essence of truth as [the] there (*als Da*)" (*SZ* 442). But this later self-criticism is evidence against, not for, a constitutivist reading of *Being and Time* itself, since it shows that Heidegger understood his own early conception of language in straightforwardly nonconstitutive terms.

Moreover, the central passages from *Being and Time* that Guignon cites in support of the constitutivist reading provide no real evidence that Heidegger regarded language as playing any essential role in constituting the basic structures of being-in-the-world. What the texts suggest instead is that language makes a crucial contribution not to Dasein's disclosedness itself, but to the particular self-interpretations Dasein finds itself with in actual historical fact. One of the key passages Guignon quotes is this:

> Language, as overt expression (*Ausgesprochenheit*), harbors in itself a way in which Dasein's understanding has been interpreted. . . . Dasein is first

---

[17] See, for example, *Holzwege* 59, *Einführung in die Metaphysik* 11, and *Unterwegs zur Sprache* 164, 166.

and within certain limits constantly delivered over to [this interpreted-ness]; it regulates and distributes the possibilities of average understand-ing and of the disposedness belonging to it. Overt expression preserves in the totality of its articulated context of significations an understanding of the disclosed world and, equiprimordially with it, an understanding of the being-there-with (*Mitdasein*) of others and of the one's own being-in. (*SZ* 167–8)[18]

What Heidegger says here, and elsewhere, is not that Dasein's disclosed-ness is, as it were, linguistic all the way down, as Guignon suggests, but that the interpretations circulated and handed down in natural lan-guage as a matter of fact have a profound effect on what Dasein is typically capable of understanding and feeling about anything. This is probably true, but it does not support Guignon's argument, since the same could be said for any number of other ontic contingencies that can make no special claim to constitutive ontological status, for example religious customs, sexual mores, marriage and burial rites, economic practices, and political and legal institutions.

Other textual evidence that Guignon enlists in favor of reading *Being and Time* as advancing a constitutive view of language is not evi-dence that clearly implicates language at all, referring as it does to dis-course and its fallen variant, "idle talk" (*Gerede*). There is no doubt that Heidegger regards discourse as a constitutive structure of disclosedness: "Disposedness and understanding are determined equiprimordially by *discourse*" (*SZ* 133); "*Discourse is existentially equiprimordial with disposed-ness and understanding*" (*SZ* 161). But this tells us nothing directly about language, and there is abundant evidence in *Being and Time* that dis-course and language are not identical, indeed that language is just one manifestation of discourse among others. Nothing Heidegger says in *Being and Time* about discourse in general, then, offers any direct or conclusive evidence concerning his conception of language.

[18] In quoting this passage, Guignon begs the question by inserting in brackets the phrase 'of the public language' after 'this interpretedness' in the second sentence and by replac-ing the term 'overt expression' (*Ausgesprochenheit*) with the bracketed word 'language' in the third. This kind of tampering with the text is tendentious in the extreme, for what Heidegger is attributing a formative power to is precisely *not* language itself, but the "interpretedness" (*Ausgelegtheit*) he says language "harbors in itself" (*in sich birgt*). Granted, Heidegger does go on to refer to "the average intelligibility that already lies in the language spoken in overt expression (*Sichaussprechen*)" (*SZ* 168). But while it may be reasonable in general to assume that "overt expression" (*Ausgesprochenheit* or *Sichaussprechen*) is equivalent to *linguistic* expression, the question is whether or not Heidegger has such an equation in mind.

Guignon is right, in any case, that Heidegger's early conception of meaning and practice still has much in common with that of the later Wittgenstein. But the affinity is owing far more to their shared sense of the contextual integration of language in our everyday practices than to the idea that all meaning is somehow essentially linguistic. *Being and Time* does advance a kind of linguistic instrumentalism, after all, but it is not at all the instrumentalism of the early modern tradition, according to which linguistic meaning is a function of decontextualized associations between external signs and inner thoughts or experiences.[19] Wittgenstein argues persuasively in *Philosophical Investigations* for the incoherence of mentalistic or psychological theories of meaning, and Heidegger too rejects any philosophical account of language resting on the mere association between outer signs and inner understandings:

> Communication is never anything like a transport of experiences, for example opinions and wishes, from the interior of one subject to the interior of another.... In discoursing, Dasein *ex*-presses itself or speaks *out* (*spricht sich* aus), not because it is first encapsulated as an "interior" over against an exterior, but because as being-in-the-world it is, in its understanding, already "outside." (*SZ* 162)

Heidegger's instrumentalism is not mentalistic, then, but pragmatic, and it warrants comparison with Wittgenstein's own observations concerning the practical heterogeneity of our various uses of language: "Think of the tools in a tool-box: there is a hammer, pliers, a saw, a screw-driver, a rule, a glue-pot, glue, nails and screws. – The functions of words are as diverse as the functions of these objects."[20]

Similarly, when Heidegger says that "words accrue to significations," it is by no means clear that what he has in mind is anything like reference or denotation. For recall that significations (*Bedeutungen*) in Heidegger's sense are not occurrent objects, but practical meanings, pragmatic connections among the with-which, the in-which, the toward-this, the in-order-to, and the for-the-sake-of-which that together constitute the "referential" totality or context of significance (*Bedeutsamkeit*) (see *SZ* §18). So, for example, when a child learns to say "milk," the

---

[19] I therefore agree with Blattner's reply to Guignon that Heidegger's conception of language in *Being and Time* is a kind of "derivativism," according to which "language is derivative of some more basic aspect of being-in-the-world." Blattner, *Heidegger's Temporal Idealism*, 69. As I argue later, however, I think Blattner misunderstands the dimension of being-in-the-world from which language derives, namely, discourse.

[20] Wittgenstein, *Philosophical Investigations*, §11.

intelligibility of the word does not just consist in a free-floating reference to the object milk. The word instead finds a functional role in an
already intelligible nexus of cartons, bottles, refrigerators, acts of re-
questing, demanding, searching, drinking, and satisfying thirst. A word
"accrues" to a signification, that is, not by referring to a bare object, but
by being an integrated part of a practice, a custom, an institution, just
as Wittgenstein says.[21] So, even if Heidegger was tempted in *Being and
Time* to assimilate words and sentences to the equipment otherwise situating our everyday activity,[22] he was still arguably in the neighborhood
of Wittgenstein's later conception of meaning and linguistic practice as
belonging to a broadly contextualized "form of life" (*Lebensform*).[23]

Guignon's distinction between instrumentalism and constitutivism,
then, fails to capture Heidegger's ambivalent remarks about language
in *Being and Time*. But even if Guignon is wrong to accord language the
same constitutive status that Heidegger attributes to discourse, he may
be right to regard the two as very closely intertwined. Language, after
all, provides Heidegger with his prime source of examples whenever
he mentions discourse in *Being and Time*. Moreover, what I am calling the linguistic model does not require that discourse be identical
or coextensive with language, only that it be very closely related to it,
perhaps by anticipating grammatical and illocutionary structures, pre-
figuring linguistic forms in the prelinguistic background of practical
significance.

And this is admittedly what Heidegger himself seems to suggest. In
§34, for example, he says of discourse, "Belonging to it as constitutive moments are: what the discourse is about (what is talked about)
(*das Beredete*), what is said (*das Geredete*) as such,[24] communication

---

[21] Ibid., §§198–9, inter alia.

[22] All Heidegger in fact offers in this regard is a series of rhetorical questions: "In the end,
philosophical research must resolve to ask what mode of being belongs to language in
general. Is it an intraworldly available [piece of] equipment, or does it have Dasein's
kind of being, or is it neither? What kind of being does language have, such that it can
be 'dead'? What does it mean ontologically for a language to grow and decay?" (*SZ* 166).
What these remarks suggest, I take it, is that language has something like Dasein's mode
of being, inasmuch as it is just an aspect of Dasein itself, who lives and dies. Granted,
plants and animals "grow and decay," too, but Heidegger gives no other indication that
the organic metaphor would be the right one for understanding language ontologically.

[23] Wittgenstein, ibid., §§19, 23, 241, pp. 174, 226.

[24] Heidegger distinguishes between "*what* is said" (was *geredet ist*), or "the said" (*das Gesagte*),
and "what is talked about" (*worüber geredet wird*) already in §7B on "The concept of *logos*"
(*SZ* 32).

(*Mitteilung*) and intimation (*Bekundung*)" (*SZ* 162).[25] Discourse, apparently, consists essentially in *saying* something *about* something *to* someone. This threefold distinction between communication, what is said, and what is talked about is a distant cousin of distinctions drawn by philosophers like Bolzano, Frege, and Husserl. Bolzano distinguishes between spoken or mental propositions, that is, speech acts or subjective ideas (*Vorstellungen*); objective ideas and what he calls "propositions in themselves" (*Sätze an sich*); and finally, the objects of ideas and propositions.[26] Similarly, Frege distinguishes between a linguistic term and its subjective psychological connotations; the term's "sense" (*Sinn*); and finally, the term's "meaning," or reference (*Bedeutung*).[27] And Husserl distinguishes in much the same way between linguistic signs and their function of intimating the "act-quality" or "thetic character" of a speaker's intentions, for example her intention to communicate; the "act-matter" or noematic core or sense (*Sinn*) of an intentional state; and finally, objects and states of affairs in the world. Heidegger's account of discourse and meaning in *Being and Time* is radically removed from the tradition of these theories, in particular the Platonist tendency they share in reifying ideal semantic content over against its realization in concrete discursive acts. Nevertheless, his sketch of the structure of discourse in this passage seems to echo the distinctions Bolzano, Frege, and Husserl draw, at least formally. And it is no accident that this threefold distinction maps almost exactly onto Heidegger's tripartite account of assertion (*Aussage*) as involving three corresponding elements:

---

[25] Why does Heidegger list both communication and intimation (*Bekundung*) as elements of discourse? I think he is echoing the distinction Husserl draws in §7 of the First Logical Investigation between the purely expressive capacity of words and their "intimating function" (*kundgebende Funktion*). Speech involves the communication of objective meanings, but it also involves an "intimation" (*Kundgabe*) of the subjective attitudes and intentions situating those meanings in their pragmatic context. When I assert that "Grass is green," for instance, I express a proposition, but I also intimate that I believe it, just as when I ask a question, I intimate, though I do not assert, that I want to know the answer (*LU* II/1, 33). What linguistic expressions intimate, that is, is the "act-quality" of one's intention, or what Husserl later called the "thetic character" or "positing character" (*Setzungscharakter*) of an intentional act (see Chapter 2). But the terms that appear in *Being and Time* here are only an echo, not an endorsement, of Husserl's theory, since Heidegger rejects Husserl's intentionalism, according to which linguistic meaning can be carved off from its communicative context and remain exclusively a function of the speaker's private expressive intentions.

[26] Bolzano, *Wissenschaftslehre*, §§19, 48–9.

[27] Frege, "On Sense and Meaning" and "Thoughts" in *Collected Papers on Mathematics, Logic, and Philosophy.*

"pointing-out" (*Aufzeigen*), predication, and communication.[28] By offering this account of assertion in §33 and then following it up in §34 with a neatly homologous description of discourse as constituted by an "about-which" (*Worüber*), "something said" (*das Gesagte*), and communication (*SZ* 161–2), Heidegger invites us to understand discourse as something like a prelinguistic set of conditions precisely anticipating the semantic and pragmatic structures of language.

But this is obviously misleading, since Heidegger says repeatedly that discourse and interpretation are more basic than assertion, that assertions often distort and conceal the true content of discourse, that assertion is but one "derivative mode of interpretation," and that the Greeks misinterpreted discourse (*logos*) as assertion and misidentified truth with the truth of assertions (*SZ* 32, 36, 149, 153–62, 165, 214, 223–6). The challenge, then, is to understand discourse as the existential basis of language and linguistic practice without thereby reducing it to a mere protolinguistic or quasilinguistic foreshadowing of all and only essentially linguistic phenomena. After all, finding in discourse nothing more than a prefiguration of language threatens to trivialize Heidegger's discussion by rendering the concept itself redundant. For why not then just describe the same semantic and pragmatic phenomena and extend the term 'language' to include whatever incipient structures precede its eventual emergence in our practices and behaviors?

The Pragmatic Model

Other readers of *Being and Time*, intent on finding in Heidegger's notion of discourse something fundamentally different from language, if only to prevent its putative grounding of language from collapsing into a tautology, have been led to divorce the concept from anything even remotely resembling grammatical or illocutionary structure. They therefore advance what I shall call the *pragmatic model*.

Following Haugeland, for example, Dreyfus opts to "translate *Rede* by 'telling,' keeping in mind the sense of telling as in being able to tell the

---

[28] Somewhat confusingly, Heidegger lists these as three "senses" or "meanings" of the *word* 'assertion' (*SZ* 154). What he means, I take it, is not that the term is ambiguous, but that these three aspects are all implied by the concept, which is to say they are the constitutive features of assertions generally. It is not as if some assertions just point something out without predicating or communicating, while others predicate or communicate without pointing anything out. An assertion may *fail* to refer or communicate and still be an assertion, but this is to be understood as a degenerate case.

time, or tell the difference between kinds of nails."[29] To tell, according
to Haugeland, is just to "respond differentially,"[30] which needn't have
anything to do with language. Consequently, "without expression, I can
tell your pawn from my rook, that the rook is threatened, and what to do
about it."[31] In the same vein Dreyfus writes, "A surgeon does not have
words for all the ways he cuts, or a chess master for all the patterns he can
tell apart and the types of move he makes in response."[32] And although
he concedes that "The language Heidegger uses" in his discussion of
discourse "is shot through with linguistic suggestions," William Blattner
tries to explain away the communicative dimension of discourse by
reducing it to something purely pragmatic. On this view, even walking
down the sidewalk is essentially discursive, for "As Smith walks on the
sidewalk, he makes known that sidewalks are for walking on."[33] Indeed,
"Every act of walking on a sidewalk tends publicly to communicate, that
is, make known, that sidewalks are to be walked upon," just as "Walking
in the street makes publicly known that streets are for walking in." Even
in our most private or solitary moments, we are constantly discoursing,
just by skillfully differentiating the equipment we use and the tasks we
pursue. Thus, "As Reiss sits in her mountain retreat writing a novel, she
makes known or manifest the workshop of the author. She writes with
the computer, thus, as it were, stating publicly that computers are to be
written with."[34] Discourse, then, is just "communicatively differentiatory
comportment."[35]

I think this minimal pragmatic account fails to do justice to the semantic and illocutionary structures Heidegger plainly has in mind in
his account of discourse, though admittedly many passages in *Being and
Time* seem to support a fully pragmatic, nonsemantic reading. For example, Heidegger introduces the term 'discourse' in §7 when he proposes
that, contrary to its customary philosophical interpretation, "the basic
meaning of *logos* is discourse," which "means the same as *dēloun,* to make
manifest what is 'at issue,' what is talked about, in talk" (*wovon in der Rede
'die Rede' ist*) (*SZ* 32).[36] The discussion of *logos* in §7 supports Blattner's
contention that we should not infer from the linguistic associations

---

[29] Dreyfus, *Being-in-the-World,* 215.
[30] Haugeland, "Heidegger on Being a Person," 17.
[31] Haugeland, "Dasein's Disclosedness," 44 n39.
[32] *Being-in-the-World,* 215.   [33] Blattner, *Heidegger's Temporal Idealism,* 72.
[34] Ibid., 73.   [35] Ibid., 75.
[36] I take some liberty with the translation here in order to capture the colloquial sense of
the German '*wovon die Rede ist.*'

of Heidegger's terminology that the phenomenon in question is itself essentially linguistic. For what is definitive of *logos,* as Heidegger conceives it, is just that it "lets something be seen (*phainesthai*)" (*SZ* 32). Moreover, as we have seen, "only *because* the function of *logos* as *apophansis* lies in letting something be seen by pointing it out (*aufweisenden Sehenlassen*) can the *logos* have the formal structure of *sunthesis*," that is, the structure of the proposition, of judgment, of assertion. Finally, "*because* the *logos* is a letting [something] be seen, *for that reason* it can be true or false" (*SZ* 33).[37] Again, the truth and falsity of assertions, and so of propositions and the propositional contents of beliefs and judgments, is parasitic on the prior disclosive capacity of *logos.*

The account of discourse proper in §34 also suggests something so general and so basic as to be distinct in principle from the semantic and illocutionary structures suggested by Heidegger's analysis in terms of something talked about, something said, and communication. To begin with, listening and keeping quiet are modes of discourse: "*Hearing* and *remaining silent* are possibilities belonging to discursive speech" (*SZ* 161; cf. 296). Listening, in particular, is not just a possibility but an essential element of discourse: "Hearing is constitutive for discoursing" (*SZ* 163). Moreover, as we shall see in Chapter 6, one of the many modes of discourse is what Heidegger describes in §§55–6 as the "call" of conscience, which one might otherwise be tempted to identify with an essentially private sphere of ethical subjectivity (*SZ* 269, 271). The strongest evidence for the pragmatic reading, however, is what looks like Heidegger's characterization of discourse as the mere complexity or differentiation of practical significance:

> Discourse is the articulation (*Artikulation*) of intelligibility. It therefore underlies interpretation and assertion. What can be articulated in assertion, thus even more primordially in discourse, we called meaning (*Sinn*). What gets articulated (*das Gegliederte*) as such in discursive articulation we call the totality of significations. This [totality] can be dissolved into significations. As the articulated [elements] of the articulable, significations are always meaningful (*sinnhaft*). (*SZ* 161)

Discourse is simply "the articulation of the intelligibility of the there" (*SZ* 161), that is, of Dasein's disclosedness. And later he repeats:

---

37 This is just to say that discourse *can* be true or false, not that it always is. Commands and requests are neither true nor false, for example. As Heidegger says, "Even a command is issued about –; a wish has its about-which. Nor does a recommendation lack an about-which" (*SZ* 162).

Discourse "articulates (*gliedert*) intelligibility" (*SZ* 271). But what exactly does the "articulation of intelligibility" amount to? What does it mean to "articulate" something?[38] For Dreyfus, "a skeleton is articulated, and so is the referential whole."[39] Does discourse, then, just consist in telling the foot bone from the leg bone, left from right, and right from wrong?

I think it cannot, for the pragmatic account of discourse fails to make sense of what Heidegger says about its specifically semantic and communicative dimensions. Indeed, it is hard to see how the solipsistic examples of communication Blattner describes (as he describes them) are genuinely communicative at all. For Heidegger, that is, discourse is not just the normative dimension of whatever purposive activities we happen to be pursuing. It is instead tied to our expressive and communicative interaction with others:

> To discourse is to articulate "meaningfully" (*Reden ist das "bedeutende" Gliedern*) the intelligibility of being-in-the-world, to which being-with belongs, and which maintains itself in each case in a definite manner of concernful being-with-one-another. This [being-with-one-another] is discursive as assenting or refusing, inviting, warning, as talking things through, consulting, recommending.... (*SZ* 161)

Blattner is right that discourse pervades our practices, that most of what we do has some discursive character. But his examples fail to show what that discursive character amounts to, in its expressive and communicative aspect. After all, the normative element that informs his account of the communicative character of discourse is already accounted for by the concept of "the one" (*das Man*), specifically Heidegger's claim that we begin by understanding even ourselves as embodying the anonymous normative authority of our received practices: "The self of everyday Dasein is the *one-self*... I am 'given' to my 'self' in the first instance in terms of, and as, the one" (*SZ* 129).

---

[38] Heidegger uses the words '*Gliederung*' and '*Artikulation*' interchangeably. I have translated both by 'articulation' (indicating the original in parentheses), since I can find no systematic distinction between them in the text. Dreyfus is mistaken in claiming that the two terms mark a distinction between the structure or, as it were, "jointedness" of practical intelligibility itself (*Gliederung*) and our making its nodes or joints manifest by discoursing, which he describes as "telling" one from another in our coping activity (*Artikulation*). See Dreyfus, *Being-in-the-World*, 215. If this was the distinction Heidegger had in mind, he could not say, as he does, that "To discourse is to articulate 'meaningfully' (*Reden ist das 'bedeutende' Gliedern*) the intelligibility of being-in-the-world" (*SZ* 161) or that discourse "articulates (*gliedert*) intelligibility" (*SZ* 271). Dreyfus's reading fails for systematic reasons, too, as I argue later. See footnote 42.

[39] Dreyfus, *Being-in-the-World*, 215.

But Blattner's claim is stronger. On his account, it is not just that we all start out with an understanding of our own actions as invested with the authority of the one; rather, we understand all our particular actions on each and every occasion as carrying with them a kind of reflexive self-endorsement *as* normatively sanctioned, *as* fitting or appropriate. But this just seems false. Even if I typically understand what I do as normal and proper, it does not follow that what I do includes as part of its own intelligibility an expression or communication of its normality or propriety, for example *that* streets are for walking in or *that* computers are to be written with. Solitary, purposive activities of the sort Blattner describes, it seems to me, typically lack any such communicative import.

Moreover, if the pragmatic model is correct, what does the concept of discourse contribute to Heidegger's account of the referential structure of significance that his notion of normatively structured practical understanding does not already describe? What does the pragmatic concept of discourse *add* to Heidegger's existential conception of understanding as competent projection into practical possibilities? If the linguistic interpretation of discourse threatens to trivialize the concept by reducing it to semantic and illocutionary structures specific to language, the pragmatic alternative is apparently in danger of letting it collapse in another direction into Heidegger's practical conception of understanding.

According to Dreyfus, for example, discourse, or what he calls "*Ontological telling*, refers to everyday coping as manifesting the articulations *already* in the referential whole which are by nature manifestable."[40] This is problematic for two reasons. First, it suggests that intelligibility is *already* "articulated" (*gegliedert*) *prior to* discourse, whereas, as we have seen, Heidegger identifies discourse with articulation (both *Gliederung* and *Artikulation*). Discourse does not *presuppose* the articulation of intelligibility; it *is* the articulation of intelligibility. The claim that discourse merely makes manifest a prior articulation of significance also runs counter to Heidegger's insistence that discourse is "equiprimordial" with disposedness and understanding. Dreyfus equivocates on this point, as we have seen.[41] When he does assign discourse a primordial role, however, he does so only by conflating it with understanding: "[T]elling refers to the way the whole current situation is Articulated *by*

---

[40] Ibid., 217 (emphasis added).   [41] See footnote 3.

coping so as to be linguistically expressible."[42] But since 'coping' is presumably also Dreyfus's term for Heidegger's concept of understanding, his account in effect collapses discourse with the merely instrumental discerning or differentiating capacities of practical skill as such. The projective character of understanding is surely what allows us to differentiate the meaningful elements in the referential context of significance and thus "tell" one thing from another. Discourse must therefore be something more than actualizing significations just by coping with them or in light of them.

The error that I suspect underlies Dreyfus's and Blattner's pure pragmatic accounts of discourse is that of supposing that if discourse is not confined to linguistic articulation, then *everything* Dasein does beyond its specifically linguistic practices also ought to exemplify what Heidegger has in mind. But this is not the case. Discourse is indeed primordial, in a certain sense perhaps even ubiquitous. It is no less basic a feature of disclosedness than disposedness and understanding; indeed, it is "constitutive" of human existence. And just as Dasein always has some mood and some understanding, so too we are in a sense always "in" discourse. But the primordiality of an existential structure does not imply that that structure will be made manifest and obvious in any and every concrete case we imagine, as we imagine it. After all, Dasein in a dreamless sleep does not provide a good example of any of the existential structures Heidegger describes in *Being and Time*. The sleeping person, if he is Dasein, will indeed be an attuned, understanding, discursive agent. But we will not be able to appreciate those aspects of his existence simply by imagining him prostrate and unconscious. So too, instances of Dasein walking down the sidewalk or using a computer are not particularly illuminating examples of discourse, though of course anyone doing such things will as a matter of fact be standing in abiding discursive relations of some kind to others. What then does it mean to stand in discursive relations to others?

Signs and the Expressive Structure of Intelligibility

What do our abiding discursive relations to others consist in, if not our specifically linguistic practices or the bare pragmatic structure of

---

[42] Ibid., 217 (emphasis added). Note Dreyfus's distinction between (lowercase) "articulation" (*Gliederung*) and (uppercase) "Articulation" (*Artikulation*). As I have said, Dreyfus leans on this verbal distinction in a way that, as far as I can tell, Heidegger does not. See footnote 38.

everyday intelligibility? To answer this question, we have to get back to the phenomenon motivating the things Heidegger says about discourse in *Being and Time*. What is he trying to describe, if not language or purposive activity?

As it happens, I believe Dreyfus's example of *telling time* opens a path back to the phenomenon. For telling time is not just a matter of telling one thing from another. To tell time is rather to know how to interpret – or in the broad, nonliteral sense, *read* – what Heidegger calls "signs," whether natural indications of the time such as shadows and the positions of heavenly bodies or artifacts such as sundials and clocks.[43] All such indicators, natural or artificial, Heidegger argues in §17, are crucially different from any other kind of available thing equipping our practical environment. Signs are unique kinds of tools, but they are tools nonetheless, for they do not belong to a different ontological category from equipment generally. It is the *ontically* distinctive function of signs to indicate, show, or make manifest, but "showing is not the *ontological* structure of the sign as equipment" (*SZ* 78, emphasis added). But although signs are indeed tools, they are unique inasmuch as they function *not* by receding inconspicuously into the background of our practical attention, as equipment generally does, but by standing out explicitly and *showing* something: "In our concernful dealings, equipment for showing (*Zeig-zeug*) gets used in a *special* (*vorzüglich*) way" (*SZ* 79); and Heidegger elsewhere refers to "the character of a special presence that is constitutive for being a sign" (*PGZ* 285). What is special about signs, according to Heidegger, is that they show not just occurrent and available things, but also the *how* of the intelligibility of the equipmental context itself, and hence the ontological contours of the world as

---

[43] I say "what Heidegger calls 'signs' " because many of the things linguists and semioticians would call signs Heidegger would not. This is because Heidegger's account of signs is phenomenological, not formal or semiotic. Consequently, only what actually stands out conspicuously in our dealings with things will count as a sign in Heidegger's sense. For a more detailed discussion, see my "The Conspicuousness of Signs in *Being and Time*." Note that Heidegger does not exclude natural signs from his concept. Indeed, in remarking on the astonishing diversity of signs, he refers explicitly to symptoms (*Anzeichen*), distinguishing characteristics (*Kennzeichen*), tracks and traces (*Spuren*), and remnants or vestiges (*Überrest*) (*SZ* 78). I think Heidegger does deny the naturalness of the meaning of natural signs, however. Smoke "means" fire, but only in virtue of the conventions governing our *use* of it as an indicator of fire. So, although nonhuman animals may recognize things, and anticipate other things causally related to them, Heidegger thinks they do not use things as tools or signs as we do. This is because there is for them no difference between an appropriate and an inappropriate use of anything, that is, there are no normative conventions governing the use of things.

such. Signs, that is, are *interpretive* tools. For interpretation consists in *showing how*, and showing how is precisely what signs do. A sign, or more precisely our use of signs, is therefore part and parcel of what I have called demonstrative practice.

Heidegger's example is an automobile's turn signal. A turn signal is a tool, and its serviceability consists in showing something, but what it shows is not an object. The turn signal does not show anything, does not *mean* anything, apart from our knowing how to attend to it and deal with it. For, as Heidegger points out, "Even if we turn our glance in the direction that the arrow shows, and look at something occurrent in the region shown, even then the sign is not authentically encountered" (*SZ* 79).[44] What the turn signal does, rather, is explicitly orient me with respect to all the various things in the situation: the driver, the car, the traffic. The signal affords me "an explicit 'overview' " (*eine ausdrückliche 'Übersicht'*) of the situation, not from some disengaged perspective, but in the midst of all its immediate practical demands. The sign does not just fit inconspicuously into an interlocking nexus of equipment; it organizes my sense of the situation as a whole:

> This circumspective overview does not grasp what is available; what it achieves is rather an orientation in our environment. . . . Signs of the kind we have described let what is available be encountered; more precisely, they let some context of it become accessible in such a way that our concernful dealings take on an orientation and hold it secure. (*SZ* 79)

Heidegger even suggests that signs have a kind of transcendental function in their capacity to highlight or organize an entire complex of equipment by establishing our circumspective orientation within it. Signs are fantastically general in their possible serviceability. To use another example of Heidegger's (which he borrows from Husserl),[45] a knot tied in a handkerchief can serve as a reminder of nearly anything, just as nearly anything can function as a sign. Signs are not embedded in their equipmental contexts in the way equipment generally is. Rather, by illuminating an entire equipmental context as such and helping us navigate through it, signs disclose the ontological structure of the world itself, namely, its worldliness: "A sign is not a thing that stands to another thing in the relation of showing; it is rather *a piece of equipment*

---

[44] Heidegger's point here warrants some comparison with Wittgenstein's claim in *Philosophical Investigations* §198 that "a person goes by a sign-post only in so far as there exists a regular use of sign-posts, a custom."

[45] See *LU* II/1, §2.

that explicitly raises a totality of equipment into circumspection, so that together with it the worldly character of the available announces itself" (*SZ* 79–80). It is not just in the wake of practical disturbances such as equipmental breakdowns, then, that the worldliness of the world manifests itself explicitly for us. Signs make manifest the worldliness of the world by casting light on the organization of the practical world as a whole and orienting us within it generally. How are signs able to do this?

What Heidegger describes as the unique practical serviceability and the ontically privileged status of signs, I believe, allows us to understand his conception of discourse. For consider what it is that allows signs to function interpretively as they do. For the turn signal to succeed in signaling a turn, we must already have a shared understanding not just of the equipmental context of cars, streets, and traffic, or of purposive acts such as driving, turning, and crossing the street. We must also know how to respond to and deal with appropriate and meaningful interpretive gestures themselves appropriately and meaningfully. The turn signal *shows* the *how* of the situation, and it does so in a way that is governed by the same standards and norms of the one that govern our demonstrative practices generally. So too, my response to the sign cannot be right and proper if I simply absorb it into the purposive structure of my own solitary activity. I must instead know how to acknowledge and reply to the gesture with meaningful and appropriate gestures of my own.

There are, in short, two fundamentally different dimensions constituting the normative structure of significance. There is, to begin with, the normativity governing our purposive activities as such, informing our ways and means of acting (our with-whiches and in-whiches) with reference both to our goals (our toward-thises and in-orders-to) and to the *point* of what we do, that is, to *who* we are (our for-the-sake-of-which). But there is also a dimension of normativity cutting across the first, governing not our pursuit of ends as such, but rather our interpretative expressions and gestures, which manage to make manifest the purposive structure of intelligibility itself. There are norms not just for *doing,* that is, but also for *showing* and *saying,* and I believe Heidegger wants to insist that the latter cannot be reduced to the former. This normativity specific to interpretation, governing the intelligibility of demonstrative practices as such, is what Heidegger means by 'discourse.'

Discourse is in this sense *the* hermeneutic condition par excellence. Every saying is in fact a doing, of course, just as the *showing how* of interpretation is a "development" or "elaboration" of the *knowing how* of understanding. Understanding is a condition of interpretation, but it is not the only one. We should not infer from the dependence of interpretation on understanding, that is, that the intelligibility of understanding as such exhausts the meaningfulness peculiar to interpretive gestures and demonstrative practice. For the proprieties and improprieties specific to expressive practice are not reducible to those of practical understanding in its merely purposive orientation.

'Discourse,' then, is Heidegger's word for the underlying normativity governing comportments that are not simply end-seeking, but instead manage to *express* what we might otherwise simply understand in its purposive aspect. The "articulation of intelligibility" that constitutes discourse is therefore not just the purposive structure, the differentiation, the skeletal "jointedness" of the referential totality itself, as Dreyfus and Blattner propose. It does not lie simply in our instituting or discerning the pragmatic structure of significance as such. *Articulation,* in Heidegger's sense, is rather the susceptibility of that pragmatic structure to meaningful and appropriate interpretation, which is to say *expression.* Our everyday world is structured not just pragmatically, but expressively as well. For there are proper and improper, sensible and senseless, common and uncommon *ways* of making our understanding explicit in demonstrative practice. There is always an indefinitely wide range of instrumentally effective means of conveying what I mean, only some of which will strike you as sensible and correct, given our shared repertoire of expressive comportments. There are purely discursive norms governing the expression of intelligibility, that is, just as there are purely pragmatic norms governing our purposive activity at large.

We are now perhaps in a better position to appreciate the pervasiveness of discourse in everyday intelligibility, in spite of the fact that not everything we do is as discursive as, say, wrinkling our noses, shrugging our shoulders, or using language. Discourse is ubiquitous not because it has no essential connection to explicitly expressive gestures of that sort, but because every intelligible situation Dasein finds itself in is intelligible in two complementary ways: first, in its directedness to purely pragmatic ends; and second, in the expressive possibilities that lie open to us in making our understanding explicit, whether to others or to ourselves. Of course, the way anything manages to be expressively intelligible is by conforming to the public and anonymous norms governing our shared background practices. Discourse, that is, is always essentially beholden to the normative authority of "the one" (*das Man*).

Deliberate Speech Acts and Communicative Rapport

On my reading, then, Heidegger's notion of discourse implies a fundamental distinction between two kinds of meaning, or rather two mutually irreducible dimensions in the structure of significance. This distinction between discursive and pragmatic intelligibility, which I am attributing to Heidegger, however, differs sharply from traditional distinctions between action and language, doing and saying, or natural and conventional meaning.

Consider, for example, Paul Grice's distinction between the natural meaning associated with causes and effects on the one hand, and what he calls the "nonnatural meaning" (or "meaning$_{NN}$") of utterances and gestures on the other. Although Grice considers and rejects what he calls "causal" accounts of meaning$_{NN}$,[46] his own theory arguably remains within a broadly causal paradigm itself. On his account, that is, we use utterances to express meanings with the intention of bringing others to a recognition of our intention to express those meanings by those means.[47] This account moves in the right direction beyond the crude notion that meaningful utterances are simply those intended to cause beliefs in the minds of others, but it too passes over the phenomenon of discourse as such by assimilating expressive comportment generally to deliberate speech acts driven by explicit communicative intentions.

So, Grice suggests, whereas I may fail a student, intend to cause him distress by doing so, "and even intend him to recognize my intention," still my failing him does not "mean$_{NN}$" anything. On the other hand, "if I cut someone in the street, I do feel inclined to assimilate this to the cases of meaning$_{NN}$," since "I could not reasonably expect him to be distressed (indignant, humiliated) unless he recognized my intention to affect him in this way."[48] It seems to me, on the contrary, that I could reasonably expect him to feel indignant, even humiliated, at my overt recklessness and self-importance, and even more so upon recognizing that I intended, in part, to annoy or offend him, just as the student recognizes that I intend him harm by giving him a bad grade. To be more than just a causal indication of my intentions, that is, my gesture

---

[46] Grice, "Meaning," in *Studies in the Way of Words*, 215–17.

[47] "'*A* meant$_{NN}$ something by *x*' is (roughly) equivalent to '*A* intended the utterance of *x* to produce some effect in an audience by means of the recognition of this intention.'" Ibid., 220.

[48] Ibid., 220.

need not rise to the level of explicit communicative intention definitive of meaning$_{NN}$. For I can reasonably expect his indignant response even if I do not intend him to understand that the purpose of my gesture was to offend him. Assuming that I did not just fail to notice him, my cutting him off in the street has an undeniable expressive and communicative character, but what I express and communicate in it may be precisely how little I care about people like him and what they think of what I do. Far from my needing to intend him to understand my act as expressing my intention, the gesture could be discursively and not just causally significant precisely in my indifference to his reaction and his understanding.

It seems to me, then, that Grice's distinction between natural and nonnatural meaning is too blunt to capture the manifest expressive dimension of much of what we do.[49] For while our actions that are not overtly communicative aim pragmatically at in-orders-to and for-the-sakes-of-which, many of them also carry discursive significance even when we do not intend them to reveal our intentions. Moreover, the fact that discourse is distinct from and irreducible to instrumental action is the reason we can never conceive of language as mere equipment. What are words *for*? Presumably, for expressing and communicating something. But if we then describe expression and communication themselves in instrumental terms, we find ourselves lapsing into the kind of intentionalistic analysis Grice favors. But the really striking fact about discourse is that it is not essentially *for* anything at all. It does as a matter of fact play a role in our pursuit of any number of different pragmatic ends, of course. When I ask you to pass the salt, my utterance is instrumental in my getting the salt. But discourse is in no way exhausted by the instrumental functions it serves. Discourse figures in the accomplishment of innumerable ends, but no end in particular defines it in the way cleaning defines brooms and mops or writing and drawing define pencils and paper. Discourse is not *for* anything, and in that sense it cuts across, though it is woven and integrated into, the purposive structure of significance.

[49] Grice concedes that his distinction is not exhaustive, but I think he underestimates how much of our discursive comportment it fails to capture: "I do not want to maintain that *all* our uses of 'mean' fall easily, obviously, and tidily into one of the two groups I have distinguished; but I think that in most cases we should be at least fairly strongly inclined to assimilate a use of 'mean' to one group rather than to the other." Ibid., 215. What I am urging is that we ought to resist that inclination, since it simplifies and as a result obscures the phenomena.

John Searle has criticized Grice for conflating what Austin calls "illocutionary" and "perlocutionary" acts, that is, speech acts proper and acts meant merely to produce effects in the attitudes of hearers.[50] Searle points out that I may "mean" something while remaining quite indifferent to the effects my utterance has on my listeners. For Searle, then, although we cannot understand speech acts simply in terms of their perlocutionary effect, we can and must understand them in terms of their intended illocutionary effect, namely, the hearer's understanding of what the speaker means. Understanding, he points out, "is not the sort of effect that is included in Grice's examples. It is not a perlocutionary effect."[51] But it is, for Searle, an effect nonetheless. And construing discursive understanding as an *effect* only, and not also as a *condition* of language use, obscures the way in which discourse already figures in our shared sense of expressive possibilities prior to the performance of any particular deliberate speech act. Discursive understanding is not created ex nihilo by speech acts themselves, after all; it is rather what conditions linguistic artifacts and deliberate speech, rendering them meaningful in the first place. So, although Searle improves on the Gricean account by tying the speaker's meaning to the public linguistic conventions determining the meanings of the sentences speakers use, he is evidently committed to the same underlying causal and intentionalistic presuppositions that deflected Grice's theory from the phenomenon of discourse as such. Searle analyzes discourse as the production of an understanding by means of the performance of speech acts, whose meaning, though informed by a commonly intelligible language, remains a function of the intentions of the speaker.

In contrast to Grice and Searle, Charles Taylor has offered an illuminating account of the discursive articulation of intelligibility that precedes and conditions deliberate speech in his description of what he calls the "expressive," as opposed to the "designative," dimension of meaning. In Taylor's example, you and I find ourselves traveling together, it is oppressively hot, and I turn to you and say, "Whew, it's hot." The sentence does not tell you anything you do not already know, nor was my point to convey information of any kind, neither that *it is hot* nor just that *I feel hot*. Indeed, although Taylor does not say so, the meaning of my gesture is strictly indeterminate, not just ambiguous, with respect to those two propositions. For neither proposition spells out exactly

---

[50] Searle, *Speech Acts*, 44, 46–9.   [51] Ibid., 47.

what my gesture conveys; indeed, each is too specific, too finely articulated, and so says at once more and less than what I mean. Rather than reporting a fact of any kind, Taylor writes, "What the expression has done here is to create a rapport between us, the kind of thing which comes about when we do what we call striking up a conversation." What Taylor regards specifically as an achievement of language, or "human symbolic communication in general," as he puts it, is what Heidegger attributes to discourse in its prelinguistic, even presymbolic manifestations. "Language," according to Taylor – *discourse,* Heidegger would say instead – "creates what one might call a public space, or a common vantage point from which we survey the world together. . . . [I]t serves to found public space, that is, to place certain matters before *us.*"

The epistemological tradition has been blind to this public space of expressive and communicative rapport, Taylor adds, since it "privileges a reconstruction of knowledge as a property of the critical individual" and "makes us take the monological observer's standpoint not just as a norm, but somehow as the way things really are with the subject."[52] Taylor charges Grice's theory of meaning with precisely that monological bias, for in focusing narrowly as it does on the individual subject understood as a kind of solipsistic observer, it in effect drives a wedge between speakers and hearers by reducing meaning to sophisticated self-referential intentions to cause effects in the minds of others. Moreover, its recognition of the importance of a publicly intelligible language notwithstanding, Searle's account, too, tends to conceal the phenomenon of discourse by construing understanding as an effect brought about by speech acts, rather than as a prior condition of their intelligibility. What Grice and Searle fail to describe, then, is discourse itself, as distinct from its specific realization in deliberate language use.

But if communication is not the kind of causal transaction that Grice and Searle describe, if it is not, as Heidegger puts it, "a transport of experiences . . . from the interior of one subject to the interior of another" (*SZ* 162), what is it? In §33 and §34 Heidegger appeals to the literal meaning of the word '*Mitteilung*' to suggest that, prior to any mere transfer of information, communication consists in *sharing* an

---

[52] Taylor, *Human Agency and Language,* 259. One could argue further, as I believe Heidegger would, that the very conception of human beings as "subjects" already obscures the phenomenon of the public expressive space of discourse in which human beings dwell together as members of a community and as inhabitants of a world, rather than as minds possessing and trading pieces of knowledge and information.

orientation and an understanding *with* others. Assertion, for example, as letting someone see something with us (*Mitsehenlassen*), "shares with (*teilt mit*) the other the entity pointed out in its determinate character. What is 'shared' is a common seeing and *being-toward* what is pointed out" (*SZ* 155). Of course, not all communication involves making assertions, and even in their absence things remain intelligible to us, just as we remain mutually intelligible to one another:

> Assertoric "communication," reporting information for example, is a special case of communication grasped in a fundamental existential way. In the latter, the articulation of being-with-one-another understandingly is constituted. It brings about the "sharing" (*Teilung*) of disposedness-with (*Mitbefindlichkeit*) and of an understanding of being-with.... Dasein-with is essentially already manifest in disposedness-with and in understanding-with (*Mitverstehen*). Being-with is *shared* "explicitly" in discourse, that is, it already *is,* but is unshared in not having been taken up and appropriated. (*SZ* 162)

Communication is an essential element of discourse, then, but is not confined to overt speech acts. Rather, the communication involved in discourse consists in our *sharing* affects and understandings *with* others. Dasein's being is always being-with (*Mitsein*), Heidegger insists, but *sharing* our being-with explicitly with one another constitutes a distinct aspect of disclosedness, over and beyond the mere fact of social community and pragmatically coherent interaction. The communicative dimension of mutual disposedness and understanding is crucial to an appreciation of the specific contribution discourse makes to the existential analytic, then, in addition to the general concept of being-with. Only in discursive communication is being-with explicitly shared, Heidegger says, and so "taken up and appropriated."

How then are we to understand this distinction between the mere sociality of being-with and its being explicitly *shared*? First, negatively speaking, to say that in discourse we come to share our being-with explicitly, to take it up and appropriate it, is not to say that discourse is a secondary or derivative mode of being-with. Discourse, as we have seen, is not a secondary or derivative mode of any other existential structure; it is a primitive constituent of disclosedness in its own right. Positively, what is distinctive about communicative sharing, over and beyond being-with as such, is its mutual transparency. A truly shared disposedness or understanding involves a shared understanding of ourselves *as* having and sharing that disposedness or understanding. Our

understanding is in that case not a mere combination or your understanding and mine, but is genuinely collective.

It may be tempting to analyze collective attitudes in terms of the
individual attitudes of those who have them, so that our sharing an attitude would just consist in my having the attitude and your having the
attitude, together with the explicit beliefs we have about each other.
For example, if we collectively believe that *p*, then I believe *p* and you
believe *p*, and I believe that you believe it, and you believe that I be-
lieve it, and I believe that you believe that I believe it, and so on ad
infinitum. But as Searle has argued, such accounts fail to capture the
peculiar transparency of collective intentionality. Searle's conclusion is
confirmed by the difference he points out between genuine cooperative
activity and the mere coordination or synchronization of actions. In the
case of real cooperation, or what Heidegger would call the "sharing of
being-with in discourse," your comportment and my comportment are
immediately intelligible to each of us as *our* doing something, not as the
mere summation of *your* doing it and *my* doing it. Of course, our doing
something cooperatively entails that we are each performing some part
of the task, but not that we are acting separately or that we understand
our actions as isolated, albeit coordinated. Instead, my contribution to
the task makes sense to me only as part of our shared effort; my own
actions are not intelligible to me by themselves or even as the basis of
our collective activity. If you and I are lifting a heavy piece of furniture
together, for example, it is not as if I understand that I am lifting it and
that you are lifting it, and that you understand the same thing. Rather,
my lifting it makes sense to me only as part of *our* lifting it.[53]

The mere coordination of social activity is what Heidegger seems to
have in mind in his description of "the deficient modes of solicitude
(*Fürsorge*)," that is, our relative indifference to one another in the course
of our daily routine:

> Being for or against or without one another, passing one another by,
> not mattering to one another are all possible forms of solicitude. And
> precisely these last mentioned modes of deficiency and indifference
> characterize everyday and average being-with-one-another. These modes
> of being exhibit again the character of inconspicuousness and obvi-
> ousness that belongs as much to everyday intraworldly being-there-with
> (*Mitdasein*) of others as to the availability of the equipment that is our
> daily concern. (*SZ* 121)

---

[53] See Searle, "Collective Intentions and Actions" and *The Construction of Social Reality*, 23–6.

Heidegger cautions us, of course, not to confuse this kind of social indifference with any conception of others as mere objects or equipment. We take other human beings for granted, just as we do our familiar tools and practical environments, but we do not simply make use of them as we do of available things. Except in extreme degenerate cases, even our most indifferent social attitudes are still *social* attitudes, and in them others do not just sink into the background as so much available stuff, but remain intelligible to us as human beings.

What the phenomenon of neutral or indifferent social coexistence suggests instead is the difference between being-with as such and discursive communication. For it is only in discourse that we can be said to share collectively whatever attitudes we might otherwise separately hold in common as individuals. Discourse establishes *rapport,* as Taylor says. More precisely, discourse just *is* the rapport we always already have with others. It is the space of intelligible expression in which we share dispositions and understandings.

Our disposedness to and understanding of the expressive significance of things, including other human beings, is what Heidegger calls "hearing" (*Hören*), and "Hearing is constitutive for discoursing. . . . Indeed, hearing constitutes Dasein's primary and authentic openness for its ownmost ability-to-be, as in hearing the voice of a friend, which every Dasein carries with it. Dasein hears because it understands" (*SZ* 163). The existential ubiquity of discourse is especially clear in our most intimate and enduring human relationships, those sustained by ongoing communicative rapport, even in the other's absence. But more generally, discourse is an appropriation or cultivation of being-with: "Listening to one another, in which being-with develops itself (*sich ausbildet*), can take the form of following, going with, or the privative modes of not listening, resisting, defying, turning away" (*SZ* 163). Comportments like these are not just actions aiming at ends, but are discursive inasmuch as they communicate and express commitment and devotion, or alternately refusal and rejection. Following, not listening, turning away – these are not just acts that achieve a goal; rather, they express and communicate something. To follow is to consent or obey, for example, not just to track and observe. So too, turning away is not just removing or reorienting oneself physically, but rejecting, surrendering, abandoning, dismissing.

In describing the discursive character of hearing, Heidegger also refers to listening or hearkening (*Horchen*), which he says is "more primordial phenomenally than what is defined 'in the first instance' as hearing in psychology, the sensing of tones and the perception of sounds. Hearkening, too, has the kind of being of a hearing that understands" (SZ 163). The kind of hearing that constitutes discourse involves a kind of understanding of and rapport with others. To say that it is "more primordial" than mere auditory perception is not to say that the latter is impossible in the absence of the former, or else we would have to conclude that cats and dogs cannot really hear anything, which is absurd. The point is rather that human perception is always imbued with understanding, so that *what* we actually hear is nothing like sensations, or even meaningless noises, but real-life, full-fledged things that we understand by dealing with them: "What we hear 'in the first instance' is never noises and complexes of sounds, but the creaking wagon, the motorcycle. One hears the column on the march, the north wind, the woodpecker tapping, the crackling fire" (SZ 163). Since, as I said earlier, I do not think that Heidegger is trying to account for biologically general conditions of intentionality, I think he is not here suggesting that auditory perception can be intentional only on a prior basis of practical understanding, but only that the intentionality of *our* perceptual experience is inextricably bound up with and conditioned by an understanding that is uniquely human. I shall have more to say in the next chapter about the receptivity of hearing and what Heidegger calls the "call of conscience" (SZ 269, 271), a mode of discourse bearing directly on the authenticity or inauthenticity of our existence.

Communication as a Condition of Expression

My main concern in this chapter is to show that discourse is vital to Heidegger's existential analytic not just as an interesting and important feature of being-in-the-world in its own right, but as a hermeneutic condition, a condition of understanding in its explicitness, that is, in its concrete expression. What does such a claim amount to? Interpretation, I have argued, is expressed understanding, whether in our overt comportment or internalized in our mental states. I have also suggested that discourse is a kind of space of expressive possibilities, a domain of expressive comportments that it makes sense to perform in some local world.

But given that interpretation is just the expression of understanding, taken in a broad sense, then if discourse were nothing more than the expressive dimension of intelligibility, the claim that it is a condition of interpretation would be trivially true. Of course, the domain of expressive possibilities conditions our expressive comportment. The claim that discourse is a hermeneutic condition would be a tautology on my reading were it not the case that *communication* is one of its essential features. But as we have seen, Heidegger insists that discourse is essentially communicative. It is far from trivial, then, to say that all interpretation, all explicit understanding, is discursive, since that means that communication is in effect a condition of expression. This, then, is the substance of the claim that discourse is a hermeneutic condition: There is expression at all only in virtue of the communicative sharing of disposedness and understanding, that is, shared disposedness and understanding are conditions of the possibility of meaningful expressive comportment as such.

To see this point, recall what Heidegger says about the semantic structure of discourse. In addition to communication, discourse involves two distinct elements: what is talked about (*das Beredete*) and what is said (*das Geredete*). These two notions mark what I have described as a semantic gap, a distinction in principle between the contents and the objects of discourse. That distinction brings Heidegger's account close, at least formally, to the semantic tradition that precedes him in Bolzano, Frege, and Husserl, though I believe it commits him to none of the more specific details of their theories of meaning. Heidegger differs from his predecessors, for instance, in that while they tended to conceive of the objective reference of words and ideas solely as a function of their sense or content, which for its part remains autonomous and readily distinguishable from its external relations to the world, Heidegger regards meaning itself as a worldly phenomenon determined by the external orientation of our actions and attitudes in everyday practice. For Heidegger, then, it is not the internal content of discourse that determines its objects, but its external, worldly context that determines its content: "In discourse," he says, "insofar as it is genuine, *what* is said is drawn *from* what is talked about" (*SZ* 32).[54] Heidegger is an externalist about meaning.

Moreover, although he does say that the semantic distinction between content and object is essential to the structure of discourse,

---

[54] Heidegger's insistence that in discourse "*what* is said is drawn *from* what is talked about" seems irreconcilable with Cristina Lafont's claim that "The thesis that meaning determines reference is an important premise of Heidegger's philosophy, if a tacit one." Lafont, *The Linguistic Turn in Hermeneutic Philosophy*, 59. See also chapters 4 and 5 of her *Heidegger, Language, and World-Disclosure*. For a critical discussion the latter, see my "Was Heidegger a Linguistic Idealist?"

Heidegger never tries to fit his account of meaning and understanding in general into a purely semantic framework, as his predecessors did. Instead, both phenomenologically and conceptually speaking, the distinction between what is said and what is talked about emerges for Heidegger only in interpretation, that is, in our understanding something explicitly *as* something. The word 'as' in that formulation marks the semantic gap: To understand *x as y* is to understand *x* (what is talked about) explicitly under the aspect *y* (what is said of it). Understanding is an intentional phenomenon, and is therefore aspectual, since it consists in our competent use or treatment of things *as* the things they are. To understand hammers is to use them as hammers, just as understanding human beings means treating them as human beings, not just as objects or equipment. In understanding, however, the aspects under which we cope with things do not typically swing free of the things themselves, but rather constitute them as the things they are. For example, hammers just *are* those items of equipment that figure into our practices in that particular way, just as we *are* the entities defined by our understanding of our being. So too, phenomenologically speaking, our absorbed skillful practices therefore do not present such entities to us as discrete occurrent objects, cleanly distinguishable from the understandings that afford us access to them. Rather, those things are constituted by the understandings in which we uncover them. What distinguishes interpretation from understanding, then, is the emergence of an explicit phenomenological difference between *what* we understand and *how* we understand it. Only in light of this difference does it become possible to draw a conceptual distinction between semantic contents and objects of reference, for only then can we genuinely countenance different ways of understanding one and the same thing, and so too the idea that one understanding may be right and another wrong or one true and another false.

Understanding thus consists in *using as* or *treating as,* which is normative and aspectual but typically tacit and unthematic. Interpretation, by contrast, consists in *taking as* or *seeing as* (in a broad, nonliteral sense of 'seeing'). Wittgenstein invokes a similar notion of interpretation in his discussion of seeing aspects in Part II of *Philosophical Investigations.* He distinguishes two uses of the word 'see,' or more precisely two kinds of objects of seeing: objects proper on the one hand, and aspects such as similarities and differences on the other. If we see lines drawn on a page *as* an illustration of a three-dimensional box, our seeing is a kind of interpretation, or reading, of what we see: "[W]e interpret (*deuten*) it, and *see* it as we *interpret* it."[55] So too, when Jastrow's ambiguous duck–rabbit illustration oscillates between looking like a duck and looking like a rabbit, it is not the object per se that is undergoing any change, but our interpretation or reading of it: First we see it as a duck, then we see it as a rabbit.

Only when we can speak of alternative or competing aspects, then – whether continuous and enduring or dawning and shifting – does it make sense to describe our perceptual reports with the qualifier '*as* such and such.' In the course of a meal, as Wittgenstein says, I cannot sensibly look at a knife and fork and say, " 'Now I am seeing this as a knife and fork.' This expression would not be understood. – Any more than: 'Now it's a fork' or 'It can be a fork too.' " In the normal course of events a fork just *is* a fork, so it is pointless to insist that one is seeing it *as* a fork. We do not normally interpret things as the things they are, then; we just understand them by dealing with them appropriately. As Wittgenstein says, "One doesn't '*take*' what one knows as the cutlery at a meal *for* cutlery; any more than one ordinarily tries to move one's mouth as one eats, or aims at moving it."[56]

Interpretation, then, defined by the explicitness of the '*as*' of understanding, the dawning or abiding of an aspect understood as one among several ways in which *this* particular thing could be taken, is what opens up the semantic gap between the content of an understanding and its object. Although Heidegger at times seems to insist that this semantic dimension of interpretation already constitutes the structure of discourse itself, it is hard to see how it could do so without reducing discourse to something derivative of understanding, which he insists it is not (*SZ* 161). What I want to suggest, then, is that the semantic gap between content and object should be regarded as an essential structure not of discourse itself, but more specifically of interpretation. The distinction between content and object does *presuppose* discourse, in particular its communicative dimension. For it is the function of interpretive expressions to highlight aspects, to show things *as* such and such, and only in the shared understanding of communicative rapport can acts amount to expressive gestures at all, for it is only against a

---

[55] Wittgenstein, *Philosophical Investigations*, IIxi, 193. The German word *deuten* means to interpret or read, in a broad sense.

[56] Ibid., IIxi, 195.

background of communication that expressions are *intelligible as* expressions, and only by being intelligible as expressions can expressions *be* expressions.

Part of the burden of Wittgenstein's *Philosophical Investigations* was to show the incoherence of the idea of a private language, that is, a language meaningful just by standing in relation to our psychological states. Wittgenstein argues that the meaning of any given expression remains indeterminate in the absence of something like a practice, a custom, an institution.[57] Suppose I write 'S' in a diary or calendar every time I have a certain sensation. Wittgenstein says, "I will remark first of all that a definition of the sign cannot be formulated." Moreover, "What reason have we for calling 'S' the sign for a *sensation*?"[58] He could have made the same point more simply (perhaps he meant to) by showing that it is communication that establishes criteria for distinguishing expressions from nonexpressions at all. It is not just that the meanings of our expressions are underdetermined by our psychological states, but that there is nothing in those mental states as such to determine what is and what is not an expression. We might wonder, that is, whether the inscribed 'S' can be a sign or expression at all just in virtue of my writing it down whenever the sensation occurs. Perhaps it is not really an expression, but merely a component of an action. More precisely, perhaps there is no way to answer the question whether it is or is not an expression, absent some account of the communicative function the sign is supposed to serve.

Perhaps the sign plays a communicative role in an internal conversation I have with myself alone. But then how am I to distinguish my communicative from my noncommunicative gestures? The distinction seems to collapse when the gesture is no more than an integrated element in my own activity. We can talk to ourselves, of course, but doing so is like paying oneself a salary: It is perfectly possible, but only by being parasitic on a social practice involving more than just one agent.[59]

---

[57] Ibid., §§198–9, inter alia.　　　　[58] Ibid., §§258, 261.

[59] Wittgenstein himself considers this analogy in connection with ostensive definitions: "Why can't my right hand give my left hand money? – My right hand can put it into my left hand. My right hand can write a deed of gift and my left hand a receipt. – But the further practical consequences would not be those of a gift. When the left hand has taken the money from the right, etc., we shall ask: 'Well, and what of it?' And the same could be asked if a person had given himself a private definition of a word; I mean, if he has said the word to himself and at the same time has directed his attention to a sensation." Ibid., §268.

Soliloquy is parasitic on dialogue, just as self-employment is parasitic on exchange. Absent the social context, it seems, there is no way to distinguish expressive from merely purposive activity.

The point suggests itself in an example Saint Augustine uses in *De Magistro* when he asks his son, Adeodatus, "if I were completely ignorant of the meaning of the word ['walking'] and were to ask you what walking is while you were walking, how would you teach me?" Adeodatus replies, "I would do it a little bit more quickly." The response is forlorn, as Augustine points out: "Don't you know that *walking* is one thing and *hurrying* another?"[60] One lesson to draw from this, whether it is the lesson Augustine intended or not, is that there is a fundamental difference between discursive and nondiscursive gestures or comportments, and that some definite communicative conditions must obtain in order for genuine expressions or explicitations of our understanding to manifest themselves in what we do. Absent that distinction, everything we do could be construed as just so much purposive activity, and we will be forced back to the problem of discursive meaning as Grice and Searle conceive it, namely, as a problem about how some purposive acts can be speech acts, that is, acts in which we *say* and *mean* something. Rather than analyze the difference between discursive and nondiscursive acts by appealing to private intentions, as Grice and Searle do, we ought to admit that the difference is already manifest phenomenally in our overt communicative comportment with one another. It is a mistake to construe discourse as a special case of a more general, more readily intelligible phenomenon, namely, goal-oriented action. For we always already recognize expressive-communicative comportments as more than just purposive activity. The phenomenon of discourse is primitive, just as Heidegger says it is. It is not a modification of purposive action or understanding, nor can it be analyzed in terms of first-person, subjective intentions.

What I conclude, then, is that expressions are discursive, and so become expressions at all, only in our shared recognition and treatment of them as such in communication. Expression presupposes communication. Discourse is therefore a hermeneutic condition, indeed *the* condition of interpretation par excellence, for it is in virtue of the communicative dimension of discourse that interpretations make understandings explicit by bringing them to expression, linguistic or otherwise. It is thanks to the communicative dimension of discourse that

[60] Augustine, *The Teacher*, 3.6.

expressive gestures *express*, rather than simply enact or embody, the understandings animating and informing our practices.

Truth as Correspondence, Truth as Unconcealment

Confusion and controversy have surrounded Heidegger's ontological account of truth ever since its initial appearance in §44 of *Being and Time*.[61] There Heidegger seems to dismiss the traditional concept of truth as an agreement or correspondence between reality and representations, mental or linguistic. In its stead, or so it appears, he advances an alternative conception of truth as the "uncoveredness" of entities, or simply "unconcealment" as such, which in turn rests on the more primordial phenomenon of Dasein's disclosedness. Many readers sympathize readily enough with Heidegger's apparent dissatisfaction with the correspondence theory, but his suggestion that we conceive of truth as mere uncoveredness or unconcealment, as opposed to representational adequacy or correctness, can seem at best an implausible analysis to put in its place, at worst a willful manipulation of language. Given the way we use the word, after all, truth involves more than things just showing up or manifesting themselves, for things can appear *other* than they are without thereby failing to appear. Indeed, in §7 of *Being and Time* Heidegger himself reserves the term 'semblance' (*Schein*) for just that phenomenon, as opposed to the right and proper kind of showing up that he calls the "primordial phenomenon of truth" (*SZ* 220). To reduce truth to the phenomenon of unconcealment is surely just to drain the concept of its essential normative import, namely, its implication of *rightness*.[62]

But do these standard reactions to Heidegger's account capture what he says about truth in *Being and Time* and elsewhere? Does Heidegger deny the intelligibility of the traditional conception of truth as agreement or correspondence, and is his own notion of truth as uncovering or unconcealment meant to challenge or supplant our ordinary notion

---

[61] Heidegger's conception of truth so pervades his philosophical thinking, both early and late, that it can scarcely even be distinguished from his more general concern with the question of being. Heidegger dwells (so to speak) on the question of truth in numerous texts, above all *Logik: Die Frage nach der Wahrheit*, "On the Essence of Truth" and "Plato's Doctrine of Truth" in *Wegmarken*, "The Origin of the Work of Art" in *Holzwege*, and "Alētheia (Heraclitus, Fragment B16)" in *Vorträge und Aufsätze*.

[62] As we shall see, this is the core of Ernst Tugendhat's critique. See *Der Wahrheitsbegriff bei Husserl und Heidegger*, 329 et passim.

of truth as correctness? No, on both counts. In *Being and Time* Heidegger says explicitly,

> The proposed "definition" of truth [as uncoveredness or unconcealment] is not a *rejection* (*Abschütteln*) of the tradition, but a primordial *appropriation:* and all the more so, if the argument can show that and how theory had to arrive at the idea of agreement (*Übereinstimmung*) on the basis of the primordial phenomenon of truth. (*SZ* 220)

The scarequotes around the word 'definition' indicate that Heidegger's purpose is not to analyze or define our ordinary concept of truth at all; moreover, he denies that his account is anything like an alternative theory competing directly with the traditional conception. The point of his phenomenological interpretation of truth is instead to shed light on the ontological structures presupposed by the phenomenon of correctness or correspondence, that is, to specify the *hermeneutic conditions* of truth conventionally understood.

I argued in Chapter 4 that Heidegger is an ontic realist, that is, a realist about occurrent entities, which he takes to exist independently of us and of our understanding of being. I also said, however, that he is not a metaphysical realist, if that means insisting that there is exactly one true ideal description of everything, and moreover construing truth as some obscure sort of correspondence between reality and representations. Heidegger's philosophical outlook is staunchly antireductionist, so he could never accept the idea of there being just one uniquely true description of everything. That notion makes no more sense than the idea of there being one best time or place from which to see things. Nature does not care when or where we stand, nor does it care what understanding, what concepts, or what language we avail ourselves of in dealing with and describing things.

But neither is Heidegger a realist out of any prior commitment to the correspondence theory of truth. He traces the conception of truth as correspondence, or "agreement" (in Greek *homoiōsis*, in Latin *adaequatio*) from Aristotle, through Isaac Israeli, Avicenna, and Aquinas, and finally to Kant.[63] Like Brentano, and contrary to the neo-Kantians of the nineteenth century and Hilary Putnam more recently,[64] Heidegger maintains that Kant never abandoned, or even meant to challenge, the correspondence theory of truth. Rather, "Kant, too, adheres to this concept of truth, so much so that he never even puts it up

---

[63] Aristotle, *De interpretatione* I, 16.6. Aquinas, *Quaestiones disputatae de veritate*, qu. 1, art. 1.
[64] See Putnam, *Reason, Truth and History*, 60–4, 74.

for discussion" (*SZ* 215).[65] Indeed, in *Kant and the Problem of Metaphysics* Heidegger argues that, far from having overturned the correspondence theory, Kant's critical philosophy in fact "grounds it for the first time" (*KPM* 13). Heidegger thus takes himself to be confronting, and no doubt attempting to "dismantle," a long tradition, including that of Kant, that is uncritically committed to the notion of truth as correspondence or agreement between subjects and objects.

A commitment can be uncritical, however, without being mistaken or unsound. That Heidegger takes the tradition to task for its impoverished conception of the ontological conditions of truth understood as correspondence, then, does not by itself imply that he denies or even doubts that propositional truth consists in the relation between the contents of our beliefs and assertions on the one hand, and entities on the other. Indeed, Heidegger does not reject the notion of agreement outright as an interpretation of truth. Instead, although he wants to set it aside as more or less theoretically vacuous and uninformative, he seems to consider it neither false nor incoherent in its own right: "The characterization of truth as 'agreement,' *adaequatio, homoiōsis* is indeed very general and empty. Yet it will have some justification if it stands up in the face of the most diverse interpretations of the knowledge bearing that distinctive predicate" (*SZ* 215). Heidegger wants not to dismiss the correspondence conception of truth out of hand, then, but rather to inquire into the conditions of our interpreting it in that way in the first place:

> We are now asking about the foundations of this "relation." *What else is implicitly posited in this relational totality – adaequatio intellectus et rei?* What ontological characteristics belong to what is posited itself?
> What does the term "agreement" mean generally? (*SZ* 215)

Like other philosophers before and after him, Heidegger wonders what more, if anything, can be said about the kind of agreement that is supposed to constitute truth:

> With regard to what do *intellectus* and *res* agree? Do they offer anything at all in their mode of being and their essential content with regard to which they can agree? If equality is impossible because of the lack of homogeneity between the two, are they (*intellectus* and *res*) then perhaps similar? (*SZ* 216)

---

[65] Kant writes, "The nominal definition of truth, namely that it is the agreement of cognition with its object, is here granted and presupposed" (*KRV* A58/B82).

This much sounds like the familiar charge that it simply makes no sense to talk about minds and things "agreeing," at least until we know what such agreement might actually consist in. But Heidegger differs crucially from philosophers like Leibniz, Hegel, Nietzsche, and others more recently, who reject the very idea of such a relation as fundamentally incoherent. Instead, he seems to accept the notion as a kind of benign metaphor that we ought neither to embrace nor defend in the form of an explicit philosophical thesis. To say that truth is a kind of agreement may be just as potentially misleading, but also just as potentially harmless, as saying that time flows like a river, or indeed that time is a series of nows or instants. Such folk-philosophical notions are not straightforwardly false or unintelligible; indeed, there are discernible structures in our preontological understanding of being that motivate them and lend them intuitive plausibility. Similarly, the notion of agreement or correspondence seems to present us with a kind of preliminary picture, at least in the domain of objective knowledge of the physical world, where we have some definite conception of the domain of objects with which something on the subject side is supposed to be in accord. Truths about values and abstract objects may be another matter altogether, of course. In any case, what remains is to ask how it is possible for such a preliminary picture to arise at all, right or wrong, and moreover come to seem so natural:

> knowledge is supposed to "give" the thing *just as* it is. The agreement has the relational character of "just as." In what way is this relation qua relation between *intellectus* and *res* possible? From this question it becomes clear that in order to shed light on the structure of truth it is not enough simply to presuppose this relational totality, rather it must be traced back to the context of being that supports the totality as such. (*SZ* 216)

Here it is quite clear that Heidegger is not repudiating the notion of truth as agreement, but rather sketching out its existential-ontological genealogy, which is to say its hermeneutic conditions.

We might say, then, that Heidegger rejects the correspondence *theory* of truth, but not the naive, pretheoretical idea of truth as a kind of harmony or agreement, which idea then gave rise to the philosophical theory. The so-called correspondence "theory" of truth apparently lacks content as a theory. Nor is any alternative theory – coherence, pragmatist, redundancy – likely to be of much help in uncovering the hermeneutic conditions Heidegger is seeking.

Heidegger points out that distinguishing, as Husserl does, between "ideal" (abstract) intentional contents and "real" (temporally concrete) mental acts and objects of knowledge does nothing to lessen the obscurity of the notion of correspondence, since such a distinction ignores the question of the *being* of the correspondence relation itself:

> Is the agreeing, in its mode of being, real or ideal, or neither of these? How is the relation between ideal entities and real occurrent things to be conceived ontologically? . . .
>
> Or is the ontological meaning of the relation between the real and the ideal (*methexis*) not to be asked about? Yet the relation is supposed to *obtain* (*bestehen*). What does obtaining (*Bestand*) mean ontologically?
>
> Why should we not be justified in asking this question? Is it an accident that this problem has made no progress for more than two millennia? Does the convolution of the question lie already at its inception in the ontologically unclarified separation of the real and the ideal? (*SZ* 216–17)

That these remarks are aimed primarily at Husserl's antipsychologistic conception of the ideality of intentional content, in contrast to the occurrent reality of psychological acts, is evident from Heidegger's final rhetorical question: "Is not psychologism right to balk at this separation, though it itself neither clarifies the mode of being of the thinking of what is thought nor even knows it as a problem?" (*SZ* 217).

Heidegger accepts Husserl's refutation of psychologism, which both philosophers dismiss as a hopeless attempt to reduce the normativity of meaning to nonnormative psychological facts. Nevertheless, contrary to Husserl, Heidegger suggests that psychologism was right to resist the metaphysical distinction between reality and ideality that has been the troubled legacy of the Platonic tradition. In short, "In the question concerning the mode of being of the *adaequatio,* going back to the division between the act of judgment and the content of judgment does not advance the discussion, but only points up the need to clarify the mode of being of cognition itself" (*SZ* 217). Heidegger therefore proceeds with his phenomenological account of the conditions of the intelligibility of truth as correspondence, which lie in our prior, preontological understanding of truth as "being-uncovering" or "uncoveredness" (*Entdeckend-sein, Entdecktheit*), which is in turn close to the literal meaning of the Greek *alētheia,* or "unconcealment" (*Unverborgenheit*) (*SZ* 219).

Heidegger's account strikes a characteristically ambivalent pose in response to its immediate predecessor, namely, Husserl's analysis of the intentional conditions of truth as "adequation" in the Sixth Logical Investigation.[66] Heidegger is clearly indebted to Husserl inasmuch as what he offers is not strictly speaking a *theory* of truth, at least not in the sense in which such theories are understood in contemporary analytic philosophy,[67] but rather a phenomenological account of the conditions of our ordinary conception of truth as something like correspondence, adequation, or agreement between minds or ideas on the one hand, and objects on the other.

Yet Heidegger is just as concerned to mark the difference between his own account and Husserl's, and he does so by reminding us that our ordinary understanding of truth makes no essential reference to the mental representations that figure centrally in Husserl's theory of intentionality. Briefly, Husserl describes the intentional conditions of truth in terms of the coincidence or "convergence" (*Deckung*) of intending acts with "fulfilling" intuitions, above all perception. Perception, that is, plays a "fulfilling function" in the constitution of knowledge, pointing up an "ideal of ultimate fulfillment" in what Husserl calls "evidence" (*Evidenz*), or "adequation to the 'thing itself' (*die 'Sache selbst'*)" (*LU* II/2, §37):

> when a representational intention has attained final fulfillment through this ideally complete perception, then the genuine *adaequatio rei et intellectus* has been established: *the objectivity is really "present" or "given" exactly as it is intended*; no partial intention is further implied that lacks fulfillment. (*LU* II/2, 118)

"Evidence itself is, we say, the act of the most complete synthesis of convergence" (*LU* II/2, 122).[68] Husserl's phenomenology of knowledge, then, rests on an analysis of "adequation" in terms of the interconnections among intending and fulfilling acts.

[66] Heidegger refers specifically to the sixth of the *Logical Investigations*, §§36–9.

[67] For a reading of *Being and Time* as advancing a literal theory of truth, indeed a verificationist theory, see Okrent, *Heidegger's Pragmatism*, 97ff. One reason to doubt that Heidegger was offering such a theory is precisely that the argument supposedly backing it up is, as Okrent himself observes, such a bad one. It should not be surprising that phenomenology read as theory makes for bad theory, just as naive, phenomenologically ungrounded theory read as phenomenology makes for bad phenomenology.

[68] For a critical account of the difficulty Husserl confronts in explaining the fulfillment of "the meant" (*das Gemeinte*) in "the given" (*das Gegebene*) in terms of a kind of intuitive content or perceptual meaning (*Sinn*), see Dreyfus, "Husserl's Perceptual *Noema*." For an account of why all such efforts are doomed to failure owing to their misguided faith in "the myth of the given," see Sellars, *Empiricism and the Philosophy of Mind*.

Heidegger follows the general spirit of Husserl's account in tracing the notion of adequation or agreement back to its phenomenological roots in our more primitive understanding of the world. Echoing Husserl, he writes: "The intended entity itself shows itself *just as* it is in itself, which is to say, *it* is in its selfsameness just as *it* is indicated as being, as it is uncovered as being, in the assertion." Yet he rejects the entire mental-representational apparatus of Husserl's theory, and therefore replaces the concept of "convergence" (*Deckung*) with its verbal opposite, his own essentially nonmentalistic notion of "uncoveredness" (*Entdecktheit*):

> Representations are not compared, neither among themselves nor in *relation* to the real thing. What stands to be revealed is not an agreement of cognition and object, nor even of the mental and the physical, *but neither is it an agreement of the "contents of consciousness" among themselves.* What stands to be revealed is solely the being-uncovered of the entity itself: *it* in the how of its uncoveredness. (*SZ* 218, emphasis added)

So, whereas Husserl's intentional analysis of adequation hinges on a conception of convergence or coincidence among representations, Heidegger's notion of truth as uncoveredness dispenses with mental vocabulary altogether and introduces in its place a properly ontological understanding of assertion as a mode of being toward entities in their being: "Asserting is a being toward the thing itself, which is," and "That the assertion *is true* means that it uncovers the entity in itself" (*SZ* 218).

Ontologically speaking, then, "Truth in no way has the structure of an agreement between cognition and object in the sense of an alignment (*Angleichung*) of one entity (subject) and another (object)" (*SZ* 218–19). Rather, "Being true as being-uncovering is a mode of being of Dasein. What makes this uncovering itself possible must be called 'true' in a still more primordial sense. *The existential-ontological foundations of uncovering show the most primordial phenomenon of truth*" (*SZ* 220). The conditions of the intelligibility of truth therefore reside in the uncoveredness of things known and the disclosedness (*Erschlossenheit*) of Dasein's being-in-the-world: "[O]nly with the *disclosedness* of Dasein is the *most primordial* phenomenon of truth attained" (*SZ* 220–1). The most primordial ontological conditions of truth consist not in any kind of correspondence among entities, then, but in the uncoveredness of things and the disclosedness of Dasein. Note that Heidegger's account draws crucially on the ontological difference between being and entities, for no mere description of entities and the relations among them – whether mental or physical, real or ideal – can by itself make sense of the possibility of some entities, say, beliefs and assertions, having meaning and being true of anything.

But does tying truth essentially to Dasein's disclosedness threaten to undermine Heidegger's ontic realism, which I have suggested is central to his fundamental ontology? Truth, for Heidegger, is a mode of being, or more precisely a mode of our understanding of being. It is therefore no more independent of Dasein than being itself is:

> *"There is" truth only insofar as and as long as Dasein is.* Entities are only uncovered *then* and only disclosed *as long as* Dasein *is* at all. Newton's laws, the law of noncontradiction, and all truths in general are true only *as long as* Dasein *is.* Before there ever was any Dasein, there was no truth, and after Dasein is no longer, there will be none, since then it *cannot* be as disclosedness, discovery and uncoveredness (*Entdeckung und Entdecktheit*). Before Newton's laws were discovered, they were not "true"; from that it does not follow that they were false, or even that they would be false if uncoveredness were no longer ontically possible. Just as little does this "restriction" involve any diminishment of the being-true of "truths." (*SZ* 226–7)

So, although truth and being depend on Dasein, occurrent entities themselves are fully independent both of us and of the truths in virtue of which they become intelligible to us. Thus, Heidegger continues:

> To say that, prior to Newton, his laws were neither true nor false, cannot mean that, at that time, the entities that those laws uncover and indicate did not exist. The laws became true *through* Newton; with them, entities became accessible in themselves for Dasein. Once entities are uncovered, they show themselves precisely as entities that already were beforehand. Such uncovering is the mode of being of "truth." (*SZ* 227)

The term 'law' is notoriously ambiguous in discussions of scientific truth, referring as it does sometimes to the expressions of theories, sometimes to natural regularities themselves, which are arguably what they are independently of the theories describing them. In the first sense of the word, laws are trivially dependent on human beings, since they are themselves artifacts of scientific practice. And indeed, this is the sense in which Heidegger is using the word. He can therefore insist that Newton's laws are strictly speaking dependent on Newton's formulation of them, but also that the entities and patterns described by those laws existed prior to scientific inquiry. For although truth and theory are both modes of Dasein's disclosedness and of the uncoveredness of entities, disclosedness and uncoveredness are not themselves essential to the ontic structure of occurrent entities themselves.

Truth as Hermeneutic Salience

Ernst Tugendhat has advanced what is perhaps the most sophisticated philosophical challenge to Heidegger's ontological interpretation of truth. Tugendhat protests, reasonably enough, that construing truth as unconcealment effectively renders falsehood unintelligible, for false beliefs and propositions as well as true ones can be said to uncover entities, though precisely *not as they are*. If Heidegger's account fails to distinguish *false* uncovering from *true* uncovering, he points out, it can hardly qualify as an interesting or plausible account of truth. It would appear, then, that Heidegger has not so much offered a new account of truth as simply changed the subject. For in moving inconspicuously from a discussion of propositional truth conventionally understood to an account of uncovering and Dasein's disclosedness, "the concept of truth is not widened, but rather no longer adhered to at all."[69] Indeed, "Heidegger does not discuss the specific concept of truth in the horizon of disclosedness at all, but instead simply thematizes disclosedness itself under the name 'truth.' "[70] Moreover, Tugendhat concludes, "if one limits oneself to the two concepts of unconcealment and concealment (*Unverborgenheit und Verborgenheit*)," as Heidegger does in his later writings, "there remains absolutely no possibility of determining the specific sense of falsehood, and therefore also of truth."[71] Tugendhat's critique has been widely influential and has impressed critics like Jürgen Habermas, who cites it approvingly and goes on to accuse Heidegger, especially in his later works, of "an uprooting of propositional truth and a devaluation of discursive thought."[72]

Some undaunted admirers of Heidegger, by contrast, have embraced what they take to be Heidegger's account, in the face of objections such as Tugendhat's, and have insisted that what Heidegger says about truth as disclosedness must apply to propositional truth as well. So, for instance, when Heidegger insists that all unconcealment involves or entails concealment, John Sallis concludes that Heidegger's account

---

[69] Tugendhat, *Der Wahrheitsbegriff bei Husserl und Heidegger,* 350.

[70] Ibid., 351.

[71] "Heidegger's Idea of Truth," *Critical Heidegger,* 233.

[72] Habermas, *The Philosophical Discourse of Modernity,* 154.

implies a rejection of the law of noncontradiction.[73] Sallis's interpretation, if correct, amounts to a reductio ad absurdum of Heidegger's
view. If Heidegger's view is not as confused or perverse as Sallis
suggests, however, then Sallis's interpretation is a reductio ad absurdum of itself.

Mark Wrathall has replied to Tugendhat and others by insisting that
Heidegger never intended his ontological account of truth as uncovering to challenge or supplant the traditional conception of truth as
correctness or correspondence. Indeed, Wrathall goes further by suggesting that Heidegger did not even mean to say that assertions uncover entities, let alone that uncovering is what makes true assertions
true. For Wrathall, "the inquiry into unconcealment, far from being
intended as a replacement for the correspondence view of truth, in
fact seeks to elucidate the way in which propositional truth is founded."
Consequently, "Heidegger never intended unconcealment as a definition of propositional truth." Indeed, "in claiming that the essence of
truth is unconcealment, Heidegger is not claiming that true or correct
expressions necessarily unconceal, but rather that unconcealment is
'what first makes correctness possible.' "[74]

I think Wrathall is right that Tugendhat and others have misunderstood the point of Heidegger's account, which is neither to offer an
analysis of propositional truth nor to contest the traditional conception of propositional truth as correspondence. Instead, as Wrathall says
and as Heidegger himself insists, he is offering an account of the ontological conditions of truth traditionally conceived. The uncovering of
entities in our practices and in our understanding, that is, is the condition for the propositional contents of assertions and beliefs being true
in virtue of their relation to the way things are. Truth as Heidegger describes it, as unconcealment, is thus the ontological condition of truth
conventionally understood, that is, as correctness or correspondence
with entities.

Wrathall's reconstruction becomes questionable, however, precisely
by rendering Heidegger's argument so unobjectionable, indeed so innocuous. For Wrathall's reading of §44 and related texts threatens to reduce Heidegger's conclusion to a virtual triviality, namely, that if no entities were disclosed or uncovered by Dasein in any way, then assertions

---

[73] Sallis, *Double Truth*, 100.
[74] Wrathall, "Heidegger and Truth as Correspondence," 70, 86 n25, 73. The embedded
quotation is from "On the Essence of Truth," *Wegmarken*, 80.

could never manage to point anything out and be either true or false with respect to them. But who would deny that our assertions and beliefs are capable of corresponding or failing to correspond to entities only if entities have been uncovered and encountered in one way or another in our practices and attitudes? If we never uncovered entities, we could neither say nor think anything true in virtue of corresponding to the way things are. Of course, I might well utter true or false assertions or entertain true or false beliefs about things that neither I nor anyone else has in fact encountered. But Heidegger's point, according to Wrathall, is not that our beliefs and assertions can be true or false only with respect to those particular entities we have encountered, merely that encountering *some* entities is a condition on our making true or false assertions about *any* entities. Rejecting Heidegger's argument, as Wrathall construes it, then, would mean not just supposing that assertions and beliefs can be true or false of entities that no one has ever encountered, or ever will, but rather that it might be possible to have true or false beliefs or make true or false assertions without our ever having encountered any entities whatever. Skeptics admit this possibility as a matter of epistemological principle, of course, but the view is hard to take seriously, if only because we have no idea of what it would mean, short of our failing to exist altogether, for us never to have encountered entities at all.

I therefore propose that Heidegger's original account of truth is neither the implausible claim often ascribed to him, that propositional truth can be either analyzed or supplanted by the concept of uncovering or disclosedness, nor the eminently plausible but philosophically uninteresting point that the practice of assertion presupposes Dasein's disclosedness. The kind of uncovering Heidegger has in mind, it seems to me, must be something more than the mere practical intelligibility of things in a referential context of significance if the notion is to shed any light on the specific way in which assertions perform their apophantic function by allowing us to communicate with one another about entities by pointing them out and saying something about them *as they are*. Of course, assertion is possible as a mode of comportment toward entities only because entities are already uncovered in our practices in other preassertoric, indeed nonlinguistic ways, prior to our making assertions about them. But something more needs to be said about how assertions can be true, not just in the sense of being correct or incorrect, but also relevant, interesting, illuminating, revelatory of the way things are. For assertions are not meaningful just by being correct or incorrect. They are, as Heidegger suggests, capable of either bringing things to light or pushing them, or letting them sink, back into darkness and obscurity. Whereas Wrathall seems to restrict the notion of uncovering to the ontological preconditions of assertion, thus distinguishing it sharply from the semantic function of assertions themselves, it seems to me that Heidegger highlights the apophantic function of assertion by arguing that assertions can be true in the sense of correct only because they serve to uncover entities in their being by throwing light on them under some definite aspect.

What then is truth as uncovering? As I understand it, it is neither simply Dasein's disclosedness nor the correctness of sentences and propositional attitudes as they correspond to the way things are. It is rather the peculiar capacity of *interpretations* – demonstrative, expressive comportments of all kinds – to bring phenomena to light against a background of prior practical uncoveredness, so that we can then understand assertions as being either correct or incorrect, that is, as either true or false relative to the way things are. Between the mere givenness of things in practical understanding and propositional truth, then, there is a third, intermediate phenomenon that discussions of Heidegger's conception of truth typically overlook. This intermediate phenomenon is what I shall call truth as *hermeneutic salience*. Over and beyond the way entities are intelligible to us in virtue of our tacit understandings and practices, that is, and yet beneath the threshold of explicit assertions and beliefs whose contents we take to be correct or incorrect, there is the way in which what we say and think is always already organized and articulated according to some dominant interpretation of things that holds sway in our local discursive community. Our understanding always has some definite cultural and historical shape, that is, not just in virtue of the instrumental organization of our everyday practices, but thanks more specifically to the particular ways in which we are prone to express and communicate what makes sense to us *as* it makes sense.[75]

75 One might object that appealing to hermeneutic salience as a condition of assertoric truth accounts only for the truth of those assertions that have been explicitly anticipated or prefigured in preassertoric interpretation. What about such random, irrelevant, or decontextualized assertions as "The moon is larger than my head" or, for that matter, G. E. Moore's "This is a hand"? I think such cases pose no threat to Heidegger's insistence that the apophantic *as* of assertion presupposes the hermeneutic *as* of interpretation. Such random assertions are intelligible, after all, in virtue of a vast network of words and phrases whose sense arguably depends on normal language use, which ordinarily remains well within the bounds of relevance, that is, hermeneutic salience. If all, or even most, of our assertions were simply bizarre utterances out of all familiar context, we might

What underlies and conditions the prevailing intelligibility that informs our cultural and personal interpretations, I have suggested, is *discourse,* which is to say the expressive-communicative intelligibility governing our meaningful gestures and marking them as sensible, reasonable, and well formed, whether they happen to be true or false, or even propositionally articulated at all.

It is the phenomenon of discourse, then, that promises to make sense of Heidegger's conception of truth as unconcealment, and it is hardly surprising that readers who have lacked a plausible account of discourse in *Being and Time* have likewise failed to understand his phenomenological interpretation of truth as unconcealment. For truth, in Heidegger's sense, is precisely the hermeneutic salience that allows expressive gestures to bring things to light as subject to sensible and relevant assertoric discourse, both true and false. Understanding his account of truth in this way thus allows us to cut a middle path between reductive and untenable readings on the one hand, and innocuous but trivializing interpretations on the other. Instead of admitting regretfully, as Wrathall does, that the text "would be clearer if Heidegger had been more careful to distinguish between truth and 'truth,' "[76] that is, between correspondence and disclosedness as such, we should instead recognize that those two phenomena lie on either side of the "primordial phenomenon of truth" that he in fact intended, namely, the *salience* in virtue of which some privileged aspects of our world emerge as worthy of our discursive concern, in contrast to the mundane and largely irrelevant background revealed by the entire scope of our practices and attitudes taken as a whole.

Consequently, as I have suggested, whereas Wrathall proposes that Heidegger is offering an account of the most basic ontological conditions of propositional truth, or the correctness of assertions, I believe he is offering an account of the hermeneutic conditions of our commonsense conception of truth *as* correctness and *as* consisting in a kind of agreement with the way things are. Putting the point in terms of hermeneutic conditions allows us to accept Wrathall's conclusion,

---

indeed have no basis for interpreting them as either true or false. But we need not take Wittgenstein's hard line against Moore and insist that even in philosophical argument such utterances are senseless. It is enough, even for Wittgenstein's antiskeptical purposes I think, to say that such utterances are perfectly meaningful, but that they mean what they do thanks only to other, necessarily more common, instances of situated, sensible speech.

[76] Wrathall, "Heidegger and Truth as Correspondence," 78.

since arguably the truth of assertions is itself possible only in virtue of Dasein's understanding truth in some particular way, for instance as agreement with the way things are. That is, it is not at all clear that beliefs or assertions could be true de facto, or indeed that there could be such things as beliefs or assertions at all, were Dasein incapable of understanding itself *as* saying or thinking anything true or false. Truth as such may therefore depend on our understanding of it. However, just as Heidegger advances neither a skeptical critique of objectivity nor an idealistic theory of time, but rather accounts of the hermeneutic conditions of our ordinary *conceptions* of objectivity and temporality, so too I believe he is not offering a novel theory of truth, either to support or to challenge the traditional conception of correspondence, but is instead describing the hermeneutic salience in virtue of which we come to understand truth prephilosophically *as* a kind of agreement between thoughts and things, between words and the world.

6

AUTHENTICITY AND ASYMMETRY

Points have we all of us within our souls
Where all stand single

Wordsworth

The concept of hermeneutic conditions, the lens through which I have been reading the analytic of Dasein in *Being and Time,* is a concept not of causal or logical conditions of intelligibility, but of the constitutive conditions of the *interpretability* of entities as such. To say that hermeneutic conditions are constitutive, rather than merely causal or logical, is to say that we always already have some understanding of them, however inarticulate or prethematic, just in virtue of understanding *what* and *that* entities *are.* The interpretability of entities is therefore tied essentially to their *being,* which is to say the conditions of their intelligibility *as entities.* Fundamental ontology, at once guiding and guided by the question concerning the meaning of being, thus has to do with the conditions of Dasein's explicit understanding of entities as such.

Moreover, the "explicitness" of understanding in interpretation, as Heidegger conceives it, lies not just in its presence before the mind, but in its *expression* in communicative practice broadly construed. I have argued that communication, also broadly construed, is a condition of expression, as contrasted with the mere purposiveness of practical activity. Discourse, which is to say the entire expressive-communicative dimension of Dasein's disclosedness, thus constitutes a hermeneutic condition – indeed, *the* hermeneutic condition par excellence. For the communicative dimension of the intelligibility of being-in-the-world is what makes possible the semantic gap between the objects and the contents of explicit understanding, that is, between the entities we talk (and think) *about* and what we *say* (and think) about them. It is discourse, then, not practical understanding as such, that constitutes the primordial phenomenon of truth understood as uncoveredness, that is, entities dawning or showing up for us explicitly *as they are.*

Yet the emphasis I have placed on the phenomenon of expression in my account of discourse and interpretation is potentially misleading. For Heidegger's account of authenticity or ownedness (*Eigentlichkeit*) as a kind of "forerunning resoluteness" (*vorlaufende Entschlossenheit*) in a concrete situation toward death (*SZ* 302) represents a radical departure from a tradition of conceptions of the self and selfhood that has dominated late modern thought. The tradition I have in mind, which Charles Taylor, taking his inspiration from Isaiah Berlin, has called "expressivism,"[1] dates back to the middle or late eighteenth century, specifically to Rousseau and Herder, and persists in the nineteenth century in such figures as Hegel, Marx, Kierkegaard, and Dilthey. All these thinkers, Taylor suggests, helped to transform the modern conception of human beings as autonomous subjects by reconceiving existence and action in terms of self-realization in expressive form. Distinctively human activities involve expression of various sorts, linguistic and nonlinguistic, and selfhood in a robust sense is not an antecedent condition of expressive activity, but its proper end and possible achievement. Human beings are not just brutely self-identical like objects; rather, in their actions, they can either fail or succeed in realizing their true selves. We can either fall into self-estrangement and alienation or come to recognize and find ourselves in our lives and works. By analyzing Heidegger's concept of interpretation as a notion of expression, however broadly construed, do I mean to include Heidegger in that expressivist tradition, as Taylor defines it?

No, although the suggestion would not be entirely unreasonable. Taylor himself, for one, reads Heidegger in this way,[2] and as we shall

---

[1] See Taylor's *Hegel,* 13n et passim; "Language and Human Nature" and "Theories of Meaning," in *Human Agency and Language*; and *Sources of the Self: The Making of the Modern Identity,* chapter 21. See also Isaiah Berlin, "Herder and the Enlightenment," in *The Proper Study of Mankind: An Anthology of Essays.*

[2] See "Theories of Meaning," in *Human Agency and Language,* and "Heidegger, Language, and Ecology," in *Philosophical Arguments.* Taylor acknowledges that Heidegger's later thought is radically antisubjectivist. What I am urging is that the account of authenticity in *Being and Time* already transcends subjectivism, too. I should add that I agree with Taylor's description of Heidegger's approach to language, early and late, as "manifestationist," manifestation being part of, but not the same as, expression in its subjective form.

see, Charles Guignon offers an interpretation of authenticity that places Heidegger squarely among the expressivist thinkers who undoubtedly influenced him. The notion is not altogether implausible, for even if Heidegger's concept of authenticity takes him beyond the expressivist paradigm, as I believe it does, his language clearly resonates with the various discourses of authenticity that have dominated late modern thought and literature. What distinguishes Heidegger from the expressivist tradition proper, however, is his radical rejection of any conception of Dasein as a finished or in principle finishable self, an integrated whole, a complete occurrent entity. Expressivism, by contrast, relies essentially on a normative ideal of completion, wholeness, totality, unity. The consummation of expressive activity, as expressivist writers and thinkers imagine it, is a whole and integrated self, transcending divisions between sensibility and understanding, and between spirit and nature, ultimately uniting human beings in a common recognition of their shared humanity. For the central figures of the Romantic age, Taylor says, expression "makes something manifest while at the same time realizing, completing it," and is moreover "what realizes and completes us as human beings."[3]

For Heidegger, on the contrary, any such ideal of total self-realization, self-actualization, or completion is incoherent and impossible in principle for an entity like Dasein. Nor can this view be understood as a mere minor disagreement within an otherwise continuous tradition. Rather, to reject the ideal posited by the expressivist paradigm as unintelligible, as unrealizable not just as a matter of social or psychological fact but essentially, as Heidegger does, is to abandon the paradigm altogether.

This is admittedly difficult to see, since so much of Heidegger's language remains indebted to the expressivist tradition from which he departs. One might suppose, for example, that the very distinction between authenticity and inauthenticity makes sense only with reference to a normative ideal of integrated selfhood, of integrity understood as *being oneself*, or *being true to oneself*. Indeed, at first glance anyway, Heidegger's descriptions of inauthenticity seem to bear this out. In everyday life, "first and for the most part Dasein *is not itself*," and this is possible only because there is "a determinate mode of being of

---

Language manifests our being-in, our being-with, and our understanding, then, but it cannot actualize anything like a fully integrated or finished self.

[3] Taylor, *Sources of the Self*, 377.

the 'I' itself" that consists precisely in "a loss of self (*Selbstverlorenheit*)" (*SZ* 116). And one of the modes of falling and inauthenticity is precisely "alienation" (*Entfremdung*) (*SZ* 178), a word that captures the normative spirit of expressivism perhaps better than any other.

But while Heidegger's negative characterizations of inauthenticity seem to remain attuned to the Romantic discourse of self-estrangement and subjective disintegration, I think it is easier to see that his positive account of authenticity as forerunning resoluteness has little in common with the corresponding ideal of wholeness, completion, or unified subjecthood taken for granted by the expressivist model. For when Heidegger talks about authentic selfhood, he has in mind something radically different from the kind of subjective integrity envisioned by philosophers like Rousseau, Hegel, Kierkegaard, and Dilthey. This is because, in short, for Heidegger, Dasein cannot be understood in terms of the ontological category of subjectivity: "subject and object do not coincide with Dasein and the world" (*SZ* 60), for "the ontological concept of the subject characterizes... *the selfsameness and constancy of something always already occurrent*. To define the I ontologically as *subject* means treating it as something always already occurrent" (*SZ* 320).

In what follows I will try to say more precisely what authentic forerunning resoluteness amounts to, how it differs from subjectivity, in particular subjectivity as conceived by expressivism, and finally, what I believe Heidegger's account of authentic existence implies for the metaphysics of the self. Division II of *Being and Time,* I shall argue, is concerned largely with the ontological irreducibility of the first-person point of view. What Heidegger's account of authenticity entails, I believe, though he does not draw the inference explicitly himself, is that there can be no fully objective, perspectivally symmetrical concept of the self. Rather, there is a radical asymmetry between first- and second- or third-person perspectives, an asymmetry, that is to say, between my own reflexive understanding of *myself* and another's understanding of me as *a self.* On Heidegger's view, our reflexive understanding of *ourselves* is irreducible to any symmetrical and impersonal conception of *the self,* nor is any metaphysically substantial or robust *self* realizable in our own authentic understanding of *ourselves.*

Selves exist, to be sure. Daseins are selves. Selves are neither fictions nor artificial constructs fabricated by anxious creatures whose selflessness strikes them as somehow problematic and unsettling. Nevertheless, the self is an essentially social phenomenon, for it emerges only in Dasein's being-with, hence only with the admixture of a second- and even a third-person point of view. We are selves above all in the eyes of others, not just directly and authentically for ourselves, by ourselves. Yet *Being and Time* seems to offer no account of this other-oriented dimension of selfhood, indeed authentic selfhood, quite apart from the anonymous other-directedness of fallen, inauthentic existence. While Heidegger was right to insist on the irreducibility of the first person to any impersonal generic concept of the self, then, he was wrong to ignore those aspects of sociality that inevitably mingle and complicate our first-person understandings with our understandings of others, and with theirs of us.

Heidegger does not call attention to the phenomenon of asymmetry in his account of authentic selfhood in *Being and Time,* at least not explicitly. Nevertheless, the idea echoes what he does say about death in §49, more specifically about the asymmetry between on the one hand "demise" (*Ableben*), or dying in what I shall call the "biographical" sense, that is, a human life's concluding by coming to an end, or coming to completion as a whole, a phenomenon experienceable by others, but not by oneself, and on the other hand "dying" proper (*Sterben*), or dying in the *existential* sense, which Heidegger defines as "the *mode of being* in which Dasein *is toward* its death" (*SZ* 247). Evidently, then, there can be no general metaphysical theory of death, only phenomenological interpretations of the relation in which one stands to the deaths of others and to one's own dying.

Similarly, I want to suggest, there can be no impersonal metaphysics of the self, only complexly interwoven and interpenetrating phenomenologies of selfhood in oneself, which Heidegger describes in Division II of *Being and Time,* and of selfhood in others, which he does not. Indeed, the existential analytic has virtually nothing at all to say about other selves. And although the peculiarly egoless or characterless quality of authentic selfhood, as Heidegger describes it, suggests that the self as such remains invisible to itself qua authentic, it may be so only from the first-person point of view, just as my own biographical death necessarily remains unexperienceable by me, though others may experience it, as I do theirs.

Even if Heidegger is right to refuse to assimilate first-person self-understanding to any second- or third-person conception of intraworldly selves, then, his account remains unsatisfying inasmuch as it tells us nothing about the hermeneutic conditions of bringing the two perspectives together in an overarching interpretation of human beings as selves. How is it possible, indeed *is* it possible, to come to understand myself as others understand me, namely, as an intraworldly character whose life concludes with my eventual earthly demise? Is it possible to come to understand myself, if only partially, as another? At some level, of course, learning to see ourselves as others do, and perhaps coming to see others as they see themselves, is a necessary condition of empathy and the most basic forms of moral awareness, and Heidegger's failure to account for it is, I suspect, bound up with his more general failure to understand ethics as a proper branch of philosophy.[4]

Heidegger is right, however, to deny that being-with is itself founded on empathy, since empathy is itself intelligible only as a particular attitude toward others, among whom one must already have found oneself situated in a common world: "'Empathy' does not first constitute being-with, but is possible only on the basis of it." But Heidegger not only denies the primordiality of empathy; he also identifies it with a wholly inauthentic mode of being-with, insisting that it is "motivated by the dominant deficient modes of being-with in their unsociability (*Unumgänglichkeit*)." Viewed positively or negatively, then, empathy has no place among the hermeneutic conditions informing the analytic of Dasein: "'empathy' is no primordial existential phenomenon, any more than cognition in general" (*SZ* 125). This is right, and yet it leaves open the question of whether and to what extent understanding oneself as others understand one may yet be a constitutive moment in understanding oneself as a *self* at all.

One further point is worth noting at the outset. It is too seldom observed that Heidegger's distinction between authenticity and inauthenticity is systematically ambiguous, and so lends itself to two completely different interpretations. Naturally, authenticity in human understanding and conduct is supposed to be something desirable, while

[4] The same could probably be said of Wittgenstein. As Strawson argues in "Persons" (chapter 3 of *Individuals*), Wittgenstein seems to lack any primitive concept of persons that might make sense of what he otherwise presents as peculiarly disconnected first- and third-person uses of pronouns and predicates describing and expressing mental states. Moore reports Wittgenstein maintaining in the early 1930s that "'the idea of a person' doesn't enter into the description of 'having toothache,'" and that "the word 'I' or 'any other word which denotes a subject' is used in 'two utterly different ways,' one in which it is 'on a level with other people,' and one in which it is not." Wittgenstein, *Philosophical Occasions*, 100–1. I think it can be no accident that, along with his antimetaphysical conception of the first person, Wittgenstein shared Heidegger's indifference, even hostility, to philosophical discussions of ethics, as distinct from aesthetics and problems about the meaning of life. See Wittgenstein's "Lecture on Ethics," op. cit.

inauthenticity is somehow undesirable. Heidegger regularly insists that such seemingly pejorative terms as 'idle talk,' 'falling,' and 'inauthenticity' have no evaluative content (*PGZ* 378; *SZ* 167, 175–6, 179; *GP* 228). But this is utterly unconvincing. No one can come away from the text with the idea that such notions are value-neutral. The problem is that terms like 'idle talk' and 'falling' do double duty both as descriptions of the indifferent ontological structures underlying the invidious distinctions Heidegger does draw between authentic and inauthentic modes of existence, and as names for the specifically negative instances or manifestations of those structures. Consequently, Heidegger's language inclines in a pejorative direction and systematically blurs the distinction between indifferent ontological conditions and the specifically undesirable ontic syndromes they condition, which wreaks havoc with the coherence of *Being and Time* as a whole, particularly in the tensions that emerge between Division I and Division II.[5]

When it comes to authenticity and inauthenticity, the ambiguity is especially acute. For in addition to denoting something desirable and something undesirable, the two terms also have purely formal senses, namely, *relating directly to oneself* and *relating to or mediated by others*. Heidegger can plausibly maintain that the distinction has no evaluative content as long as it simply points up a formal distinction between Dasein's ontologically distinctive relation to itself and its relations to others, or to itself as mediated by the actions and interpretations of others. So, for example:

> We understand ourselves daily, as we can formulate it terminologically, *not authentically* in the strict sense, not constantly in terms of the ownmost and most extreme possibilities of our own existence, but *inauthentically*, our selves indeed, but as we are *not our own*, rather as we have lost ourselves in the everydayness of existing among things and people. 'Not authentically' means: not as we *can* at bottom be our own to ourselves. Being lost, however, has no negative, derogatory significance, but means something positive, something belonging to Dasein itself. (*GP* 228)

It is probably impossible to hear the phrase "being lost" as having no negative connotations. Still, there is an intelligible formal distinction underlying the normative difference: Dasein sometimes understands

---

5 Dreyfus has made this point most forcefully in *Being-in-the-World*, chapter 13 and the Appendix coauthored with Jane Rubin. See also my response to the problem in "Must We Be Inauthentic?"

itself directly or authentically as its own, sometimes obliquely or inauthentically as others interpret it, as it appears to others.[6] Making the formal point, it seems to me, is Heidegger's chief philosophical purpose in Division II of *Being and Time*. Yet the evaluative contrast between better and worse modes of existence impinges on the entire discussion and throws it off course. For conflating the descriptive sense of the distinction with the normative sense suggests that there is something *wrong* with understanding oneself through, by means of, in relation to, in terms of – in short, *as* – another. But surely some ways of doing so are good and some are not.

This terminological and conceptual ambiguity thus feeds into what I believe is the principal flaw in Heidegger's account of selfhood, namely, that it neglects the hermeneutic conditions underlying one's capacity to understanding oneself as another, an exercise in empathy and imagination that is arguably essential to our mundane ethical self-understanding.

Wholeness and Wholeheartedness

Commentators have read Heidegger's account of authentic selfhood in Division II of *Being and Time* in widely, sometimes wildly, different ways. For example, whereas Charles Guignon ascribes to Heidegger what seems to me an overly robust or metaphysically optimistic account of the ontological structure of the self, Hubert Dreyfus sees in the account of forerunning resoluteness what I think is an overly impoverished or pessimistic conception of authentic existence. Steering a middle course between these two readings suggests an alternative view of the philosophical implications of Heidegger's account of authenticity at large. I will comment briefly on Guignon's view here and then consider Dreyfus's reading later in the chapter in connection with Heidegger's discussion of guilt.

Guignon argues that, like Paul Ricoeur more recently,[7] Heidegger conceives of the temporality of human existence as exhibiting

---

[6] Heidegger's blurring of the descriptive and evaluative senses of '*eigentlich*' and '*Eigentlichkeit*' is echoed in the ambiguity of the English word 'proper': What is proper is what belongs intrinsically to something, but also what is right and appropriate for it.

[7] In "Narrative Time" Ricoeur proposes "that narrativity and temporality are closely related – as closely as, in Wittgenstein's terms, a language game and a form of life. Indeed, I take temporality to be that structure of existence that reaches language in narrativity and narrativity to be the language structure that has temporality as its ultimate referent. Their relationship is therefore reciprocal" (165). More explicitly, in the first volume of

an essential narrative structure. Living authentically, according to Guignon, sheds light on that narrative structure and lends it greater coherence and intelligibility: "[A]n authentic life is lived as a unified flow characterized by cumulativeness and direction." Indeed, "such a life is lived as a coherent story."[8] An authentic life is a life made meaningful by its temporal unity and coherent purpose: "Like a well-crafted story, there is a beginning, a development, and an ending that gives the whole its *point*."[9] The unifying meaning or purpose of one's life, moreover, becomes clear only in light of one's temporal finitude: "[T]he individual who faces up to death lives each moment as part of the totality of life, and carries forward the past as part of a coherent, cumulative narrative." Authentic Dasein "lives each moment as an integral component of the overall story it is shaping in its actions."[10]

Guignon is right that the difference between authenticity and inauthenticity is the difference between focused, coherent activity and the dispersal and distraction of leveled everydayness. I think he is wrong, however, to describe what Heidegger calls the existential "moment" (*Augenblick*) as one "in which the whole of life – stretched out from beginning to end – is transparent in its temporal structure."[11] On the contrary, as we shall see, Dasein's relation to its own death renders any such view of its own life impossible. I cannot understand my own existence as anything like a "finite life span"[12] organized by a beginning, a middle, and an end. The problem with such a conception of existence is not just the obvious fact that I will no longer be around to experience my life once it has ended, but that the kind of interpretive or biographical distance necessary for comprehending an adequate global

---

Time and Narrative, he writes, "time becomes human time to the extent that it is organized after the manner of a narrative" (I: 3). It should be pointed out, however, that Ricoeur does not share Guignon's reading of Heidegger. Indeed, I think Ricoeur is right to say that narrative per se does not figure into the existential analytic of Dasein at all: "Heidegger's text," he observes, "seems to leave no place for it, inasmuch as the tie between history and time occurs, in *Being and Time,* at the level of historicality, not at that of within-time-ness" (I: 63; cf. III: 60–96). Beyond his account of Dasein's primordial ecstatic temporality, that is, Heidegger never offers an account of the temporal structure of human affairs as events occurring *within* time, let alone in narrative form. Ricoeur's point seems to run parallel to my own worry that Heidegger says almost nothing about selves understood from a second- or third-person point of view.

[8] Guignon, "Authenticity, Moral Values, and Psychotherapy," 230, 229.

[9] Guignon, "Philosophy and Authenticity: Heidegger's Search for a Ground for Philosophizing," 85.

[10] Ibid., 89.   [11] Ibid., 89.

[12] Ibid., 90.

narrative of a life is structurally unavailable to me as the one whose being is at issue in the interpretation. Its being *my* life, that is, formally
and so necessarily precludes me from approaching it hermeneutically
in anything like the way another might approach it, or I the life of
another.

Although, as I said, Heidegger does not himself draw this distinction
between first-person and third-person perspectives on lives or selves, he
always insists that Dasein cannot coherently aspire to any kind of complete or total understanding of itself in its existence. As early as 1920
in his "Comments on Karl Jaspers's *Psychology of Worldviews*," he explicitly denies that human existence can be intelligible to itself as anything
like a whole entity, complete and unified. Jaspers analyzes breakdowns
or extreme existential conditions, which he calls "limit situations"
(*Grenzsituationen*) – for example, struggle, death, contingency, guilt –
by way of sketching out a general metaphysical account of the structure
of human life. The interpretations of death, guilt, and conscience in
Division II of *Being and Time* testify to the decisive influence Jaspers's
methodological appeal to such special cases obviously exerted on
Heidegger's project.[13]

Yet Heidegger objected at the outset to the ontological assumptions
informing Jaspers's argument. For example, Jaspers makes repeated
reference to unity, totality, and infinity in his positive characterization
of life, which is therefore in principle vulnerable to division, opposition,
and destruction. Having cited a number of such passages, Heidegger
remarks,

> It should be clear enough by now that it is from this "whole" ("unity,"
> "totality"), taken up as a prior conception (*Vorgriff*), that the talk of
> "destruction," "division," "opposition" derives its meaning. Man stands
> within antinomies insofar as he sees himself as a "whole," and so has
> *this* aspect of life in his prior conception, sees himself as essentially fit-
> ted into this whole as something final, experiences his being (*Dasein*) as
> "bounded" by this unbroken "medium." (*Weg/GA9* 12)

But Heidegger maintains that Jaspers's notion of understanding human life "as a whole" is fatally obscure: "What this 'seeing as a whole'
and experiencing the antinomies in infinite reflection is supposed to
mean, nothing definite about this is worked out" (*Weg/GA9* 13). Jaspers

---

[13] There are five references in *Being and Time* either to Jaspers or to his concept of a limit
situation (*SZ* 249n, 301n, 308, 338n, 349).

"persists in the untested opinion that he can grasp the problem of existence with the help of the prior conception explicitly exposed above," namely, the notions of unity and totality (*Weg/GA9* 15). Indeed, for Jaspers, according to Heidegger,

> Life "is there" as something that is to be had by looking at it, and which, in this mode of having, is attained as the encompassing whole.... The whole of life, life *itself*, is something about which we can say nothing directly. Yet it must be intended somehow, since consciousness of existence arises precisely from looking *at it*. (*Weg/GA9* 24–5)

But, Heidegger objects, even if we concede that philosophical observation has an unavoidable theorizing effect, nevertheless "that does not entail that the meaning of the being of what is observed as such must be primarily accessible in observation" (*Weg/GA9* 24). Indeed, as Heidegger would go on to argue in greater detail in *Being and Time*, Dasein's understanding of itself differs profoundly from observational attitudes such as perception or intuition. In an only very thinly veiled reference to Husserl's conception of "regional ontologies,"[14] Heidegger refers to "the specific foreignness of the 'I' to any region or subject domain (*die spezifische Regions- und Sachgebietsfremdheit des 'ich'*)" (*Weg/GA9* 29). Heidegger thus infers "*the need for radical suspicion ... concerning all regional objectifying prior conceptions, concerning the networks of concepts arising from them, and the various ways in which they arise*" (*Weg/GA9* 30).

Moreover, anticipating the fully existential orientation of the analytic of Dasein in *Being and Time*, Heidegger argues that all notions of a purely observational or contemplative access to the ontological structures of human existence must give way to a phenomenology of engaged practical concern:

> The sense of existence is acquired ... not from the ... cognitive, explicating, and thereby somehow objectifying "is," but from the basic experience of a *concerned* (*bekümmert*) relation to itself, which is enacted *prior to* any possible, but extraneous, subsequent "is"-type ("*ist*"-*mässig*) objectifying cognition. To the extent that I seek such knowledge, the observational attitude will become decisive, and all my explications will have an objectifying character, but will repel existence and any genuine relation to it (concern). (*Weg/GA9* 30)

---

[14] See *Id I*, 19, 112, 134, et passim. For Husserl, "transcendental consciousness" is an ontological region, indeed "the primal region (*Urregion*) ... in which all other regions of being are rooted, to which they are related according to their *essence*, on which they are all therefore essentially dependent" (*Id I*, 141).

Our everyday existential understanding of ourselves is distinct from and prior to any contemplative or cognitive attitude, so no generically conceived regional ontological framework can do it justice:

> In the basic experience related to the I, its facticity becomes decisive; [it is] lived as one's own, *hic et nunc*. . . . Factical life-experience itself, in which I can relate to myself in various ways, however, is nothing like a region in which I stand, not the universal whose individuation would be the self. (*Weg/GA9* 32)

Our most basic understanding of ourselves lies in an immediate and engaged concern (*Bekümmerung*) "in which the specific past, present, and future of the self are experienced not as temporal schemata for an objective order of facts" (*Weg/GA9* 32–3), but in another, more primordial way.

In the review of Jaspers, Heidegger does not say explicitly what that primordial sense of self amounts to, but he does insist that it differs profoundly from the observation or contemplation of anything like a whole, complete, unified occurrent object. Not until Division II of *Being and Time* would he spell out the positive account of authentic selfhood with which he intended to supplant the method and the metaphysics still evidently informing Jaspers's philosophical anthropology. Although *Being and Time* begins with a hermeneutic of everydayness, the ultimate aim of the book, even in Division I, was always "to acquire a phenomenal basis for answering the guiding question concerning the being of the totality of the structural whole of Dasein," and moreover "to grasp the totality of the structural whole ontologically" (*SZ* 191).

Division II begins, however, with an admission that the hermeneutic of everydayness, precisely because of its phenomenological immersion in the mundane world of quotidian concern, was incapable of providing an account of Dasein's being *as a whole*. Recall that Dasein's own everyday understanding of itself always tends toward averageness, superficiality, and obscurity. Any naively credulous hermeneutic phenomenology of mundane existence is thus in imminent danger of inheriting that same partiality and inadequacy from the phenomenal Dasein it interrogates. Heidegger concludes, "*the foregoing existential analysis of Dasein cannot sustain the claim to primordiality*. Present in its fore-having was always only the *inauthentic* being of Dasein, and this as a *nonwhole*" (*SZ* 233).

How then are we to grasp the being of Dasein as a whole? How are we to do so, moreover, without lapsing back into the traditional methodological and metaphysical preconceptions that led Jaspers astray? Heidegger's response to this problem is in effect to change the subject in a subtle but profound way by replacing the very idea of human existence understood *as a unified whole* with a concrete internal interpretation of Dasein *owning up wholly* – that is, *wholeheartedly* – to itself in its existence. To own up to oneself in one's existence is to exist authentically. It is Dasein in its authentic aspect, then, that promises to reveal the deep structure of human existence as falling, thrown projection.

This is not to say that what is primordial is simply what is authentic, though Heidegger does seem to conflate the two notions in Division II of *Being and Time*.[15] It is rather that the authentic mode of existence, which is ontically contingent, is authentic precisely in its ability to uncover or cast light on the primordial structures of being-in-the-world that obtain whether Dasein exists authentically or inauthentically. Moreover, to focus on one particular existentiel mode of existence is in effect to refuse to retreat to any preconceived methodological or metaphysical standpoint external to Dasein's own concrete self-understanding. In this way, Heidegger continues to probe the phenomenon of existence from the inside, as it were, asking what Dasein's understanding of itself *as a whole* might amount to – *for* Dasein itself, internal to the understanding it has of its *own* being, solely in virtue of having "its being, as its own, to be" (*SZ* 12).

Grasping Dasein as a whole, of course, still means comprehending human existence in its finitude. Indeed, Heidegger maintains that it is precisely in the face of its own death that Dasein is capable of understanding itself wholly, or authentically, absent the generic distortions and banalities of common sense and received opinion. Division II therefore begins with an account of death.

Death as the Constant Closing Down of Possibilities

An enormous amount of confusion has resulted from the fact that by 'death' Heidegger does not mean quite what is commonly meant by the word. But neither is his existential conception of death wholly alien to our ordinary understanding. Heidegger's account of death is in fact an account of the hermeneutic conditions rendering intelligible

---

[15] Blattner is right to insist that primordial temporality is not the same as authentic temporality. See *Heidegger's Temporal Idealism*, 98–102, 117 n31.

our ordinary notions of death, which he distinguishes from existential dying.

To understand death not just as some contingent or impersonal event, but as a hermeneutic condition internal to and constitutive of our understanding of ourselves as being-in-the-world, it is necessary to make clear what death is *not*. For example, death is not the event of dying:

> For Dasein to achieve its wholeness in death is at once for it to lose the being of the there (*das Da*). The transition to no-longer-being-there (*Nichtmehrdasein*) lifts Dasein right out of the possibility of experiencing this transition, and of understanding it as something experienced. This is precisely what is denied to any particular Dasein in relation to itself. The death of others is therefore all the more haunting. The termination of Dasein in this way becomes "objectively" accessible. (*SZ* 237)[16]

In the existential sense, death is always *my own*; it is not external to my existence: "With death Dasein stands before itself in its *ownmost* ability-to-be" (*SZ* 250); "Death is Dasein's *ownmost* possibility" (*SZ* 263). Hence it cannot be anything like an episode falling within the temporal boundaries of my life: "In dying, what is revealed is that death is ontologically constituted by mineness and existence. Dying is not an occurrence, but a phenomenon to be understood existentially" (*SZ* 240). Hence the radical asymmetry between the deaths of others and my own death. More precisely, there is an essential asymmetry between *my* relation to the deaths of others and my relation to *my own* death, just as there are asymmetries between my relation to my own body and mind and the relation in which I stand to the bodies and minds of others.[17]

Neither therefore is death in the existential sense the same as the state of being dead. Strictly speaking, Dasein cannot *be* dead, since to *be dead* is, for Dasein, precisely *not to be*. Once dead, Dasein no longer

---

[16] Cf. Wittgenstein in the *Tractatus:* "Death is not an event in life. One does not experience death." *Tractatus Logico-Philosophicus*, 6.4311.

[17] Herman Philipse tries to play down the importance of the mineness of death precisely by assimilating it to what he regards as trivial mental and bodily analogues: "[M]y death is not *more* mine than the thoughts that I have, or the pain I feel in my body." *Heidegger's Philosophy of Being*, 359. Philipse is right that Heidegger's refusal to include any discussion of the body in *Being and Time* (see *SZ* 108) prevents him from taking seriously the mineness of embodiment as an ontological structure of being-in-the-world. But, as Wittgenstein and Merleau-Ponty have shown, there is nothing trivial about the mineness of bodily and mental phenomena; indeed, failing to take seriously the first/third-person asymmetries constituting them is sure to yield profound philosophical confusion.

exists qua being-in-the-world. After death, it appears, there *is* no more Dasein, just a corpse: "The *end* of the entity qua Dasein is the *beginning* of this entity qua something merely occurrent" (*SZ* 238). The human being has become an occurrent entity, though Heidegger remarks that even a corpse is not *just* an occurrent object, for it is intelligible not solely in terms of its objective properties, but in terms of its once having been alive:

> the entity that remains presents us with no purely corporeal thing. Even the occurrent corpse, viewed theoretically, is still a possible object of pathological anatomy, whose understanding tends to remain oriented around the idea of life. What is merely occurrent (*das Nur-noch-Vorhandene*) is "more" than a *lifeless* material thing. In it we encounter something *unliving* that has lost its life. (*SZ* 238)

Nevertheless, death in this sense remains at some level a kind of transition or transformation from being-in-the-world to being occurrent, though it remains problematic whether we ought to say it is the same entity that formerly had being-in-the-world and that is now merely occurrent.[18]

Yet even if we treat corpses *as* corpses, whether human or animal, and not just indifferently as mere objects, we also treat dead human beings *as human beings,* not just as corpses. We think they deserve a proper burial, for instance, and this is not obviously based on any inability to appreciate their nonexistence qua being-in-the-world. The deceased are "no-longer-in-the-world," as Heidegger says, and of course we understand this. Our respect for the dead is arguably more primordial

---

[18] Philipse concludes rather hastily from the fact that one does not survive one's own death that Epicurus was right that my own death ought to be of no concern to me. But the Epicurean view is phenomenologically broken-backed precisely because of its cultivated (indeed, therapeutically motivated) foreignness to our ordinary understanding of death, and it is the ordinary understanding that Heidegger is interpreting. Philipse therefore argues that Heidegger's approach to the problem of death is misguided because "the problem itself is a sham." Strangely, he then insists that Heidegger's phenomenology rests on a *failure* to appreciate the asymmetry between my own death and the deaths of others: "Such a phenomenological project is nonsensical, because one cannot experience or 'suffer' anything when one is dead. Heidegger misconceives death as an inner state of the dead person, whose dead body is the outer appearance of her or his death. He imagines this inner state as one of bereavement, as if the dead person is bereaved of herself or himself." Ibid., 365. This is an astonishing misreading, since, as we have seen, Heidegger himself is at pains to insist that, for Dasein, *being dead* is precisely *not being*, even if others may in a sense still *be with* me after I have died. For Heidegger, that is, existential death is something utterly different from the state of being dead.

ontologically than any literal beliefs we might entertain about dualism and the survival of the soul; indeed, atheists are no more indifferent to these practices and attitudes than religious believers. Characteristically attentive to the phenomena, Heidegger therefore distinguishes the "deceased" (*der Verstorbene*), the dead Dasein understood qua Dasein, from the "dead" *tout court* (*der Gestorbene*), the mere corpse:

> The "deceased," who, in contrast to the dead, was torn away from those "left behind," is an object of "concern" (*Besorgen*) in the ways of funeral rites, interment, and the cult of graves. And this moreover because in his mode of being he is "still more" than a manageable (*besorgbar*) piece of equipment available in the environment. In abiding by him mournfully, in remembrance, those left behind *are with him* in a mode of respectful solicitude (*Fürsorge*). The relation of being that one has to the dead therefore cannot be defined as *concernful* being amidst something available. (*SZ* 238)

This distinction between the deceased and the dead *tout court* corresponds to Heidegger's distinction between two kinds of dying, what I shall call *biological* and *biographical* dying. Biological dying is what Heidegger calls "perishing" (*Verenden*) (*SZ* 240).[19] Heidegger insists that "Dasein never perishes" (*SZ* 247), presumably because, although our bodies do eventually stop functioning biologically, being-in-the-world cannot be understood just in terms of biological function. So, the collapse of the biological infrastructure of our existence is not the same as the end of our existence qua Dasein, which is to say *death*, properly understood.

A concept of death minimally appropriate to human beings as such must therefore be a biographical notion, a notion of the conclusion or resolution of a human life understood as a series of actions, events, episodes, life experiences, and so on. Biographical dying is the ending of a life inasmuch as that life can be understood retrospectively as a whole, perhaps narrated in part as a story. Dying, biographically understood in this way, is what Heidegger calls "demise" (*Ableben*) (*SZ* 247).

---

[19] Actually, Heidegger distinguishes even further between perishing, which he defines as "the ending of anything living," and the "physiological-biological" or "medical concept of *exitus*" (*SZ* 240–1), but he does not explain what he means by this distinction. It could simply be the difference between our ordinary, untutored notion of a thing's being dead, for example when it stops breathing or when its heart stops beating, and more precise medical definitions of death, which might refer explicitly to the cessation of brain activity. I take the liberty of simplifying here by identifying perishing with the mere cessation of life biologically understood, whether theoretically or pretheoretically.

But demise is always the demise of others, for no Dasein can enjoy any settled or stable biographical perspective on itself, if only because, as long as you are still alive, the book of your life is still open, as it were. Again, your death can never be an experience falling within the compass of your life, for it is in principle not something you could live to tell about. In remarking that Dasein cannot experience its own death, and so cannot understand its own death as mere demise, Heidegger is not just reiterating the familiar platitude that, even when you're on your deathbed, it's not too late for important things to happen that will change the meaning of your life. The point is rather that the very structure of being-in-the-world as my own and as falling thrown projection makes it impossible in principle for me to take up a merely observational or biographical point of view on myself and my existence. It is not that I might convert or divorce or win the lottery an hour before I die, but that just in virtue of my existing at all, my existence remains an issue for me, not a settled matter of objective fact – not even a settled matter of objective biographical fact, as it may well be for others.

Existential death, then – that is, death understood as essentially *one's own* – is something different from both perishing and demise, for it can be understood neither biologically nor biographically. Existential dying is neither the mere cessation of the biological functions of life nor the settled conclusion or resolution of the events and episodes constituting a human life. Death in the existential sense must be something phenomenologically accessible to oneself, something immanent in the structure of being-in-the-world understood as my own and as falling thrown projection. But how is my own death manifest and accessible to me while I am still alive? Not in my being-*at*-an-end (*Zu-Ende-sein*), Heidegger says, but in my being *toward* the end (*Sein zum Ende*). Being *toward* the end means projecting into it, which is to say that my death is something with the ontological status of an existential possibility. Indeed, as we have seen, it is *my* possibility in a radical and irreducible sense: "Death is Dasein's *ownmost* possibility." No one else can die for me; rather, death "has to be taken over by Dasein itself." My death – like my body, or indeed my mind – is primitively my own; it cannot in principle be traded or transferred to another. It is, as Heidegger puts it, radically "nonrelational" (*unbezüglich*) (*SZ* 263).

What kind of possibility is my death? It is, Heidegger says, "the possibility of no-longer-being-able-to-be-there" (*SZ* 250), the possibility "*of the utter impossibility of existence*" (*SZ* 262). What does this mean? It is tempting, but it would be a mistake, to read this as meaning simply that it is *possible,* that is, it *might* happen to me, that it will henceforth be *impossible* for anything to happen to me, because I will be dead and will therefore not exist. But to construe possibility simply as what might happen is to take for granted a categorial understanding of modality. Heidegger at times seems to slip into the categorial mode himself, for example when he insists that *"The nearest nearness of being toward death as possibility is as far as possible from anything actual"* (*SZ* 262). This appears to conflate existential possibility, which is a primitive phenomenon constitutive of Dasein's being, with categorial possibility, which contrasts with, and is derivative of, actuality. A more charitable reading, however, suggests that Heidegger's point is rather that death understood as *existential* possibility differs ontologically and in principle from anything *categorially* "real" (*wirklich*), either possible or actual, which Dasein might conceivably encounter in the world. And this seems right, for indeed my own death is precisely not *categorially* possible for me, since we have no notion of what it would be for it to be categorially *actual* for me, and what cannot be actual is (by definition) not possible. I encounter my own death nowhere in my environment, neither in skeletons and graveyards nor even in the deaths of others close to me, but solely in my immanent relation to my own being-in-the-world – which is nothing at all like categorial actuality.

Understood existentially, then, what does the possibility of "no-longer-being-able-to-be-there," or the possibility of "the utter impossibility of existence," amount to? A possibility is something into which I project. So, what am I projecting into in projecting into my own death? The impossibility of existence. But again, this cannot mean being dead. Impossibility, like possibility, must be an existential notion, and if possibilities are what define me, then impossibilities must be what define me negatively. They are what or who I *am not,* or more precisely *cannot be.* And indeed, all projecting into possibility is at once a projecting into impossibility, that is, negative determinations of what or who I am. By projecting into being a student, I project into *not* being an autodidact or a dropout. By projecting into being a husband, I project into *not* being a cloistered monk or a flirtatious bachelor. For every possibility that opens up for Dasein, others are constantly being closed off. What Heidegger's existential account of death reveals, then, is that Dasein's projection into future possibilities turns out to have a twofold structure: Every possibility open to Dasein leaves in its wake other possibilities that have been shut down, rendered null and void. All possibility is bounded and conditioned by impossibility.

Our possibilities are constantly dropping away into nullity, then, and this is what Heidegger means when he says – what might sound otherwise hyperbolic or simply false – that "Dasein is factically dying as long as it exists" (*SZ* 251). To say that we are always dying is to say that our possibilities are constantly closing down around us. Heidegger adds, "but first and for the most part in the mode of *falling*" (*SZ* 251–2). To add that our dying is a kind of *falling* is to say that we are thrown into this possibility. It is given to us. Yet we must also project into it, and the way in which we do so marks our existence as either authentic or inauthentic. Here I want to draw a distinction between two kinds of dying, that is, two ways of projecting into death. The involuntary and, as it were, *disintegrated* mode consists of two discrete projections, the projection into possibility and the projection into impossibility, but the two moments do not form a whole into which Dasein projects as such. This is what Heidegger calls inauthentic dying, or merely "expecting" (*Erwarten*) death. And this much is simply given to us: We all expect death, we are thrown into expecting it, and there is no escaping the expectation.

A resolute or *integrated* projection into death, by contrast, involves a projection into the twofold structure of death itself, that is, into the divide or watershed that is constantly, unrelentingly separating our possibilities from our impossibilities, illuminating the former, extinguishing the latter. This projection into a unified future horizon, defined simultaneously by possibility and impossibility, is what Heidegger calls "authentic being-toward-death" (*SZ* §53). One might object that such a distinction between authentic and inauthentic projections into death is just an empty verbal distinction, a distinction without a difference. But just as there is a difference between a conjunction of two beliefs or two desires on the one hand, and a single belief or desire whose unified content includes a conjunction on the other, so too there is a difference between simultaneously *projecting* into possibility and *projecting* into impossibility on the one hand, which is unavoidable, and projecting simultaneously into *possibility and impossibility* on the other, which would constitute a distinctively integrated attitude or style of comportment. Existential comportments, like intentional states, are opaque, so it makes a difference whether their contents are parceled out across separate attitudes or integrated in a single perspective. Dasein's self-understanding, that is, can be either scattered and dispersed or focused and unified. And although we have no choice but to accept the extinction or nullification of possibilities, which necessarily attends the dawning and abiding of possibilities, we can choose either to embrace it or to flee from it. Of course, fleeing it is ultimately futile, since it is an essential structure of projection, and so of being-in-the-world. But the futility of the effort does not make the effort itself impossible. Embracing death in an integrated way as the essential double aspect of projection into possibility and impossibility, then, is what Heidegger calls authentic "forerunning into death" (*Vorlaufen in den Tod*) (*SZ* 263).

Heidegger's account of existential death therefore departs significantly from commonsense beliefs and attitudes about death, but he has not simply redefined the word in a willful or arbitrary way. Indeed, Heidegger's conception of death as the essential finitude of projection and the constant closing down of possibilities arguably cuts right to the heart of what we find so disturbing and depressing about the prospect of our own death. It is true that the discussion of death in *Being and Time* sets aside what is incoherent in many commonsense worries about death – for example, worries about what will happen to me qua being-in-the-world when I am dead. But Herman Philipse is wrong to insist that Heidegger "is merely stating that death is final so that there is no afterlife," hence that he "might have done better to list the convincing scientific arguments against the doctrine of afterlife."[20] This suggestion is refuted by the text itself. Heidegger writes:

> If death is defined as the "end" of Dasein, that is, of being-in-the-world, this implies no ontical decision about whether yet another, higher or lower, being is possible "after death," whether Dasein "lives on," or even "outlasts" itself and is "immortal." No more is decided about the "other-worldly" and its possibility than about the "thisworldly," as if norms and rules of conduct toward death should be propounded for "edification." The [present] analysis of death, however, remains in this sense purely "thisworldly" inasmuch as it interprets the phenomenon solely as it *impinges upon Dasein* as a possibility of any given Dasein's being. We can only even sensibly and rightfully *ask* with any methodological assurance what *may be after death* once it has been grasped in its full ontological essence. (*SZ* 247–8)

What may come of us *after* death, that is, after the event of our demise, is simply not what Heidegger is talking about. His point is rather that

---

[20] Philipse, *Heidegger's Philosophy of Being*, 368, 367. One wonders what "convincing scientific arguments against the doctrine of afterlife" there could be. In any case, as Heidegger says, that is a *completely* different issue.

questions about survival or immortality will remain ontologically obscure if we have not already understood death in its immanent existential significance. Indeed, "Whether such a question represents a possible
theoretical question at all remains here undecided," and it may well be
that a proper existential understanding of death will expose all talk of
life after death as nonsense. But this is simply not Heidegger's concern:
"The thisworldly ontological interpretation of death comes before all
ontic-otherworldly speculation" (*SZ* 248).

But although Heidegger is not talking about the state of being dead,
or indeed any state following our demise, he does nonetheless understand death as a kind of bereavement. Existential bereavement is neither
the loss of vital functions nor the end of a life story, but a deprivation of
possibilities constitutive of one's existence. This may not be what people have in mind when they worry, probably incoherently, about being
dead, but it is emphatically what they have in mind when they feel their
possibilities falling away from them into nothing, as if their lives were
effectively over. It is also the source of our talking about not just persons
but projects, loves, hopes, epochs, cultures, and worlds dying off. Loves,
hopes, and worlds die, and not just in a secondary metaphorical sense
transferred from a more basic literal concept of the perishing of organisms or the demise of persons. Rather, such things die by dying to us, or
rather by our dying to them as possibilities. To say that Dasein is always
dying is to say that you can be dying, even dead, precisely when you are
in perfectly good health and in the middle of a career, a marriage, a
life.[21]

Far from departing perversely from ordinary understanding and
common sense, then, Heidegger's existential account of death captures
precisely what we might call its *tragic* dimension. And the tragic structure of existence is, ontologically speaking, something fundamentally
different from and irreducible to any set of objective facts about human
beings, their vital functions, or the quality or value of their lives.

---

[21] What does the title of Arthur Miller's *Death of a Salesman* refer to? There is a sense in
which Willy Loman has died before the action of the play even begins. His possibilities
have dried up, and his eventual demise merely punctuates the existential death that he is
already living out in his final days. Loman is already existing his death, though arguably
in the disintegrated, inauthentic mode of fleeing from it. Similarly, *Malone Dies*, like
so many of Beckett's works, is a living record of the existential death of the narrator,
Malone, whose world has shrunk down to include little more than his bed, his pencil,
and a steady trickle of random, mostly empty thoughts. Malone's demise lies outside the
text, but his existential dying is the substance of the narration.

Guilt as Being Thrown into Assuming Responsibility

To define death as the possibility of the impossibility of existence, as Heidegger does, and moreover to interpret existential impossibility as the constant closing down of possibilities, which is an essential structural feature of all projection into a future, as I have suggested, effectively draws the account of death in Chapter 1 of Division II of *Being and Time* into close connection with the discussions of conscience and guilt that follow in Chapter 2. Indeed, as I shall suggest, on Heidegger's account, death – understood as the finitude, indeed the *nullity* of projection – must itself be understood as an aspect of guilt, which Heidegger defines as "being-the-ground of a [mode of] being defined by a not (*ein Nicht*) – that is, *being-the-ground of a nullity* (*Grundsein einer Nichtigkeit*)" (*SZ* 283).[22]

Like his notion of death, Heidegger's conception of guilt departs widely, but not completely or perversely, from received opinion. Following Aristotle, Heidegger often takes received opinion as his point of departure: "All ontological investigations of phenomena like guilt, conscience, death must begin with what the everyday interpretation of Dasein 'says' about them." But, unlike Aristotle, Heidegger concludes that the true ontological meaning of such phenomena tends to "get perverted by everyday interpretation" (*SZ* 281). The German word for guilt (*Schuld*) also means debt, fault, liability. Existential guilt is not debt or responsibility in any ordinary sense, however, since these are all ontic contingencies: Just as you might or might not be biologically or biographically dying, so too you might be indebted to someone, or responsible for something, or you might not be. But just as Dasein is always dying existentially, so too guilt in the existential sense, Heidegger insists, "lies in the being of Dasein as such, so that it *is* already guilty, just insofar as it factically exists" (*SZ* 281). Guilt is no accidental occurrence, for "*Dasein is as such guilty*" (*SZ* 285). "Dasein is essentially guilty, not *sometimes* guilty and *then sometimes not*" (*SZ* 305).

To uncover the abiding ontological phenomenon underlying, and systematically belied by, guilt conventionally understood, Heidegger says, "the idea of 'guilty' must be *formalized* to such an extent that the

[22] It is important to keep in mind throughout this discussion that the German word '*Grund*,' even more so than the English word 'ground,' means the reason, cause, or occasion for something. '*Auf Grund von*,' for example, means *in virtue of*. To say that Dasein is the "ground" of a nullity, then, is to say that Dasein is the reason for it, the cause or occasion. Why the nullity? Because of Dasein.

ordinary phenomena of guilt related to concernful being-with with others *drop out*." Once guilt in the ordinary sense drops out, what is left
over?

> in the idea of "guilty" lies the character of the *not*. If the "guilty" is ca-
> pable of defining existence, then this raises the ontological problem of
> clarifying existentially the *not-character* of this not. Moreover, to the idea
> of "guilty" belongs what is expressed indifferently in the concept of guilt
> as "having responsibility for": being the reason for such-and-such. We
> define the formal existential idea of "guilty" thus: being-the-ground of
> a [mode of] being defined by a not – that is, *being-the-ground of a nullity*.
> (*SZ* 283)

Hubert Dreyfus has read these passages in what, as I said earlier,
I believe is an overly pessimistic vein. What anxiety reveals, he suggests, is "that Dasein has no possibilities of its own and that it can
never acquire any."[23] Hence, "anxiety is the revelation of Dasein's basic
groundlessness and meaninglessness."[24] On Dreyfus's reading, "Dasein
as transcendence *can never make* any possibilities its own," which is to
say, "no possibilities can be given meaning by becoming my defining
possibilities."[25] Dasein "is a *nullity* in that it can make no possibilities its
own."[26]

But is this what Heidegger means in *Being and Time* when he defines
guilt as Dasein's "being a nullity," or in his lectures of 1928 when he
refers to "the inessentiality of the self" (*MAL* 176)? To say that Dasein
in truth has no possibilities of its own, all appearances to the contrary,
and moreover that it can never make any possibilities its own, sounds
dangerously close to saying that Dasein cannot *be* its own, that is, cannot
be authentic (*eigentlich*). But this is not what Dreyfus has in mind. Rather,
existential guilt, he says, "reveals an essentially unsatisfactory structure
definitive of even authentic Dasein. Even if Dasein has done nothing
wrong there is something wrong with Dasein – its being is not under its
own power."[27]

This last point is surely right. Dasein's guilt lies in the fact that its
being is not under its own power; it is not a self-creating, nor even a
self-determining entity; there is no such thing as radical autonomy.
But in what sense is there anything essentially "wrong" with this

[23] Dreyfus, *Being-in-the-World*, 305.   [24] Ibid., 308.
[25] Ibid., 310.   [26] Ibid., 311.
[27] Ibid., 306.

condition or with the entity thrown into it? Existential guilt, as op-posed to contingent indebtedness or moral responsibility, consists in our always only partial, radically conditioned self-possession, self-determination, and self-understanding. Dreyfus is right to point out that this notion owes much to Kierkegaard. The repeated refrain of the "ultimatum" or "last word" that concludes *Either/Or*, for instance, is the "edifying" realization that "Against God we are always in the wrong."[28]

But while *Being and Time* is strictly speaking neutral or open-ended on substantive theological matters, it remains a resolutely secular work, methodologically speaking. Indeed, Heidegger insists that fundamen-tal ontology cannot even do so much as suggest the possibility of sin as a distinct interpretation of existential guilt, although of course it is existential guilt that makes the very idea of sin intelligible in the first place:

> The primordial being-guilty belonging to the constitution of the being of Dasein must be sharply distinguished from a *status corruptionis*, theologi-cally understood. Theology can find in being-guilty, existentially defined, an ontological condition of its own factical possibility. The guilt contained in the idea of this *status* is a factical indebtedness (*Verschuldigung*) of an utterly peculiar sort. It has its own attestation, which remains closed off in principle to any philosophical experience. The existential analysis of being-guilty proves nothing either *for* or *against* the possibility of sin. Strictly speaking, one cannot even say that the ontology of Dasein *of itself* leaves open this possibility, since, as philosophical questioning, it "knows" nothing in principle about sin. (*SZ* 306n)

Existential guilt is not sin. But then it is problematic in what sense Dasein could be said to be essentially "in the wrong," for it need never have understood itself as a creature or subject standing over "against God." As Dreyfus says, since the analytic of Dasein cannot invoke any positive thesis about God as the ground of human existence, Heidegger in effect "excludes the possibility of faith" à la Kierkegaardian Religiousness B.[29] But if the analytic of Dasein cannot in principle describe Dasein as standing over against God, it is unclear how Heidegger could be arguing that our essential and abiding guilt consists in there being anything fundamentally "wrong" or "essentially unsatisfactory" with us.

I think the notion of *wrongness* is, in a word, the wrong notion with which to try to capture Heidegger's concept of guilt. More precisely, to

[28] Kierkegaard, *Either/Or: A Fragment of Life*, 597–609.
[29] Dreyfus, ibid., 312.

say that guilt involves a kind of wrongness is not yet to have "*formalized*" the concept, as Heidegger puts it, "to such an extent that the ordinary phenomena of guilt related to concernful being-with with others *drop out*." The positive definition of guilt, after all, says only that "in the idea of 'guilty' lies the character of the *not*." What kind of *not* does Heidegger have in mind? Again, guilt is "being-the-ground of a [mode of] being defined by a not – that is, *being-the-ground of a nullity*" (*SZ* 283). This definition is formal indeed, almost to the point of sounding empty. But to construe the nullity as a kind of wrongness threatens to read something ontically contingent back into the formal existenti*al* structure Heidegger is trying to isolate and describe in its own terms, prior to any particular existenti*el* interpretation.

The nullity of guilt is in fact twofold, for just as we simultaneously project and are thrown into death, so too we are simultaneously thrown and project into the nullity of guilt. Dasein is

> the ground of its ability-to-be. Even though it has *not itself* laid the ground, it reposes in its weight, which its mood makes manifest to it as a burden.
>
> And how *is* it this thrown ground? Just by projecting itself into possibilities into which it is thrown. The self, which as such has to lay the ground for itself, can *never* get it under its power, and yet, in existing, has to take over being-a-ground. To be one's own thrown ground is the ability-to-be that is at issue for care.
>
> Being a ground, that is, existing as thrown, Dasein constantly lags behind its possibilities. It is never existent *before* its ground, but always only *from it* and *as it*. Being-a-ground, then, means *never* having one's own being in one's power from the ground up. This *not* belongs to the existential meaning of thrownness. Being a ground *is* itself a nullity of itself. (*SZ* 284)

The not (*Nicht*) of our nullity (*Nichtigkeit*)

> constitutes this *being* of Dasein, its thrownness. The not-character of this not is defined existentially: being a *self*, Dasein is the entity that has been thrown *as* a self. It has been *discharged* from its ground, *not by* itself, but *to* itself, in order to be *as this ground*. Dasein is not itself the ground of its being in the sense that this ground first springs from its own projection, though, to be sure, as being-a-self, it is the *being* of the ground. This ground is always only the ground of an entity whose being has to take over being-a-ground. (*SZ* 284–5)

Existential guilt is not just being the ground of a nullity, then, but rather "being the (null) ground of a nullity" (*SZ* 285). Dasein is not fully autonomous or spontaneous. It is not the unconditioned condition, the uncaused cause, of its own nullity. We are not unmoved movers. Our existence is instead thoroughly conditioned, caused, moved in ways we can never bring fully under our own control. This is what Heidegger means when he says that *"Care itself is in its essence permeated with nullity through and through"* (*SZ* 285). The point is not that something must always be wrong or unsatisfying about Dasein's being, but that not even being the ground of its own nullity affords Dasein any fixed, positive metaphysical character, independent of the way its being shows up for it as an issue to be worked out in the course of existing. Being the positive, determinate ground of one's own groundlessness, after all, would be to enjoy a kind of radical freedom, as for example Sartre describes in *Being and Nothingness,* and Heidegger's conception of thrownness is precisely a denial that Dasein is free in any radical, unconditioned sense.

The *not* in Dasein's nullity "belongs to the existential meaning of thrownness." That is, just by being thrown into being anything or anyone, I am thereby thrown into *not* being something and someone else. Moreover, Heidegger adds, "Being a ground *is* itself a nullity of itself." That is, I am the ground of my own nullity precisely by *not being able to be* anything like a metaphysical ground or determinate reason for not being what and who I am not. There is always something or someone I am *not;* moreover, I am the ground or reason for my not being what I am not, even though I am the reason for not being so precisely by *not being* any kind of fixed or settled reason for my being or not being anything. I am constantly thrown into taking on responsibility for my being, though the very fact that I am thrown into it means that I am not in fact ontically responsible for my own being as any kind of fixed metaphysical matter of fact. My responsibility for my own being is thrust upon me; it accrues to me just in virtue of my being-in-the-world as thrown projection. I have to take on a kind of responsibility for myself and my situation, for which I am not in any ordinary sense strictly speaking responsible. I am handed my existence, but then I have to face up to it or not: "To be or not to be," as Hamlet says. Dasein "has its being, as its own, to be" (*SZ* 12). Indeed, "The 'essence' of this entity lies in its to-be (*Zu-sein*)" (*SZ* 42).

If being the ground of a nullity consists in being thrown into projecting what one projects into, it might appear that the nullity of guilt is just Dasein's thrownness. But this is not quite right. It is not enough to equate nullity with thrownness, for the projection that is thrown is null qua projection. And what is the nullity of projection? In a word, death:

> in being-able-to-be, [Dasein] always stands in one possibility or another, it is constantly *not* another and has relinquished it in existentiel projection. Projection, as always thrown, is not only defined by the nullity of being-a-ground, but as *projection* is itself essentially *null.* (*SZ* 285)

Forgoing some possibilities as nullified by others, the constant closing down or extinction of possibilities as impossibilities, I have suggested, is existential death. I therefore conclude that death, on Heidegger's account, is itself simply a constituent element of guilt. The two phenomena overlap in the nullity of projection.

Dasein's existential situation is in this way like Joseph K.'s in Kafka's novel, *The Trial.* K. is politely informed that he is under arrest, but no charges are pronounced against him, nor does he suffer any overt coercion from the legal authorities. He is told, "you're under arrest, certainly, but that's not meant to keep you from carrying on your profession. Nor are you to be hindered in the course of your ordinary life."[30] As the priest tells him at the end of the scene in the cathedral, "The court wants nothing from you. It receives you when you come and dismisses you when you go."[31] The novel, that is, presents almost no tangible manifestation of the court at all, nor any hint of the power or authority of "the law." K.'s guilt, that is, has no ontic concreteness, no legal or psychological reality.

And yet he is guilty. Wherein lies his guilt? Precisely in his constantly rising to the occasion of the putative charges against him to proclaim his innocence. K. assumes responsibility for himself, that is, by insisting a priori that he is not guilty. Indeed, it is precisely his own repeated categorical denial that he is in any way guilty, and moreover his insistence that the court and the law are themselves illegitimate, that embodies and confirms his guilt, which is to say the fact of his being called upon to answer for himself. K.'s confirmed guilt, one might say, consists in denying and obscuring the existential guilt that lies simply in his being thrust into assuming responsibility for himself, which constantly motivates him to answer the charges against him, even before they have been spelled out and given any determinate content. Hence, as the priest explains, "the proceedings gradually merge into the judgment."[32] In the

---

[30] Kafka, *The Trial*, 17.   [31] Ibid., 224.
[32] Ibid.,213.

world of *The Trial,* as K. is told, the court is "attracted by guilt."[33] But the law has no content, the court no reality. K.'s "guilt" is thus ontologically prior to any form of indebtedness or responsibility according to determinate laws and in conformity with effective legal institutions. As Heidegger puts it,

> The phenomenon of guilt, which is not necessarily related to "being in debt" (*Schuldenhaben*) and violating the law, can be elucidated only if we first inquire fundamentally into Dasein's *being*-guilty. . . . The idea of guilt must not only be raised above the domain of concern of the settling of accounts, it must also be detached from any connection with a law or an ought, in violation of which someone brings guilt down upon himself. (*SZ* 283)

Ontic indebtedness and responsibility are contingent affairs, in principle avoidable. Existential guilt, by contrast, is our being thrown into answering for ourselves and taking up the responsibilities into which we have been thrown. As such, it is an abiding structure of being-in-the-world, an existential structure that indebtedness and responsibility presuppose and moreover tend to obscure. Only because we are existentially guilty can we understand ourselves as susceptible to ethical or moral guilt:

> An entity whose being is care can not only be laden with factical guilt, but rather *is* guilty in the ground of its being, and this being-guilty above all provides the ontological condition for Dasein's ability to become guilty, factically existing. This essential being-guilty is equiprimordially the existential condition of the possibility of "moral" good and evil, that is, for morality in general and its factically possible outward forms. Primordial being-guilty cannot be defined by morality, since morality already presupposes it for itself. (*SZ* 286)

Although this primordial being-guilty "first and for the most part remains undisclosed, is kept closed off by the falling being of Dasein," it is nevertheless the abiding condition of our explicit understanding of ourselves as thrown, and so of the possibility of authentic existence. For "only because Dasein is guilty in the ground of its being, closing itself off from itself as thrown and falling, is conscience possible" (*SZ* 286). What then is "conscience" (*Gewissen*), and how does it disclose the primordial guilt of which we are by and large ignorant?

---

[33] Ibid., 9, 39.

The Call of Conscience and the Structure of Authenticity

Authenticity consists in part, as we shall see, in resoluteness, which Heidegger describes as facing or owning up to guilt: "Resoluteness means letting oneself be called forth to one's ownmost *being*-guilty" (*SZ* 305). Owning up to guilt manifests itself in conscience, or more precisely "*wanting to have a conscience*" (*Gewissenhabenwollen*), which Heidegger also describes as "choosing choice" (*Wählen der Wahl*) (*SZ* 270).

Like death and guilt, however, conscience in the existential sense does not coincide with its more familiar mundane counterpart phenomenon, namely, unpleasant feelings of remorse. And just as existential death and guilt are hermeneutic conditions of our ordinary concepts of death and guilt, so too conscience in the existential sense is what makes possible our ordinary ethical notions of conscience and conscientiousness. So, whereas "the everyday interpretation remains within the dimension of concernfully reckoning and counterbalancing 'guilt' and 'innocence,'" and so places heavy emphasis on the subjective experiences or feelings of "'good' conscience" and "'bad' conscience" (*SZ* 292), the existential account of conscience is an attempt to dig down beneath such distinctions by way of uncovering the conditions of their intelligibility. Consequently, Heidegger says, "This existential interpretation necessarily lies far afield of everyday ontic common sense (*Verständigkeit*), even though it lays its ontological foundations" (*SZ* 269). What then does conscience in the ontological-existential sense amount to?

To begin with, taking the metaphor of a "call" (*Ruf*) or "voice" (*Stimme*) as his common, received point of departure, Heidegger insists that conscience is a mode of discourse. Of course, "vocal utterance is not essential" (*SZ* 271). Rather, to say that conscience is discursive is to say that it is an expressive and communicative phenomenon, more specifically a kind of "appeal" (*Anruf*) or "summoning" (*Aufruf*) (*SZ* 269). What is talked about (*das Beredete*) in conscience, Heidegger says, is "Dasein itself." That is, we understand conscience as being *about* or *concerning* ourselves. Moreover, the call is communicative in that we understand it as being *addressed to* us. But who is "us"? Recall that the "who" of everyday Dasein is "the one" (*das Man*). The call of conscience therefore calls one precisely in one's average understanding of oneself in the indifference or the inauthenticity of the everyday. Dasein "always already *understands itself,*" so that "The call reaches Dasein in this everyday-average concernful always-already-understanding-itself. The one-self of concernful being-with with others is reached by the call" (*SZ* 272).

What then is the content of the call? Perhaps, Heidegger wonders rhetorically, "it remains at most an occasion for Dasein to take notice of itself" (*SZ* 272). But that would render it virtually meaningless. One hears the call as being *about* oneself and as *addressed to* one, but what does it *say*? "But how are we to define *what is said* (*das Geredete*) in this discourse? *What* does conscience call out to the one appealed to? Taken strictly – nothing. The call asserts nothing, offers no information about world events, has nothing to tell us." The call has no determinate propositional content. Nevertheless, one understands it as calling one *to* something. What does the call call one *to*? "To one's *own self*." Yet it does so precisely not by articulating any determinate semantic content, but by saying nothing: "*Conscience discourses solely and constantly in the mode of remaining silent*" (*SZ* 273). Of course, as we have seen, saying nothing is not the same as not saying anything. That is, remaining silent is one way of being in discourse with oneself and others.

What the silence of conscience expresses and communicates, then, is an explicit recognition of the distinction between the everyday self of the one, in terms of which one ordinarily understands oneself, and the *proper* self, or one's *own* self, which is an ontological structure formally distinct from any of its own self-interpretations. The call undercuts all such ordinary self-interpretations and refers directly to, one might say rigidly designates, Dasein in its sheer *mineness*: "Dasein, as it is understood in a worldly way for others and itself, gets *passed over* in this appeal. The call to the *self* takes not the slightest cognizance of it." On the contrary, "only the *self* of the one-self is called upon and brought to hear." The self itself "is brought to itself by the call" (*SZ* 273); "Conscience summons the self of Dasein out of its lostness in the one" (*SZ* 274). Conscience calls Dasein away from all its ordinary self-interpretations back to itself, but not back to any substantive or determinate conception of itself, just back to the bare fact of its existence in all its concrete particularity: "*That* it factically is may be obscure with respect to the *why*, but the '*that*' itself is disclosed to Dasein" (*SZ* 276).

Finally, what, or rather who, is the source of the call of conscience? Where does the call come from? Lest the account begin to sound supernatural, or for that matter merely sociological or psychoanalytical, Heidegger assures us that "the caller is Dasein" (*SZ* 277). Conscience has no otherworldly source, nor is it merely the internalization of contingent external influences. Ontologically, that is, "conscience, in its ground and essence, is *always mine*," and is so "because the call comes from the entity that in each case I myself am" (*SZ* 278). More specifically, the caller is myself in the utter strangeness of my existence: "The caller is, in its who, definable by *nothing* worldly. It is Dasein in its uncanniness (*Unheimlichkeit*), primordially thrown being-in-the-world as the not-at-home (*Un-zuhause*), the naked 'that' in the nothing of the world" (*SZ* 276–7).

The apparent foreignness or faraway quality of the voice of conscience, then, is neither an echo of some real transcendent power nor the mere mundane effect of society and the family. It is instead a function of the relative unfamiliarity of the bare fact of one's existence as such, which is typically covered over and obscured by routine and generic forms of intelligibility: "The caller is unfamiliar to the everyday one-self – thus it is something like an *alien* voice" (*SZ* 277). Moreover, the silence of the call is a function both of its source and of its content. That is, not only is the caller Dasein itself, stripped of the usual content of its own self-interpretations, but what the call calls one back to is precisely the fact of one's existence, which is something formally distinct from and so irreducible to the substance of any of those interpretations. "The call discourses in the uncanny mode of *remaining silent* (*Schweigen*)"; moreover, it "*calls one back into the reticence (Verschwiegenheit) of one's existent ability-to-be*" (*SZ* 277). The call calls silently, then, precisely in calling one back to silence.

In what sense, then, is conscience a mode of discourse? To say that conscience is discursive, I have suggested, is just to say that it is essentially expressive and communicative. But conscience does not literally have the structure of dialogue or conversation, or even of inner monologue, for the voice of conscience does not in fact articulate any definite interpretation of anything. Moreover, conscience cannot even be distinguished from Dasein's response to it. Rather, I want to suggest, *the call* is identical with Dasein's *hearing* and responding to it, either by owning up to its guilt in resoluteness or by fleeing from it into distraction and inauthenticity. Dasein hears the call of conscience only by *freely letting itself* hear it, and this amounts to choosing itself as a self: "Letting oneself be called forth to this possibility understandingly involves Dasein's *becoming free* for the call: readiness for the ability to be called. In understanding the call, Dasein is *in thrall to its ownmost possibility of existence*. It has chosen itself" (*SZ* 287). Authenticity consists in Dasein's freely choosing itself against a background of indifference and inauthenticity: "Resoluteness means letting oneself be called out of the lostness of the one" (*SZ* 299).

Conscience, I therefore conclude, is nothing more or less than Dasein's responsiveness to the fact of its own singularity, or mineness. At some level Dasein always understands itself as an existing concrete particular, and it understands this primitive aspect of itself as something distinct from and irreducible to any of its particular self-interpretations. To say that conscience is discursive is not to say that it has the structure of conversation, or even soliloquy, but simply that it consists in one's expressive relation to the fact of one's own concrete particularity. Discourse is a condition of interpretation generally, and a fortiori a condition of one's own interpretive relation to oneself. Conscience, which is to say my expressive responsiveness to my own particularity, is a hermeneutic condition of explicit self-understanding generally.

While it would obviously be a crude mistake, then, to take the metaphor of the call or voice of conscience so literally as to suppose that there must be some other entity in the world, or beyond it, telegraphing moral messages to Dasein about itself, it is less crude but no less mistaken to suppose that Heidegger's account draws a distinction between, on the one hand, some positive normative fact pertaining to Dasein, some fact belied or concealed by our inauthentic self-interpretations, but that cries out for substantive recognition, and on the other hand our proper or improper, correct or incorrect response to that fact. The distinction Heidegger draws is not literally between a call and a response, or speaking and hearing, but between the formal fact of Dasein's mineness, that is, its concrete particularity as such, and its expressive response or responsiveness to that particularity. For the sheer fact of Dasein's particularity carries no definite normative implications, no objective value. It is therefore not something that could literally be reported or said informatively in a call with determinate content. It is instead a bare fact about the concrete existential structure of Dasein's being-in-the-world. Nor does it have any ethical implications, though it is a feature of existence arguably taken for granted by all ethical discourse.

It is not, then, as if we all have true selves generating substantive normative demands on us. Rather, our finite particularity constitutes a kind of boundary condition or limit point past which we cannot in principle continue to lose ourselves, or lose track of ourselves, in the banality of everydayness. To say that we are called back to ourselves by the call of conscience is not to say that an underlying authentic self is crying out for some positive evaluative recognition, but rather that we have run up against a limit past which we cannot become further dispersed and lost in the one.

Of course, there is no such thing as existing without some definite self-understanding that goes beyond the mere mineness of being-in-the-world; the bare recognition of one's particularity does not by itself constitute any substantive self-interpretation. Authentic selfhood, Heidegger insists, does not consist in conceiving of oneself apart from all concrete worlds and self-interpretations: "Resoluteness, as *authentic being-oneself*, does not detach from its world, nor does isolate it as a free-floating I" (*SZ* 298). There is no such hermeneutically substantive I; there is only the mineness of existence, which I always have before me to understand and interpret in some particular way. Though a leash tied to a stake does not literally tell a dog where to go, at its limit it does pull the dog back in the direction of the stake. So too, while the call of conscience does not tell us in any definite way how we ought to interpret ourselves, it does pull us back in the direction of our radical particularity, even though that particularity by itself provides us with no determinate content in which to interpret ourselves. There is no such thing as being an unconditionally autonomous individual, then, since there is no way of shrinking oneself down to the vanishing point of one's sheer particularity, which is a formal structure of existence and so by itself hermeneutically empty.[34]

Dasein's response or responsiveness to its own particularity, then, is both the call of conscience and Dasein's interpretation of it, be it authentic or inauthentic. Conscience is an openness to guilt, which is to say a readiness to assume responsibility for what or who one is *not*. Hence the call itself, which is at once articulated and heard in Dasein's openness to guilt, that is, in the self-interpretation in which

---

[34] See my "Must We Be Inauthentic?" It is true, of course, that Heidegger's concept of authenticity includes a further account of the way in which we can and do fill in the formal structure of mineness with some determinate content or other, some particular thing we might live or die for. Dreyfus is therefore right to say that I overstated my case in claiming that "authenticity consists in nothing over and beyond our ongoing resistance to the banalizing, leveling pressures that pull us away from any explicit recognition" of our finite particularity (25, 309). I should have said that there is nothing more to the formal structure of authenticity than that resistance, though of course living authentically means living for the sake of some particular thing. What sort of thing that might be, though, can in no way be anticipated or prescribed by fundamental ontology. There is simply nothing to say a priori about what kinds of things are worthy of our wholehearted devotion.

Dasein acknowledges its irreducible mineness, is already constitutive of authentic selfhood.

The full formal concept of authenticity in *Being and Time,* however, comprises two distinct but equally important elements: forerunning and resoluteness. What do these two notions amount to, and how is the one related to the other? Forerunning and resoluteness are clearly distinct, even partly separable aspects of authenticity, yet Heidegger insists there is an essential connection between them, so that an adequate account of authenticity must make reference to both. Forerunning means projecting willingly or wholeheartedly into the double aspect of possibility and impossibility that constitutes an essential structure of existence. Forerunning, that is, amounts to being toward death in such a way as to grasp death as one's ownmost existential possibility: "Being toward possibility as being toward death . . . is to comport itself toward *it* in such a way that it reveals itself in this being and for it *as possibility*" (*SZ* 262). At the same time, authenticity consists in resoluteness, that is, owning up to the concrete situation in which one finds oneself and understanding one's being explicitly *as* one's own. Resoluteness is a kind of focused engagement with things in the world and with other Daseins: "Resoluteness brings the self directly into its current concernful being amidst the available and thrusts it into solicitous being-with with others" (*SZ* 298). What resoluteness reveals, precisely by constituting it for Dasein, is what Heidegger calls the concrete "situation" (*Situation*) itself: "[T]he situation *is* only through and in resoluteness," Heidegger says. "*For the one, by contrast, the situation is essentially closed off.* It knows only the '*general state of affairs*' (*allgemeine Lage*)" (*SZ* 300).

But if authenticity involves both forerunning into death and resolute engagement in the concrete situation, Heidegger now asks, "How are these two phenomena to be brought together?" That is, "What can death and the 'concrete situation' of action have in common?" Heidegger worries that "forcing together resoluteness and forerunning" has perhaps yielded an altogether "unphenomenological construction that can no longer lay claim to the character of a phenomenally grounded ontological projection." The crucial question is whether the one phenomenon harbors in itself any essential reference to the other: "*Does resoluteness itself, in its ownmost existentiel tendency of being, point toward forerunning resoluteness as its ownmost authentic possibility?*" (*SZ* 302).

To see that and how resoluteness does indeed already involve an indication of the possibility of forerunning, one need only recall how closely death and guilt are themselves intertwined. Since authentic dying is just

an integrated projection into possibility-cum-impossibility, it is plainly
bound up with a resolute appreciation of the concrete situation into
which one has been thrown. Indeed, in its commitment to the exigencies of the concrete situation defining it, resoluteness is essentially an
acknowledgment and acceptance of guilt: "Resoluteness means letting
oneself be called forth to one's ownmost *being*-guilty" (*SZ* 305). To be
called forth to being guilty means taking on responsibility for the nulli-
ties defining one, that is, interpreting oneself as the ground or reason
that one is not what or who one is not. Recall that I am thrown into
not being what or who I am not, and though I take up that nullity as
my own, it is not as if I have full autonomy or spontaneity. I am not the
uncaused cause of my own being. Nevertheless, that being is essentially
mine to be, and realizing that, and moreover integrating the realization into the content of my self-interpretation, in effect frees me to take
up a new, radically open stance on my own possibilities as my own, as
opposed to feeling oppressed or thwarted by them as if they were alien
entities somehow external to myself. Resoluteness means knowing con-
fidently what one is about, which is a kind of certainty, or more precisely
a noncognitive *being*-certain (*Gewiß*sein) about oneself, and this makes
it possible to take up a new, freer relation to the concrete situation itself:

> *What then does the certainty belonging to such resoluteness mean?* It is to main-
> tain itself in what is resolved in the resolution. But this means that it
> precisely cannot become *fixed* to the situation, but must understand that
> the resolution ... must be free and *held open* for the given factical possi-
> bility. The certainty of the resolution means *holding oneself free for* one's
> possible, and always factically necessary, *taking back*. (*SZ* 307–8) [35]

Genuine openness to possibility is an openness to the double aspect
of possibility and impossibility, and an integrated projection into possibility and impossibility is precisely forerunning into death. On my
account of death as the constant closing down of possibilities understood as an essential moment of projection into possibility as such, that
is, it becomes perfectly understandable that and how resoluteness itself
involves an essential reference to forerunning as its proper end or fulfillment. For being fully resolved to oneself and one's situation ultimately
means projecting wholeheartedly into the dying off of possibilities that
necessarily attends and defines one's being anything or anyone at all.

---

[35] It is not clear whether "taking back" (*Zurücknahme*) here means revoking a resolution or
rather withdrawing or extricating oneself from a situation.

Consider Shakespeare's *Hamlet*. It is a popular misconception that Hamlet is wracked by indecision, that he cannot make up his mind, that he is irresolute. The suggestion is not obviously right even in the ordinary sense of the word 'resolute,' but it is plainly false given Heidegger's account of resoluteness as an owning up to the nullity of guilt. For already by the end of Act 1, immediately after conversing with his father's ghost, Hamlet confronts his situation directly and knows exactly what it calls him to do: "The time is out of joint – O cursed spite, / That ever I was born to set it right" (1.5.188–9). What is true of Hamlet is rather that, for whatever psychological (or theatrical) reasons, he does not carry that resoluteness forward into a forerunning into his own death until Act 5, when he accepts the challenge to fight Laertes in a wager: "I am constant to my purposes" (5.2.200); he now says, "If it be now, 'tis not to come; if it be not to come, it will be now; if it be not now, yet it will come – the readiness is all" (5.2.220–2).

These words might sound like mere passive resignation or fatalism, but in fact they express an active embrace of the loss and impossibility that define *forerunning* resolute commitment. It was that sense of loss to which Hamlet was unable to reconcile himself, in spite of the resoluteness in guilt he had already plainly achieved. It is fitting, then, by Heideggerian lights, that he should seem to undergo a kind of courageous transformation at around the time he encounters the skull of Yorick at Ophelia's grave. For only then is his resoluteness carried forward in an acceptance of death as the price one pays for being-in-the-world at all.[36] Resoluteness and forerunning are distinct moments of authentic existence, then, yet a full acknowledgment and acceptance of the nullity of guilt is realizable only in an active projection into the utmost possible impossibility of death.

Subjectivity as the Abiding Presence of the Self to Itself

What I have described so far is what one might call the formal concept of authenticity, abstracting from the concrete content that any particular authentic self-interpretation might have. Formally, authenticity is simply forerunning resoluteness, which means facing up to the nullity of guilt and projecting into the nullity of death as one's ownmost possibility. The existential analytic of Dasein is meant to be fully general,

---

[36] Hence the pun on 'debt' in *1 Henry IV*, when Prince Hal says to Falstaff, "Why, thou owest God a death"(5.1.126).

culturally and historically universal, hence neutral with respect to the content of ontically specific self-interpretations, which of course vary widely from time to time and from place to place. Moreover, there will be variation not just among specific interpretations, but among locally dominant schemas for such interpretations. Global conceptions of what is worthy and unworthy, what is desirable or admirable for human beings, have drifted historically from notions of nobility and moderation in antiquity, to blessedness and humility in the Middle Ages, to autonomy, maturity, sincerity, and authenticity in modernity, to the maximization of potential or self-fulfillment in our contemporary technological culture.

Being and Time is no doubt implicated in Romantic and post-Romantic discourses of authenticity and self-realization, if only by the vocabulary and the rhetorical tenor of the text. But whatever surface continuity may run from such characteristically late modern themes to Heidegger's existential analytic, the ontological conception of selfhood that emerges in Division II of *Being and Time* nevertheless represents a radical break from the expressivist tradition of the eighteenth and nineteenth centuries, as Isaiah Berlin and Charles Taylor have described it. For Heidegger interprets human existence in such a way that the dichotomies drawn in the service of expressivist conceptions of the self – between, say, unity and fragmentation, whole and part, completeness and incompleteness, integration and alienation – notwithstanding their undeniable resonance at an ontic-existentiel level, fail in principle to apply to Dasein ontologically. Dasein can achieve no kind of real unity over and beyond its formal unity as a concrete particular, nor therefore can it literally be broken into fragments. Neither can it be made whole by any of its commitments or projects, nor is it ever merely part of some larger whole. Dasein is in principle neither complete nor completable, and so cannot be incomplete. Finally, it cannot enjoy any kind of integration beyond its own resolute forerunning into death, for its estrangement in everydayness is always only a failure to own up to the exigencies of its concrete situation.

Heidegger's position is therefore more radical and more original than the departure from expressivism alone suggests. Indeed, his existential account of selfhood seems to imply that there can be no fully objective, impersonal metaphysics of the self at all. For any general metaphysical theory would have to remain indifferent to the distinction between the first-person point of view from which one understands oneself either authentically or inauthentically in relation to guilt and death, and the second- and third-person points of view from which one understands others as intraworldly characters whose lives conclude with their eventual earthly demise. And to blur that distinction, or to assimilate the former to some version of the latter, would simply be to fail to grasp the structure of selfhood from the only point of view we can ever have on ourselves, namely, our own.

Heidegger's existential conception of selfhood is concerned primarily with the irreducibility of the first-person perspective, as I hope the foregoing discussions of death, guilt, and forerunning resoluteness have made clear. That there can be no general account of the self at all, however, is a deeply unsettling idea. In the remainder of this chapter I will try to spell out Heidegger's notion of the irreducibility of the first person and then conclude by saying why I believe his bifurcated ontological conception of the self remains problematic, if only because it omits something arguably essential about us ontologically, namely, our existence as discrete selves.

My point is not that philosophy ought to be in the business of providing us with complete, systematic theories of everything, including ourselves. It is rather that Heidegger's account of the self supplies none of the conceptual resources necessary for making sense of ourselves *as selves,* that is, as intraworldly characters whose lives conclude with our eventual earthly demise, notwithstanding the fact that we also understand ourselves existentially, that is, as negatively defined situated particulars whose defining possibilities are constantly dying off to us and who must perpetually assume responsibility for the situations and histories into which we have been thrown. Heidegger's account of selfhood is not incoherent, then, but incomplete, for it fails to describe our characteristically human understanding of ourselves *as* others understand us. What it omits, in short, is an account of the hermeneutic conditions for understanding oneself *as* another.

There is a gap between our understanding of ourselves as bare particulars, then, and the impersonal or perspective-neutral conception we acquire of ourselves as persons or characters on a par with others. Modern philosophy has tried to bridge that gap, or has taken it to be already bridged, by the structure of subjectivity itself. The concept of subjectivity, that is, offers an interpretation of ourselves as always already standing in a certain epistemic or normative relation to ourselves. It is difficult to say exactly what that putative relation amounts to, but philosophers and intellectual historians have been mulling the question over since Descartes, and then with increasing earnestness and intensity after Kant. In any event, it is undeniable that philosophical conceptions of the self and selfhood changed profoundly during the seventeenth and eighteenth centuries with the emergence of problems about subjectivity, in a way they had not since antiquity, even if it is hard to say exactly what the change consisted in or how we should understand its philosophical significance.

I will therefore say something about subjectivity by way of situating Heidegger's conception of the self and the phenomenological problem I believe it leaves us with. Heidegger presents his account of authentic selfhood as part of a wholesale rejection of the concept of subjectivity, which he regards as the ontological foundation stone of modern philosophy. What precisely does he take himself to be rejecting? What does it mean to understand human beings as subjects? In the course of his critique of Kant, Heidegger says bluntly, "To define the I ontologically as *subject* means to determine it as something always already occurrent. The being of the I is understood as the reality of the *res cogitans*" (*SZ* 320). But this seems much too crude, for it simply equates the concept of subjectivity with Descartes' philosophy of mind. It certainly seems unfair to Kant, as we shall see.

More precisely, then, what is the subjectivism Heidegger is trying to avoid? What do Descartes and Kant have in common, in spite of their differences? Descartes' conception of subjectivity, for its part, centers around two internally connected notions: one ontological, the other epistemological. First, the subject is identical with the soul or mind, understood as a simple substance, a thing with properties but no parts, the *res cogitans*. Second, the subject stands in an epistemically privileged relation to itself and its modes: My mind and its contents are directly present to me and so are immediately knowable by me in a way external bodies and other minds are not. The two ideas go together naturally and complement each other. The Cartesian subject is thus for itself an ideally unified object of knowledge. In the Paralogisms of the first *Critique* Kant rejects Descartes' rational psychology and argues that, though it may be unobjectionable as a matter of metaphysical principle to call the soul a simple substance, the assertion nevertheless adds nothing to our knowledge of ourselves. The subject is not intuitively present to itself as a thing, nor is theoretical knowledge of the noumenal self possible, any more than we can know God or spatiotemporal objects as things in themselves. Nevertheless, the I constitutes the formal unity of consciousness, so that I can at any time explicitly represent myself to myself as the subject of my experience. As Kant puts it, "The *I think* must *be able* to accompany all my representations" (*KRV* B131).

It would appear, then, that Kant departs more decisively from the Cartesian conception of the self and self-knowledge than Heidegger is willing to admit. Indeed, it has struck many readers as uncharitable of Heidegger to criticize Kant's notion of the subject as if it differed only superficially from Descartes' substantialism. Kant, he writes,

> shows that the ontic theses about the soul-substance inferred from the specified characteristics [simplicity, substantiality, personality] are without justification. But to do so is merely to reject a flawed *ontic* explanation of the I. The *ontological* interpretation of selfhood is in no way thereby achieved, nor even secured and positively prepared. (*SZ* 318)

Notwithstanding such a modest advance at a merely ontic level of description, Heidegger argues, Kant "slips back into *the same* inappropriate ontology of the substantial, whose ontic foundations he has theoretically denied to the I" (*SZ* 318–19).

How so? By generalizing an ontically particular relation in which we sometimes stand to ourselves, namely, in self-conscious reflection, and construing it as the most fundamental structure of our relation to the world at large. The I is thus the ultimate ground of our relation to entities, a relation Kant still conceives in terms of mental representation:

> The I is . . . the subject of logical comportment, of binding together (*Verbinden*). The "I think" means: I bind together. All binding together is "*I* bind together." In every gathering-together (*Zusammennehmen*) and relating, the I always underlies – *hupokeimenon*. The subject is thus "consciousness in itself" and not a representation, but rather the "form" of representation. . . . A form of representation is neither a framework nor a general concept, but that which, as *eidos,* makes everything represented and every representing what it is. (*SZ* 319)

To say that Kant conceives of the I as *hupokeimenon* is to say that for him, as for Descartes, subjectivity has inherited and retained the function of substance in ancient Greek ontology. Like the English word 'substance,' the Greek '*hupokeimenon*' and the Latin '*substantia*' literally mean what underlies or stands beneath as a kind of ground. A substance, that is, underlies, supports, and unifies a thing's attributes. In ancient and medieval philosophy human beings enjoyed no privileged place in the general scheme of things, and the concept of substance had nothing to do with human subjects or subjectivity. It was Descartes who radically reoriented ancient and medieval ontology, so that the human subject came to be understood as the ultimate metaphysical principle grounding and explaining the being of entities as such.

So, according to Heidegger, although Kant denies that the I appears to itself as an object accessible in intuition,[37] he nonetheless conceives of it as underlying or standing beneath all its representations as the unifying principle of consciousness, and in this sense it remains literally a kind of *sub-stance*. In this respect, then, Kant's conception of the self remains enmeshed in Cartesian ontology:

> Kant fundamentally retains Descartes's definition. As essential as Kant's own investigations in the ontological interpretation of subjectivity have been, and forever remain, the I, the ego, is for him, as for Descartes, *res cogitans, res, something* that thinks, i.e. represents, perceives, judges, affirms, denies, but also loves, hates, strives, and the like. (*GP* 177)[38]

Similarly, in his critique of Kant's "Refutation of Idealism" in the B edition of the first *Critique,* Heidegger writes, " 'Consciousness of my existence (*Dasein*)' means, for Kant: consciousness of my being occurrent in Descartes' sense. The term '*Dasein*' means as much the being occurrent of consciousness as the being occurrent of things" (*SZ* 203). There is less difference than there appears to be, then, between the Cartesian *res cogitans* and the Kantian unity of apperception:

> It seems at first as if Kant has given up the Cartesian assumption of an iso- lated, antecedently given subject. But it only seems so. That Kant demands

---

[37] In a footnote to the Paralogisms in the B edition, Kant does say that "the proposition *I think* ... expresses an indeterminate empirical intuition, i.e. a perception." However, he goes on to say that "An indeterminate perception here signifies only something real that is given, and indeed only to thinking in general, thus not as appearance, and also not as a thing (*Sache*) in itself (noumenon), but rather as something that in fact exists and is designated as such in the proposition *I think* ... the *I* in this proposition is ... purely intellectual, since it belongs to thinking in general" (*KRV* B422–3). It seems, then, that although the proposition *I think* expresses an empirical intuition, the intuition it expresses is one we lack, since the self is given to itself only in thought. If the ambiguity of this text is what led Fichte to insist that his own concept of intellectual intuition is just the same as Kant's notion of the unity of apperception, then Kant was right to deny it, and so to repudiate Fichte's system.

[38] Nor is Husserl exempt, of course. Citing his claim that "Between consciousness and reality there yawns a veritable abyss of meaning" (*Id I* 93), Heidegger remarks, "Husserl con- stantly refers to this distinction, and precisely in the form in which Descartes expressed it: *res cogitans – res extensa*" (*GP* 176).

a proof for the "existence of things outside me" at all already shows that he takes the subject, the "within me," as the starting point of the problematic. . . . What Kant proves – assuming that the proof and its basis are correct at all – is the necessary being-occurrent-together of changing and permanent entities. (*SZ* 204)

Heidegger points out that even this much fails to prove that objects exist in addition to subjects. And even if it did, it obscures the question concerning the mode of being of the subject itself, for "*The being-occurrent-together of the physical and the mental is ontically and ontologically completely different from the phenomenon of being-in-the-world*" (*SZ* 204).

So, although Heidegger concedes that Kant "sees the impossibility of the ontic reduction of the I to a substance" (*SZ* 319–20), he nevertheless presses the question, "How does it happen that Kant is unable to evaluate the true phenomenal starting point of the 'I think' ontologically and must fall back on 'substance,' that is, the substantial" (*SZ* 320–1)? The point seems to be that Kant still regards the I as something constantly abiding, something present in the very structure of experience, if not as an intuitable object, then as a logical accompaniment, or adhering element, in the structure of cognition. Kant insists that the I does not simply occur alongside and in addition to its representations. Nevertheless,

These representations are for him the "empirical" that is "accompanied" by the I, the appearances to which it "adheres." But Kant nowhere shows the mode of being of this "adhering" and "accompanying." At bottom, however, it is understood as the constant being-occurrent of the I along with its representations. (*SZ* 321)

Although the I does not occur materially in my experience, it nevertheless accompanies or adheres to my representations in the very form of my thinking. It is not that I continually self-consciously represent myself to myself as the subject of my thoughts, only that I *can* always in principle make the I explicit in the proposition *I think*.[39]

---

[39] Kant equivocates somewhat, referring at one point to the I as "a mere consciousness that accompanies all concepts" (*KRV* A345–6/B404). It is important to recognize that Heidegger is not simply exploiting an uncharitable reading of the text to suggest that Kant implausibly depicts us as constantly reflective or hyperconscious of ourselves as subjects. In his 1927 lectures, having quoted the remark about the *I think* being *able* to accompany all my representations, Heidegger observes, "This proposition, however, is not to be taken as though with every comportment, with every thinking in the widest sense, there is also always the representation I, rather I am conscious of the connectedness of

Why does Heidegger object to this notion of the I residing in experience as a purely formal structure, and so as a possible explicit accompaniment to any of my representations? Why does he insist that Kant's conception of subjectivity is little more than a minor ontic variation on Descartes' substantialism? What kind of permanent structural accompaniment or adherence of the I in relation to its representations, after all, is in question in Kant's understanding of the I as the mere unity of apperception?

The answer, I believe, is that although in Kant's view the I is not present to itself as an object of intuition, hence not as a substance in the received sense, it is nevertheless immanent in its own thinking activity as a kind of ever-present normative guide or governing agency. The I does not appear before me empirically, but it does constantly inform my actions and my thoughts by legislating the norms according to which I conduct myself at all times. The self is essentially autonomous, which is to say self-legislating, both theoretically and practically. Kant's conception of selfhood thus purifies and preserves the structure of subjectivity by first dismissing the *res cogitans* as an intuitable object in consciousness and then reinstating it as the self-legislating agency immanent in free thought and action as such. The self thus retains a kind of abiding presence to itself, not as a thing with properties, but as normative guide constantly informing its own cognitive and practical behavior.

The concept of subjectivity that has dominated modern philosophy, and that is arguably common to Descartes, Kant, and Husserl – perhaps to Hegel, Kierkegaard, and Nietzsche, too – notwithstanding the many undeniable differences among them, might therefore be described, albeit schematically, as the idea of a self constituted by a direct abiding presence to itself, whether descriptively in its awareness of itself as a mind or prescriptively in its capacity to determine its thoughts and actions autonomously, independently of external authority or coercion. Subjectivity is supposed to be a kind of metaphysically essential, formally guaranteed self-presence or self-possession, quite apart from the contingent ways and means we have of coming to know ourselves and

---

all my comportments with my I, i.e. I am conscious of them in their multiplicity as *my* unity, which has its ground in my I-hood (as *subiectum*) as such" (*GP* 179). Heidegger's objection is thus not just phenomenological, but ontological. That is, it is not that Kant misdescribes ordinary experience as hyperreflective, but that he takes the phenomenon of reflective self-consciousness as his paradigm in interpreting the fundamental structure of selfhood as such, whether it is overtly self-conscious or not.

learning how to steer our actions effectively in a world of objects. Subjectivity thus amounts to a kind of short circuit in which the self stands in relation to itself, whether as an object of unmediated knowledge for itself or as an authoritative source of norms governing its own actions. In either case, that is, for both Descartes and Kant, the idea of subjectivity is the idea of an abiding internal relation to oneself that grounds some positive epistemic or normative value. In Descartes the subject is the self understood as ideally present to itself as an object of knowledge. In Kant the subject ceases to be an ideal object of theoretical knowledge and becomes instead the abiding normative authority over its own actions, including the operations of its own understanding.

It is this common underlying idea of abiding self-presence, I want to suggest, that Heidegger rejects as an interpretive model for the ontology of selfhood. The self can come to stand in any number of theoretical and practical relations to itself, of course, but there is no source of knowledge or normativity purely immanent in the self's relation to itself. All sources of epistemic and normative value are worldly through and through, embedded in the contingencies of historical tradition and social life. This, once again, is why the account of authenticity in *Being and Time* has nothing to do with theoretical self-knowledge or substantive action-guiding norms, but is instead simply a description of the relation in which Dasein stands to itself in the bare recognition of the *that* of its existence. Kant could interpret the self's relation to itself as establishing substantive normative principles only because, like Descartes, he had already lost sight of the essentially worldly context of Dasein's comportments, even those most purely related to itself as a concrete particular: "Kant did not see the phenomenon of world," Heidegger writes; "consequently the I was once again pushed back to an *isolated* subject, which accompanies representations in an ontologically quite indefinite way" (*SZ* 321).

The Asymmetry of the Self

Far from being grounded in any prior concept of subjectivity, then, Heidegger's own account of authentic selfhood is precisely meant to ground and explain the traditional notion of subjecthood as it has figured ontologically in modern philosophy since Descartes. Subjectivity is precisely *not* the phenomenon we should appeal to in trying to understand the self existentially. Rather, we ought to contrast the self in its authentic and inauthentic modes of existence in order to understand how modern philosophers ever came to conceive of the self as a subject to begin with.

It would be simplistic to argue, as one might expect Heidegger to do, that the philosophical tradition seized upon our everyday inauthentic conception of ourselves as the indifferent "one" (*das Man*) and then simply let that interpretation harden until it became entrenched dogma. Indeed, the story he tells in §64 of *Being and Time* is much more subtle, for he suggests instead that the concept of subjectivity emerged as a conflation of two different sorts of self-interpretation: one authentic, the other inauthentic. Subjectivity, it turns out, is not just the projected image of an inferior form of self-understanding, but rather an illegitimate hybrid that combines elements of inauthentic everydayness and authentic selfhood without explaining how such a combination is possible or even intelligible.

Tracing the idea of subjectivity back to an inauthentic self-understanding would seem to be more in keeping with Heidegger's usual insistence on the fallenness of traditional philosophy and its forgetfulness of the question of being. In our ordinary self-interpretations, Heidegger suggests, we typically fail to grasp ourselves explicitly *as* being-in-the-world, that is, as thrown, falling, projecting particulars whose existence is radically our own, to own up to or not:

> In saying I, Dasein indeed means the entity that it in each case is. Everyday self-interpretation, however, has the tendency to understand itself in terms of the 'world'[40] of its concerns. In intending itself ontically it *mistakes* itself with respect to the mode of being of the entity that it itself is. (*SZ* 321)

This kind of self-misrecognition is grounded in Dasein's inevitable falling into the world of its concerns:

> What motivates this "flighty" (*flüchtig*) I-saying? The falling of Dasein, in which it *flees* in the face of itself into the one (*das Man*). "Natural" I-discourse is carried out by the one-self (*Man-selbst*). What expresses itself in the "I" is the self that, first and for the most part, I am *not* authentically. (*SZ* 322)

What explicit conception of the self does this fallen, anonymous form of self-expression constitute? A purely empty, formally self-identical

---

[40] 'World' in inverted commas denotes the first of the four senses Heidegger distinguishes in §14, namely, the mere collection of occurrent entities (*SZ* 65).

subject: "[T]he self of the self-forgetful I-am-concerned shows itself as the constantly selfsame, but empty-indeterminate simple [something]" (*SZ* 322) – in short, a mere thing, ontologically on all fours with any other thing, which then finds explicit philosophical expression in the Cartesian conception of a substantial *res cogitans* and the Kantian notion of a simple logical subject, the merely formal principle of the unity of experience.

But however plausible or implausible that derivation story may be on its own, it is by no means the whole story Heidegger tells. In addition to expressing our average inauthentic understanding of the self, the concept of subjectivity incorporates an authentic understanding of selfhood, too. Our ordinary way of saying "I" is not authentic, Heidegger insists: "Care expresses itself with 'I' first and for the most part in the 'flighty' I-discourse of concern. The one-self says 'I-I' the loudest and the most frequently because at bottom it *is not authentically* itself and evades its authentic ability-to-be" (*SZ* 322). Again, to say that our ordinary understanding of the first person is "inauthentic" could be either an evaluative or a descriptive claim, implying either that it is deficient and undesirable in some way or just that it is not directly reflexive but mediated by some general or impersonal conception of selves that is indifferent to the fact of my being this particular one. To be sure, evading your authentic ability-to-be sounds like a bad thing. Nevertheless, it is plausible to construe Heidegger's claim in a descriptive sense, since he goes on to say that inauthentic self-understanding must itself be understood in terms of Dasein's being itself authentically: "[T]he ontological constitution of the self can be traced back neither to an I-substance nor to a 'subject'; the everyday-flighty I-I-saying must on the contrary be understood in terms of the *authentic* ability-to-be" (*SZ* 322). This cannot mean that Dasein must already have achieved an authentic self-understanding in order to understand itself inauthentically, since the inauthentic understanding is precisely the one Dasein has "first and for the most part" in its everydayness. Falling does not mean falling *from* a prior authentic self-understanding into inauthenticity. Instead, it means being always already embroiled and entangled in the world of quotidian concerns: "The fallenness of Dasein must neither therefore be taken as a 'fall' from a purer and higher 'primal status' " (*SZ* 176).

To say that the inauthentic self must be understood in terms of the authentic self must instead mean that Dasein can interpret itself indirectly and impersonally only because it is the sort of entity whose first-person dimension is primitive and irreducible, whether it itself understands that fully and explicitly or not. In any case, Heidegger wants to insist that the self is not any kind of underlying ground of being-in-the-world, according to which human existence is intelligible to itself immanently or autonomously in abstraction from its worldly involvements. The self is not an autonomous or self-sufficient hermeneutic condition. This is what Heidegger means by denying that the self is a *subject*. Rather, selfhood is an irreducible aspect of being-in-the-world that is itself interpretable only against a background of hermeneutic conditions realized in a wide range of existential structures and worldly phenomena. It does not follow, that is, that "the self is thus the constantly occurrent ground of care. Selfhood is to be discerned existentially only in the authentic ability-to-be-a-self (*Selbstseinkönnen*), that is, in the authenticity of Dasein's being *as care*" (*SZ* 322).

This is not to say that Dasein becomes a self at all only once it attains forerunning resoluteness, but rather that selfhood as an abiding ontological structure of being-in-the-world lies in the existential *possibility* of achieving an authentic relation to oneself, in Dasein's "*ability*-to-be-a-self." Once realized, however, authenticity casts interpretive light back on that structural possibility of selfhood as *having been* a possibility all along. It is only because Dasein is already a self that it can exist either authentically or inauthentically, as its own or not its own. And it can fully appreciate that fact only retrospectively, as it were, from a forerunning-resolute point of view. Moreover, the constancy of resolute commitment is what then feeds into the illicit notion of an abiding subject as having been present to itself all the while, whether as a thinking substance or as an autonomous source of normative authority:

> The *constancy of the self* as the supposed persistence of the *subiectum* is to be clarified in terms of care. The phenomenon of the authentic ability-to-be, however, opens our eyes to the *constancy of the self* in the sense of having gained standing. *The constancy of the self* in the dual sense of constant steadfastness is the *authentic* counter-possibility of the non-self-constancy of irresolute falling. Existentially, *self-constancy* means nothing other than forerunning resoluteness. The ontological structure of the latter reveals the existentiality of the selfhood of the self. (*SZ* 322)

Selfhood in the *formal* sense of standing in a uniquely direct relation to oneself, then, is what makes possible the achievement of selfhood in the *evaluative* sense of having achieved authentic forerunning resoluteness. The modern concept of subjectivity thus combines two distinct preontological notions of selfhood: an *inauthentic* conception of a self as a simple occurring thing, and an *authentic* understanding of a self as constant, or resolute in its commitments.

The concept of subjectivity is illegitimate, however, Heidegger insists, since it simply takes for granted the phenomenological interconnectedness of those two forms of self-understanding. I do not mean there is no story to tell about how Dasein manages to lift itself out of its indifferent or inauthentic state, to pull itself together, as it were, and become authentic. Heidegger himself tells a story of that sort in the second chapter of Division II of *Being and Time* in his account of Dasein's spontaneous, boot-strapping response to the call of conscience. Dasein reverses its unchosen entanglements in its average everyday existence by "fetching itself back to itself from its lostness in the one," and it does this by "*reclaiming a choice.* Reclaiming a choice, however, means *choosing this choice,* deciding on an ability-to-be, out of one's own self. In choosing the choice Dasein first *makes possible* its own authentic ability-to-be" (*SZ* 268). Authentic selfhood in the evaluative sense means forerunning resoluteness, and "Resoluteness means letting oneself be called out of the lostness of the one" (*SZ* 299).

The concept of subjectivity is a response not to that evaluative difference between authenticity and inauthenticity, or to the problem of becoming resolute, but to the formal distinction between our immediate or authentic relation to ourselves and our mediated or inauthentic understanding of ourselves as anyone, just any old self. For the idea of subjectivity, as I have suggested, is the idea of a self being in some way constantly present to itself as such. And that direct internal relation to oneself as a self already combines the first-person point of view with a kind of second- or third-person perspective, since in the immanence of self-consciousness we are supposed to be present to ourselves either as mere things or as self-legislating practical authorities. Heidegger rejects such notions since they threaten to cut the self off ontologically from the world constitutive of its being. They fail, that is, to acknowledge the worldly hermeneutic conditions necessary for having any understanding of oneself at all. This is how I understand Heidegger's notorious hostility to the very idea of subjectivity, which he believes has cast such an ominous shadow over the whole of modern thought.

Absent the concept of subjectivity, however, we are left once again with the ontologically perplexing asymmetry of the self, to which the idea of subjectivity first arguably arose as a response. That is, how does our first-personal self-understanding overlap and interact with our

second- and third-person interpretations of selves as intraworldly entities? To what extent and in what ways is it possible or impossible to
understand and relate to oneself *as* one understands and relates to others? I show up and make sense to myself in my situated activity in a
way radically different from the way in which others show up and make
sense to me. How could it ever have occurred to us to try to unify and
harmonize those two incongruent sides of our perceptions and understandings so as to regard ourselves as intelligible from a multiplicity of
perspectives, rather than just authentically as our own, or inauthentically as just any old self? Managing to see ourselves in terms of more
complex social points of view was no doubt a momentous achievement
somewhere in the early chapters of human history, or prehistory, and
various refinements of that perspectival sensitivity probably continue to
insinuate themselves in subtle ways in our contemporary evolving self-
undertanding. What concerns me here, however, is not the social and
psychological effects of such archaic and ongoing innovations in our
discursive interaction, but the very possibility, the primitive hermeneutic conditions, of a more fully integrated concept of persons, which
must as a matter of principle comprise an abiding asymmetry between
one's relation to oneself and one's relation to others.

Strawson's argument for the primitiveness of the concept of a
person[41] is at once a denial of Cartesian dualism and a response to
Wittgenstein's emphasis on the asymmetry of first- and third-person
concepts of experience, which invites comparison with the asymmetry
of authentic and inauthentic, reflexive and other-oriented modes of
self-interpretation in Heidegger. But simply pointing out that we have
an overarching concept of persons connecting and comprising those
asymmetries does not yet tell us how the concept is possible, which is
to say, what its hermeneutic conditions consist in. How is it possible
that we have an understanding of selves that is flexible enough to apply
both to myself and to others, yet sufficiently sensitive to the underlying asymmetries inherent in our social interaction? How am I able to
understand myself as I understand others without simply erasing the
first-person perspective without which I could not be said to have *my
own* understanding of anything? How can an interpersonally sensitive
understanding of myself as another avoid being simply "inauthentic"
in the pejorative sense of the word, which is to say depersonalized and
generic?

<hr/>

[41] Strawson, *Individuals*, chapter 3.

Heidegger's analytic, it seems to me, does not even address, let alone answer, this problem of the hermeneutic conditions of our robust, socially perspectival concept of the self. I hope I have made it clear, however, that the account of authenticity in *Being and Time* leaves us with this problem precisely because it departs so radically from subjectivist interpretations of the self that have dominated philosophy from the early modern rationalists and empiricists to the expressivists of the Romantic and post-Romantic age. For notwithstanding their undeniable advances beyond the "worldless" subject in Descartes and Kant (*SZ* 211), thinkers from Rousseau and Herder to Dilthey arguably failed to describe the self in its concrete situatedness in the world, including its primordial dependence on others, as Heidegger does. Just as the self is neither an object of intuition nor an autonomous source of normative authority, neither is it a creative achievement, consummated and reconciled with others and the world in, and in virtue of, its own expressive activity. Rather, on Heidegger's view, Dasein becomes itself, or comes into its own, as it were, only in its wholehearted immersion in and engagement with the concrete situations confronting it, thrown into assuming responsibility for itself, pushing forward into possibilities constantly closing down around it.

REFERENCES

Works by Husserl

Logische Untersuchungen. Tübingen: Niemeyer, 1900–1; 6th ed. 1980. *Logical Investigations.* 2 vols. J. N. Findlay, trans. London: Routledge, 1970. Roman and Arabic numerals refer to the volumes and page numbers of the German edition.

Die Idee der Phänomenologie: Fünf Vorlesungen. W. Biemel, ed. 2nd ed. *Husserliana* II. The Hague: Nijhoff, 1950; rev. ed. 1973.

"Philosophy as Rigorous Science." In *Phenomenology and the Crisis of Philosophy.* Q. Lauer, trans. New York: Harper & Row, 1965. Reprinted in *Husserl: Shorter Works.* F. Elliston and P. McCormick, eds. Notre Dame: University of Notre Dame Press, 1981.

Ideen zu einer reinen Phänomenologie und phänomenologischen Philosophie, Erstes Buch: Allgemeine Einführung in die reine Phänomenologie. K. Schumann, ed. *Husserliana* III. The Hague: Nijhoff, 1976. *Ideas Pertaining to a Pure Phenomenology and to a Phenomenological Philosophy. First Book: General Introduction to a Pure Phenomenology.* F. Kersten, trans. The Hague: Nijhoff, 1983. Page references are to the first German edition, given in the margins of the translation.

Ideen zu einer reinen Phänomenologie und phänomenologischen Philosophie. Zweites Buch: Phänomenologische Untersuchungen zur Konstitution. W. Biemel, ed. *Husserliana* IV. The Hague: Nijhoff, 1952.*Ideas Pertaining to a Pure Phenomenology and to a Phenomenological Philosophy. Second Book: Studies in the Phenomenology of Constitution.* R. Rojcewicz and A. Schuwer, trans. Dordrecht: Kluwer, 1989.

Ideen zu einer reinen Phänomenologie und phänomenologischen Philosophie. Drittes Buch: Die Phänomenologie und die Fundamente der Wissenschaften. M. Biemel, ed. *Husserliana* V. The Hague: Nijhoff, 1952. *Ideas Pertaining to a Pure Phenomenology and Phenomenological Philosophy. Third Book: Phenomenology and the Foundations of the Sciences.* T. E. Klein and W. E. Pohl, trans. The Hague: Nijhoff, 1980.

Analysen zur passiven Synthesis: Aus Vorlesungs- und Forschungsmanuskripten (1918–1926). M. Fleischer, ed. *Husserliana* XI. Dordrecht: Nijhoff, 1970. *Analyses Concerning Passive and Active Synthesis: Lectures on Transcendental Logic.* A. J. Steinbock, ed. Dordrecht: Kluwer, 2001.

Erste Philosophie (1923/4). Erster Teil: Kritische Ideengeschichte. Husserliana VII. *Zweiter Teil: Theorie der Phänomenologischen Reduktion. Husserliana* VIII. R. Boehm, ed. Dordrecht: Nijhoff, 1965.

Phänomenologische Psychologie. W. Biemel, ed. *Husserliana* IX. The Hague: Nijhoff, 1968. *Phenomenological Psychology: Lectures, Summer Semester, 1925.* J. Scanlon, trans. The Hague: Nijhoff, 1977. See also *PTP.*

Psychological and Transcendental Phenomenology and the Confrontation with Heidegger (1927–1931). T. Sheehan and R. E. Palmer, eds. and trans. Dordrecht: Kluwer, 1997.

Formale und transzendentale Logik: Versuch einer Kritik der logischen Vernunft. 2nd ed. Tübingen: Niemeyer, 1981. *Formal and Transcendental Logic.* D. Cairns, trans. The Hague: Nijhoff, 1978.

Cartesianische Meditationen und Pariser Vorträge. 2nd ed. S. Strasser, ed. *Husserliana* I. Dordrecht: Kluwer, 1963. *Cartesian Meditations.* D. Cairns, trans. The Hague: Nihjoff, 1960.

Erfahrung und Urteil: Untersuchungen zur Genealogie der Logik. L. Landgrebe, ed. Prague: Academia Verlagsbuchhandlung, 1939. *Experience and Judgment: Investigations in a Genealogy of Logic.* J. S. Churchill and K. Ameriks, trans. Evanston: Northwestern Univeristy Press, 1973.

Die Krisis der europäischen Wissenschaften und die transzendentale Phänomenologie: Eine Einleitung in die phänomenologische Philosophie. W. Biemel, ed. 2nd ed. *Husserliana* VI. The Hague: Nijhoff, 1962. *The Crisis of European Sciences and Transcendental Phenomenology: An Introduction to Phenomenological Philosophy.* D. Carr, trans. Evanston: Northwestern University Press, 1970.

Works by Heidegger

Frühe Schriften. Gesamtausgabe 1. F.-W. von Herrmann, ed. Frankfurt: Klostermann, 1978.

Zur Bestimmung der Philosophie. Gesamtausgabe 56/57. B. Heimbüchel, ed. Frankfurt: Klostermann, 1987.

Ontologie (Hermeneutik der Faktizität). Gesamtausgabe 63. Marburg lectures, summer 1923. K. Bröcker-Oltmanns, ed. Frankfurt: Klostermann, 1988. *Ontology: The Hermeneutics of Facticity.* J. van Buren, trans. Bloomington: Indiana University Press, 1999.

Einführung in die phänomenologische Forschung. Gesamtausgabe 17. Marburg lectures, winter 1923–4. F.-W. von Herrmann, ed. Frankfurt: Klostermann, 1994

Der Begriff der Zeit. H. Tietjen, ed. Tübingen: Niemeyer, 1989. *The Concept of Time.* W. McNeill, trans. Bilingual ed. Oxford: Blackwell, 1992.

Prolegomena zur Geschichte des Zeitbegriffs. Gesamtausgabe 20. Marburg lectures, summer 1925. P. Jaeger, ed. Frankfurt: Klostermann, 1979. *History of the Concept of Time: Prolegomena.* T. Kisiel, trans. Bloomington: Indiana University Press, 1985.

Logik: Die Frage nach der Wahrheit. Gesamtausgabe 21. Marburg lectures, winter 1925–6. W. Biemel, ed. Frankfurt: Klostermann, 1976.

Sein und Zeit. Tübingen: Niemeyer, 1927; 15th ed. 1979. *Being and Time,* J. Macquarrie and E. Robinson, trans. New York: Harper & Row, 1962.

Grundprobleme der Phänomenologie. Gesamtausgabe 24. Marburg lectures, summer 1927. F.-W. von Herrmann, ed. Frankfurt: Klostermann, 1975. *The Basic Problems of Phenomenology.* A. Hofstadter, trans. Bloomington: Indiana University Press, 1982; rev. ed., 1988.

Phänomenologische Interpretation von Kant Kritik der reinen Vernunft. Gesamtausgabe 25. Marburg lectures, winter 1927–8. I. Görland, ed. Frankfurt: Klostermann, 1977; 3rd ed. 1995. *Phenomenological Interpretation of Kant's "Critique of Pure Reason."* P. Emad and K. Maly, trans. Bloomington: Indiana University Press, 1997.

Metaphysische Anfangsgründe der Logik im Ausgang von Leibniz. Gesamtausgabe 26. Marburg lectures, summer 1928. K. Held, ed. Frankfurt: Klostermann, 1978. *The Metaphysical Foundations of Logic.* M. Heim, trans. Bloomington: Indiana University Press, 1984.

Kant und das Problem der Metaphysik. Gesamtausgabe 3. F.-W. von Herrmann, ed. 5th expanded ed. Frankfurt: Klostermann, 1991. *Kant and the Problem of Metaphysics.* 5th, expanded ed. R. Taft, trans. Bloomington: Indiana University Press, 1997.

Die Grundbegriffe der Metaphysik: Welt-Endlichkeit-Einsamkeit. Gesamtausgabe 29/30. Freiburg lectures, winter 1929–30. Frankfurt: Klostermann, 1983. *The Fundamental Concepts of Metaphysics: World, Finitude, Solitude.* W. McNeill and N. Walker, trans. Bloomington: Indiana University Press, 1995.

Aristoteles, Metaphysik Θ *1–3: Vom Wesen und Wirklichkeit der Kraft. Gesamtausgabe* 33. Freiburg lectures, summer 1931. Frankfurt: Klostermann, 1981. *Aristotle's "Metaphysics" Θ 1–3: On the Essence and Actuality of Force.* W. Brogan and P. Warnek, trans. Bloomington: Indiana University Press, 1995.

Einführung in die Metaphysik. Tübingen: Niemeyer, 1953; 3rd ed. 1966. *Introduction to Metaphysics.* G. Fried and R. Polt, trans. New Haven: Yale University Press, 2000.

Beiträge zur Philosophie (Vom Ereignis). Gesamtausgabe 65. F.-W. von Herrmann, ed. Frankfurt: Klostermann, 1989. *Contributions to Philosophy (From Enowning).* P. Emad and K. Maly, trans. Bloomington: Indiana University Press, 1999.

Holzwege. Frankfurt: Klostermann, 1950; 6th rev. ed. 1980. *Off the Beaten Track.* J. Young and K. Haynes, trans. Cambridge: Cambridge University Press, 2002.

Vorträge und Aufsätze. Pfullingen: Günther Neske, 1954; 6th ed. 1990. English translations of the essays in *Holzwege* and *Vorträge und Aufsätze* can be found in *The Question Concerning Technology and Other Essays,* W. Lovitt, trans. New York: Harper & Row, 1977; *Poetry, Language, Thought,* A. Hofstadter, trans. New York: Harper & Row, 1971; and *Early Greek Thinking: The Dawn of Western Philosophy,* D. F. Krell and F. A. Capuzzi, trans. New York: Harper & Row, 1975.

Identität und Differenz. Pfullingen: Günther Neske, 1957. *Identity and Difference.* J. Stambaugh, trans. New York: Harper & Row, 1969.

Unterwegs zur Sprache. Pfullingen: Günther Neske, 1959. *On the Way to Language.* P. D. Hertz, trans. New York: Harper & Row, 1971.

Nietzsche. 2 vols. Pfullingen: Günther Neske, 1961. *Nietzsche.* 4 vols. *Volume I: The Will to Power as Art. Volume II: The Eternal Recurrence of the Same. Volume III: The Will to Power as Knowledge and as Metaphysics. Volume IV: Nihilism.* D. F. Krell, ed. New York: Harper & Row, 1979–87. Reference is to the English translation.

Die Technik und die Kehre; 3rd ed. Pfullingen: Günther Neske, 1962. The essay "Die Kehre" is translated as "The Turning" in *The Question Concerning Technology and Other Essays*, W. Lovitt, trans. New York: Harper & Row, 1977.

Wegmarken. Gesamtausgabe 9. F.-W. von Herrmann, ed. Frankfurt: Klostermann, 1976. *Pathmarks.* W. McNeill, ed. Cambridge: Cambridge University Press, 1998. Page references are to the first edition of *Wegmarken* (1967), which appear in the margins of *Gesamtausgabe* 9 and in brackets in the English translation. In the case of the additional material in the 1976 edition, references are to *Gesamtausgabe* 9, cited as *Weg/GA9*.

Zur Sache des Denkens. Tübingen: Niemeyer, 1969. *On Time and Being*, J. Stambaugh, trans. New York: Harper & Row, 1972; Chicago: University of Chicago Press, 2002.

Martin Heidegger/Karl Jaspers. *Briefwechsel 1920–1963.* W. Biemel and H. Saner, eds. Munich: Piper, 1992.

Works by Other Authors

Allison, H. E. *Kant's Transcendental Idealism: An Interpretation and Defense.* New Haven: Yale University Press, 1983.

———. *Idealism and Freedom: Essays on Kant's Theoretical and Practical Philosophy.* Cambridge: Cambridge University Press, 1996.

Ameriks, K. "Kantian Idealism Today." *History of Philosophy Quarterly* 9 (1992): 329–40.

———. *Kant and the Fate of Autonomy: Problems in the Appropriation of the Critical Philosophy.* Cambridge: Cambridge University Press, 2000.

Augustine, St. *Against the Academicians* and *The Teacher.* P. King, trans. Hackett, 1995.

Berlin, I. *The Proper Study of Mankind: An Anthology of Essays.* H. Hardy and R. Hausheer, eds. New York: Farrar, Straus & Giroux, 1998.

Biemel, W. "Husserl's *Encyclopaedia Britannica* Article and Heidegger's Remarks Thereon." In *Husserl: Expositions and Appraisals.* F. Elliston and McCormick, eds. Notre Dame: University of Notre Dame Press, 1977.

Blattner, W. D. "Existential Temporality in *Being and Time* (Why Heidegger Is Not a Pragmatist)." In *Heidegger: A Critical Reader.* H. L. Dreyfus and H. Hall, eds. Oxford: Blackwell, 1992.

———. "Is Heidegger a Kantian Idealist?" *Inquiry* 37 (1994): 185–201.

———. *Heidegger's Temporal Idealism.* Cambridge: Cambridge University Press, 1999.

Bolzano, B. *Wissenschaftslehre.* J. Berg, ed. In *Bernard Bolzano. Gesamtausgabe.* E. Winter et al., eds. Stuttgart–Bad Cannstatt: Friedrich Frommann Verlag; G. Holzboog, 1969. *Theory of Science.* R. George, ed. and trans. Berkeley: University of California Press, 1972.

Bourdieu, P. *Le sens pratique.* Paris: Éditions de Minuit, 1980. *The Logic of Practice.* R. Nice, trans. Stanford: Stanford University Press, 1990.

Brandom, R. B. "Heidegger's Categories in *Being and Time*." *Monist* 66 (1983): 387–409. Reprinted in *Heidegger: A Critical Reader.* H. L. Dreyfus and H. Hall, eds. Oxford: Blackwell, 1992.

———. *Making It Explicit: Reasoning, Representing, and Discursive Commitment.* Cambridge, MA: Harvard University Press, 1994.

Burge, T. "Individualism and the Mental." *Midwest Studies in Philosophy,* vol. IV. P. A. French, T. E. Uehling, Jr., and H. K. Wettstein, eds. Minneapolis: University of Minnesota Press, 1979.

———. "Individualism and Psychology." *Philosophical Review* 95 (1986): 3–45.

Carman, T. "The Conspicuousness of Signs in *Being and Time."* *Journal of the British Society for Phenomenology* 22 (1991): 158–69.

———. "On Being Social: A Reply to Olafson." *Inquiry* 37 (1994): 203–23.

———. "Heidegger's Concept of Presence." *Inquiry* 38 (1995): 431–53.

———. "What Is Intentionality? Heidegger's *via media."* *Ars interpretandi: Journal of Legal Hermeneutics* 3 (1998): 241–8.

———. "The Body in Husserl and Merleau-Ponty." *Philosophical Topics* 27 (1999): 205–26.

———. "Must We Be Inauthentic?" In *Heidegger, Authenticity, and Modernity: Essays in Honor of Hubert L. Dreyfus, Volume 1.* M. Wrathall and J. Malpas, eds. Cambridge, MA: MIT Press, 2000.

———. "Normativity and Social Skill in Searle and Bourdieu." *Yearbook for Philosophical Hermeneutics* 1 (2000): 41–50.

———. Review of William D. Blattner, "Heidegger's Temporal Idealism." *Journal of Philosophy* 97 (2000): 308–12.

———. "On Making Sense (and Nonsense) of Heidegger." *Philosophy and Phenomenological Research* 63 (2001): 561–72.

———. "Was Heidegger a Linguistic Idealist?" *Inquiry* 45 (2002): 205–16.

Carnap, R. "Empiricism, Semantics, and Ontology." *Meaning and Necessity: A Study in Semantics and Modal Logic.* Supplement A. 2nd ed. Chicago: University of Chicago Press, 1956.

———. "The Elimination of Metaphysics Through Logical Analysis of Language." In *Logical Positivism.* A. J. Ayer, ed. New York: Free Press, 1959.

Cerbone, D. "World, World-Entry, and Realism in Early Heidegger," *Inquiry* 38 (1995): 401–21.

Churchland, P. M. "Eliminative Materialism and the Propositional Attitudes." *Journal of Philosophy* 78 (1981): 67–90. Reprinted in *A Neurocomputational Perspective: The Nature of Mind and the Structure of Science.* Cambridge, MA: MIT Press, 1989.

Davidson, D. *Inquiries into Truth and Interpretation.* Oxford: Oxford University Press, 1984.

———. "The Social Aspect of Language." *The Philosophy of Michael Dummett.* B. McGuiness and G. Oliveri, eds. Dordrecht: Kluwer, 1994.

———. *Subjective, Intersubjective, Objective.* Oxford: Oxford University Press, 2001.

Dennett, D. C. *Content and Consciousness.* London: Routledge, 1969; 2nd ed. 1986.

———. "On the Absence of Phenomenology." In *Body, Mind and Method: Essays in Honor of Virgil Aldrich.* D. Gustafson and B. Tapscott, eds. Dordrecht: Reidel, 1979.

———. *The Intentional Stance.* Cambridge, MA: MIT Press, 1987.

———. *Consciousness Explained.* Boston: Little Brown & Co., 1991.

————. "Real Patterns." *Journal of Philosophy* 88 (1991): 27–51. Reprinted in *Brainchildren: Essays on Designing Minds.* Cambridge, MA: MIT Press, 1998.

————. "Back from the Drawing Board." In *Dennett and His Critics.* B. Dahlbom, ed. Oxford: Blackwell, 1993.

————. *Darwin's Dangerous Idea: Evolution and the Meanings of Life.* New York: Simon & Schuster, 1995.

Derrida, J. *Speech and Phenomena and Other Essays on Husserl's Theory of Signs.* D. B. Allison, trans. Evanston: Northwestern University Press, 1973.

Descartes, R. *Selected Philosophical Writings.* J. Cottingham et al., trans. Cambridge: Cambridge University Press, 1988.

Diemer, A. *Edmund Husserl: Versuch einder systematischen Darstellung seiner Phäenomenologie.* 2nd rev. ed. Meisenheim am Glan: Verlag Anton Hain, 1965.

Dostal, R. J. "Time and Phenomenology in Husserl and Heidegger." In *The Cambridge Companion to Heidegger.* C. Guignon, ed. Cambridge: Cambridge University Press, 1993.

Dreyfus, H. L. "Husserl's Perceptual *Noema.*" In *Husserl, Intentionality, and Cognitive Science.* H. L. Dreyfus and H. Hall, eds. Cambridge, MA: MIT Press, 1982.

————. *Being-in-the-World: A Commentary on Heidegger's "Being and Time," Division I.* Cambridge, MA: MIT Press, 1991.

Dreyfus, H. L. and C. Spinosa, "Coping with Things-in-Themselves: A Practice-Based Phenomenological Argument for Realism." *Inquiry* 42 (1999): 49–78.

————. "Robust Intelligibility: Response to Our Critics." *Inquiry* 42 (1999): 177–94.

Fell, J. P. "The Familiar and the Strange: On the Limits of Praxis in the Early Heidegger." In *Heidegger: A Critical Reader.* H. L. Dreyfus and H. Hall, eds. Oxford: Blackwell, 1992.

Field, H. " Realism and Relativism." *Journal of Philosophy* 79 (1982): 553–67.

Fine, A. "The Natural Ontological Attitude." In *The Shaky Game: Einstein, Realism, and the Quantum Theory.* 2nd ed. Chicago: University of Chicago Press, 1986.

Fodor, J. "Methodological Solipsism Considered as a Research Strategy in Cognitive Psychology." *The Behavioral and Brain Sciences* III, 1 (March 1980): 63–72. Reprinted in *Husserl, Intentionality, and Cognitive Science.* H. L. Dreyfus and H. Hall, eds. Cambridge, MA: MIT Press, 1982.

Føllesdal, D. "Husserl and Heidegger on the Role of Actions in the Constitution of the World." In *Essays in Honour of Jaakko Hintikka.* E. Saarinen, R. Hilpinen, I. Niiniluoto, and M. P. Hintikka, eds. Dordrecht: Reidel, 1979.

————. "Husserl's Notion of *Noema.*" *Journal of Philosophy* 66 (1969): 680–7. Reprinted in *Husserl, Intentionality, and Cognitive Science.* H. L. Dreyfus and H. Hall, eds. Cambridge, MA: MIT Press, 1982.

Förster, E. "Kant's Notion of Philosophy." *Monist* 72 (1989): 285–304.

Frege, G. *Collected Papers on Mathematics, Logic, and Philosophy.* B. McGuiness, ed. Oxford: Blackwell, 1984.

Gadamer, H.-G. *Wahrheit und Methode.* Tübingen: J. C. B. Mohr, 1960. *Truth and Method.* 2nd rev. ed. J. Weinsheimer and D. G. Marshall, trans. New York: Crossroad, 1989.

Grice, P. *Studies in the Way of Words.* Cambridge, MA: Harvard University Press, 1989.

Guignon, C. *Heidegger and the Problem of Knowledge.* Indianapolis: Hackett, 1983.

———. "Authenticity, Moral Values, and Psychotherapy." In *The Cambridge Companion to Heidegger.* C. Guignon, ed. Cambridge: Cambridge University Press, 1993.

———. "Philosophy and Authenticity: Heidegger's Search for a Ground for Philosophizing." In *Heidegger, Authenticity, and Modernity: Essays in Honor of Hubert L. Dreyfus, Volume 1.* M. Wrathall and J. Malpas, eds. Cambridge, MA: MIT Press, 2000.

Guyer, P. *Kant and the Claims of Knowledge.* Cambridge: Cambridge University Press, 1987.

Habermas, J. "Wahrheitstheorien." In *Wirklichkeit und Reflexion: Festschrift für Walter Schulz zum 60.* H. Fahrenbach, ed. *Geburtstag.* Pfüllingen: Neske, 1973.

———. *The Theory of Communicative Action, Vol. 1.* T. McCarthy, trans. Boston: Beacon Press, 1984.

———. *The Philosophical Discourse of Modernity: Twelve Lectures.* F. Lawrence, trans. Cambridge, MA: MIT Press, 1987.

Hall, H. "Was Husserl a Realist or an Idealist?" In *Husserl, Intentionality, and Cognitive Science.* H. L. Dreyfus and H. Hall, eds. Cambridge, MA: MIT Press, 1982.

Haugeland, J. "Heidegger on Being a Person." *Noûs,* XVI (1982): 15–26.

———. "Dasein's Disclosedness." In *Heidegger: A Critical Reader.* H. L. Dreyfus and H. Hall, eds. Oxford: Blackwell, 1992.

———. "Pattern and Being." In *Dennett and His Critics.* B. Dahlbom, ed. Oxford: Blackwell, 1993. Reprinted in *Having Thought.* Cambridge, MA: Harvard University Press, 1998.

Hoffman, P. "Heidegger and the Problem of Idealism." *Inquiry* 43 (2000): 403–11.

Kafka, F. *The Trial.* B. Mitchell, trans. New York: Schocken, 1998.

Kant, I. *Kritik der reinen Vernunft.* R. Schmidt, ed. Hamburg: Felix Meiner, 1956. *Critique of Pure Reason.* P. Guyer and A. W. Wood, eds. and trans. Cambridge: Cambridge University Press, 1997.

———. *Prolegomena zu einer jeden künftigen Metaphysik.* K. Vorländer, ed. Hamburg: Felix Meiner, 1969. *Prolegomena to any Future Metaphysics that Will Be Able to Come Forward as Science.* P. Carus and J. W. Ellington, trans. Indianapolis: Hackett, 1977. Page references are to the Akademie edition, given in the margins of these editions.

———. *Theoretical Philosophy, 1755–1770.* D. Walford and R. Meerbote, eds. and trans. *The Cambridge Edition of the Works of Immanuel Kant.* P. Guyer and A. W. Wood, eds. Cambridge: Cambridge University Press, 1992.

Kern, I. *Husserl und Kant: Eine Untersuchung über Husserls Verhältnis zu Kant und zum Neukantianismus. Phenomenologica* 16. The Hague: Nijhoff, 1964.

Kierkegaard, S. *The Sickness Unto Death.* A. Hannay, trans. New York: Penguin, 1989.

———. *Either/Or: A Fragment of Life.* A. Hannay, trans. New York: Penguin, 1992.

———. *A Literary Review.* A. Hannay, trans. New York: Penguin, 2001.

Kisiel, T. "Heidegger (1907–1927): The Transformation of the Categorial." In *Continental Philosophy in America.* H. J. Silverman, J. Sallis, and T. Seebohm, eds. Pittsburgh: Duquesne University Press, 1983.

Kripke, S. *Naming and Necessity.* Cambridge, MA: Harvard University Press, 1980.

Kuhn, T. S. *The Structure of Scientific Revolutions.* 2nd ed., enlarged. Chicago: University of Chicago Press, 1962.

———. *The Essential Tension: Selected Studies in Scientific Tradition and Change.* Chicago: University of Chicago Press, 1977.

Lafont, C. *The Linguistic Turn in Hermeneutic Philosophy.* J. Medina, trans. Cambridge, MA: MIT Press, 1999.

———. *Heidegger, Language, and World-Disclosure.* G. Harman, trans. Cambridge: Cambridge University Press, 2000.

McGinn, C. *The Problem of Consciousness: Essays Toward a Resolution.* Oxford: Blackwell, 1991.

Merleau-Ponty, M. *Phénoménologie de la perception.* Paris: Gallimard, 1945. *Phenomenology of Perception.* C. Smith, trans. London: Routledge, 1962.

Miller, I. *Husserl, Perception, and Temporal Awareness.* Cambridge, MA: MIT Press, 1984.

Mohanty, J. N. "The Development of Husserl's Thought." In *The Cambridge Companion to Husserl.* B. Smith and D. W. Smith, eds. Cambridge: Cambridge University Press, 1995.

Mulhall, S. *Routledge Guidebook to Heidegger and "Being and Time."* London: Routledge, 1996.

Nagel, T. *Mortal Questions.* Cambridge: Cambridge University Press, 1979.

———. *The View from Nowhere.* Oxford: Oxford University Press, 1986.

Neske, G. and E. Kettering, eds. *Martin Heidegger and National Socialism: Questions and Answers,* L. Harries, trans. New York: Paragon House, 1990.

Okrent, M. *Heidegger's Pragmatism: Understanding, Being, and the Critique of Metaphysics.* Ithaca: Cornell University Press, 1988.

———. "The Truth of Being and the History of Philosophy." In *Heidegger: A Critical Reader.* H. L. Dreyfus and H. Hall, eds. Oxford: Blackwell, 1992.

Olafson, F. A. *Heidegger and the Philosophy of Mind.* New Haven: Yale University Press, 1987.

Ott, H. *Martin Heidegger: A Political Life.* A. Blunden, trans. New York: Basic Books, 1993.

Philipse, H. "Heidegger's Question of Being and the 'Augustinian Picture' of Language." *Philosophy and Phenomenological Research* 52 (1992): 251–87.

———. "Transcendental Idealism." In *The Cambridge Companion to Husserl.* B. Smith and D. W. Smith, eds. Cambridge: Cambridge University Press, 1995.

———. *Heidegger's Philosophy of Being: A Critical Interpretation.* Princeton: Princeton University Press, 1998.

Putnam, H. "The Meaning of 'Meaning.'" *Philosophical Papers II: Mind, Language, and Reality.* Cambridge: Cambridge University Press, 1975.

———. *Reason, Truth and History.* Cambridge: Cambridge University Press, 1981.

———. *The Many Faces of Realism.* La Salle: Open Court, 1987.

Reinhardt, K. *Parmenides und die Geschichte der griechischen Philosophie.* Bonn: Friedrich Cohen, 1916.

Richardson, J. *Existential Epistemology: A Heideggerian Critique of the Cartesian Project.* Oxford: Clarendon Press, 1986.

Richardson, W. J. *Heidegger: Through Phenomenology to Thought.* The Hague: Nijhoff, 1963.

Ricoeur, P. "Narrative Time." In *On Narrative.* W. J. T. Mitchell, ed. Chicago: University of Chicago Press, 1981. Originally in *Critical Inquiry* 7 (1980).

———. *Time and Narrative.* 3 vols. K. Blamey and D. Pellauer, trans. Chicago: University of Chicago Press, 1984–88.

Rorty, R. *Philosophy and the Mirror of Nature.* Princeton: Princeton University Press, 1979.

Rouse, J. *Knowledge and Power: Toward a Political Philosophy of Science.* Ithaca: Cornell University Press, 1987.

———. *Engaging Science: How to Understand Its Practices Philosophically.* Ithaca: Cornell University Press, 1996.

Ryle, G. Review of Martin Heidegger, *Sein und Zeit. Mind* 38 (1929): 355–70. Reprinted in *Collected Papers*, vol. 1. London: Hutchinson, 1971.

Safranski, R. *Martin Heidegger: Between Good and Evil.* E. Osers, trans. Cambridge, MA: Harvard University Press, 1998.

Sallis, J. *Double Truth.* Albany: State University of New York Press, 1995.

Sartre, J.-P. *L'Être et le néant: Essai d'ontologie phénoménologique.* Paris: Gallimard, 1943. *Being and Nothingness.* H. Barnes, trans. New York: Philosophical Library, 1956.

———. *L'Existentialisme est un humanisme.* Paris: Nagel, 1946, 1970.

Searle, J. R. *Speech Acts: An Essay in the Philosophy of Language.* Cambridge: Cambridge University Press, 1969.

———. *Intentionality: An Essay in the Philosophy of Mind.* Cambridge: Cambridge University Press, 1983.

———. "Collective Intentions and Actions." In *Intentions in Communication.* P. Cohen, J. Morgan, and M. E. Pollack, eds. Cambridge, MA: MIT Press, 1990. Reprinted in *Consciousness and Language.* Cambridge: Cambridge University Press. 2002.

———. *The Rediscovery of the Mind.* Cambridge, MA: MIT Press, 1992.

———. *The Construction of Social Reality.* New York: Free Press, 1995.

Sellars, W. *Empiricism and the Philosphy of Mind.* Cambridge, MA: Harvard University Press, 1997.

Shakespeare, W. *The Riverside Shakespeare.* 2nd ed. G. B. Evans et al., eds. Boston and New York: Houghton Mifflin, 1997.

Simons, P. "Meaning and Language." In *The Cambridge Companion to Husserl.* B. Smith and D. W. Smith, eds. Cambridge: Cambridge University Press, 1995.

Stalnaker, R. *Inquiry.* Cambridge, MA: MIT Press, 1984.

Stewart, R. M. "Intentionality and the Semantics of 'Dasein.'" *Philosophy and Phenomenological Research* 48 (1987): 93–106.

Strawson, P. F. *Individuals: An Essay in Descriptive Metaphysics.* London: Methuen, 1959.

Taylor, C. *Hegel.* Cambridge: Cambridge University Press, 1975.

———. *Human Agency and Language: Philosophical Papers*, Vol. 1. Cambridge: Cambridge University Press, 1985.

———. *Sources of the Self: The Making of the Modern Identity.* Cambridge, MA: Harvard University Press, 1989.

———. *Philosophical Arguments.* Cambridge, MA: Harvard University Press, 1995.

Tugendhat, E. *Der Wahrheitsbegriff bei Husserl und Heidegger.* Berlin: de Gruyter, 1967.

———. "Die sprachanalytische Kritik der Ontologie." *Das Problem der Sprache.* H.-G. Gadamer, ed. Munich, 1967.

———. "Heideggers Idee von Wahrheit." *Heidegger.* O. Pöggeler, ed. Berlin, 1969. "Heidegger's Idea of Truth." C. Macann, trans. *Critical Heidegger.* C. Macann, ed. London: Routledge, 1996.

———. *Selbstbewußtsein und Selbstbestimmung: Sprachanalytische Interpretationen.* Frankfurt am Main: Suhrkamp, 1979. *Self-Consciousness and Self-Determination.* P. Stern, trans. Cambridge, MA: MIT Press, 1986.

Waelhens, A. de. *La philosophie de Martin Heidegger.* 7th ed. Louvain: Nauwelaerts, 1971.

Wittgenstein, L. *Tractatus Logico-Philosophicus.* London: Routledge, 1922.

———. *Philosophical Investigations.* 3rd ed. G. E. M. Anscombe, trans. New York: Macmillan, 1953.

———. *On Certainty.* G. E. M. Anscombe and G. H. von Wright, eds. New York: Harper & Row, 1972.

———. *Philosophical Occasions, 1912–1951.* J. Klagge and A. Nordmann, eds. Indianapolis: Hackett, 1993.

Wrathall, M. "Heidegger and Truth as Correspondence." *International Journal of Philosophical Studies* 7 (1999): 69–88.

———. "Practical Incommensurability and the Phenomenological Basis of Robust Realism." *Inquiry* 42 (1999): 79–88.

———. "Social Constraints on Conversational Content: Heidegger on *Rede* and *Gerede.*" *Philosophical Topics* 27 (1999): 25–46.

INDEX

Lightning Source UK Ltd.
Milton Keynes UK
UKOW041056241012

201110UK00001B/132/A